GLYNN CHRISTIAN'S
CONTEMPORARY
HOME COOKING

GLYNN CHRISTIAN'S
CONTEMPORARY HOME COOKING

OCTOPUS BOOKS

First published in Great Britain in 1986 by
Octopus Books Limited
59 Grosvenor Street
London W1

© Glynn Christian
© Octopus Books Limited
All rights reserved

ISBN 0-7064-2547-2

Editorial: Tessa Rose, Diana Vowles, Barbara Croxford
and Carole Edwards

Production Controller: Maryann Rogers
Photography: Jan Baldwin and Vernon Morgan (jacket)
Food Styling: Marian Price
Index: Hilary Bird

Printed by Graficromo SA, Cordoba, Spain

CONTENTS

Key to symbols
Ⓔ Entertaining in bulk
Ⓕ First course option
Ⓠ Quick
Ⓢ Special
Ⓣ Time-consuming to prepare

PREFACE

Isn't it time we stopped feeling guilty that we can't cook the way restaurants and hotels do? The explosion of interest in food and cooking during the past 15 years has confused a great number of people and put many perfectly nice square pegs into uncomfortable round holes. There are thousands of professional chefs who should never have left home, and hundreds of thousands of home cooks who feel guilty if they have not achieved something that might be found in a restaurant. Of course there is inspiration for the home cook to be gained from catering professionals who, in turn, should never forget the flavours and simplicity of honest home cooking as their touchstone, but apart from mutual appreciation the two should hardly meet. In any case, the more they do, the less excitement there is in eating out, the less satisfaction there is to be derived from being a good home cook – hence this book.

Contemporary Home Cooking is planned to ease the confusion that exists about so many things, from sauces and presentation through to wok cooking and healthy eating. It is a summary of the fads, fashions and movements of the '80s moulded into what I hope you will find the single practical book that will enable you to be a modern and exciting home cook but without needing radically to change your life-style or give up the things you like. And that's the first thing to get abundantly clear – the question of what is and what is not bad for you. It's simple: unless you have a specific medical condition which dictates that you should avoid sugar, fat, dairy products, red meat or salt, none of these foods is a poison or dangerous to health if

they form part of a sensible diet. Anything can be bad for you if you have too much of it. People have died of eating too many carrots or from drinking too much water. It's simply a matter of moderation and ensuring that you do not have too much of any one ingredient in your diet: it is imbalance that is the major problem, rarely the ingredients themselves.

Once you have understood this properly you will see how unnecessary it is to give up eating steamed puddings with custard and cream, or vow never again to eat roast beef. If you like these foods, eat them and enjoy them. But you may like to put the philosophy of balanced eating into practice by serving a poached chicken or a light fish dish before the steamed pudding, or considering serving a baked potato and salad with the beef instead of fatty roasted vegetables. You see, it's simply a matter of balance.

Contemporary Home Cooking contains traditional puddings, cakes and biscuits as well as the most modern style of low-fat dishes. For food should be fun as well as nutritious and nothing is truer than 'a little of what you fancy does you good'. I will never criticise a family who choose to eat only vegetarian or fat-free food, but I'm very sorry if they have cut themselves off from so much pleasure for the wrong or for faddish reasons.

Although these sweet treats are here in abundance, you'll find them well balanced by the chapters on fish, pasta, grains, pulses and poultry, which numerically far outweigh the recipes using red meat and thus reflect contemporary culinary practice. These alternative proteins are very much cheaper than meat. Equally important, most of them also cook much faster than meat, enabling busy men and women to prepare and serve nutritious and attractive fresh food quickly without having to resort to the processed, the packaged and the additive-laden.

There are honourable exceptions, but in my view most convenience food is convenient only for the manufacturer, who uses it to stretch quality produce as far as possible without actually being dishonest, by first putting it in a convenient form in which to artificially inject the natural colour and flavour lost in the 'convenient' process and, conveniently, to sell it for much more money than is otherwise possible. The most convenient foods I know are fresh vegetables and fruit, fish and poultry, cooked in minutes with almost no preparation, no defrosting, no struggling with plastic packs and little to fear from hidden extra fat, sugar, salt or artificial colour and flavour.

The charts that accompany the major chapters should be seen as rich reference sources for simple meals, as they tell you how to cook the most common ingredients just as they come. The recipes written in full are an extension of these, for those days when you have more time or would like to make more effort. I have only a small kitchen and few gadgets and very little workspace. It is in that kitchen that these recipes were created and tested. All will repay both the money you spend on ingredients and the time required to make them. It is my belief that unless every ingredient and every minute of effort put into preparation can be tasted, the cook is wasting his or her time.

My helpers were many but the most important has been Jill Foster, who is a brilliant creative cook with a marvellous ability to recognise culinary absurdity. Jill has a wealth of family life experience so I always listened carefully when she thought something was too fiddly or wasn't relevant to home cooking. She was always right. I also appreciated the enthusiasm of Brigit Banham, whose American background and sophisticated international culinary experience contributed enormously. Thanks. There wasn't a single tester who didn't add his or her own ideas to the recipes, notably Anne Moginie from New Zealand and Katerina Gounaraki from Greece.

When deadlines got out of hand I was saved by these three much-valued friends: Beryl Childs of the Tante Marie School of Cookery in Woking and Caroline Waldegrave and Sally Proctor of Prue Leith's School of Cookery, who offered facilities, advice and support so spontaneously and generously that it encouraged everyone to bigger and better things. If you like the book and the recipes, all those mentioned above should be included in your appreciation.

Of course not every recipe has been created just for this book. Some have been published in my monthly pages in *Over 21*, some were constructed for *Breakfast Time* and for *The Gloria Hunniford Show*, and latterly a few have appeared in articles for *Taste* magazine. I thank them all for permission to use the recipes again.

Now it's up to you. Forget trying to copy the last restaurant meal you enjoyed and be a Contemporary Home Cook with pride.

SOUPS

Soups can be thick and nourishing, a meal in themselves, or delicately flavoured starters to titillate the palate. Here you'll find ideas for both – for all seasons.

Virtually any vegetable can form the basis of a soup, either on its own or with other vegetables, pulses or grains, with meat, or even with fruits. Most soups taste better if made with good stock, but judicious use of stock cubes with water or wine can be almost as good. If using cubes, add 50 per cent more liquid than recommended for each cube, so they do not dominate the soup. The flavour of any hot or cold soup will improve if it is made a day in advance.

A STOCK-MAKER'S PRIMER

Rich beef or veal stocks made by simmering pounds of bones for hours are no longer part of the modern household and are also disappearing from many modern restaurants, well, in their old guise at least. Nowadays chefs tend to base sauces and soups on a reduction of a dish's own cooking juices, and that is a far more practical technique for the home cook.

Poultry and Game Bird Stocks
It is a shame to throw away the carcasses of chickens, game birds or turkeys, for these stocks are very useful and can be used to make a risotto, a Velouté sauce (see page 15), to cook vegetables – and even to poach more poultry.

You'll quickly discover how you like your chicken stock – here's what you need to know to set you on the right road.

First break up the bones or flatten the carcass if it is a small game bird. Remove any nice pieces of breast meat, slice into very thin matchsticks, cover and reserve. For a brown stock, roast or fry the bones with a little oil but do not let them become too dark in colour or they will taste burnt.

Extra colour can be added with onions, either by frying some onions in butter until golden brown but not bitter or, for a light golden coloured stock, simply cut unpeeled onions into quarters and the skins will give a lovely colour to the stock.

Combine the browned bones and your chosen onions and cover with cold water. Add some herbs and spices – a few bay leaves, 6 black peppercorns, lots of parsley (stalk only), some pieces of lemon rind, 6 whole allspice berries. A few pieces of carrot or celeriac are worth adding but celery is better still, since root vegetables may cloud the stock. I always add a few leeks, too.

Simmer, uncovered, until well flavoured and reduced by about half. Strain and cool if you are going to clarify the stock. Otherwise strain and continue to reduce the stock until very strong. Cool, and remove the solid fat that sets on the surface. Then either freeze individually in ice-cube trays or store in the refrigerator.

Clarified Stock
Clarifying will make a stock crystal clear, perfect for clear soup or consommé. I find it best to do this after the initial cooking, once the stock has cooled and the fat has been skimmed.

To clear about 1 litre/1¾ pints of well strained, cold chicken or game stock, lightly beat 2 egg whites and a crushed egg shell into a

> ### GLYNN'S TIP
> *If you are in a hurry to remove the fat from a stock, let it cool in a wide-rimmed bowl. Gently scoop off most of the fat, then take off the rest by gently laying sheets of absorbent kitchen paper on the surface. If carefully done, this will lift the fat and almost none of the stock.*

large cupful of the stock until frothy. Stir that into the rest of the stock, then cook over medium heat, stirring continuously. The egg whites will solidify and collect the impurities. At this stage, the mixture looks worse than when you started but eventually the scum and residue will clump together and form a crust on top of the stock. Once this has happened, stop stirring and continue heating until the stock breaks through the crust. Cook for another minute or so until you are certain that the egg-white layer is cooked through; do not boil furiously or you will break the egg crust and ruin the whole process. Remove from the heat and prepare a large sieve lined with scalded muslin, or the scrupulously clean filter of a coffee-maker lined with a paper filter. With great care, using a slotted spoon, remove most of the egg layer, then very carefully ladle the stock through the muslin or coffee filter.

You can now reduce the clarified stock to obtain the required strength. Season to taste; the most common flavouring is a couple of slurps of dry Madeira or sherry. Most consommé will form a jelly when it is chilled. If it does not, use a little gelatine to encourage it to set.

Hot Consommé and Garnishes
A clear chicken or game consommé, particularly one with a little colour produced by browned bones or onion skins, is the basis of hundreds of fragrant, rather Oriental, soups. First ensure that you have reduced the consommé sufficiently; it must have a strong flavour. Then prepare 1 teaspoon or so per serving of very fine matchsticks of raw vegetables. Use at least three vegetables of contrasted texture and colour or two vegetables and thin strips of the flesh from which the consommé was made. Carrots, red or green peppers, lettuce, beetroot, turnip – anything you can eat raw, or lightly cooked, will do. If you enjoy a real Oriental flavour, include

some shreds of garlic and fresh ginger, too.

Place the matchsticks in the bottom of each warm bowl and pour a little of the boiling consommé into each bowl: let it sit for a few minutes to draw out the flavour of the vegetables. Fill the bowls with consommé and serve.

COLD SOUPS

Cold soups are a delightful way to start a meal at any time of the year. Well chilled, they are cooling and refreshing in summer and make a light taste-teaser before winter's heavier meals – but they should be only lightly chilled. It cannot be the climate which prevents them being more popular in Britain, since the Russians and Scandinavians are devotees of chilled soups, particularly those based on fruits.

Many single-vegetable soups (parsnip, carrot, tomato, beetroot) are suitable for serving cold but they must be thin, diluted with a little single cream or more stock.

In the following recipes you will find fresh ginger used a great deal, simply because I think it is the best way to add the 'bite' that makes chilled soups so refreshing. Ginger has far more flavour than, say, cayenne pepper, and won't discolour soups as Worcestershire sauce does.

TWO MELON SOUP

I have also made this with one type of melon flavoured with the juice of fresh ginger and left to marinate overnight. Serve it in clear glass bowls, so that your guests can appreciate the glorious swirls of colour. Use only very ripe fruit.

Serves four to six

1 small ripe cantaloupe melon, peeled, deseeded and roughly chopped
2-3 tbls lemon juice
1/2 ripe honeydew melon, peeled, deseeded and roughly chopped
2-3 tbls lime juice
1 tbls chopped fresh mint
mint sprigs, soured cream and fresh fruit to serve (optional)

Purée the cantaloupe with the lemon juice in a food processor or blender, and chill for several hours, preferably overnight. Purée the honeydew with the lime juice and chopped mint and chill for several hours. (Be sure to cover the bowls carefully with plastic film before putting them into the refrigerator, or they will taint other foods.)

To serve, ladle equal amounts of the two purées at the same time into chilled bowls. Garnish with a swirl of soured cream and a sprig of mint and perhaps a perfect raspberry, strawberry or, better still, wild strawberry. Ⓕ Ⓥ Ⓔ
Photograph p. 42.

CHILLED STRAWBERRY-GINGER SOUP

Chilled fruit soups can be served as a first course or, if a little sweeter, as a refreshing dessert. Try using other fruit, especially raspberries, or a combination of raspberries and strawberries.

Serves four

250 g/8 oz ripe strawberries, hulled
125 g/4 oz caster sugar
150 ml/1/4 pint plain yoghurt
150 ml/1/4 pint light red wine (see below)
300 ml/1/2 pint iced water
extra yoghurt to finish (optional)
1 cm/1/2 inch peeled fresh ginger, roughly chopped
fruit and mint leaves to decorate

Select strawberries which have bright red flesh, as they both look and taste better. Crush and force them through a fine nylon sieve. Add sugar (start with a little and add more later) and then the yoghurt. Once blended, mix in the red wine (a fruity young Beaujolais would be excellent, or one of the dry rosé wines from Provence). Chill very well and, just before serving, dilute with the iced water. Ladle into small chilled bowls and spoon an extra dollop of strained, plain yoghurt into each (if used).

Using a garlic press, squeeze ginger juice into each soup or over each garnish of yoghurt and serve at once decorated with mint leaves or extra fruit. Ⓕ Ⓔ Ⓥ

Option
Pears poached with just a little vanilla essence, cloves and a cinnamon stick and then puréed and spiked with ginger juice make a fascinating soup which can be served warm or chilled – make sure it is not too thick.

CHERRY SOUP

This classic Hungarian dish is best made using cherries preserved in a light syrup rather than fresh. Although I specify black cherries, you can use the rather more sour red morello cherries – indeed, you should do so if your guests are not fond of sweetness. In any case, add the sugar carefully – you may find that you need far less than the given quantity.

Serves four to six

500 g/1 lb jar black cherries, stoned
thinly pared rind of 1 lemon
6 cloves
cinnamon stick
90-125 g/3-4 oz white sugar
1 tbls cornflour
200 ml/1/3 pint red wine
150 ml/1/4 pint soured cream
ground cinnamon

Put the cherries with their juice (made up to 900 ml/1½ pints with water), lemon rind, cloves, cinnamon and sugar into a saucepan and heat gently to simmering point. Cook uncovered for 15 minutes, then thicken with the cornflour mixed to a paste with 2 tablespoons of water. Continue to simmer, stirring frequently, for 2-3 minutes, remove from the heat, stir in the wine and allow the soup to cool. Strain into a bowl, cover and refrigerate for several hours.

To serve, ladle the soup into chilled bowls and swirl a spoonful of soured cream into each. Dust with a little ground cinnamon. Ⓕ Ⓥ Ⓔ

ICED AVOCADO SOUP

It is important to scrape out the bright green lining to the skins of the avocado. If you don't do this, the soup will be sludge-coloured rather than a delicate pale green.

Serves six

1 kg/2 lb ripe avocados
600 ml/1 pint chicken stock
300 ml/1/2 pint single cream or milk
1 tbls lemon or lime juice
1/2 tsp finely crushed garlic juice
2 tsps salt
up to 2 tsps Worcestershire sauce
double cream or strained yoghurt to finish

Make a purée of the avocado flesh. Blend well and gradually add the chicken stock and enough cream or milk to give the preferred texture. Flavour with lemon or lime, garlic juice, salt and just enough Worcestershire sauce to give a subtle 'bite'. Chill thoroughly and check the seasoning before serving in chilled bowls, with a dollop or swirl of double cream or strained yoghurt. Ⓕ

Options
Sprinkle with finely chopped green pepper, finely chopped fresh ginger, or sprigs of young mint. For a more tropical flavour try chopped fresh green coriander leaves. For a spicy tang, heat a little of the stock with some curry paste or powder before incorporating it. You can replace the lemon juice with orange juice and include a little finely grated orange rind.

GLYNN'S TIP

If the avocado used in Iced Avocado Soup is a little under-ripe and has a raw flavour, sweeten with honey (never with sugar, as it doesn't work) or with a sweet wine, sherry or vermouth.

COLD MINTED PEA SOUP

This perfect summer soup improves by being chilled for a day or two in the refrigerator. You *can* make it using frozen peas, but be sure to do so with the best quality frozen *petits pois* you can find.

Serves six

1.2 litres/2 pints chicken stock
300 ml/½ pint water
1 small onion stuck with 2 cloves
1 garlic clove, peeled
1 tbls fresh, or 1 tsp dried tarragon
1.5 kg/3 lb shelled peas, or frozen petits pois
450 ml/¾ pint plain yoghurt
½ tsp salt
½ tsp freshly ground black pepper
150 ml/¼ pint double or soured cream or strained yoghurt
fresh mint leaves to garnish

Put the chicken stock and water in a saucepan with the onion, garlic, tarragon and peas. Cook until the peas are just tender. Remove and discard the onion. Purée in a blender or food processor, stir in the yoghurt and season to taste. Chill well, for at least 24 hours. Stir in the cream or yoghurt. Alternatively, swirl the cream or yoghurt into the soup just before serving. Spoon into chilled bowls and top with a sprinkling of chopped mint or a whole sprig. Ⓕ Ⓥ Ⓔ

LETTUCE and GINGER SOUP

Even the colour of this soup is refreshing and the bite of fresh ginger adds just the spice needed to perk you up on a hot day.

Serves four

1 tbls finely chopped onion
30 g/1 oz butter
30 g/1 oz fresh ginger root, peeled and thinly sliced
500 g/1 lb lettuce leaves, with stalks removed
1 chicken or vegetable stock cube
900 ml/1½ pints water or water and milk mixed
salt and pepper
lemon slices and cream to serve

Soften the onion well in the butter without browning, then add the ginger and lettuce. Cook gently until the lettuce has wilted. Add the stock cube and the water or water and milk mixed and simmer for 30 minutes. Purée in a blender and strain through a fine sieve (in this case a blender will work better than a food processor). Season to taste; it can be served hot but, if it is to be served cold, wait until it is well chilled before seasoning.

Serve with a slice of lemon and a swirl of cream. Ⓕ Ⓥ

GLYNN'S TIP

It is possible to make an almost instant Gazpacho soup of a kind by cooking frozen Ratatouille (see page 56) in a rich stock for a short while and puréeing it. Don't forget the olive oil.

You will notice that there is no onion in the Gazpacho. If it is included, it makes the mixture turn sour easily and, at the same time, overpowers the flavours of the other ingredients.

ANGELES KENNEDY'S GAZPACHO

There are dozens of Gazpacho recipes in Andalusia, whence it came, so it is pointless to give a definitive one. But this was served to me by Angeles Kennedy when we made some films about Spanish food for BBC-TV, and it was the best I'd ever eaten.

Serves four generously

250 g/8 oz very ripe, red tomatoes, peeled
125 g/4 oz soft white breadcrumbs
1 or 2 garlic cloves, peeled
125 g/4 oz green pepper, chopped
125 g/4 oz cucumber, peeled or unpeeled, chopped
4 tbls olive oil
6 tbls white wine vinegar
900 ml/1½ pints water
salt and extra vinegar to taste
GARNISH
finely chopped peeled tomato
chopped pepper
chopped cucumber
chopped onion (optional)
croûtons

Put all the ingredients except the water into a blender or food processor and reduce to a purée. Slowly add the water until you have the texture you prefer and adjust the flavour by adding salt and a little more vinegar, but no more oil as it will not blend but simply make 'eyes'. Chill well and serve with small bowls of finely chopped peeled tomato, chopped pepper, cucumber, and onion (if liked), plus croûtons fried in olive oil, which your guests add to their own tastes. Ⓕ Ⓥ Ⓔ

Options
Gazpacho may be frozen until slushy and served as a savoury sorbet. If you feel that the soup needs a 'little something', a measure of vodka will do nicely . . .

HOT SOUPS

The most basic and often the best soup to serve hot is made from leftover or fresh vegetables. The technique is simplicity itself. You need about 125 g/4 oz chopped or roughly sliced vegetables for each person. Sweat these in butter or butter and oil in a closed saucepan until soft. Butter gives by far the best flavour and you need at least 30 g/1 oz for every two servings. Some finely chopped onion can also be softened in the butter for extra savour.

Add milk, or stock and milk, water and stock cubes (1.2 litres/2 pints for four servings) and simmer for 20-30 minutes before puréeing in a blender or food processor. Sieve or strain the soup to obtain a satisfying, smooth texture. If you want something more rugged, purée only half the mixture and chop the remainder, so you have a smooth soup with some texture.

I have always found that the combination of milk, water and stock cubes give a better texture and flavour than all stock, which produces a glue-like consistency with root vegetables. Always check the seasoning before serving.

Some Ideas
Beetroot Soup Grate raw beetroot and sweat with a little onion and some chopped carrot. Cook in a mixture of stock and orange juice with a couple of bay leaves for flavour. Remove the leaves before blending, then stir in strained yoghurt until you have a good consistency.
Broad Bean Soup Cook broad beans in stock and milk (600 ml/1 pint to 500 kg/1 lb) until tender, then purée. Sweat chopped onion with a little garlic in butter until soft, then add a round lettuce (roughly chopped) and sweat until it is very limp – purée that, too. Blend the two purées, adding milk or single cream to give the consistency you prefer. Stir in chopped fresh parsley or summer savory before serving, hot or cold.
Carrot Soup Cook peeled carrots as above, with a little onion and a bay leaf, purée, blend with thick, plain yoghurt and serve strewn with fresh dill.
Celery Soup Make a celery soup. Brown 60 g/2 oz ground almonds in a small pan over a low heat. When the nuts are golden brown and smell delicious, stir them into the soup with as much single cream as you like.
Courgette Soup Grate courgettes and sweat in butter for 2 minutes only. Stir 1 heaped tablespoon of dried tarragon into warm chicken stock and let it stand for 10-15 minutes before straining over the softened courgettes. Simmer for 15 minutes (no longer, or you will lose the lovely green colour), then purée in a blender. Stir in single cream before reheating gently without boiling.
Jerusalem Artichoke Soup Cook peeled Jerusalem artichokes in half milk, half chicken stock. Serve with chopped cooked bacon mixed

with tomato and masses of parsley and garlic; top with soured cream.

White Onion Soup Sweat sliced onions in butter without allowing them to colour. Add milk with a glass of white wine and a couple of bay leaves and simmer gently for 20-30 minutes. (Remove the leaves before puréeing.) Purée and thicken with a little cornflour or arrowroot mixed to a paste with water. Add single cream for richness, if you like, or adjust the consistency with more milk. Serve sprinkled with chopped fresh coriander or parsley.

Mushroom Soup Wipe and slice mushrooms (field or flat-capped are best) and sweat with some finely chopped onion and a very little garlic if you like it. Simmer in stock and milk, then thicken with 1 teaspoon of cornflour mixed to a paste with water. Season the soup with salt, pepper and nutmeg, adding a little lemon juice to taste. Serve with 1 spoonful of cream and chopped fresh parsley.

Parsnip Soup Prepare a parsnip soup with a bay leaf in a milk and chicken stock combination. Serve with cream and a sprinkle of cinnamon or some grated orange rind. This is excellent cold, too.

Potato Soup Sweat peeled, chopped potatoes and a generous amount of sliced onion. Cook in a well-flavoured chicken or fish stock (salmon stock makes a wonderful soup); blend, then stir in single cream to achieve the right consistency (it should be fairly thick). Serve piping hot, with lots of freshly ground nutmeg.

Pumpkin Soup Sweat chopped pumpkin and the same amount of chopped parsley, then purée. Serve sprinkled with 60 g/2 oz toasted chopped pecan nuts.

Watercress Soup Chop 90-125 g/3-4 oz watercress (including the stalks) and sweat in butter. Add about 500 g/1 lb defrosted frozen peas, 2 tablespoons of chopped fresh mint and ½ teaspoon of sugar. Simmer in stock and milk for 10-15 minutes (don't overcook or the soup will be khaki-coloured and not green). Blend, and swirl 1 tablespoon of yoghurt or cream into each bowl to serve.

MINESTRONE

If your Minestrone contains pasta, tomato, garlic and oil, you'll be in the south; if beans are in evidence, you'll be in central Italy; and towards the north, rice and herbs are used. This version comes from Milan and dates from the nineteenth century.

Serves six as a light meal and ten as a first course

250 g/8 oz bacon, chopped
60 g/2 oz raw ham (Bayonne, Parma, etc.) cut into strips (optional)
1 medium Savoy cabbage, roughly sliced
2 × 397 g/14 oz cans haricot beans
3.5 litres/6 pints water or stock
60 g/2 oz celery, finely chopped
60 g/2 oz white cabbage, finely diced
125 g/4 oz broad beans, shelled
125 g/4 oz fresh or frozen peas, shelled
125 g/4 oz fresh, canned or frozen asparagus tips (optional)
1 tomato, peeled and chopped
375 g/12 oz Italian rice
2-3 smoked sausages
freshly grated Parmesan cheese

Place the bacon in a large saucepan with the ham, if included, the cabbage, one can of haricot beans with their liquid and the water or stock. (If you are using a stock cube, dilute to twice the recommended amount or the soup will be too salty.)

Bring the soup to the boil and simmer gently for 10 minutes. Chop the remaining can of beans and add to the soup with the celery and chopped cabbage. Continue simmering for another 8-10 minutes. Stir in the remaining ingredients, except the cheese, and simmer gently until the rice is cooked. Remove the sausages, chop them into chunks and return to the soup. Test the seasoning and serve in warm soup bowls, generously sprinkled with the cheese. Ⓕ

GAELIC FARMHOUSE BROTH

Mutton is the ideal meat for this soup, but it is very hard to find nowadays, so use lamb, stewing beef or even ham or bacon, depending on what's available; some bones are essential, though.

Serves eight to ten

750 g/1½ lb lamb, beef, ham or bacon (with bones)
1 tbls dried split peas
125 g/4 oz pearl barley or rice
2 tbls salt
125 g/4 oz onion, chopped
250 g/8 oz carrots, peeled and chopped
1 or 2 sticks celery, chopped
125 g/4 oz leeks, cleaned and sliced
125-185 g/4-6 oz turnips, peeled and thinly sliced
125-185 g/4-6 oz fresh or frozen peas
chopped parsley to serve

Remove the meat from the bones and trim off any fat and gristle. Chop the meat into small pieces. Put the bones into a large saucepan and cover with cold water. Bring to the boil and simmer gently while you prepare the vegetables. Put the chopped meat into a large saucepan with the split peas and pearl barley (if used). Strain the stock off the bones and make up to about 2.25 litres/4 pints with water and add it to the meat. Season and bring slowly to the boil, skimming if necessary, then cover and cook gently for 30 minutes. Add the prepared vegetables and continue simmering for another 30 minutes. Add the peas and rice (if used) and simmer for a further 10-15 minutes.

Serve in warm soup-bowls, sprinkled with plenty of chopped parsley. Ⓕ

COCK-A-LEEKIE

Serves six as a main-course soup

1 boiling fowl, dressed
3.5 litres/6 pints water
bay leaf
sprig of thyme
parsley stalks
salt and pepper
250 g/8 oz onions, finely chopped
625 g/1¼ lb leeks, finely chopped, with the green and white parts separated
60 g/2 oz rice
chopped parsley to serve

Put the fowl in a large pan and add the water. Bring slowly to the boil, skim and reduce the heat to a gentle simmer. Tie the herbs and add, with the salt and pepper, onions and white part of the leeks. Simmer for up to 2 hours, until the chicken is tender. About 30 minutes before the end of cooking time, add the rice. Remove the bird from the pan and add the green leek and continue to simmer for 10 minutes. Take some of the flesh from the bird, chop roughly, then return to the saucepan and heat through. Remove the herbs and check the seasoning.

Serve in warm soup-bowls, garnished with chopped parsley. You can serve the remaining flesh from the chicken at the same time, moistened with a little of the broth.

IRISH LEEK and OATMEAL SOUP

Leeks are the sweetest members of the onion family; their delicate flavour makes them perfect for composite soups, where no ingredient should dominate, as in this very old Irish soup, known in Gaelic as *Brachan rua*.

Serves six to eight

6-8 large leeks, roughly chopped
30 g/1 oz butter
1.5 litres/2½ pints milk and stock mixed
4 heaped tbls flaked oatmeal
salt and freshly ground black pepper
pinch of mace
2 tbls chopped parsley
cream to serve (optional)

Wash the leeks carefully. Heat the butter in a saucepan, add the leeks and leave to 'sweat' for 5 minutes. Add the milk and stock, then sprinkle on the oatmeal and stir well. Bring to the boil and simmer for about 15 minutes, until the oatmeal is cooked. Season to taste. Either serve the soup as it is, or purée in a blender if you prefer a smoother texture. Just before serving, stir in the chopped parsley. Ladle into warm soup-bowls and swirl in a spoonful of cream. Ⓕ

BORTSCH

There are numerous recipes for Bortsch; this one includes chopped celery and beer with water, rather than beef stock.

Serves six

125 g/4 oz onion, sliced
2 tbls oil
500 g/1 lb beetroot, peeled and chopped
125 g/4 oz celery, chopped
125 g/4 oz carrots, chopped
2 garlic cloves, chopped
2 tbls tomato purée
1.5 litres/2½ pints water
300 ml/½ pint beer
salt and pepper
250 g/8 oz red cabbage, shredded
½ tsp sugar
1 tbls chopped parsley
1 tbls lemon juice
soured cream or yoghurt to finish

Sweat the onion in the oil for 5 minutes, then add the prepared beetroot, celery and carrot with the garlic, tomato purée, water and beer. Season with salt and pepper, bring to the boil, then simmer for 30 minutes. Stir in the cabbage and sugar and continue to simmer until the cabbage is tender. Check seasoning and add the parsley with lemon juice to taste. To serve, swirl a spoonful of soured cream or plain yoghurt into each bowl of soup and sprinkle a little extra chopped parsley on top. Ⓕ Ⓥ

PRAWN and ARTICHOKE SOUP

This is a posh soup that is equally delicious hot or cold, but don't over-chill it or you will lose the subtle flavours which make it special.

Serves four

250 g/8 oz cooked unshelled prawns
150 ml/¼ pint white wine (sweetish for preference)
2 tbls brandy
2 tsps tomato purée
1 sachet saffron powder
1 tsp sweet paprika
1 garlic clove, crushed
300 ml/½ pint double cream
salt and pepper
ground mace to taste
425 g/15 oz can artichoke hearts, drained
150 ml/¼ pint milk or single cream
fresh dill to garnish

Shell the prawns and set aside. Put the heads, shells and debris into a saucepan with the wine, brandy, tomato purée, saffron, paprika, garlic and double cream. Season with salt and pepper and a little ground mace. Bring to the boil and simmer uncovered for 15 minutes, then allow the liquid to cool before straining. Reserve 8 even-sized prawns for decoration and chop the remainder.

Rinse the artichoke hearts and purée them in a blender with a few tablespoons of milk or single cream. Sieve the purée into the sauce, mix thoroughly and stir in the chopped prawns. Adjust the consistency by adding a little more milk or single cream and check the seasoning. To serve hot, re-heat gently but *do not* boil. If serving cold, cover and cool completely, then chill lightly. Decorate each bowl of soup with whole prawns and a little fresh dill. Ⓕ Ⓢ

GLYNN'S TIP

When washing leeks, remember to hold their heads downwards at all times, so that any grit they contain is washed down and out of the vegetable, rather than being pushed further in by the pressure of water.

SOUPE DE POISSON VICTORIA

This recipe was devised by a talented young chef in Aberdeen, called William Gibb, whose showpiece fish soup is topped with a soufflé which is encouraged by the steam generated beneath it. After such a triumphal start to a meal, serve a selection of high-quality cold cuts and some special fruit, for nothing could excel or compete with this soup. Make sure that your soup-bowls are ovenproof and have saucers.

Serves four

1 lemon sole
185 g/6 oz scampi, prawns or shrimps
90 g/3 oz butter
1 litre/1¾ pints water
15 g/½ oz flour
2 egg yolks, beaten
4 scallops
4 medium tomatoes, skinned and diced
2 tbls finely chopped parsley
60 g/2 oz celery, finely chopped
60 g/2 oz fennel, finely chopped
60 g/2 oz carrots, finely chopped
3 tbls Pernod
3 tbls white vermouth
salt and pepper
3 egg whites

Skin and fillet the sole and shell the scampi, prawns or shrimps, if necessary. Sauté the shells and fish trimmings with a knob of the butter, then add the water and simmer for no longer than 20 minutes. Strain the stock, return to a clean pan and bring to the boil. Add the sole and sea food and simmer gently for 5 minutes. Remove the sole and mince finely, or chop in a food processor.

To make the soufflé topping, melt 1 table-spoon of the butter and add the flour, cook for 2 minutes without browning, then add 150 ml/¼ pint of the strained fish stock. Cook, stirring continuously, until the mixture leaves the sides of the pan. Turn into a bowl and add the beaten egg yolks and the minced sole, mixing well.

Put a scallop and a quarter of the shellfish seafood in each of the four soup-bowls and top with the tomato and chopped parsley. Sauté the celery, fennel and carrots in the remaining butter in a large pan for about 5 minutes. Then add the Pernod and vermouth with the rest of the strained fish stock and adjust the seasoning. Divide between the soup bowls.

Whisk the egg whites until stiff and fold them into the soufflé mixture. Divide the soufflé between the four bowls, making sure the mixture reaches the edges of the dishes. Cook at 220°C/425°F/Gas Mark 7 for 15 minutes and serve immediately. Ⓕ Ⓢ

Recipe courtesy of William Gibb and the TSB/British Gas Cook 'n' Save Competition.

SAUCES

No longer the mysterious prerogative of the trained chef, sauces made the modern way add colour to your dishes, frame your masterpieces, win friends and influence people.

There's no question about it – a good sauce is vital to many dishes, savoury and sweet. A well-balanced sauce of just the right texture is also a palpable demonstration of the love and care which you are prepared to put on the plate. But don't be deceived by disciples of the past or by practitioners of restaurant food. Sauces based on stocks which start with half a cow and end up with half a pint belong only to the professional kitchen and, anyway, are merely the dying gasps of a style of food brought to perfection by Careme in the 1870s, but already being criticised as old-fashioned 30 years later by Escoffier. This alone should be proof enough that to regard French recipes or techniques as graven in stone, or to believe there is somewhere an academy that officially protects them in the same way the French protect their language, is a gross misunderstanding, indeed an insult to France. The fame of French cooks and their food is based on their brilliant ability always to change and to create. It is only those who are the wrong shape for the professional hole they have chosen who hide between the musty pages and (usually) reheated food of *haute cuisine*. They most certainly have nothing to say to the home cook.

A sauce should do several things. It should, naturally, add welcome moisture and texture contrast. But it must also complement and extend the flavour of the main ingredients that it accompanies. Every contemporary chef with some thought for what he or she is doing, largely dismisses the tactic of using just a few meat stocks as the basis for an entire battery of sauces. Instead they use the essence of the food being presented, often using the combination of ingredients included in the cooking medium, no matter how unorthodox, to make a light purée, or make a quickly reduced sauce from the cooking liquid and thicken that with butter rather than with flour. The particular advantage to the home cook about such sauces is that

nothing is wasted and they are an impeccable reflection and extension of the dish rather than an additional flavouring.

When it comes to presentation it's worth taking an important serving tip from the top professionals. Whether serving steamed pudding and custard, an elegant ice cream or a supreme of chicken, a grilled chop or warm mousselines of fish, serve the sauce under the food rather than over it. This simple technique allows the diner more easily to appreciate how nicely you have prepared and cooked the main part of the dish – why hide your efforts under a sauce? It also gives everyone far more interesting food. Served like this you can enjoy the main part by itself, the sauce by itself or the two in any combination that takes your fancy. It's a small difference of technique that makes a major difference both to the presentation and to enjoyment: it's the latter that is far more important, of course.

Take a new look at sauce making and their uses, and remember you cook at home and not at the Savoy. You'll find you spend less time making more individual sauces.

CREAM *and* BUTTER THICKENED SAUCES

Sauces, cream or butter thickened, referred to collectively as Mounted sauces, are usually based on the cooking liquids and juices you have in the pan, so you don't need quantities of stock.

The principle is that used for Hollandaise sauce and Beurre Blanc. The base is a highly flavoured and seasoned reduction of pan juices or of wine, wine vinegar or stock. Cold butter is beaten into the base by degrees until the desired thickness is achieved – about 125 g/4 oz is needed for 2 tablespoons of reduced liquid. The butter emulsifies the other ingredients to make a coherent sauce out of what looked a mess.

BLUEBERRY STEAK SAUCE

This butter-mounted vinegar sauce is wonderful with steak. The following recipe is sufficient for four people.

185 g/6 oz each (approx) 4 steaks (fillet, sirloin, etc.), trimmed
60 g/2 oz butter
SAUCE
8 tbls dry vermouth or red wine
1½ tbls blueberry vinegar
1-2 garlic cloves, crushed
4 tbls double cream
salt and pepper

Mix the vermouth or wine and vinegar and add squeezed garlic to taste. Reduce this in a small pan over high heat to half the original volume. Stir in the cream and reduce again. (Meanwhile, if the sauce is to accompany steak, cook the steaks in a little of the butter for 2-5 minutes on each side, depending on how you like them. When they are cooked, remove from the pan and keep them warm.) Add the sauce to the pan and mix with the cooking juices. Reduce the heat and add the remaining butter, in small pieces, whisking with a fork. Season with salt and pepper and serve the sauce beside or under the steak, scattered with a few blueberries.

Options
As this is the technique for a butter-mounted vinegar sauce, the recipe can be varied *ad infinitum*. Use raspberry vinegar and scatter with raspberries, or try a herb vinegar – thyme is especially good with steak. You can also omit the cream and simply reduce some alcohol, or alcohol and flavoured vinegar then stir butter into the pan.

HEALTH-CONSCIOUS MOUNTED SAUCE

Concern about levels of cholesterol in foods and growing preferences for lighter sauces, which complement rather than overpower food, have led to a new breed of sauce which excludes floury thickeners. It is important that the sauce doesn't get too hot, so use a double saucepan or a bowl sitting over a pan of *simmering* water.

Makes about 300 ml/½ pint

6 tbls white wine or vermouth
1 tsp black peppercorns
1 bay leaf
a few parsley stalks, crushed
sprig fresh thyme (if available)
30 g/1 oz unsalted butter, chilled
200 g/7 oz Greek strained yoghurt or fromage blanc (quark)
salt and pepper
lemon juice to taste

Place the wine or vermouth in a small pan with the peppercorns, bay leaf, parsley stalks and thyme. Bring to the boil and simmer, unco-vered, until reduced to about 2 tablespoons. Strain into a basin and stand over a pan of simmering water. Beat in the butter, a little at a time, then stir in the strained yoghurt or *fromage blanc* and stir while heating through gently. Season and add lemon juice to taste.

Options
Use fish or chicken stock instead of the wine or vermouth, but take care when seasoning as it will be very highly flavoured when reduced.

SIMPLE CREAM SAUCE

Some of my favourite (but rich!) sauces are made by reducing double cream over medium heat until very thick and then flavouring (see page 17). You can also combine the cream with white wine in equal quantities and reduce the two together. Any fears you may have about boiling double cream are totally unfounded.

Another simple sauce is made by cooking vegetables in cream, then puréeing them together. Leek is my favourite; it is especially good with seafood and fish, but you can also do this with celeriac, carrots, parsnips, peas and mushrooms.

To make a cream leek sauce, simmer 375 g/ 12 oz thinly sliced leeks with 300 ml/½ pint double cream until tender. Purée in a blender or food processor and strain, season and serve warm rather than hot.

> ### GLYNN'S TIP
> *Use thick, strained, Greek yoghurt as an alternative to cream in sauces. Don't use ordinary yoghurt, which tends to separate. The fat-free fromage blanc or quark, which the French first used to make such sauces, is excellent but is harder to obtain and costs more than yoghurt. Boursin, plain or flavoured, is wonderful whisked into stock to make sauces.*

BEURRE BLANC

Lukewarm and slightly foamy, this sauce is almost the signature of France's Loire region. Because the butter must be slowly worked into the base, it is not a sauce which can be made in the food processor. It is perfectly marvellous with poached or grilled fish or with any of the vegetable specialities of the Loire, particularly asparagus or broccoli spears.

Serves four to six

150ml/¼ pint good, dry white wine
4 tbls white or red wine vinegar or cider vinegar
1 tbls finely chopped onion or shallot
up to 375 g/12 oz chilled, unsalted butter

In a heavy-based saucepan which will hold the heat, simmer together the wine, vinegar, onion or shallot until there is no more than 2 tablespoons of liquid left. Cut the butter into walnut-sized pieces. Take the saucepan off the heat and after adding a couple of butter pieces start whisking. Once the butter begins to melt return to a low heat and, whisking continuous-ly, slowly beat in more butter. Keep whisking and it will thicken.

> ### GLYNN'S TIP
> *If a Beurre Blanc sauce becomes liquid and transparent, it cannot be saved. If you see the slightest sign of this happening, plunge the saucepan into a sink of very cold water and whisk in some lemon juice. Alternatively, always take the precaution of having ice-cubes to hand and, if the sauce shows any sign of overheating, drop one into the sauce as you beat furiously off the heat.*

BLENDER HOLLANDAISE SAUCE

This butter sauce is thickened with egg yolks and reduced lemon juice or vinegar. It can be tricky to make by hand but is easy in a blender or food processor.
Hollandaise can be made well in advance and it is always safer to serve the sauce warm rather than hot. Never add more than 60 g/2 oz of butter for each egg yolk.

Serves four

1 tbls lemon juice or a good tarragon or cider vinegar
2 tbls water
155 g/5 oz unsalted butter
3 egg yolks
lemon juice and seasoning to taste

Combine the lemon juice or vinegar and water in a small saucepan and reduce over heat until just 1 teaspoonful remains. Meanwhile, melt the butter until hot but not browning. Mix the egg yolks together in the blender until very smooth and, with the machine running, pour in the vinegar first and then the hot butter in a very slow and steady stream. The texture should be like a thick mayonnaise. Add lemon juice and seasoning to taste. Remove from the blender and keep only just warm over hot water but with no heat under the lower saucepan.

Options
Sauce Maltaise is a classic sauce for serving with asparagus and uses the juice of blood oranges to finish a Hollandaise. You could also use ordinary orange juice and/or grated rind. Fresh lime Hollandaise is excellent with fish.
Sauce Mousseline Add 150 ml/¼ pint of lightly whipped double cream to the completed sauce. A contemporary cook will probably use plain, strained yoghurt instead or could whip up some or all three egg whites lightly and incorporate those. Sauce Mousseline is especially good with masses of watercress or fresh herbs.
Herb Hollandaise Add a good teaspoon of a herb to the vinegar and water mixture.

BASIC WHITE SAUCE

Makes 300 ml/½ pint

300 ml/½ pint milk
flavourings
30 g/1 oz butter
20 g/¾ oz plain flour
salt and white pepper

If time permits, infuse the milk with a bay leaf, a piece of celery stalk, slice of onion or lemon, a few peppercorns and a sprig of thyme – these will give you the basis of a worthwhile sauce.

Bring the milk and flavourings *very slowly* to the point where bubbles appear around the edge of the pan, turn off the heat and allow to cool before straining.

Melt the butter in a medium saucepan, then add the flour and stir to blend. Cook over a medium heat for 2-3 minutes, taking care not to allow the mixture to brown. Take the pan off the heat and strain in the flavoured milk. Return to the heat and bring to the boil, stirring continuously, until the mixture thickens and is smooth. Season with salt and pepper. Continue to cook over a low heat for 2-3 minutes.

If you are not using the sauce immediately, cover the surface with plastic wrap which will prevent a skin forming. Check the seasoning again before serving; you can give the sauce extra gloss and flavour if you whisk in a few knobs of butter; a few walnut-sized pieces will polish as much as 600 ml/1 pint of sauce.

This recipe gives a sauce of coating consistency. If you prefer it thinner, add a little more milk or, better still, some single cream. If it needs to be thicker, cook it for a few minutes over a medium heat (stirring frequently, or it will stick) until the correct consistency is reached.

Options

Cheats' White Sauce Thicken strained, flavoured milk with 2 tablespoons of cornflour that has been slaked (mixed to a paste) with a little of the milk. Cook for a few minutes after it has thickened, and serve. A sauce thickened with cornflour tends to thin if you keep it hot too long.

Cream Sauce Make the basic sauce with only half the amount of milk; when it has thickened, dilute it to the texture you want by adding single or double cream. Delicious as it is, it is also the perfect base for adding almost anything – reconstituted dried mushrooms, prawns, potted shrimps, finely sliced baby artichokes, horseradish, garlic, and so on.

Slimmers' Sauce It won't make that much difference to the calories in these quantities, but you can use skimmed rather than full-fat milk. Instead of enriching it with cream, stir in thick, strained, plain yoghurt just before serving.

White Wine and Cream Sauce For this more elegant version, make the basic recipe with only half the quantity of milk and, once thickened, stir in 150 ml/¼ pint of white wine and let it reduce to the thickness you want. Then add about the same amount of cream and reduce again, or leave it thin. If the sauce is to be served with fish, flavour the wine by first warming it with the trimmings.

Flavour options

Cheese Sauce When the basic sauce is smooth and fully cooked, add 60-90 g/2-3 oz finely grated hard cheese. Use only the best quality, strongly flavoured cheese and finish with grated Parmesan, Pecorino or Gruyère. So-called cooking cheese, a very mild Cheddar, is useless for flavouring; you will end up using an enormous quantity, so it is better to use a more flavoursome cheese. Reheat gently, but don't allow the sauce to boil, or the cheese may turn to oil making the sauce stringy and unpleasant. Season to taste but be sparing with the salt. The flavour of cheese is improved by the addition of mustard – *either* add ½ teaspoon of mustard powder with the flour when making the roux, *or* stir 1 teaspoon made French or Dijon mustard into the finished sauce with the seasoning. Otherwise add freshly grated nutmeg.

Mushroom Sauce For a dark, rather rugged sauce, slice 90 g/3 oz mushrooms and sauté them over a high heat in 45 g/1½ oz butter before stirring in the flour. Then proceed as above. The addition of cream is good, and just 1 teaspoon of wine vinegar stirred in with the seasoning gives an extra dimension.

A paler, more elegant mushroom sauce can be made with the cream, or white wine and cream, sauce to which very finely sliced button mushrooms are added just before serving.

Onion (Soubise) Sauce Place 250 g/8 oz sliced onions in a pan with 30 g/1 oz butter and 2 tablespoons of water. Cover and cook over the lowest possible heat until the onions are soft and transparent, but not brown.

Make the basic white sauce and stir in the softened onions with 2 or 3 tablespoons of cream or milk. I prefer to purée the onions, but they should be so meltingly soft that they are acceptable as they are. This sauce is delicious if seasoned with a ¼-½ teaspoon of dried mint. Adding colour with a little tomato purée can help to lift this sauce out of the ordinary, too.

Caper Sauce Add 1 tablespoon capers and 1-2 teaspoons of lemon juice to the basic sauce.

Citrus Sauce Add 2 teaspoons finely grated lemon, orange or lime rind and 1 or 2 tablespoons of the same juice to the basic sauce. Adjust the sharpness by adding either extra juice or a little cream. This sauce is particularly delicious with fish.

Herb Sauce Stir lots of chopped fresh herbs (at least 3 tablespoons) into a plain, cream or white wine sauce. Let the herbs macerate over very low heat for 10 minutes or so, then strain them out just before serving and stir in some fresh ones. Most herbs are suitable – tarragon, parsley, dill, chervil, marjoram, fennel and mint.

Velouté Sauce This is an important variation of White Sauce made, not with flavoured milk, but with a flavoured stock. Cream or milk is usually added to improve its appearance and give a richer flavour.

If making a Velouté to serve with poached chicken, strain and reduce the cooking liquid and use this as your liquid together with a little cream, wine, and extra flavouring. Conversely, you could make a thickish white sauce and thin it with this stock. To a fish stock Velouté add some cream and dry white vermouth and reduce or cook down and finally add some saffron for colour and flavour.

PARSLEY SAUCE

Most recipe books will tell you to make parsley sauce by adding 1-2 tablespoons of finely chopped parsley to a basic white sauce. By following this advice you lose out on the fine flavour and superb colour of the herb, so try my method instead.

3 or 4 tbls finely chopped parsley
salt and black pepper
300 ml/½ pint creamy milk, plus 2 tbls
1 tbls cornflour
knob of butter

Put the parsley into a saucepan with 6 tablespoons water, ½ teaspoon of salt and plenty of freshly ground black pepper. Simmer *very gently* for 3 minutes to extract lots of green colour. Add 300 ml/½ pint milk and heat to just below boiling point. Mix the cornflour with 2 tablespoons milk to a smooth paste. Add it to the sauce and continue cooking, stirring continuously, until the sauce thickens. Beat in the knob of butter, check the seasoning and serve. You could also add some chopped parsley just before serving.

COCKLE and HORSERADISH SAUCE

A wonderful accompaniment to all sorts of white fish, steamed or braised. If possible, use some of the fish juices in making the basic white sauce. Add 250 g/8 oz drained cockles (don't use the ones preserved in vinegar, just those which have been brined) and 1 teaspoon of creamed horseradish. Test the seasoning, adding salt and pepper and a little lemon juice to taste. Heat gently to warm through, without letting the sauce boil, and serve immediately or the cockles will toughen.

GLYNN'S TIP

The secret of cream and wine sauces is to cook them at a low temperature for a long time, adding stock, wine and cream to thin the sauce and letting it reduce and concentrate again. Putting a cream sauce through a fine strainer always improves the texture.

TOMATO SAUCE

When really ripe, red-skinned tomatoes are plentiful, use them to make a fresh tomato sauce. At other times, use canned plum or crushed tomatoes with a little extra tomato concentrate if you think it needs more flavour. The secret of both kinds of tomato sauce is to simmer slowly.

Makes about 300 ml/½ pint

1 tbls olive oil
1 garlic clove
500 g/1 lb ripe, red tomatoes, peeled, seeded and chopped, or 397 g/14 oz can plum tomatoes
pinch of dried thyme
1 bay leaf
2-3 tsps tomato paste
salt and pepper
pinch of sugar (optional)

In a saucepan heat the oil over a low heat and soften the garlic for one minute. Add the tomatoes, thyme, bay leaf and stir. Bring to the boil, then simmer, uncovered, over a low heat, stirring occasionally, until the sauce is thick and the tomatoes are very soft.

Remove the bay leaf and either blend the sauce in a food processor or push it through a sieve. Return to a clean saucepan, stir in the tomato paste and season to taste. Simmer for a further 10 minutes and serve hot or cold.
Photograph, p. 115.

Options
Spicy Tomato Sauce Stir 2 teaspoons of ground cumin and 1 teaspoon of ground coriander into the blended or sieved sauce with the tomato paste. This is a good sauce for vegetables and transforms something as boring as cauliflower into a marvellous first course.
Spicy Tomato and Coconut Sauce Blend 90 g/3 oz creamed coconut with 200 ml/⅓ pint boiling water and add to the sieved or blended sauce with 2 teaspoons of ground cumin and 1 tablespoon of tomato paste. Simmer for 15-20 minutes. This sauce is best made 24 hours in advance.
Fast-cooked Tomato Sauce When you need a sauce in a hurry, take advantage of the emulsifying properties of boiling oil. Turn a can of plum tomatoes in their own juices into a saucepan, mash, and bring them to the boil. Pour in a few tablespoons of good, strong olive oil and keep boiling. It will emulsify with the tomato juices and appear to thicken them. Season, with salt, pepper and a little onion and garlic, and keep boiling until you are ready to serve it or it is thick. I like to make it look more professional by sieving before serving and giving it a final boil again, with a sprig or two of a fresh herb — mint is particularly good and unexpected in a tomato sauce.

GLYNN'S TIP

I sometimes manage to grow tomatoes in my patch of London garden. I save the best ones to make an uncooked tomato sauce to serve with cold meats or as a dip.

Plunge the ripe tomatoes into boiling water and then into cold water so they are easy to peel. Peel, then purée them in a blender or food processor with a little vodka, season — and that's all there is to it! Add a few sprigs of thyme or basil and leave to infuse for a day or so; remove before serving. Alternatively, add chopped herb leaves and serve them in the sauce.

BARBECUE SAUCE

It is difficult to estimate exactly how much barbecue sauce you will need at a party but this quantity will be sufficient to cook 1 dozen thick pork spare-ribs or 8 pork chops or 8 chicken breasts or 3 dozen chicken wings (see page 88).

Makes about 150 ml/¼ pint

2 tbls butter
1 medium onion, very finely chopped
4 celery sticks, trimmed and finely chopped
1 medium green pepper, very finely chopped
2-4 garlic cloves, finely chopped
2 tbls wine vinegar
2 tbls fresh lemon juice
2 tbls Worcestershire sauce
2 heaped tbls dark brown sugar
1 tbls mustard powder
1 tsp salt
300 ml/½ pint tomato ketchup
water or tomato juice as needed

Melt the butter in a medium pan; soften and brown the onion well. Add the other chopped vegetables and stir until softened. Add all the other ingredients and simmer for 30 minutes, then dilute with water or tomato juice to a coating consistency that is not too gooey.

GLYNN'S TIP

Pour my Barbecue Sauce over chicken wings or thighs, pork spare-ribs, chicken breasts or whatever, and bake at 150°C/300°F/Gas Mark 2 until tender.

SPICY CHERRY SAUCE

Best served warm, this sauce can be made from fresh cherries but is equally successful with canned or bottled fruit. Good with chicken and turkey, ham and tongue or tenderloin of pork.

Makes about 600 ml/1 pint

450 ml/¾ pint red wine, or half red wine and half port wine
1 cinnamon stick
1 or 2 whole cloves
1 tsp grated orange rind
1 bay leaf
2 level tbls cornflour
500 g/1 lb red cherries, stoned
OPTIONAL EXTRAS
sugar
redcurrant jelly
orange or lemon juice
dark rum or brandy
butter

Simmer the wine gently with the spices, grated rind and bay leaf in a covered pan for 5 minutes, then allow to cool completely. Strain the spiced wine into a clean pan and thicken with the cornflour mixed to a paste with 3-4 tablespoons of water or juice from the cherries. Stir the sauce until it thickens, then add the cherries and heat through. Taste and sweeten with a little sugar or redcurrant jelly if you wish, or add citrus juice to sharpen. A few tablespoons of dark rum or brandy add richness, and a knob of butter beaten in just before serving gives the sauce a glossy shine.

ONION-RAISIN SAUCE for POULTRY

A combination of old and new Middle Eastern cooking, this recipe from Jerusalem gives a rich, sweet-sour savour to hot chicken, duck, turkey or guinea fowl. It is also delicious hot or cold with cold meats such as ham and tongue. Cooked down until really thick it could be served as a vegetable rather than a sauce.

Serves four to eight or more depending on reduction

500 g/1 lb onions
185 g/6 oz butter
600 ml/1 pint water or stock
150 ml/¼ pint orange juice
1 tsp hot paprika
2 tsps ground cinnamon
1 tbls ground allspice
2 tbls honey
2 tbls Cognac
250 g/8 oz seedless California raisins

Peel and cut the onion into thin rings and brown lightly in the butter. Add all the remaining ingredients and simmer gently for 15-20 minutes until well-blended and savoury, and as thick as you would like. Stir from time to time, taking care not to let the sauce burn. Orange juice can be used in a higher proportion, to replace some or all of the stock or water; this will make a rather sweeter sauce.

GRAVY

I've nothing against gravy except when it is poured all over everything on the plate, negating all the textures and flavours that some poor cook has struggled to make. If you are a cook who suffers thus, the answer is in your own hands – don't make so much!

The best meat sauces (a better name than gravy) are made in the pan in which meat has been roasted. So, plan ahead and always have a few slices of onion and a bay leaf and some carrot or a similar flavouring in the base of the pan; masses of parsley stalks are among the best, because they absorb the fat while flavouring the juices. If you like garlic, one or two crushed garlic cloves are a good addition.

Unthickened Remove the meat and let it rest for 15 minutes or so, which makes it more succulent and easier to carve. For 10 minutes of this time, let the roasting-tin sit quietly so that the fat rises to the top, then gently pour off most but not all of it. Put the tin over a medium heat on top of the cooker and add about as much liquid as there is already in the pan – you can add red or white wine, or some of the cooking liquid from a vegetable that you are serving. Scrape everything from the bottom and boil furiously until it has reduced by at least a quarter. Taste, and add a little salt or pepper. That's the best gravy of all.

Thickened If you want more gravy, or a thicker one, add more cooking liquid and thicken with a little cornflour slaked with water. Leave it warm on the cooker and when you have carved, tip any juices from the carving into the gravy. Strain into a warmed gravy boat.

Alternatively, stir about a tablespoon of flour into the remaining fat and cooking debris, turn up the heat and, stirring and scraping like mad, brown everything including the flour. Pour in vegetable water, still stirring, until you get the thickness you want. Don't worry about lumps and nasty looking bits. Adjust the flavour, and strain into the gravy boat.

MAYONNAISE

Mayonnaise isn't *real* mayonnaise unless at least half the oil used is olive oil. Use the very best olive oil you can find or afford, for it is the olives' flavour that makes mayonnaise.

Mayonnaise is simpler to make than most people imagine, especially in small quantities.

> ### GLYNN'S TIP
> *If, by any chance, the mayonnaise curdles before you have finished beating in the oil, beat up an egg yolk in a clean bowl and slowly whisk the curdled mayonnaise into that.*

Although it is very satisfying to make by hand with nothing but a wooden spoon, a large bowl, time and strength, an electric beater, blender or a food processor can do the work for you. Dry mustard powder is added not as a flavouring but as an aid to emulsification and should not be omitted; it will not be detectable by the palate.

The only absolute essential about making mayonnaise is that everything *must* be the same temperature, either cold, at room temperature or slightly warm.

Electric Beater Mayonnaise Beat three egg yolks until creamy in a large bowl together with a good pinch of dry mustard. Gently dribble in some oil, a teaspoonful or so at a time, and beat it in well before adding more. Soon you will see the mayonnaise forming but continue to pour the oil in slowly. If it gets too thick, add a few spoonfuls of water, cream or any other liquid to thin it, and continue. Three egg yolks will take at least 300 ml/½ pint of olive oil and can take up to 50 per cent more; you can use half sunflower, safflower or other good-quality vegetable oil and half olive oil, or use only enough olive oil to give a slight flavour. Once the mayonnaise is made, adjust the flavour with seasoning and perhaps with a touch of lemon juice or vinegar. If you are not using it straight away, stir in 1-2 tablespoons of boiling water, which seems to 'set' it. Provided it is well sealed, mayonnaise will keep for several weeks in a refrigerator.

Processor Mayonnaise When making mayonnaise in a processor or blender, start off with one whole egg and an egg yolk with the mustard and then proceed as above. Again, use half vegetable oil and half olive oil.

FLAVOURINGS for MAYONNAISE

Over the years I have created and published many recipes for flavoured mayonnaise – here are just a few with some ideas of how to use them.

Garlic Mayonnaise (Aïoli) Either make your mayonnaise and flavour it highly with garlic juice or finely chopped garlic, or beat the egg and egg yolk in a processor with 6 decent-sized cloves of peeled garlic; once they are a paste, dribble in the olive oil in the normal way.

Herb Mayonnaise Snip in masses of fresh herbs, either just one variety or a mixture. To add colour, whisk in some puréed raw or cooked spinach. This is good served with white meats and fish and with vegetables and eggs.

Nut Mayonnaise For each 150 ml/¼ pint mayonnaise, add 60 g/2 oz of finely chopped or ground toasted nuts. If you use walnuts, add a touch of vinegar and some garlic; with almonds, add a touch of orange rind or orange-flower water. Nut mayonnaise is excellent with raw vegetables as a *crudité* dip and with poultry.

Pear and Tarragon Mayonnaise Start with very thick mayonnaise; to every 150 ml/¼ pint fold in up to 185 g/6 oz of puréed or finely chopped fresh ripe pears and a teaspoon of tarragon vinegar. Add tomato purée for colour if the sauce is not too thin.

Saffron Mayonnaise This is one of the most important flavoured sauces for cold fish and for vegetables. Stir in 1 sachet of powdered saffron and allow it to sit with the mayonnaise for a few hours so that the maximum effect is obtained. Garlic is always good in this and if you have some hot sauce (*harissa* perhaps, or a Chinese chilli sauce), add the merest drop; this is just right to use as a *rouille* to spread on rounds of toast to accompany some fish soups.

Watercress Mayonnaise Add the finely chopped leaves of a bunch of watercress; marvellous on cold poached fish or chicken.

GREEN PEPPER SAUCE for POULTRY SALADS

375 g/12 oz (1-2) whole sweet green peppers
1 or 2 fresh green chilli peppers
1 large ripe papaya
150 ml/¼ pint mayonnaise
150 ml/¼ pint soured cream

De-stalk the sweet green peppers and scoop out the seeds. Slice them thinly and cook in boiling water until they start just to soften – they must remain a very bright green. Drain well and while still warm purée the sweet peppers with the chilli peppers in a blender. The seeds of the chilli peppers are the hottest part so you may like to remove them – but use rubber gloves because their oils can act as a painful irritant to the skin or eyes. You might have to add a little liquid – water would do well or a little mayonnaise or soured cream. Force the pepper purée through a sieve, using the back of a soup ladle.

Blend together the mayonnaise and the soured cream then fold in the green pepper purée. It needs to stand for a couple of hours for the flavour to develop properly. This quantity is enough for about 500 g/1 lb of cold turkey, chicken or duck and is very good served with mango, papaya, pineapple or lychees.

AVOCADO DRESSING

Especially good with cold fish, but also perfect for dips and as a *crudité* sauce. Provided the avocados are really ripe, you can scrape up every bit of the bright green flesh directly inside the skins, which gives a sensational colour and flavour. Avocado dressing will save the day when you want something similar to a mayonnaise but don't have the necessary ingredients.

Serves four to eight

250 g/8 oz ripe avocado flesh
1 tbls orange juice
2 tsps lemon juice
3 tbls ground almonds
2 tbls olive oil
1 tsp orange-flower water
salt to taste

In a blender or food processor, purée all the ingredients and strain if necessary. If you have no orange-flower water, add a little finely grated orange rind.

Options

This dressing is particularly suited to the addition of yoghurt, soured cream or whipped double cream.

You can omit the orange juice and add 2 tablespoons lemon juice and 2 tablespoons of roughly chopped fresh mint. Let it sit for a few hours to develop the flavour fully and add some garlic if you like. It is good with almost anything but particularly with chilled new potatoes.

SALAD DRESSINGS

Nowadays, many people find traditional oil and vinegar salad dressings compete too fiercely with wines and so they leave them off altogether. In any case, those which contain mustard and sugar as well as oil and vinegar often make salad taste like pickle or some congealed Chinese takeaway! Here are some modern ways to make less intrusive additions to your salads. See also the salad section, page 57.

Oil and Vinegar Other than a little garlic, which you have rubbed around the bowl, and salt and pepper, you need nothing but oil and vinegar. The oil should be olive oil and the vinegar should be the finest you can afford, but it certainly should *not* be malt vinegar. The proportions of oil to vinegar are a matter of taste but if your ingredients are both top quality, they can vary from three to five parts of oil to one of vinegar. Although the combination can be shaken together before being poured on to washed, dried and chilled salad leaves, this coats them with an opaque sauce that can hide the fresh colours. Sprinkle the oil and the vinegar

directly into the bowl, season lightly, toss quickly and serve. Even better (and easier) is when you provide small bottles of olive oil and vinegar on the table and let people sprinkle on what they prefer in the European style.

No-vinegar dressing To keep vinegar off the plate and off your palate you must turn to citrus flavourings. But don't use the juice; instead, finely grate a light shower of rind directly over each serving of salad. Fresh lime is the most impressive, but lemon or orange is equally good. Any of the three can be used to balance a vodka dressing – plain vodka with grated lime, dill vodka with lemon and so on.

Don't use too much and *do* grate directly over the plates so you use all the citrus oils which contain the flavour and have little bitterness.

Oil dressings If you develop an interest in the different flavours of olive oils, you'll soon find that you need no other flavourings for your salad. Other flavourful oils, particularly walnut, hazelnut and almond oil, can be used with discretion to flavour safflower, sunflower or soya oil, or they can be sprinkled lightly directly on to salads with no vinegar or lemon juice. Walnut oil is a revelation on sliced tomatoes. Nut oils must be kept dark and cool; but let them warm to room temperature before serving, so their full flavour can be appreciated.

Oil-free dressings The best alternative to oils is vodka, especially on salads which contain such bitter leaves as radicchio or curly endive. Sprinkle it on with a teaspoon. For a real sensation, the vodka should be flavoured by warming it with a suitable herb or a little onion or garlic. For four servings you will need only 4 tablespoons vodka and perhaps 1 teaspoon of dried dill. Saffron is marvellous for flavouring vodka, too.

Don't let the vodka get more than slightly warm, cool it with the herb still in it, then strain through a very fine sieve or a piece of muslin before using it.

COMPOUND BUTTERS

If you don't fancy yourself as a saucemaker yet feel that some foods should be moistened, flavoured butters are your saviours. Simply made, using leftovers of butter and flavourings, they can be stored in the freezer and brought out in an emergency. Try beans with a red pepper butter, or poached fish with an olive and olive oil butter, ham sandwiches with a seed mustard

GLYNN'S TIP

At Christmas time, pots of flavoured butter make really nice gifts.

GLYNN'S TIP

Margarine is cheaper than butter but does not have the flavour or texture. The new low-fat spreads that contain some butter are more convincing in flavour and as they are soft straight from the refrigerator, they can be flavoured very quickly by simply stirring in goodies.

butter, salmon with dill and lemon butter, and almost anything with a vodka butter!

All the following flavourings are given in quantities sufficient for 125 g/4 oz butter. Use a good quality unsalted or slightly salted butter, and soften but *do not* melt it before beating in the other ingredients. Spoon the savoury butter into a ramekin or other small dish, cover with plastic wrap and chill well.

Anchovy Mix into the butter 4 teaspoons anchovy essence and a pinch of cayenne pepper.

Currants and Cumin Seed Heat 1 tablespoon cumin seeds in a small non-stick pan until they turn a light golden brown. Cool before beating into the butter with 2 tablespoons of chopped currants. Marvellous on most vegetables but especially on cabbage and carrots.

Curry and Lemon Stir in 1 heaped tablespoon curry paste with 1 tablespoon finely grated lemon rind. Don't use curry powder, or the butter will have an unpleasant floury taste.

Green Olive and Orange Chop 2 tablespoons of green olives very finely and beat into the butter with 2 teaspoons finely grated orange rind. Great on fish.

Ground Almonds Toast 60 g/2 oz flaked almonds and grind them in a food processor. Beat the almonds into the butter with ½ teaspoon grated lemon rind.

Hazelnut Grind 2 tablespoons toasted hazelnuts in a food processor. Add a ½ teaspoon finely grated orange rind. Especially good on green beans and cauliflower.

Olive Oil and Black Peppercorn Mix 3 tablespoons good olive oil into the butter with 1 teaspoon roughly ground black peppercorns. Have your pepper-mill on its coarsest setting, or use a pestle and mortar to grind the peppercorns.

Orange and Coriander Seeds Beat into the butter 1 tablespoon finely grated orange rind, 1 teaspoon lemon juice, 1 teaspoon orange juice and 2 tablespoons crushed coriander seeds.

Green Peppercorn and Walnut Mix 1 tablespoon crushed green peppercorns with 2 tablespoons chopped walnuts and beat into the butter.

Red Pepper and Garlic Chop 125 g /4 oz of sweet red pepper roughly and plunge into fast-boiling water. Bring back to the boil, then drain in a colander and run cold water through until cold. Chop very finely, mince or process before beating into the butter with a crushed garlic clove.

Seed Mustard Toast 2 teaspoons mustard seeds by putting them into a small non-stick pan and heating until you hear the seeds popping. Cool before mixing with 1 heaped tablespoon Dijon mustard and beating into the butter. You can use 1 tablespoon of seed mustard instead of the toasted mustard seeds.

Tomato, Garlic and Olives Beat into the butter 2 teaspoons tomato paste, 2 teaspoons minced garlic, and 4 black Calamata olives, stoned and minced or very finely chopped. This is excellent on poached cod, or on hot toast or cold biscuits as a drinks snack.

Vodka Honestly, you can't believe how good this is. Put 2 tablespoons vodka and the softened butter into a food processor or blender and whizz until emulsified. Add a little salt to taste.

If ever you get bored, add chopped walnuts or toasted hazelnuts, crushed green peppercorns, fresh tarragon leaves, mint leaves, grated orange rind or red lumpfish caviare. All these combinations are wonderful on everything!

CUSTARD SAUCES

What most people tend to call 'custard' is probably sweetened milk thickened with cornflour and flavoured with vanilla. There is nothing wrong with this sauce – where would most trifles and steamed puddings be without it? A *real* custard, called *crème Anglaise* by snobs, should be thickened with egg yolks. If you've never made or eaten one before, try it; the difference in flavour is surprising and well worth the effort.

Serves four to six

4-5 egg yolks
90 g/3 oz caster sugar
450 ml/3/4 pint full cream milk
flavouring

Before you start, decide how confident you are. If you are unsure or are in a rush, add a teaspoon of cornflour to the above ingredients. This will prevent the mixture from turning into scrambled eggs if you don't get the method quite right.

Beat the egg yolks and the sugar well until pale and creamy, then beat in the cornflour (if used). Heat the milk to boiling point and pour it into the egg mixture in a stream, beating all the time. Return the mixture to the saucepan and stir continuously over medium-to-low heat until the mixture coats the back of the spoon. Keep the temperature low – if the mixture bubbles at all it is probably about to burn or turn to scrambled egg on the base. It will

appear rather thin but thickens as it cools to lukewarm, which is the best temperature to serve it. Strain it through a fine sieve and then flavour it lightly.

Options

The most common flavouring is vanilla – about a teaspoon of essence is enough. Such spirits as brandy or whisky or rum are festive and rich but you can also add almost any liqueur, very strong black coffee, orange-flower water or rose water.

Bay Custard A wonderful, old-fashioned flavouring for custard is bay leaf. Macerate 1-2 bay leaves in the milk until it is flavoured, then remove. This recipe is especially good with baked apples.

Foamy Custard This is equally old-fashioned and a charming change in texture from the usual custard. Make 600 ml/1 pint custard with 2 egg yolks and 2 tablespoons of cornflour; it will be slightly thicker than you usually expect. Flavour in your favourite way, cool, then whisk up the 2 egg whites and fold them into the warm custard.

Rich Custard Sauce This richer version is perfect to serve with Christmas pudding, or serve it cold with fresh fruit. Blend 2 egg yolks with 1 or 2 tablespoons sugar and 1 tablespoon cornflour in a bowl. Pour over 300 ml/1/2 pint hot milk, then return to the heat and thicken, stirring continuously. Remove from the heat and add 300 ml/1/2 pint double cream that has been reduced to half its original volume. You can stir in a little rum, brandy or orange liqueur.

MRS BEETON'S WINE and BUTTER SAUCE

The definitive accompaniment to plain sponge puddings, baked or steamed, this sauce is equally good with baked fruit. Ring the changes by replacing the sherry or port with any liqueur, brandy or rum; try adding some finely grated citrus rind, too, for extra flavour.

125 g/4 oz butter
2 tsps plain flour
150 ml/1/4 pint milk or water
1 level tbls caster sugar
150 ml/1/4 pint sherry or port
grated nutmeg to taste
finely grated orange or lemon rind (optional)

Chop the butter into small pieces, put into a saucepan and sprinkle the flour over. Add the milk or water and stir while bringing slowly to the boil, then stir in the sugar and wine. As soon as it is well blended, add a little grated nutmeg and finely grated citrus rind (if used). If there are lumps, strain the sauce. Serve immediately.

ORANGE ZABAGLIONE SAUCE

Serve this light sauce warm, freshly made, or make in advance and serve cold. It is particularly good with Christmas pudding, mince pies and similar rich puddings.

3 large egg yolks or 2 medium eggs
30 g/1 oz caster sugar
150 ml/1/4 pint orange juice and white wine, mixed
finely grated rind of half an orange

Beat the yolks or eggs with the sugar in a bowl until light and creamy. Meanwhile, have simmering a pan of water into which your bowl will fit. Once the sugar has dissolved and the eggs are fluffy, add the orange juice, wine and rind and put the bowl over the simmering water. Using an electric hand-mixer (or whisk and a lot of elbow-grease), keep beating fast until the foam thickens. As soon as the mixture drops from the beaters in blobs, rather than a dribble, it is ready. Take the bowl off the heat and continue beating furiously until the mixture cools and stops setting. Serve immediately, or cover and allow it to get cold.

FRUIT COULIS

Thin purées of fruit, known as *coulis*, have become fashionable for puddings, and very nice, too. The most popular by far is a raspberry *coulis*, made simply by puréeing fresh or frozen raspberries, sieving out the pips and then flavouring. You need sugar, but not much, and nothing improves raspberries better than a little rose water. That's all there is to it, although you could add vodka or brandy to lift the sauce.

The next most popular *coulis* is made from mango but, once it is puréed, mango seems to change flavour and I've decided that it does not do justice to such a wonderful fruit. Strawberries don't react well to being puréed either.

One of the most interesting sauces of this kind is of dried apricots. Cook them until they are soft in just enough water, white wine or orange juice, then purée in a blender. Adjust the flavour with a little lemon juice and some orange-flower water.

GLYNN'S TIP

Instead of custard, try hot fruit sauces: apple with spice or citrus peel and honey goes with most heavy puddings, baked fruit sponges and baked fruits, or add other stewed fruits.

CHEESE-BASED STUFFINGS

These deliciously fragrant stuffings based on soft cheese are placed between the skin and the breast of chicken, guinea fowl or turkey. They don't set too solidly and keep the breast meat wonderfully moist. With the addition of two eggs, they can be baked separately to set like a savoury tart and sliced as an accompaniment to plainly roasted poultry or meats.

For very large chickens or small turkeys (3.6-4.5 kg/8-10 lb) double the recipes; for the usual Christmas type turkey 5.5 kg/12 lb or more, treble the recipes at least.

COURGETTE with TARRAGON

250 g/8 oz courgettes, trimmed
salt
60 g/2 oz butter
1 tbls chopped fresh tarragon (or 1 tsp dried)
185 g/6 oz curd cheese
salt and pepper
grated nutmeg

Grate the courgettes coarsely. Sprinkle with salt, let drain and then squeeze with your hands to expel all moisture. Melt the butter in a large saucepan, add the courgettes and tarragon and stir to coat them evenly. Cook gently for 2 or 3 minutes. Let cool a little then fold in the cheese and flavour with salt, pepper and nutmeg. Stuff between the skin and breast of the bird.

CELERIAC with HORSERADISH

250 g/8 oz peeled celeriac
60 g/2 oz butter
150 ml/¼ pint single cream or milk
185 g/6 oz curd cheese
1 tbls creamed horseradish
1 tbls lemon juice
salt and pepper

Cut the celeriac into small chunks and cook gently, uncovered, in the butter and milk or single cream until soft. Allow to cool completely then process with the remaining ingredients and season to taste.

Options

Grate the celeriac and soften in butter and 5 or 6 tablespoons of single cream. Cool and fold into the curd cheese with the horseradish and lemon juice. Check the seasoning and add more horseradish or lemon juice if needed. Garlic is a good addition and chopped parsley would add both flavour and colour.

Leeks with Mustard Substitute leeks for the celeriac and 2 teaspoons of seed mustard for the creamed horseradish. Slice the leeks thinly and cook as above; leave a few whole and purée the remainder with the other ingredients.

CARROT with CARDAMOM

250 g/8 oz peeled carrots, coarsely grated
60 g/2 oz butter
150 ml/¼ pint single cream or milk
185 g/6 oz curd cheese
1 tsp whole cardamom seeds, removed from the pods and lightly crushed
60 g/2 oz fresh breadcrumbs
1 tbls orange juice
salt and pepper

Cut the carrot into small chunks and cook gently, uncovered, in the butter and milk or single cream until soft. Blend the cool, softened carrots, coated in butter and milk or cream, with the remaining ingredients.

CHICKPEAS, PIMENTO, SPINACH and CUMIN

440 g/14 oz cooked chickpeas
90 g/3 oz canned red pepper, sliced
250 g/8 oz frozen leaf spinach, defrosted and well drained
1 tsp roasted cumin seeds
salt and pepper
orange juice and rind (optional)
45 g/1½ oz softened butter

Mash some of the chickpeas slightly, stir in the sliced red pepper (equal to about half the usual small can of cooked red peppers). Pull the spinach apart and add to the mixture together with the roasted cumin seeds, salt and pepper; mix thoroughly. Add a little orange juice or orange rind, too, and stir in the butter.

GLYNN'S TIP

The curd-cheese stuffings are excellent fillings for parcels of phyllo pastry. Cigar-shapes are the most attractive: cut sheets of phyllo into strips about 5 cm/2 in wide and paint with olive oil. Put stuffing at one end, roll a few times then hold in the sides and continue rolling. Bake only until pastry is lightly browned and filling has set.

FRUIT AND NUT STUFFINGS

These stuffings are specially suited for placing in the neck end of all poultry. Unlike the usual stuffings, these are loosely textured, but full of flavour and colour. These quantities given are sufficient for an average-size chicken (2 kg/4 lb approx.). For turkeys or geese, you will need to double the quantities.

Use the mixture to stuff the neck end of the bird then secure the neck flap under the body with toothpicks; don't do it too tightly or, as the stuffing swells with the heat, the skin might burst.

These recipes are also suitable for rolling into belly of pork, or for stuffing into pork loins and chops.

CRANBERRY, APPLE and PECAN

Especially good for those who don't like sweet sauces.

125 g/4 oz Cox's Orange Pippin apple, cored but not peeled
185 g/6 oz fresh or defrosted cranberries
60 g/2 oz toasted pecan nuts, roughly chopped
2 tbls orange-flavoured liqueur
ground allspice to taste
45 g/1½ oz softened butter

Grate the apple coarsely and mix with the cranberries, nuts and liqueur. Flavour with allspice, then stir in the butter. Use for stuffing as suggested above.

PINEAPPLE, WATER CHESTNUT, COCONUT and LYCHEE with GINGER

The rosemary is a surprise in this Oriental mixture but works wondrously well.

185 g/6 oz canned pineapple chunks, drained
185 g/6 oz canned lychees, drained and stoned
125 g/4 oz canned water chestnuts, drained
1 tbls peeled and grated fresh ginger
60 g/2 oz desiccated coconut
2 tsps fresh rosemary, chopped
2 tbls white or dark rum
45 g/1½ oz butter

Slice the pineapple chunks and lychees in half, grate the water chestnuts and mix all the ingredients together. Use for stuffing as suggested above.

BLACK CHERRIES, PRUNES, TOASTED NUTS, BREADCRUMBS

425 g/15 oz can black cherries, drained and pitted
8 dried prunes, pitted and chopped
2 tbls toasted pecans, hazelnuts or almonds
2 heaped tbls fresh white breadcrumbs
2 tbls or more dark rum
cinnamon to taste (1/2 tsp or more)
60 g/2 oz softened butter.

Mix all the ingredients together and use for stuffing as suggested.

MEAT-BASED STUFFINGS

This is the most useful style of stuffing for poultry, for being pork based they will baste the flesh as they sit under the skin during the cooking; the flavourings in the pork or sausage base are also able to perfume the flesh, unlike stuffings inside the bird. As the stuffings firm up during cooking, they will carve beautifully with the breast meat, giving multi-coloured slices under a contrasting golden brown skin.

These can be used for stuffing pork, lamb or veal though they can be rather rich and would be better with very lean cuts.

SAVOURY PORK STUFFING

Each recipe is sufficient for a 1.75-2 kg/3½-4 lb chicken (approx), but for a turkey you should double or treble the recipe.

500 g/1 lb coarse pork sausages (Toulouse or bratwurst) or coarsely minced belly of pork
125 g/4 oz finely minced sausage meat
1 tsp ground cinnamon
1/2 tsp ground nutmeg
1/4 tsp ground cloves
1/4 tsp ground mace
1 garlic clove, chopped or 1 tbls chopped onion

Remove the skins from the sausages (if using) and mix with the sausage meat. Mix in the spices and the garlic or onion. (If you are using belly of pork you might like to add a little more garlic or onion and some salt and pepper.)

Options

Chili and Green Pepper Add 250 g/8 oz cooked red kidney beans, 1 teaspoon or more chili seasoning and 125 g/4 oz chopped green pepper.

Apricot and Mint Add 125 g/4 oz dried apricots, the rind and juice of half a large orange, 1 heaped teaspoon dried mint and brandy, Cognac or orange liqueur to taste.

Chestnuts, Celery and Orange Add 250 g/ 8 oz unsweetened chestnut purée, 250 g/8 oz cooked whole chestnuts, grated rind and juice of half a large orange, 2 tablespoons coarsely chopped celery leaf, port or brandy to taste (optional).

Dried Banana and Coconut Add 60 g/2 oz dried bananas, chopped, 2 tablespoons desiccated coconut, 2 tablespoons raisins, dark rum and lime juice to taste. Soak the desiccated coconut in a little boiling water to rehydrate it. Soak the raisins in rum and lime juice for 24 hours if you can, or mix all in together. In this version I should follow the Caribbean habit of using rather more nutmeg and leaving the cinnamon out of the basic mixture. Use onion rather than garlic.

Prunes, Orange and Port Add 125 g/4 oz chopped prunes, grated rind and juice of half an orange, port to taste. To this, you might like to add some chopped toasted nuts, too.

Cashew and Indian Spices Add 125 g/4 oz toasted unsalted cashews, chopped green pepper, 1/4 teaspoon each of ground cardamom, cumin and coriander.

Cranberries These may be put whole or chopped raw into any stuffing. They are specially good in the Chestnut, Celery and Orange stuffing; add as many as you like.

EGGS

What would we do without eggs? Perfect as a quick, nourishing
snack, they also lighten cakes, enrich soups, thicken sauces, make
sophisticated custards and delicious desserts, give pastry a shine. . .

Nowadays, dieticians are giving more and more consideration to eggs. A major recommendation, in order to keep our cholesterol intake low, is that we limit the number of eggs we eat to three or four a week within a balanced diet. Vegetarians can eat rather more than red meat eaters.

The age-old reputation of eggs causing constipation is true only if your diet is very low in fibre. When eaten in balanced meals, or simply with wholemeal bread or toast, eggs are no more or less binding than other fibre-free foods.

The latest worry is the way in which eggs are produced. Eggs from battery hens are virtually identical, from a dietary point of view, to eggs produced by free-range chickens but concern over mass-production and cruelty to chickens has led to a growth in the production of eggs from free-range chickens. It is accepted that brown-shelled eggs are no different from white-shelled and the days of having to pay more for the former are past – or they should be.

Free-range egg farms have more scope for flexibility and many now supply different types of eggs – tiny bantam eggs, brown Maran eggs, goose, guineafowl, pheasant and duck eggs. All may be used in the same way as chickens' eggs with some adjustment for size, of course. The exceptions are ducks' eggs. They have exceptionally thin shells and, as ducks tend to lay them in very wet and often unhygienic places, they can contain harmful bacteria which have been absorbed through the shell. They must be well cooked and should never be served soft-boiled or poached; but they are superb in baking, giving extra lightness, colour and flavour, especially to sponge cakes.

Eggs keep far longer than most people think, and will last for several weeks in a refrigerator but they have porous shells and absorb smells easily. Many eggs considered 'off' have merely been tainted by some other food.

POACHED EGGS

This method of cooking eggs has attracted a fair degree of nonsense, the worst of which is adding vinegar to the poaching water; this is done to set the egg white quickly and prevent it from running. This is evidence that the cook has not enough confidence in the freshness of the eggs. It is criminal to ambush an egg's rich, round flavour with the sharpness of vinegar.

My method is to bring a few inches of water just to the boil in a saucepan. Swirl the water to give a good shape to the egg just before you slide it in. (Fresh eggs always adopt a nice shape anyway.) Return the pan to low heat and let the water do no more than 'smile' at you with the occasional small bubble – boiling is out. The egg will be done in just over 3 minutes; during the cooking time you can cut off any ragged bits of white by poking at the edges with a sharp knife. Lift the egg out with a slotted spoon or fish slice, angling the edge of the implement to the side of the pan to allow the water to drain off fully before you put the egg directly on to crisp, generously buttered toast.

Once a poached egg has cooled, its yolk will not cook any further, so if you have several dozen to prepare, poach in advance, drain and set aside in cold water, reheating in hot water to order.

SCRAMBLED EGGS

Patience and a gentle heat produce the best results; high heat makes eggs tough and you will end up with them separating and swimming in liquid.

In general, allow 2 eggs per person but for a larger number average it out to 1½ large eggs per person.

Scrambled eggs wait for no-one, so first make your toast, and prepare the table.

Beat the eggs lightly with a fork, and add at least 30 g/1 oz chopped butter for every 4 eggs. Pour the eggs into a pan, and cook gently, stirring, until the butter is melted and combined with the eggs. Now either keep stirring to make a very even texture (which I find a little boring) or make long scoops with a wooden spoon to form light cushions of curd. Either way, serve *just before* the texture has reached the stage you prefer, for it will continue to cook with its own heat. The addition of milk or cream is popular and gives a lighter curd. Add no more than 1 tablespoon per egg in addition to the butter.

Many ingredients may be used to flavour scrambled eggs – herbs, spices, vegetables. I like the flavour of tarragon or *fines herbes*, and chives are very popular. Some people even add garlic. In Australasia, tomato is often included but this generally curdles the eggs before they are cooked.

H.R.H. the Prince of Wales has popularized scrambled eggs with smoked salmon. You need only 1 tablespoon or so per person of salmon cut into matchsticks and stirred in just before the eggs are ready. A little dried or fresh dill makes this a magical lunch or supper. If you have plenty of smoked salmon, serve dill-flavoured scrambled eggs on top of thick slices, or twist the salmon slices into a nest and serve the eggs in the middle.

Cold scrambled eggs are an excellent accompaniment to smoked fish of all kinds. Just as the eggs are almost cooked, stir in some good quality seed mustard. This unexpected combination is also superb served hot with sweet-cured bacon.

FRIED EGGS

For the health-conscious, these are a nightmare of temptation, for they only taste good if fried in bacon fat, lard or butter. Vegetable oil does nothing for fried eggs, the only exception being olive oil which is outstandingly good.

'Sunny-side-up' eggs are cooked without

being turned over. You can fry them in very shallow fat, until the whites are cooked through and the yolk is how you like it. Alternatively, you can use deeper fat and, using a spoon, splash it over the egg as it cooks. Either way, the eggs can be flipped over and cooked on the other side. The best way of preparing fried eggs is in a non-stick pan. You need no grease at all, but I use just a smidgen of butter for flavour.

BOILED EGGS

There are two basic ways to boil an egg.

Boiling water method Boil the water, reduce it to a simmer and lower the eggs into the pan on a spoon. Simmer for 3-3½ minutes for lightly cooked eggs, 4-5 minutes for firm white and soft yolks, and 10 minutes for hard-boiled eggs. These times must be adjusted according to the size of your eggs and how cold they were when they went into the water.

Cold water method The best way is to put them into a pan of cold water and bring it slowly to the boil. Simmer for just 1 minute, then turn off the heat and put the pan to the side. Allow them to stand for 7 minutes and you will have perfect eggs – still slightly runny in the middle, with firm but not rubbery whites. This method automatically adjusts itself for eggs directly from the refrigerator by taking longer to arrive at boiling-point. For a hard-boiled egg, simmer for 4-5 minutes after the water comes to the boil.

To finish hard-boiled eggs, run them under cold water until they are completely cold (it is no good simply plunging them into a basin of water). Crack the eggs lightly while cooling to prevent an unsightly black ring from forming around the yolk.

Spiced Eggs Middle Eastern countries shell hard-boiled eggs and then fry them in olive oil; this creates an attractive webbed veil of gold around each egg. Plain or fried boiled eggs are then dipped into spices: ground cinnamon or cumin and salt, or coriander and salt, or into a mixture of all four, with, perhaps, chopped parsley or fresh coriander for good measure.

Hamine Eggs The eggs are simmered overnight, or for at least eight hours until both white and yolk develop a melting tenderness. Hamine Eggs are often cooked in water to which a little onion skin or coffee grounds have been added to lightly colour the shells and the whites. Herbs added to the water will perfume the whole egg.

STUFFED EGGS

A stalwart of buffet tables and summer weddings for decades, the stuffed egg is generally more promise than performance. They often taste musty and dry, especially versions that incorporate curry powder. The answer is butter. Butter gives texture, moistness and richness to the mixture. Stuffings made with butter also set

---

GLYNN'S TIP

If eggs to be boiled are not at room temperature, they may crack. To avoid this, you can use an egg piercer, an inexpensive item, which punches a small hole in the rounded end of the egg, allowing the air inside to expand without cracking the shell.

well. Each of the following suggestions is made with 6 eggs and serves 6.

Blue Cheese Stuffed Eggs Hard boil 6 fresh eggs, carefully centring the yolks. Cool the eggs, then cut in half lengthways with a very sharp knife. Whizz together in a blender or food processor 90 g/3 oz soft butter, 185 g/6 oz soft blue cheese and egg yolks until even and smooth. Pile into the prepared whites, then shape attractively with the prongs of a fork. This is one occasion when I *am* persuaded that piping looks worthwhile, but it always reminds me of the cookery style that believes that food will taste good as long as it is attractively presented and garnished. Ⓕ Ⓠ

Bacon and Mustard-stuffed Eggs Replace the cheese with lean smoked back bacon cut into matchsticks and cooked gently until the fat has been rendered down and the bacon is really crisp. Drain and cool on paper. Whizz up the egg yolks, butter and 2 teaspoons of Dijon mustard in a blender or food processor, then add the bacon and process just enough to break up the strips into smaller pieces. Pile the mixture into the egg whites; the bacon makes it difficult to pipe.

Prawn-stuffed Eggs Replace the cheese with peeled prawns. Roughly chop about 30 g/1 oz of the prawns and reserve. Whizz the rest in a blender or food processor with the softened butter and egg yolks, then season with a little lemon juice. Add a little parsley, dill or mint, too, if you like. Pile or pipe the mixture into the egg whites and top with the reserved chopped prawns.

EGGS MAYONNAISE

Here are two ideas that might inspire you to think up more interesting ways to serve Eggs Mayonnaise than to put them on a plate with a slurp of warm mayonnaise and a wet lettuce leaf.

Options

For 4 people, cut 3 hard-boiled eggs into 12 quarters. Add 15 g/½ oz fresh herbs (dill, basil, mint and fresh watercress are the best) to 3 generous tablespoons of chilled mayonnaise. Whizz this all up in a blender or food processor, then season, perhaps adding a squeeze of crushed garlic.

Slice some large, ripe, well-chilled tomatoes into thick slices from top to bottom. Sprinkle the tomatoes with a little lemon juice, oil and seasoning, then arrange the quartered eggs on them. Coat the eggs with the green mayonnaise, leaving lots of the tomato visible. Ⓕ Ⓠ

Measly Eggs In place of the herbs, add a tablespoon of soured cream or thick strained plain yoghurt and 1 tablespoon of red lumpfish roe to the mayonnaise. Serve this over the quartered eggs on a base of coarsely grated raw cucumber. The roe will lose some of its dye into the mayonnaise. If you use black rather than red lumpfish roe, the mayonnaise goes blue.

QUAILS' EGGS

Tiny quails' eggs don't taste very different from hens' eggs but are smashing added to cold or warm salads, served on their own with dips or celery salt as a first course, or as an elegant snack with drinks. They are delightful half-peeled as a garnish for smoked fish or other fish dishes, or fully peeled and halved lengthways and added to a prawn cocktail.

Cook quails' eggs by putting them into cold water, bringing them to the boil and simmering for just 1 minute. Cool in running cold water, cracking each one gently.

SCOTCHED QUAILS' EGGS

This is an up-to-the-minute version of the heavy, deep-fried Scotch egg. Hard-boiled quails' eggs are surrounded with a paste of smoked salmon which needs no cooking. They make a spectacular special snack with drinks or can be served as part of a buffet. With help you could easily make them by the dozen.

12 quails' eggs
125 g/4 oz smoked salmon pieces
30 g/1 oz fresh brown breadcrumbs
60 g/2 oz melted butter, cooled
1 tsp lemon juice
salt and pepper
fresh or dried dill or parsley (optional)

Hard boil the quails' eggs. Trim the salmon and use it to make a paste with the breadcrumbs, butter and lemon juice in a blender or food processor, and season lightly. Chill for about 30 minutes then, using wetted hands, form a coating round the shelled eggs. Leave plain or roll lightly in chopped fresh or dried dill or parsley.

Chill really well and serve whole or cut in half to reveal four layers of colour – the green herbs, pink salmon coating, and the white and yellow of the eggs. Don't use too much of the herb or the other flavours will be swamped. Ⓔ
Photograph, p. 44.

ROLLED and FOLDED OMELETTES

Allow 2-3 eggs per person; the best results come out of a pan that is only just big enough to hold this amount. Season and beat the eggs lightly and, if you like, add 1 teaspoon of water for each one. Melt a good knob of butter in the pan over quite high heat and pour in the eggs just as it is about to brown.

Work fast, using a wooden spatula, to draw the cooked eggs from the bottom and sides through the uncooked eggs. When two-thirds of the eggs are cooked, stop stirring and let the base form a golden skin. Sprinkle on any warmed filling ingredients. Tilt the pan and either fold the omelette in half and slide it on to a warm plate, or fold only a third of it over and tip it out on to a plate to give the second fold. The centre of the omelette should still be slightly runny; you can cook it a little longer if you prefer, but don't allow the eggs to toughen. Favourite fillings are smoked, flaked fish; chopped, sliced or grated cheese; cooked ham; pre-cooked bacon or chicken; mushrooms; tomatoes; cooked diced vegetables; and the gamut of fresh herbs.

FLAT OMELETTES

Flat omelettes are found in all the countries bordering the Mediterranean. A mixture of eggs, cooked meats and vegetables, and herbs cooked together, they are always served flat, never folded. Made thinly, they are used as pancakes to sandwich a filling, but more usually they are made thick and served in wedges. Most flat omelettes are particularly good when cold, especially if they have been cooked in olive oil.

One large egg will bind together at least 185 g/6 oz of cooked vegetables or meat. If the mixture is more than 1 cm/½ inch deep, it is usual to cover the pan. Cook for 5 minutes until virtually set, then place the omelette under a grill to finish. Alternatively, turn the omelette in the pan and cook on the second side for the same amount of time. A generous pinch of saffron beaten in for each egg gives a wonderful colour.

SPANISH OMELETTE

There are only three ingredients in a real Spanish omelette and it is vital that all three are of the best quality. Eggs, of course, potatoes and, most important of all, olive oil.

Serves two

3-4 tbls olive oil
500 g/1 lb uncooked potatoes cut in 1 cm/½ inch cubes
4-5 large eggs
salt and freshly ground black pepper

Heat the olive oil in a medium frying-pan. There should be enough to generously cover the bottom of the pan and to come *at least* a quarter of the way up the potato. Add the potatoes and, once they have started to soften, turn them, trying not to break them too much. A little browning is acceptable, but not necessary.

Once the potatoes are cooked, beat the eggs with the seasoning and pour them into the pan. Cook undisturbed until the bottom is light brown and the eggs are almost set. If you have a non-stick pan, slide the omelette off on to a large plate, invert the pan on top of that and invert again so that the omelette is turned over for browning on the other side. If you don't dare attempt this, brown the top under the grill. A Spanish omelette is better served warm than hot, and even better cold. Ⓠ Ⓥ

LENTIL OMELETTE

Vegetarian cooks often pre-cook a quantity of lentils and keep them in the refrigerator as we keep meat in the freezer. If you don't have cooked lentils at hand, use canned.

Serves one

60 g/2 oz cooked brown or green lentils
garlic to taste
1 tsp seed or other mustard
roughly chopped parsley
2 eggs, lightly beaten
salt and freshly ground black pepper
olive oil for frying

Flavour the cooked lentils with garlic, mustard and parsley, bind with the eggs, season, and cook as for Spanish Omelette in quite a generous amount of olive oil. Ⓥ Ⓠ

SOUFFLE OMELETTES

Soufflé omelettes can be sweet or savoury and are thus doubly useful for using leftovers.
Savoury Soufflé Omelette For two people, use 4 eggs. Mix 4 egg yolks with 1 tablespoon water and as much seasoning and cheese as you think you'd like: 30 g/1 oz of strong cheese is about right. Stiffly whisk the 4 egg whites and fold them into the yolk and cheese mixture. Melt a decent-sized knob of butter in a pan (larger than an ordinary omelette pan), pour in the mixture and cook over low heat for 10 minutes without turning. Then place under a preheated hot grill until the omelette turns a light golden brown – no more than 1-2 minutes. Cut through the centre and serve a half to each person, or lightly cut down the centre, fold the omelette and cut in half with a very sharp knife.

It is usual to fold filling ingredients into the mixture itself: cubed, cooked ham or bacon; lightly cooked broccoli florets; chopped, cooked spinach with grated nutmeg; very thinly sliced leeks and some seed mustard; herbs. Include cheese, too, for these omelettes are quite bland and need a lot of flavouring.
Sweet Soufflé Omelettes are made in the same way with a little sugar and vanilla or other essence beaten into the egg yolks in place of the seasoning and savoury fillings. Finely chopped fresh or dried fruit may be folded in with the egg whites. Hot jam or fruit purées, with some sort of alcohol to thin them, can be spread on these omelettes before serving or folding. I also like to squeeze over some orange or lemon juice in the same way I might flavour pancakes.

LES TOURTONS DES PENITENTS

This delightful summer first course perfectly illustrates the wonderful food being cooked in France without fuss, publicity and fancy names. Using fresh, seasonal local produce plus exotic nuts from other Mediterranean shores, Christian Millo of the Auberge de la Madone in the hill-top village of Peillons regularly creates dishes that make a mockery of those who believe good French food must be 'traditional' and expensive, or eccentric and expensive.

Serves four

1 large bunch mixed fresh herbs (see below)
1 or 2 garlic cloves
a few drops of onion juice
125 g/4 oz pine kernels
250 g/8 oz curd or cream cheese
185 g/6 oz soured cream/crème fraîche
6 eggs
olive oil, peanut oil or butter for frying

Your mixed herbs should include plenty of parsley, such available herbs as chervil, sorrel, fennel fronds, basil and tarragon, plus a snippet of chives and some leaves of fresh mint; a few thyme flowers are good, too. Wash and drain the herbs; slice the sorrel finely and chop the herbs roughly but evenly with a couple of garlic cloves and a little onion juice, extracted by squeezing some chopped onion in a garlic press. To this mixture add the remaining ingredients, blend well then season with a very little salt and pepper.

Heat the mixture of olive and peanut oils with some butter, or just one of them if you prefer, then spoon in the mixture to make small *tourtons* or fritters about 10 cm/4 inches across and at least 1 cm/½ inch thick. Cook gently for about 4 minutes on each side. Serve perfectly plain, dribbled with olive oil or lemon juice, or with a thin tomato sauce. Although served as a starter, they would make a brilliant accompaniment to grilled fish or poultry. Ⓥ

THE SOUFFLE

Soufflés are unquestionably the best way to make a few eggs go a long way. The health conscious should remember that it is the egg whites which give soufflés their lift, so if you make soufflés just from the whites you will please everyone.

From a presentation point of view, and for speed, I now tend to serve individual soufflés in ramekins rather than take portions from one large one. If these are cooked all the way through, they become firm, rather than the *baveuse* style with a sauce-like centre, and if savoury can be tipped out and served as superior dinner-party side-dishes, with or without sauce. To compensate or allow for mis-timings, my individual sweet soufflés are always cooked on top of fruit, alcohol or cream and the top opened up just before serving.

If cooking one large sweet or savoury soufflé, use a white, straight-sided soufflé dish and always bring it to the table so that your guests can appreciate its magic. Although a soufflé will fall, it is not as fragile as generally believed and can stand being carried through a draughty hallway from the kitchen to the dining-room.

The best way to serve a whole soufflé is to spread out warmed plates, lift some of the crust on to each plate, then scoop out the body of the soufflé, giving everyone a share of the runny centre. If you cannot spread out the plates, divide the top into equal portions.

There are many ways of making soufflés – here is the range I use.

BASIC SAVOURY SOUFFLE

This is the version to use when you will be flavouring the mixture with something solid.

Serves four to six as a first course; two to four as a main course

300 ml/½ pint hot flavoured milk (see below)
60 g/2 oz butter
45 g/1½ oz plain flour
4 egg yolks
5 egg whites
salt and pepper to taste

GLYNN'S TIP

If making the soufflé in advance, place plastic film directly on to the surface of the sauce and keep it in a cool place; when you are ready to continue, warm the sauce and beat in the egg yolks, then the flavouring and whisked egg whites.

Bring the milk to the boil with whatever flavouring ingredients you have on hand, some chopped onion, a bay leaf, parsley stalks, and set aside. Butter and lightly flour a 1.5 litre/3 pint soufflé dish.

Melt the butter in a saucepan over a gentle heat. Stir in the flour all at once and cook for 2 minutes, being careful not to let the mixture (called a roux) brown. Take from the heat, then strain in the hot milk. Whisk or beat with a wooden spoon until thick, return to the heat and let it bubble gently for another couple of minutes. Beat in the egg yolks and keep the mixture warm. At this point add the flavouring of your choice – see Options below. Whisk the egg whites until they form soft peaks; if you beat them too much they will not blend in neatly. Stir about one-quarter of the egg whites into the warm sauce mixture to lighten it, then fold in the rest slowly and gently. Don't over mix – it does not matter if the whites do not mix in evenly. *Ladle* the mixture into the prepared soufflé dish. (This takes a little time but keeps the air trapped in the mixture.) Although the soufflé mixture can be left to stand for some time, you will get much better results by putting the dish immediately into the oven preheated to 200°C/400°F/Gas Mark 6, then reducing the temperature to 190°C/375°F/Gas Mark 5.

Cook for 24 minutes, or until risen and golden brown, without opening the door, after which the soufflé will be perfectly *baveuse* (runny in the middle). Cook the soufflé for 30 minutes if you prefer it more solid or if you plan to serve it with a separate sauce.

Options
Pink Salmon Soufflé Don't bother using the more expensive red salmon – the pink fish really does give the better flavour. Remove the bones and skin from a 200 g/7 oz can of drained salmon and mash well. Add to the sauce before the egg yolks with 1 teaspoon of dried tarragon and 30 g/1 oz strongly flavoured cheese. If it is not too salty, the juices from the tin may be added to the milk, which further enhances the flavour.
Cheese Soufflé Add 50 g/2 oz strong cheese and 2 teaspoons of made mustard.

SAVOURY SOUFFLE BASE *for* PUREES

When you want to make a savoury soufflé using a liquid or a bulky flavouring, such as a vegetable purée, you must strengthen the base by adding extra flour. For about 300 ml/½ pint of purée flavouring, I add 15 g/½ oz flour to the basic sauce and an extra egg white to ensure lightness, but you could stick to the usual proportion of 4 yolks to 5 whites. Proceed as for the Basic Savoury Soufflé given above.

Many classic soufflés are based on this recipe

GLYNN'S TIP

You can make a soufflé from almost anything and you certainly don't have to start with a flour-based sauce. Indeed, some of the best soufflés can be made with the simple addition of whisked egg whites only. The ploy is based on choosing a vegetable or fruit which is suitable for being made into a purée all by itself.

but remember, when making a vegetable soufflé, that the vegetables will be cooked twice, once to prepare them for the base and again in the oven, so overcooking is unavoidable and many such soufflés are not worth making because they have lost the flavour of the original vegetable. Wherever you can, barely cook the vegetable that is to be puréed or use a vegetable that has a strong basic flavour. I don't think that it is worthwhile making a cauliflower soufflé. For something so delicate, use the egg-white soufflé base and bake it in individual ramekins.

Pulses make excellent savoury soufflés and have the advantage of being available ready-cooked. Try the next recipe; it's marvellous!

CHILI-BEAN SOUFFLE

Drain a 439 g/15½ oz can red kidney beans thoroughly and liquidise with ½ teaspoon of hot chili seasoning (not chilli powder) and 1 tablespoon of tomato paste. Make the soufflé base for purées and stir in the bean mixture. Add the egg whites, bake and serve.

This is particularly good served with hot ham or hot, smoked sausages. Baked in ramekins, you could serve this version with turkey.

WHOLEMEAL SOUFFLE BASE

Until I started to experiment for this book, I considered a soufflé made with wholemeal flour to be heavy and soggy. When I looked hard at most of the published recipes I found that they all seemed to use too few eggs. If you follow either the Basic Savoury Soufflé or the Soufflé Base for Purées recipes above, using wholemeal rather than white flour, you will add fibre and flavour without losing lightness. The sweet grittiness of the wholemeal flour adds extra interest but the mixture tends to be a little more bland, so whatever your recipe you will find it improved by adding 30-60 g/1-2 oz grated strongly flavoured cheese and perhaps 2 teaspoons strong, made mustard.

LENTIL and COURGETTE SOUFFLE

A vegetarian's dream, full of goodness but light and colourful, too. Because the base is substantial and heavy, I have used an extra egg white to ensure a light result.

Serves four to six as a first course; two to four as a main course, depending on accompaniments

2 tsps salt
375 g/12 oz courgettes, finely grated
250 g/8 oz cooked green lentils
1 garlic clove
60 g/2 oz chopped onion
3 tbls strained plain yoghurt
2 tsps ground cumin
60 g/2 oz strong cheese, grated
4 egg yolks
6 egg whites
salt and pepper to taste

Butter and lightly flour a 1.75 litre/3 pint soufflé dish.

Sprinkle the salt on to the grated courgettes, let them drain about 30 minutes and press out all the liquid. Purée two-thirds of the cooked lentils with the garlic, onion, yoghurt, cumin and most of the cheese. Fold in the remaining lentils and grated courgettes. You may prepare the recipe up to this stage well in advance.

Put the base mixture into the oven at 200°C/400°F/Gas Mark 6 until warmed through. Stir the egg yolks into the mixture. Whisk the egg whites until firm but not dry, stir about a quarter into the base, then fold in the remainder. *Ladle* the mixture gently into the prepared dish, sprinkle with the remaining cheese and put directly into the oven. Reduce the temperature to 190°C/375°F/Gas Mark 5 and bake for 24 minutes for a soft centre, 30 minutes for a firm one.

CHILLI-SWEETCORN SOUFFLE

This store-cupboard soufflé is simplicity itself to make.

Serves four to six as a starter; two to four as a main course, depending on accompaniments

1 or 2 small fresh green chillies
329 g/11½ oz can of creamed sweetcorn
30 g/1 oz plain flour
60 g/2 oz butter
4 egg yolks
5 egg whites
salt and pepper to taste

Butter and flour a 1.75 litre/3 pint soufflé dish.

Split the chillies and remove the seeds (preferably wearing rubber gloves). Slice or chop the de-seeded chillies and add them to the contents of the can of sweetcorn in a saucepan. Mix in the flour evenly, then turn on the heat and, stirring constantly, add the butter as the mixture thickens. Remove from the heat and stir in the egg yolks. Whisk the egg whites until firm but not dry, stir in about a quarter, then fold in the remainder. *Ladle* the mixture into the prepared soufflé dish and put into the oven at 200°C/400°F/Gas Mark 6. Reduce the temperature to 190°C/375°F/Gas Mark 5 and bake for 24 minutes for a *baveuse* centre or 30 minutes for a firm one.

Options

Try adding 2 tablespoons of chopped fresh coriander leaves, or 2 tablespoons of chopped green sweet peppers and 4 tablespoons of crisped bacon pieces. These options can be made with or without the chillies. Also try adding 2 or more chopped garlic cloves.

EGG-WHITE SOUFFLES

These are the simplest soufflés of all, for you do not have to make a thickened sauce or go shopping. With eggs and a can of fruit from the cupboard, you can entertain effortlessly. Cooked through, these soufflés can be turned out and served cold with a little fresh fruit or sauce. This mango version is one of the most rewarding, but virtually any canned fruit may be used.

Serves six

397 g/14 oz can mango slices
lemon, lime or orange juice to taste
3 egg whites

Lightly butter 6 small ramekins and sprinkle with caster sugar.

Drain the mangoes, retaining the syrup. Mash or purée roughly and, if too sweet, add a little lemon, lime or orange juice to taste. Whisk the egg whites until stiff but not dry, stir about a quarter into the fruit purée and carefully fold in the remainder. Ladle evenly into the ramekins, place on a baking-sheet and cook at 200°C/400°F/Gas Mark 6 for 8 minutes. They will cook through totally, and may be turned out hot or cold.

Options

If serving hot, add a liquid or fruit purée to the bottom of the ramekins before adding the soufflé mixture, which will form a coating sauce when turned out. It could be as simple as a spoonful of coconut-flavoured liqueur or dark rum swirled with double cream, or simply double cream. If you are serving them cold, use a purée of fruit or bake them plain. Either way, the best possible sauce is the Rich Custard (page 19), flavoured with an orange liqueur and very well chilled.

SWEET SOUFFLES

Remembering the number of people who have approached me for advice on sweet soufflés, I was determined to get these right! The major decision I made was to advise you not to bother with soufflés made with purées of soft fruits – raspberries, blackberries and the like. It's a superb idea, but I've never seen it work, even in Michelin-rated restaurants. To ensure that the flavour is strong enough, a reduced purée of the fruit must be made, which often ends up tasting like jam.

The best method is to use flavoured soufflé mixtures over a base of fresh fruit. If you don't want to use fruit, or can't get any that are suitable, put a pool of jam or cream and alcohol under the soufflé instead, or cook through and pour such a mixture into the soufflé just before you serve it.

BASIC VANILLA SOUFFLE

This basic vanilla soufflé is delicious by itself but makes the perfect foil for almost any fruit, spirit or liqueur.

There are other ways of making sweet soufflés, but this is the simplest and most reliable technique. Before you can begin making a soufflé, study the variations on the basic theme, all of which are excellent, and in this small section you have the bases for hundreds of flavour combinations.

Serves six

1 tbls cornflour
4 tbls caster sugar
3 egg yolks
300 ml/½ pint milk
1 tbls butter
2 tsps vanilla essence
4 egg whites

Lightly butter 6 small ramekins and dust with caster sugar. Blend the cornflour, sugar and egg yolks in a bowl. Heat the milk until bubbles appear round the edge of the saucepan, then pour it over the mixture, stirring as you do so. Return the sauce to the milk-pan and bring to the boil, stirring continuously. It will go through a depressingly lumpy stage which is only disastrous if you panic and stop stirring.

When the smooth, thickened sauce has bubbled for a minute, remove from the heat and beat in the butter. Stir in the vanilla essence and turn the mixture into a large bowl and allow it to cool a little.

Meanwhile, whisk the egg whites until stiff but not dry. Fold these quickly but gently into the cooled sauce, then ladle the mixture into the prepared ramekins. Put them on to a baking-sheet and cook at 200°C/400°F/Gas Mark 6 for just 8 minutes.

Options

Add cream to the bottom of the ramekins before the mixture, or pour it into the soufflé to serve. Add a layer of fresh or cooked fruit at the bottom; raisins soaked in rum, a single prune soaked in brandy afloat in double cream, raspberries or strawberries sprinkled with orange or orange-flower water in Cointreau, pineapple with Crème de Menthe, gin or Galliano.

Polka Dot Soufflé An attractive dish which solves the problem of chocolate soufflés tasting floury. Serve by itself or over fruit, especially sliced fresh pears with Maraschino or Poire William, cherries with or without black rum, or raspberries and rose water. Stir 60 g/2 oz chocolate drops into the cooled custard before folding in the egg whites.

Liqueur Soufflés Reduce the sugar to 2 tablespoons, omit the vanilla and instead stir in 6 tablespoons of liqueur. If you are not using a sweetened liqueur but a spirit – Cognac, rum or such *eaux-de-vie* as Framboise or Poire William – you can also reduce the sugar so that your soufflé is rather sharp, but remember that some sugar enhances the fruit flavour, so I should put in at least half the basic recipe's quantity.

Fruit Syrup Soufflé An extraordinarily simple way to make a soufflé with the flavour of fruit but without fruit! It is enormous fun to watch guests spoon into something looking like a simple vanilla soufflé only to find that it explodes into another flavour in the mouth. Use the range of pure fruit syrups now in the supermarkets, which includes strawberry, raspberry, orange, lemon, mandarin, grenadine or mint. Omit the sugar. Reduce the vanilla essence to 1 teaspoon and add with 4-5 tablespoons of fruit syrup. This is especially good with cream at the bottom, or with fruit at the bottom and cream poured in when serving.

Caramel Soufflé Caramel is another important ally when catering for those without a sweet tooth. Omit the sugar in the basic recipe and instead make caramel with 125 g/4 oz granulated sugar and 2 tablespoons of water. Let it turn a rich brown, then remove from the heat and add the milk – take care as it splutters. Return to a low heat and stir until the caramel dissolves. Pour over the egg yolks and cornflour and proceed as above, using just 1 teaspoon of vanilla essence. This is particularly good over rum-soaked raisins or an apple purée flavoured with cinnamon and raisins.

Citrus Soufflés These are the classic soufflés and make perfect foils for all fruits or cream. An orange soufflé is marvellous with chocolate drops in it. Reduce the vanilla essence to 1 teaspoon and add 1 teaspoon of finely grated orange rind with 3 tablespoons of orange juice and 2 tablespoons lemon juice.

BLACK CHERRY SOUFFLE

A store-cupboard recipe.

Serves six

397 g/14 oz can stoned black cherries
1 tbls cornflour
3 egg yolks
7 tbls Kirsch or black rum
4 egg whites

Lightly butter 6 small ramekins and sprinkle with caster sugar.

Drain the stoned cherries well, keeping the syrup. Purée half the cherries. Mix the cornflour with a few spoonfuls of the juice until smooth, stir it into the cherry purée and cook over gentle heat, stirring constantly until thick. Cool slightly, and beat in the egg yolks and 1 tablespoon of Kirsch or black rum. Whisk the egg whites until soft peaks form, stir a quarter into the mixture, then fold the remainder in slowly and evenly.

Spoon the remaining cherries into the prepared ramekins and pour 1 tablespoon of Kirsch or dark rum into each one. Ladle the soufflé mixture evenly into the ramekins, stand them on a baking-sheet and immediately bake at 200°C/400°F/Gas Mark 6 for 8 minutes.

Options

The syrup left over from the can may be reduced over heat (but beware of caramelizing) and also shared between the ramekins. As a precaution against overcooking these soufflés, keep the liquid warm, and when the soufflés come from the oven, make a hole in the top of each one and quickly dribble in some of the sauce and top with a dollop of whipped double cream.

SPINACH ROULADE

If you don't want to serve a hot soufflé but need something which can be prepared in advance and kept warm for a while, a roulade is perfect. This is an ideal first course for large numbers and serves ten easily and more if you provide a salad. It is delicious served hot or cold filled with a tangy cheese sauce.

500 g/1 lb defrosted frozen or fresh spinach, cooked, chopped and very well drained
3 eggs, separated
1 tbls butter, softened
freshly grated nutmeg
freshly ground black pepper
a little Parmesan or finely grated hard cheese

Prepare a Swiss roll tin approximately 30 × 25 cm/12 × 9 inches by lining it with greaseproof paper and brushing it liberally with melted butter or oil.

Make sure that the spinach is really well drained. Beat in the egg yolks and butter and season generously with nutmeg and pepper. Beat the egg whites until stiff but not dry and stir 1 tablespoon into the spinach mixture. Fold in the remaining whites as quickly and gently as possible to avoid knocking air out of the mixture. Spoon into the prepared tin, spread into the corners and level off. Bake at 180°C/350°F/Gas Mark 4 for 12-15 minutes. The roulade should be firm but not over-cooked or it will be tough.

Have ready a large sheet of greaseproof paper, lying on a clean teatowel or sheet of foil. Brush the greaseproof paper with oil and sprinkle with a little Parmesan or finely grated hard cheese. When the roulade is cooked, turn it out on to the greaseproof paper. To serve hot, spread with the filling and roll up, picking up the ends of the teatowel or foil to help you. To serve cold, cover with a sheet of greaseproof paper and roll up while warm. Allow to cool then unroll, fill and re-roll. Ⓔ Ⓕ

Options

A hot roulade is usually filled with a white sauce studded with goodies, or with a savoury purée. A spinach roulade is good with a rich cheese sauce or a white wine sauce with cubes of tongue, ham and mushrooms. Flaked fish, such as salmon, also looks very pretty in a white wine sauce. Make the sauce rather thick or it will squirt out.

I prefer roulades cold, for the variety of fillings is much wider. Flavour soured cream or thick drained yoghurt with garlic, or mix soured cream or a good mayonnaise with lots of herbs, salad and roughly chopped prawns. The best version I ever made, as a first course to a wedding banquet, was a spinach roulade sprinkled with a little extra nutmeg and then spread with a smoked salmon pâté which you can buy from your local supermarket.

Salmon Roulade Mash the drained contents of a small can of pink salmon (about 200 g/7 oz) with 1 teaspoon dried or 1 tablespoon of fresh tarragon or dill. Beat in 3 egg yolks, 2 tablespoons of single cream and 1 tablespoon of Parmesan cheese. Whisk 3 egg whites, fold them in and spread the mixture over the prepared tin. Bake, then roll while hot with a sheet of greaseproof paper inside – from the short or long end, depending on the number and thickness of slices you want. When cool, unroll, spread with a small carton of soured cream mixed with a little grated, drained cucumber or with such fresh herbs as dill, fennel fronds, basil, parsley and a little mint. Re-roll and slice to serve.

GLYNN'S TIP

Generally cornflour is a better thickener than wheat flour when using fruit, and it's much easier to work with, too.

PASTA

Conventional pasta partnerships and creative new ideas combine to give you a wide range of dinner party and family meal treats – just what the contemporary cook needs to make the most of this popular and nourishing food.

No one is certain when pasta first came to Britain; it was probably sometime in the 17th century. Originally it was known by the name of the most common shape – tubes called macaroni. Pasta was never a very important part of the British or American diet until after the great migrations from southern Italy to the United States at the turn of this century. Since then, pasta has suffered under two misconceptions: that it was brought to Italy by Marco Polo from China, and that it is fattening.

Call it pasta, noodles or macaroni, this dough of wheat flour and water quickly became a staple food wherever wheat was an important crop. The Ancient Greeks enjoyed it, and introduced it to the south of Italy during their period of colonization, centuries before the Roman Empire. The Arabs also made it and so did the Chinese. It existed in the areas where wheat grew well in central Europe, but not in northern Italy where the staple grain was millet, or in Britain where wheat was unreliable. Marco Polo may have brought noodles to Venice, but it was not until Italy was unified by Garibaldi that pasta began generally to spread north from Naples and the south.

Is pasta fattening? Like potatoes, pasta becomes a problem in a diet only when you lavish too many high-calorie sauces, fats and creams upon it. In Italy, pasta is mostly served as a first course and it is more likely that what follows the pasta causes weight problems. Italians also use far less sauce, which reduces pasta's contribution to flab.

Pasta has always been used in pudding dishes but it is hard not to overcook it and it is rarely appreciated. I have left sweet pasta dishes out of this book as so many more of us are eating pasta as a starter or a main course that I don't think we would welcome it as a pudding as well.

FOOD FACT

Essentially, pasta need only be made from flour and water, but the flour must be of a very hard wheat, usually durum, which has a high proportion of the elastic protein gluten. This gluten enables the dough to be rolled out thinly without breaking. The addition of a little oil or egg makes the dough richer-tasting and easier to work with.

Choosing pasta shapes

Although variations of thickness and shape will give slight differences in flavour, you should not assume that only one particular shape can be served with a certain sauce. There is no need to pursue strange shapes with unpronounceable names; use whatever shapes appeal to you, following these two guidelines:

Smooth shapes, including noodles of all kinds, are more suited to smooth sauces.

Chunky, twisted and fantasy shapes, such as bows, twists, spirals and shells, are more suitable for textured sauces as their cavities catch the lumps and stop them sliding off. It's fun to serve a seafood sauce with pasta shells, but it would be equally attractive and tasty over bows or spirals. These short-cut pasta types also add extra interest to smooth sauces.

Cooking technique

You should always cook pasta in far more water than you think it needs and in a very large saucepan, for it invariably foams up. You can avoid this somewhat by dribbling a little olive oil on to the water before adding the pasta, but sometimes even that won't prevent a mess if the saucepan is too small for the amount of pasta. A good guideline is 600 ml/1 pint of well-salted water per serving.

Fresh pasta is cooked enough when it rises to the top of the water; dried pasta generally follows the same pattern but varies according to the quality of the flour and its age; 7-8 minutes is probably enough boiling for it to be *al dente* or still firm to the bite. Large pasta shapes may take longer.

Serving pasta

The best way to serve pasta is to put it directly from the saucepan on to individual plates with two forks, a slotted spoon, or special tongs, depending on its shape. The pasta will quickly absorb the remaining water which clings to it and it will be left with a thin coating of the oil. Strange shapes, especially shells, should be drained, turned gently in the colander and left for a few minutes to ensure that there are no hidden ponds. Spoon the sauce on to each serving and let each person mix the two. If you wish to mix the sauce with the pasta in advance, drain the pasta quickly in a colander. If you are serving pasta tossed in olive oil or butter, heat this in a saucepan and mix with the pasta using two forks, off the heat. *NEVER* rinse any cooked pasta except lasagne and cannelloni.

BASIC EGG PASTA

Making pasta yourself is simple and rewarding, but there is such a good choice of ready-made pasta, both fresh and dried, that it is pointless unless it is something you have always wanted to do. Even so, there are now excellent pasta-making machines which do it for you; these come with recipes, which need to be followed carefully. But here is my favourite recipe, which can be made entirely by hand or, more speedily, in a food processor.
This quantity makes enough fresh pasta for a main course for two or a starter for four – but all depends upon how much pasta and sauce you like.

250 g/8 oz strong white bread flour
1 egg
2 tsps olive oil
up to 150 ml/1/4 pint water

Put the flour, egg and olive oil into the food processor, turn on and immediately begin to dribble water through the spout until the dough spins in a ball around the centre spindle. Remove the dough and cover with a damp cloth for an hour.

If you are making pasta by hand, put the flour on to a table or work-surface and make a well in the centre. Pour the olive oil and the beaten egg into this well and gradually mix together. Add small quantities of water until you have a firm, smooth dough. Knead the dough for 5-10 minutes; cover with a damp cloth and leave for an hour to enable the gluten to develop.

The dough may then be rolled out on a lightly floured surface and shaped. Use this dough for making any pasta dish, including noodles, lasagne or ravioli. Ⓣ Ⓥ

FLAVOURED PASTA

This sounds better than it usually tastes, for who can taste the spinach or tomato which colours green or pink pasta? It is better to regard them as coloured rather than flavoured pasta. Even so, a change or a mixture of colours adds interest to a dish.

The main problem with flavouring pasta is that the boiling water quickly leaches out the flavouring. The addition of fresh herbs sounds a brilliant idea but the cooked pasta generally ends up a khaki colour and tastes like it looks. Dried herbs might stand the pace, but it is better to use them to flavour the sauce. I have found some flavours which do work and I'm sure that you can think of others. Prepare and cook only a small amount of flavoured pasta before you commit yourself, however, to ensure that the trouble and expense is really worthwhile.

Options
To the basic egg pasta mixture, add the following flavourings.
Citrus pasta Add 1½-2 tablespoons of coarsely grated orange, lemon or lime rind. This is really excellent, whatever the sauce, but particularly good with tomato or seafood sauces and most sauces made with cream.
Pepper pasta Add 1½-2 tablespoons of lightly crushed green or black peppercorns. This is especially good when served with creamy sauces.
Spiced pasta Add 1½-2 tablespoons of cumin seeds which have been tossed in a non-stick pan until toasted. Good with tomato-based sauces.

You can also try adding 1½-2 tablespoons of one of the following: caraway seeds, lightly crushed coriander seeds, lightly toasted poppy seeds or lightly crushed and toasted mustard seeds. These are suitable for most sauces, but come into their own when served *al bianco* (see page 30), especially with a flavoured or garlic butter.
Sweet pepper pasta Add 1½-2 tablespoons of very finely chopped sweet red or green pepper.
Mushroom pasta Add 1½-2 tablespoons of finely crumbled dried mushroom. This is great topped with a simple cream sauce.
Nut pasta Add 1½-2 tablespoons of chopped toasted hazelnuts – very good combined with 1½-2 tablespoons grated orange rind – or walnuts. Walnut-flavoured pasta is specially good with tomato sauces.

LENTIL GNOCCHI

Gnocchi are really pasta dumplings and go marvellously with any stewed meat. I made these to go with boiled bacon and they were an enormous success. Their main purpose is to make the meat go further, so when you serve them you can reduce the amount of meat by about a quarter.

439 g/15½ oz can green or brown lentils, drained
1 egg yolk
2-3 heaped tbls wholemeal flour
1 tsp hot paprika
1 tsp ground cumin
salt

Mash the lentils and egg yolk with a fork. Mix in the flour, the spices and a little salt; the mixture should leave the sides of the bowl but be slightly sticky. Leave it to rest and firm up for an hour.

Knead the mixture for a few minutes, then take walnut-sized pieces in floured hands and roll into balls using your palms. Press each ball on to the back of the tines (prongs) of a fork, then roll off across the tines, which will give a ridged, slightly folded shape. Leave the gnocchi to dry, separated from one another. They are safe, unrefrigerated, for about 24 hours.

Cook the lentil gnocchi in boiling salted water or stock until they float to the surface. Provided that the accompanying meat or poultry has a good stock to spoon over the plate, you don't need butter or oil on the gnocchi. Ⓥ

BASIC SAUCES

The tomato was among the greatest of all the treasures brought back from the New World. At last there was something to make pasta colourful and interesting! Tomato-based sauces are always popular and can be quick and easy to make. All these recipes are suitable for two large or four small helpings (as a first course), depending on your appetite. Canned plum tomatoes will give better results than most fresh varieties.

BASIC TOMATO SAUCE

397 g/14 oz can plum tomatoes
1-2 tbls olive oil
1-2 garlic cloves, crushed

Turn the canned tomatoes into a saucepan with their juices. Add the olive oil and garlic, bring to the boil, mashing a little. Simmer until the liquid is well reduced (or not – depending on how thick you like your pasta sauces). Push the pulp through a sieve to remove the pips, simply because it looks much more professional, and add any extra flavours you like. Ⓠ Ⓥ

Options
If you would rather use onion in place of garlic, chop one small onion and soften it in the olive oil before adding the tomato.

The herbs which so improve these sauces are best put in after the initial cooking, to keep their flavours fresh. Use oregano, bay leaves, tarragon, or a mixture. The sauces look best if the herbs have been strained out before the sauce is added to the pasta. If the olive oil is sitting in puddles on the sauce, boil it fiercely for a few seconds to emulsify the mixture.

You will get really good results by using fresh herbs which sit in the sauce for 5-10 minutes: mint gives a refreshingly different flavour to the tomato; or you can stir masses of coarsely chopped parsley into the sauce and heat it just long enough to turn the parsley a very bright green. There is no need to strain these sauces.

You can add almost anything from the cupboard or vegetable rack to a herb-flavoured sauce. One of my most popular sauces is made from *vongole*, baby clams which are readily available in cans. Once you have made a rich, thick tomato sauce, highly flavoured with garlic or onion, tip in some of the juice from the can and let the sauce reduce again; toss in the clams to heat through at the last minute.

FAST TOMATO SAUCE

Although canned plum tomatoes in their own juice make fabulous pasta sauces, they need to be cooked for some time to reduce them to the right consistency. Fast cooks can't wait that long, so open a can of *chopped* tomatoes and bubble them over high heat with 1-2 tablespoons of olive oil. Stir constantly so that the oil and the tomato liquid amalgamate into one unctuous mixture that will coat and cling to your pasta. Now quickly flavour this with a tomato's best friends – finely chopped garlic and lots of fresh herbs.

Flavouring idea: add 1 heaped teaspoon dried mint, 2 tablespoons of tomato purée and freshly grated nutmeg.

Here are some other easy flavouring ideas for you to try:
Matchsticks of smoked ham or tongue, perhaps with sliced gherkins.
Sliced red peppers, raw or from cans, with black olives.
Canned cockles, brined, not in vinegar.
Canned Danish mussels.
Sliced mushrooms, just heat through.
All are improved by masses of chopped fresh parsley.

AL BIANCO

This is how the Italians describe pasta served with just butter and finely grated Parmesan cheese. It is delicious and forms a simple start to dozens of other pasta sauces. For instance, melt butter with a little garlic, or melt half butter and olive oil (my favourite). A handful of chopped parsley makes this special – but do make sure that you have plenty of Parmesan to contrast with the blandness of the pasta and the butter.

It's easier than ever to make such dishes seem clever – and taste tantalizingly different – by buying and using any of the range of flavoured butters that may be found on sale in supermarkets.

PUREE MAGIC

One of the most useful products available in supermarkets is the range of flavoured purées in tubes: *herbes de Provence*, garlic, onion, and anchovy are the four most interesting ones for the five-minute cook. Simply mix a squirt or two into melted butter for each serving, serve the pasta and pour the sauce over and toss lightly. A mixture of the anchovy and garlic purées gives you an authentic Mediterranean flavour, as does a mixture of the herb, onion or garlic purées. You may not even need to add any cheese.

ALLA CARBONARA

This is another very fast sauce, so fast that it can be ruined if you are not careful, for it relies on lightly set eggs to give a creamy finish to the pasta. As long as you do the mixing off the heat you will be successful.
I find it one of the most flexible and interesting of all sauces; the version without bacon is the one I use most.

Serves two

2 slices of bacon, cut into small pieces
2-3 tbls butter or oil
3 eggs, lightly beaten

Cook the bacon in a little butter or oil until the bacon fat is running. Add a knob of butter or a tablespoon of oil so that there is a decent amount of oil or fat in the bottom of the saucepan; keep this warm until the pasta is cooked, then remove from the heat.

Once the pasta is cooked, drain it in a colander and turn it into the saucepan with the bacon pieces. Beat the eggs, tip them into the pan and quickly mix through using two forks to lift and turn the pasta. Once it is coated with the egg and looks creamy, you should serve it immediately.

Options
If you are a vegetarian, you can make an equally good sauce by leaving out the bacon, coating the cooked pasta in a mixture of hot melted butter and olive oil, and adding a handful or so of fresh herbs before mixing in the eggs. It's terrific! You might also add some cream to the oil and butter and let it reduce a little before you add the pasta and the beaten eggs. Strips of smoked salmon are particularly good in this mixture especially when accompanied by fresh or dried dill. Ⓠ Ⓥ

CREAM SAUCES

Wicked but wonderful, these are no trouble to make or to eat. Indeed, for those days when you are allowing yourself to be indulgent, you don't have to do anything more than reduce some double cream until it is thick, pour it over pasta and sprinkle it with some Parmesan cheese. Allowing 150 ml/¼ pint double cream per person, put the cream in a saucepan and keep over a medium heat until the liquid has reduced by half.

Options
Here are some variations that I have enjoyed. The quantities don't matter too much, for I regard this as a thrilling way to eat leftovers, without them seeming to be so. Each serving is for two and is based on 300 ml/½ pint of double cream:

Artichoke and pimento Slice 6-8 canned artichoke bottoms and half a small can of red peppers; add garlic, too.
Blue cheese and broccoli Melt 1-2 tablespoons of blue cheese (Danish is best) into the cream, then add florets from the tips of fresh or frozen broccoli.
Mushroom and potted shrimp Add very thinly sliced button mushrooms and potted shrimps.
Saffron with garlic Add a pinch of saffron with crushed garlic and finish with masses of parsley.
Smoked salmon Add 30 g/1 oz of smoked salmon per person, sliced into strips, and finish with chopped fresh dill or mint.
Seafood cream For a special seafood sauce, add the liquid from a 250 g/8 oz can of baby clams or mussels to the reduced double cream with a blush of tomato purée, a little garlic and a splodge of white wine or dry white vermouth. Once reduced to the original volume, add the clams and heat the sauce only long enough to warm them through before pouring over the cooked pasta. The following recipe provides a less expensive way of making this sauce.
Wild mushroom Rinse 15 g/½ oz dried mushrooms quickly in cold water and place in a pan with the cream. Simmer very gently until the cream has reduced its volume by half, at which stage the mushrooms will have become reconstituted and flavoured the cream. The process usually takes about 15 minutes, but to be sure, and to allow the mushrooms sufficient time to become tender, leave the mixture in a warm place for another 15 minutes. *Do not* follow the usual advice and reconstitute the mushrooms before you use them, or all the flavour will go into that soaking liquid. Although this recipe is normally good enough for me, I have sometimes added a little white wine or vermouth to the sauce and let it bubble a minute. Also, some diced ham or tongue would make it prettier and more substantial. Ⓕ Ⓠ Ⓥ

FOOD FACT

In Britain we see wild mushrooms most frequently in the dried state, and even then they have come from Italy or Poland. Usually they are ceps, called porcini *by the Italians, and I think that they actually taste better when dried. The crinkled morels or* morilles *of France run a close second on flavour, but beat them hollow in appearance. Either type of mushroom, or a mixture of both, make my favourite pasta sauce (see above).*

MEAT SAUCES

For meat sauces, the meat should be lean, but need not be of grilling quality. Ordinary mince is good provided that it is not all fat, but you can't expect to make a sauce with it in 10 minutes. Mince is made from stewing beef and thus must have a long, slow cooking time, until each morsel of meat can be crushed against the roof of the mouth with your tongue.

For a main course these sauces will feed from two to four people depending on the proportion of pasta to meat that you like. Or you can double or treble the ingredients to serve a crowd.

GLYNN'S TIP

If necessary, pasta can be cooked in advance. Reheat by plunging the cooked pasta into boiling water for a few seconds. Drain and serve.

GLYNN'S TIP

For a richer red coloured ragú, fry the tomato purée in a little olive oil until it thickens and brightens. Add some of the ragú mixture and stir evenly, then pour it back into the main saucepan. Somehow this prevents the tomato purée giving a brown rather than a red cast to the sauce.

VELVETY SEAFOOD SAUCE

When you would like a seafood sauce to appear luxurious but not cost the earth, or want a change from tomato sauces with seafood, here is the answer. It's essentially a Béchamel sauce of coating consistency.

45 g/1½ oz butter
3 tbls plain flour
1 small onion, finely chopped (optional)
1 tbls tomato purée
1 bay leaf
1 small garlic clove, chopped
250 g/8 oz can baby clams
250 g/8 oz can Danish mussels
300 ml/½ pint milk
150 ml/¼ pint dry white wine
chopped fresh parsley or dried oregano to serve

Melt the butter, add the onion if used, and cook gently for a few minutes to soften. Stir in the flour and cook gently for a couple of minutes. Stir in the tomato purée, bay leaf and chopped garlic, and leave over a very low heat while you prepare the next stage. Open your cans of shellfish, reserving the liquid. Make this liquid up to 600 ml/1 pint with milk and bring the mixture to the boil. Pour it all on to the roux and whisk vigorously until thickened. Leave to simmer very slowly, covered. It will be rather thick at this stage and will burn easily.

Cook the pasta and toss it in butter; put it into a serving-dish, cover and keep warm. Remove the bay leaf from the sauce and thin the sauce to a coating consistency by adding white wine. Leave it slightly thicker than necessary, for when you add the seafood their residual liquid will thin it further. Adjust the seasoning, tip in the seafood and warm through. Pour the sauce over the pasta and serve at once with a scatter of fresh parsley or dried oregano. Ⓔ Ⓠ

Options
Prawns or crabmeat are excellent ingredients, but must be added with great care at the end. Chunks of cod or similar white fish may replace some of the shellfish, or you might make the dish with half fish and half vegetables. Try prawns and cubes of cooked celeriac, cod and smoked oysters; also you could replace the tomato purée with saffron.

BOLOGNESE RAGU

500 g/1 lb beef mince or minced chuck steak
3 tbls olive oil
1 very small onion, finely chopped
½ celery stalk, trimmed and chopped
2 × 397 g/14 oz cans plum tomatoes in juice
2 bay leaves
salt to taste

Brown the mince in the olive oil, cooking it until all excess liquid has evaporated and the meat starts to smell appetizing. Add the vegetables and cook until they have a little colour. Add the tomatoes with their juice and the bay leaves, but don't add salt until the mixture has reduced dramatically. Simmer, uncovered, over a very low heat for at least an hour, stirring from time to time. Once the liquid from the tomatoes has all but disappeared, salt lightly and cook long enough to let the salt penetrate each morsel (about 15 minutes). Ⓠ Ⓔ

Option
If allowed to cook until dry, Bolognese Ragu is a superb stuffing for ravioli.

RED WINE RAGU

Although wine and garlic are not part of a genuine Bolognese sauce, they do help to create an even more savoury flavour.

500 g/1 lb beef mince or minced chuck steak
1 small onion, chopped
½ celery stick, trimmed and chopped
397 g/14 oz can plum tomatoes in juice
2-4 garlic cloves
150 ml/¼ pint robust red wine
2-3 tbls tomato purée
2 bay leaves

Follow directions for the Bolognese Ragu, above. Ⓠ Ⓔ

PASTA with PARSLEY, PROVOLONE and MUSSELS

Here parsley bridges the gap between the sharp and rich flavours of the Provolone cheese and the mussels.

Serves two as a main course or four as a starter

2 tbls butter
2 generous tbls olive oil
125 g/4 oz canned mussels in brine, drained
1 garlic clove, crushed (optional)
30 g/1 oz parsley, including stalks, coarsely chopped
60 g/2 oz Provolone, Pecorino or Parmesan cheese, finely chopped but not grated

While the pasta is cooking, melt the butter and the oil, add the mussels and warm them through. Add the garlic, if used, and parsley. Stir gently without damaging the mussels. Add the small pieces of cheese. Leave the saucepan over a very low heat so that the cheese does not melt. Toss the drained pasta in a little extra olive oil, top with the sauce, and serve. Ⓕ Ⓠ

Options
Prawns, clams or cubed ham may be substituted for the mussels. Salty Feta cheese is very good, too, but use less of it.

If you can get it, the large-leaved variety of parsley looks better in this sauce.

GLYNN'S TIP

The fresh flavour of parsley is often wasted when it is used simply as a garnish, but coarsely chopped parsley is a wonderful way to finish sauces, absorbing excess liquid and thickening the sauce while adding sharp flavour and vibrant colour.

SMOKED SALMON SHELLS on WATERCRESS SAUCE

I found this wonderful, fresh watercress sauce at the Château de Montreuil, close to Le Touquet. Christian Germain, who created it, serves local scallops on top of it, but in this recipe the watery theme goes off in another direction. Pasta shells can be delicate and split, so always cook more than you need to allow for wastage. For the sake of appearance always serve an odd number. The pasta shells can be cooked and stuffed in advance to be served cold on the warm base.

Serves four to six as a first course

about 30 white pasta shells (2.5 cm/1 inch long)
1 tbls oil
60 g/2 oz smoked salmon, roughly chopped
185 g/6 oz Ricotta cheese
150 ml/1/4 pint double cream
2 bunches watercress
125 g/4 oz butter

Cook the pasta shells gently in salted water with the oil. When only just cooked, remove them from the water with a slotted spoon and allow to drain. Mix the smoked salmon with the Ricotta, adding a few spoonfuls of cream to make a smooth, thick paste. Stuff the mixture into the cooked pasta shells and keep cool.

Wash and dry the watercress and pull off all the best leaves from the stems. Chop the stems roughly and toss in a hot pan until most of the liquid exuded has evaporated. Pour in the rest of the cream and simmer for 10 minutes. Strain off the liquid into a clean pan, pressing the stems hard. Discard the stems, then whisk 90 g/3 oz of the butter, lump by lump, into the sauce and keep warm.

Melt the remaining butter (you can use the same pan in which you started the sauce) and toss the cress leaves until they just start to wilt. Immediately arrange beds of cress leaves in the centres of small, hot plates. Arrange the stuffed shells in a star pattern on each, surround the cress with the warm sauce, and serve. Ⓕ *Photograph, p. 149.*

GLYNN'S TIP

The best pasta shape to use for this is conchiglie, *the shells, for they pocket the pieces of fish so that each mouthful has hidden treasures. But noodles or any other substantial shape will do well. Small or very thin pasta would be overpowered.*

GRAPE, ORANGE and BLUE CHEESE PASTA SALAD

A delicious and brightly coloured salad which will serve up to twelve as part of a buffet, but serves four to six as a summer main course with a green salad.

250 g/8 oz dried pasta shapes
olive oil and lemon juice to taste
2 large oranges
500 g/1 lb white grapes (preferably seedless)
185 g/6 oz black olives, halved and stoned
125 g/4 oz Danish Blue cheese, crumbled
450 ml/3/4 pint mayonnaise
3 tbls lemon juice
garlic purée to taste (optional)

Cook the pasta until just tender in a large pan in masses of boiling salted water; drain, and toss in a generous amount of olive oil and lemon juice.

Peel the oranges with a sharp knife so that there is no white pith left. Make segments with no membrane by cutting to the centre of the oranges with a very sharp knife just inside the walls of each segment.

Mix the grapes, olives, orange segments and blue cheese into the pasta. Flavour the mayonnaise quite highly with lemon juice, and squeeze in garlic. Mix with the pasta combination, trying not to break the pieces. Chill for several hours to allow the flavours to blend, but do not serve directly from the refrigerator. Ⓔ Ⓥ

GREMOLATA VEGETABLES and WHOLEWHEAT PASTA

The clean taste of Italy's curiously named *gremolata*, a mixture of garlic, lemon rind and parsley, is usually used to enhance meat dishes but here it adds zing to a healthy mixture of grated vegetables and wholewheat pasta. I first served this recipe baked in a soufflé dish, but on later occasions I halved the mixture and cooked it in individual ramekins as an unusual starter. It is as good served cold as it is hot, and thus makes an ideal, portable, picnic dish.

Serves six as a main course

185 g/6 oz thin wholewheat noodles or spaghetti
2 tbls chopped parsley
1 generous tbls finely grated lemon rind
1 tsp finely chopped garlic
2 tbls olive oil
60 g/2 oz butter, softened
250 g/8 oz curd cheese
3 eggs
150 ml/1/4 pint soured cream
750 g/1 1/2 lb vegetables, grated (see Options)
grated sharp cheese (Parmesan or Pecorino) for topping (optional)

GLYNN'S TIP

Pasta Salads *Cold mixed salads based on pasta are a party-giver's dream; they can be simple or spectacular and so varied that you never need to make the same one twice. Combine colours and shapes of pasta, use fruit, vegetables, fish, meat or poultry.*

Cook the pasta in a large pan in masses of boiling salted water; drain, and toss in the parsley, lemon rind, garlic and olive oil.

Make a sauce by mixing the butter, cheese and the eggs with 2 tablespoons of the soured cream. In a soufflé dish, layer the noodles and grated vegetables (see below), pouring on the sauce as you go. Press gently to ensure the sauce is distributed evenly. Cover with the remaining soured cream, and sprinkle with a sharp cheese if you like, but this is not essential. Put in the oven and bake at 190°C/375°F/Gas Mark 5 for 20 minutes.

Allow the dish to settle for 10 minutes; it will not set firmly but can be cut neatly even when warm. Served with a salad and perhaps a baked potato, you will have a spectacularly good meal. Ⓥ Ⓔ *Photograph, p. 80.*

Options

Use whatever vegetables you prefer; courgettes and carrots are especially good. Try using about twice the amount of courgettes to carrots. Sliced blanched leeks, grated beetroot, celeriac or turnip, chopped fennel or spinach can all be used. Freshly grated lime rind substituted for the lemon gives a sharper and more fashionable flavour.

REAL LASAGNE

Real lasagne is a moist creamy mixture of Béchamel sauce and meat sauce layered generously between flat broad sheets of cooked pasta and then baked in the oven. It is not watery mince spread between those same layers of pasta. To make lasagne for four people first prepare one recipe of ragù, with or without red wine, and a generous 600 ml/1 pint of plain Béchamel sauce. Then boil 250-345 g/8-11 oz dry weight of lasagne in masses of boiling water, cool in running cold water and lay on drying up towels, side by side.

Choose an ovenproof dish about 25 cm/10 inch square. Scoop some of each sauce into the corners of the dish and swirl them together over the base. Cover with a layer of pasta then add more sauce and swirl them again. Never blend the two sauces totally as the marbled effect is one of the greatest treats of lasagne. Strew the sauces with a generous amount of freshly grated Parmesan or Pecorino cheese then lay on more pasta. And so on, ensuring you finish with a decent layer of the sauce topped with Parmesan and Pecorino.

Frankly, the exact proportions of béchamel, ragu and pasta don't matter that much and in any case are a matter of personal taste; mine is for rather more béchamel than ragu, which should be particularly well reduced. If you have a good layer of sauces on top it is nice to hide thin slices of Mozzarella cheese beneath it. Bake the lasagne in the oven at 180°C/350°F/Gas Mark 4 for 30 minutes.

LENTIL and SPINACH LASAGNE

Rich and satisfying, this is a dish to convert your family to vegetarian food or to serve at a party when you have vegetarian guests. The warm, exotic flavour of cinnamon mixes perfectly with the tomatoes and spinach and adds mystery.

Serves six generously

250 g/8 oz dried green or brown lentils
2 tbls oil
2 × 397 g/14 oz cans plum tomatoes in juice
1 tsp ground cinnamon
salt and pepper
60 g/2 oz butter
60 g/2 oz plain flour
600 ml/1 pint milk
250 g/8 oz frozen leaf spinach
½ tsp ground nutmeg
60 g/2 oz strong cheese (Pecorino or Parmesan), grated
185 g/6 oz dried wholemeal or spinach lasagne sheets

Cover the lentils with boiling water and leave for a couple of hours. Drain, cover with fresh water, add the oil and cook in a pressure-cooker for 15 minutes, or in an ordinary saucepan for about 45 minutes. Drain the lentils but save the liquid.

Purée the lentils with about 5 tablespoons of the juice from the can of tomatoes; if it still looks rather thick, use some of the lentil cooking liquid. The texture should be like a thickish Béchamel. Flavour with cinnamon, salt and pepper.

Make a simple white sauce: melt the butter, add the flour and cook without browning, then add the milk and whisk over heat until thick. Put the *frozen* block of leaf spinach into the sauce and allow it to defrost – the water and vitamins will be retained and the sauce will acquire a thinnish texture; remember that it will thicken in the oven while the dish is being baked. Season with nutmeg, salt and pepper and add three-quarters of the cheese.

Cook the lasagne sheets in a very big

saucepan with masses of boiling salted water and a tablespoon or two of oil. Drain, and run cold water over the pasta to cool and separate it.

Run a little of the spinach sauce around the edges of the bottom of a large greased ovenproof dish, then put in a layer of pasta. Spoon in some of both sauces, and swirl with a spoon to make an even layer but without mixing the two sauces completely. Put on a layer of tomatoes, which you have gently squashed, and sprinkle with a little salt and pepper. Continue layering as you fancy, but leave enough of the spinach sauce to finish on top. Sprinkle this with the remaining cheese. Bake at 200°C/400°F/Gas Mark 6 for 25 minutes. Ⓥ Ⓔ

COD, LEEK and PRAWN LASAGNE

This dish is pretty to look at and delightful to eat. You could halve the quantities to serve as a first course for a substantial meal, especially if you took the trouble to make individual portions in ramekins. It is important that the cod is cut into generous pieces; but the prawns are a luxury that you can do without.

Serves six as a main course

500 g/1 lb cod fillet
300 ml/½ pint dry white wine
1 bay leaf
60 g/2 oz butter
60 g/2 oz plain flour
600 ml/1 pint milk
salt and pepper
750 g/1½ lb leeks, trimmed and thinly sliced
2 tsps seed mustard
125 g/4 oz butter
185-250 g/6-8 oz plain dried lasagne sheets
250 g/8 oz peeled prawns
chopped fresh parsley to garnish

Poach the cod in the wine with the bay leaf until tender, adding a little extra water if needed. Remove the fish and flake into fairly large pieces, removing any skin or bone. Melt the butter in a pan, add the flour and cook for a few minutes. Measure the poaching liquid from the fish and make up to 600 ml/1 pint with milk. Mix into the flour mixture, whisking all the time until thickened. Adjust the flavour with salt and pepper and add the flaked cod.

Place the leeks in a saucepan with the rest of the milk (but no more than 300 ml/½ pint) and cook until the leeks begin to soften but still have a bright green colour. Reserve a quarter of the leeks and purée the rest with the mustard and butter. Stir in the reserved leeks.

Cook the lasagne in a large pan with masses of boiling salted water and 1-2 tablespoons of oil. Drain, and run cold water over them.

Cover the bottom of a large, greased, oven-

proof dish with a thin layer of the cod sauce, then a layer of lasagne. Cover with a layer of both sauces and swirl with a spoon to cover the lasagne completely without mixing the two sauces too much. Sprinkle with some of the prawns. Continue layering, leaving some of the fish sauce to make a final topping. Bake for about 25 minutes at 190°C/375°F/Gas Mark 5. Serve sprinkled with chopped parsley. Ⓔ

DILL and CRABSTICK CANNELLONI

Serves four as a starter or two as a main course with salad

8 cannelloni shells

FILLING
1-2 shallots, chopped
125 g/4 oz curd cheese
60 g/2 oz crab sticks (4 sticks)
1 tsp dried dill
½ tsp grated lemon rind
2 tbls soured cream or strained yoghurt
SAUCE
60 g/2 oz butter
50 g/1¾ oz flour
750 ml/1¼ pints milk
salt and pepper
½ tsp grated nutmeg
90 g/3 oz Parmesan or Pecorino cheese, grated

Disregard any instructions on the packet and cook the cannelloni shells for 8 minutes in fast-boiling water. Run cold water over the pasta to cool and then drain.

Make the filling: press the shallots in a garlic press to extract the juice (about 1 teaspoon is needed) and mix with all the other ingredients.

Make the sauce: melt the butter in a pan and stir in the flour. Cook without browning until it looks granular. Add the milk and stir until thickened. Season to taste, add the nutmeg and stir in 30 g/1 oz of the cheese.

Put a thin layer of sauce in the bottom of a shallow, greased, ovenproof dish. Lay the filled shells on top, making sure that they are not touching, then pour over the rest of the sauce. Sprinkle the remaining grated hard cheese on top and bake for 30-35 minutes at 180°C/ 350°F/Gas Mark 4. Ⓕ Ⓥ

Options
Mozzarella and black olive filling To the curd cheese add 60 g/2 oz chopped Mozzarella cheese; 30 g/1 oz blanched and chopped black olives; 1 teaspoon dried oregano; 2 tablespoons soured cream or strained yoghurt.
Spinach and pine-nut filling To the curd cheese add 60 g/2 oz drained, chopped spinach; 30 g/1 oz roughly chopped pine-nuts; 1 teaspoon dried mint; ½ teaspoon grated nutmeg.

MACARONI CHEESE

It is widely supposed that by pouring a cheese sauce over cooked macaroni you can produce an edible macaroni cheese – you can't. But such macaroni cheese recipes must be responsible for turning more people away from pasta dishes than anything else. You will find that the little trouble it takes to make this dish colourful and tasty is amply repaid by the final result.

Serves four generously

250 g/8 oz dried macaroni
75 g/2½ oz butter
60 g/2 oz plain flour
900 ml/1½ pints milk
salt and pepper
½ tsp ground nutmeg
125 g/4 oz bacon, cut into strips
1 small red or green pepper, sliced
185 g/6 oz strong Cheddar cheese, grated
125 g/4 oz fresh white or wholemeal breadcrumbs
8 slices tomato to garnish

Cook the macaroni in a large saucepan in masses of boiling salted water until almost tender (remember it will be cooked further in the oven). Drain the macaroni and cover and reserve. (For extra flavour, you might like to toss it in a little melted butter off the heat.)

Make a white sauce in the usual way with the butter, flour and milk (see page 14). Season lightly with salt, pepper and nutmeg and allow the sauce to simmer gently over a low heat.

Gently fry the bacon in a saucepan until the fat is running freely. Add the pepper slices and cook until they are softened and brighter in colour. Stir the bacon and peppers into the warm sauce, then stir in the cheese. Fold the sauce into the macaroni, spoon into a 1.75 litre/3 pint ovenproof dish and cover with the breadcrumbs. Arrange the tomato pieces on top and bake at 180°C/350°F/Gas Mark 4 for 20-25 minutes. The top should be crisp and golden. For added effect sprinkle on a little more grated cheese a few minutes before serving.

Options

The sauce will taste even better if you flavour the milk by heating it gently with some onion, parsley and carrots and leaving this to infuse for 20 minutes or so before using.

If you cannot obtain really strong Cheddar, use two-thirds mild Cheddar and one-third Parmesan or Pecorino.

PIZZA MACARONI PIE

Here's something truly hearty for winter days. All the flavour and colour of a pizza is baked into macaroni. This dish tastes very good reheated.

Serves six to eight

250 g/8 oz dried macaroni
olive oil
90 g/3 oz onion, sliced
900 ml/1½ pints milk
60 g/2oz butter
75 g/2½ oz flour
2 tbls tomato purée
garlic purée to taste
125 g/4 oz Parmesan or Pecorino cheese
185 g/6 oz Mozzarella cheese, thinly sliced
250 g/8 oz ripe tomatoes, thinly sliced
12-18 black olives, stoned
50 g/1¾ oz can anchovy fillets, drained and halved lengthways (optional)
1 tsp dried oregano
60 g/2 oz fresh white or wholewheat breadcrumbs

Cook the macaroni in a large pan in masses of boiling salted water until almost tender; drain, and toss in a generous amount of olive oil. Cook the onion gently in a little of the milk, then purée the mixture (if you prefer pieces of onion, you can leave the softened onion as it is).

Melt the butter, stir in the flour and cook for a few minutes before adding the onion purée and the rest of the milk. Whisk until thickened, then simmer gently while you finish the ingredients. Blanch the black olives in boiling water for at least 5 minutes. Stir the tomato purée and garlic purée into the sauce to give a rich colour and flavour – in this case it is not necessary to fry it first.

Grate the hard cheese into the sauce and mix with the macaroni; spoon it into a 1.75 litre/3 pint ovenproof dish. Interleave the Mozzarella and tomato slices on top and add the olives and anchovy fillets if you are using them. Sprinkle evenly with the oregano and put the breadcrumbs around the inside edge of the dish where they will absorb the liquids which bubble up during baking. Sprinkle with a generous amount of olive oil – 2-3 tablespoons at least. Bake at 180°C/350°F/Gas Mark 4 for about 25 minutes. Ⓥ Ⓔ *Photograph, p. 41.*

PRAWN, LIME and ARTICHOKE MACARONI

In this elegant macaroni dish the proportion of pasta to sauce is lower than usual and the subtle colours and topping of flaked almonds makes it perfect for a smart lunch for four or a first course for eight guests.

185 g/6 oz dried macaroni
75 g/2½ oz butter
60 g/2 oz plain flour
900 ml/1½ pints milk
150 ml/¼ pint white wine
1 fish stock cube
1 tbls tomato purée
250 g/8 oz frozen peeled prawns, thawed
185 g/6 oz cooked or canned artichoke hearts
1 tsp grated lime rind
60 g/2 oz flaked almonds

Cook the macaroni in a large saucepan in masses of boiling salted water until almost tender, drain and toss in a little additional butter.

Melt the butter, stir in the flour and, after cooking gently for a few minutes, add the milk, wine and stock cube. Stir and cook until thickened. Add the tomato purée for colour.

Dry the prawns and cut the artichoke hearts into strips as wide as the prawns. Stir both into the sauce, add the lime rind and mix evenly with the macaroni. Turn into a lightly greased ovenproof dish (a straight-sided white soufflé dish is the most elegant container for this recipe). Bake at 180°C/350°F/Gas Mark 4 for 10 minutes by which time a light skin will have formed on the surface. Scatter the almonds evenly over the top and bake for another 10 minutes or until heated through and the almonds are starting to colour. Do not overcook or the prawns will toughen. Ⓔ
Photograph, p.43.

RICE, GRAINS *and* PULSES

Risottos, pilaffs and pulaos, exotic dhals, hot salads and warming casseroles – international recipes offer partners and alternatives to expensive meats.

Welcome the revolution. In just a few years grains and pulses have come out of the scrubbed-pine kitchen and on to the supermarket shelf. Quite right too, for not only is the human body and mouth designed to eat these rather than meat, but they bring immeasurable variety to the diet.

They can be used as an alternative to meat and poultry or combined with them to balance both meat intake and your budget. There is an additional advantage, too, in that grains and pulses can be cooked once a week and stored in the refrigerator. I always have a few cans of cooked ones in my larder as back-up, for they are great for making dips and snacks or for filling out soups, stews and vegetable dishes at the last minute.

Start by introducing them slowly to your diet, as part of a salad or as a substitute for, say, potatoes and as your system adapts you'll gradually be able to move to complete dishes based upon them.

RICE

I always keep more than one type of rice in my store cupboard, so that I can ring the changes on a favourite recipe and, more important perhaps, use the right rice for the selected dish. Have the following on hand: short-grain rice for puddings; Italian *Arborio* rice for risottos; Indian long-grain *Basmati* rice as a fragrant accompaniment to curries and stews, for rice salads and pilaffs; patna or American long-grain rice for stuffings and flavoured rice dishes; and brown rice for main-course dishes and vegetarian meals. There are countless other types of rice available in speciality and ethnic shops – sticky or sweet Thai rice, wild pecan rice from Louisiana, Iranian rices, Chinese rices, and wild rice, which is not a rice at all but a water grass.

LONG-GRAIN WHITE RICE

There is an avalanche of advice on cooking rice. I've tried all the methods, only to find that the simplest is best. Washing the rice before cooking seems to be the most pointless advice. In the Western world anything bought in a packet is relatively clean and uncontaminated enough not to have to be washed or picked over. A quick rinse if you insist, but only if you promise that you will not rinse the rice after it is cooked, which removes what little goodness might be left in it. The one exception is brown rice, which should be rinsed before cooking.

Rice cooked by the following absorption method retains whatever vitamins may have washed into the cooking water and requires only that you keep a sharp eye on the time.

First put the amount of rice that you are using into a measuring jug, or failing that, mark the side of a bowl or jug. I usually allow 60 g/2 oz per person as an accompaniment; 125 g/4 oz as a main dish. You will need twice that volume of water or other cooking liquid, such as a light stock.

Heat some butter (if the rice is to be served hot) or some oil (if it is to be served cold) in a saucepan with a lid. Add the rice and stir until all the grains are well coated and looking somewhat translucent; do not brown them. Pour in the cold liquid, season lightly with salt and pepper, give it *one* stir and bring it to the boil. I usually add a bay leaf.

Simmer it over a moderate heat until the liquid is level with the rice and you can see a few bubbling craters on the top. Place a clean, dry folded tea-towel over the top of the saucepan and clamp the lid on top very firmly. Fold the cloth so that it cannot touch the heat source and burn. Turn down the heat to the lowest possible setting; use a wire diffuser if you have one on a gas flame and stand the pan to one side of an electric hob. Leave it for 7 minutes, and then you will discover the rice is ready. Fluff it up with a fork or wooden spoon and serve.

If the rice is overcooked and a bit sticky after the cooking time (we all have days when even the foolproof methods go wrong), or if you want to keep your rice warm, turn it into a sieve, cover it with a cloth and a lid and steam it over a pan of simmering water.

Options

Rice for savoury dishes tastes better if cooked in a good chicken stock, or a mixture of water and white wine. This is worth doing even if the rice is served simply as an accompaniment. If the rice is to be served cold, nothing is quite as good as rice flavoured with several bay leaves.

Saffron Rice Saffron gives both a glorious colour and flavour to rice, especially when the rice is cooked with a generous amount of butter. You may not like saffron as much as I do, so it is tricky to give exact amounts, but for four servings I usually add two sachets of saffron to the liquid and stir well before bringing it to the boil. Excellent for stuffing.

Lemon Rice Cook the rice as above, then for every two servings stir in 2 tablespoons of lemon juice and 1 tablespoon of chopped parsley. Season with a little grated lemon zest, salt and ground white pepper. This is particularly good with chicken and fish dishes; any fresh herb can be added that goes well with lemon, especially thyme. Use orange as an alternative to the lemon.

Nutty Rice To flavour four servings of cooked rice, stir in 125 g/4 oz roughly chopped salted cashew nuts, freshly ground black pepper and a few chopped spring onions if you like them.

Fruity Rice To flavour four servings of cooked rice, stir in 90 g/3 oz sultanas or raisins which have previously been plumped up in a little water, stock, wine or, best of all, melted butter.

Tomato Rice Cook the rice in diluted tomato purée or with crushed canned plum tomatoes in their own juice. Alternatively, turn the cooked rice in a little of either. I usually include some olive oil or butter and a sliver or two of garlic.

Spinach Rice Once the rice is cooked, prepare some hot, very well drained and pressed chopped spinach. Toss the rice in lots of melted butter, then stir in the spinach. You can use just a little spinach to give the rice an unexpected green colour as an accompaniment to a pale-coloured fish dish, or you can use almost equal quantities of rice and spinach to make a really substantial accompaniment, but ensure that it is well flavoured with butter, grated nutmeg and black pepper. Spinach tastes so good with orange that you might try grating in some rind, especially if serving it with fish and chicken salads.

RICE STUFFINGS

Rice stuffings are excellent in boned meat joints and vegetables such as courgette, peppers, marrow and tomatoes. Any of the flavoured rice options would be suitable. I like to add whole almonds and currants to cooked rice, seasoning with a little cinnamon and cardamom. Or cook the rice in a mixture of orange juice and stock or water which can be further enhanced by adding finely grated orange peel, orange-flower water and flaked almonds or pine-nuts. Try adding drained, canned crushed pineapple with lots of fresh chopped mint; drained, canned apricots, chopped, with chopped walnuts; chopped soaked prunes with hazelnuts, all of which are particularly good in pork, lamb and veal dishes.

WILD RICE

Wild rice isn't a true rice but the seeds of a fresh-water grass that grows along rivers in northern parts of the USA. It is extremely expensive because it steadfastly refuses to be cultivated and thus must be harvested by hand from canoes by a few American Indian tribes.

The seeds are long and thin and coloured a lustrous deep-brown. They may be cooked by the absorption method (see page 35) and the cooking time will fall somewhere between the times taken by white and brown rice. I like them a little chewy but unless they are cooked through and splitting open they are dreadful, almost dangerous, for their sharp ends get stuck into palates and gums. A little wild rice is strong enough in flavour to be mixed with white rice or with vegetables but cook it separately first and combine just before serving.

The American Indian way to cook wild rice is the slowest but is the most attractive as the grains split into butterfly shapes. Pour boiling water over the seeds and let it cool. Pour off the cold water and repeat this at least once more.

FOOD FACT

Brown Rice *consists of the whole rice grain with the high-fibre husk layer still intact, so it is the best type to eat from a dietary point of view. Always use the absorption method so that you retain all its valuable vitamins too. Brown rice is best cooked uncovered and may take as long as 45 minutes – just leave it to simmer gently,* don't stir.

RICE SALADS

Cold rice makes an excellent base for salads, but only if it is well flavoured both during cooking and immediately afterwards. Use *Basmatti* rice for preference and stir it in oil rather than butter or it will clump together when cold; include a couple of bay leaves in the cooking water. Once the rice is ready, let it cool to lukewarm and then lightly stir in a mixture of good oil and vinegar or lemon juice, as you would for a potato salad. The exception to this rule is when you want a spiced rice, in which case you warm oil and use it to heat saffron or a mixture of ground cumin and coriander, then turn the warm rice evenly in it. Flavour with lemon juice only when cold.

Now you can add any other ingredients in any proportion. The most elegant rice salads have only three or four ingredients and these are cut in varying shapes and sizes. In summer, combine strips of cooked chicken or turkey with fresh pineapple cubes and grate in fresh ginger; combine water-melon balls and cucumber cubes with fresh or dried mint; mix firm pieces of de-seeded, skinned tomato with segments of sweet orange and small black olives.

MINTED RICE MOULD

This is a favourite recipe for serving rice with casseroles. You must pack the rice tightly into the mould so that it can be sliced and arranged on the plate.

Serves six

blanched lettuce leaves
1 tsp sweet paprika
1 kg/2 lb American long-grain rice, cooked (about 375 g/12 oz uncooked weight)
3 eggs
150 ml/¼ pint double cream
1½-2 tbls chopped fresh mint, or prepared, preserved mint, well-rinsed and drained
salt and pepper

Lightly oil a 25 cm/10 inch ring-mould and line it with the blanched lettuce leaves. Sprinkle the paprika over the lettuce evenly. Mix together the rice, eggs, cream and mint and beat well to combine. Season to taste, then spoon the mixture into the mould and press it down *very firmly*. Fold over any excess lettuce to cover the rice, put a foil cap over the mould and cook at 180°C/350°F/Gas Mark 4 for 35 minutes. Allow it to stand for 2-3 minutes before turning it out on to a hot plate, then serve or chill it. Serve cut into slices. Ⓔ *Photograph, p. 113.*

AUBERGINE and BROWN RICE TIMBALE

This is a surprising combination that promises blandness but which actually delivers a satisfying flavour. It's so good that most people don't realise that it is a vegetarian dish. Make sure the rice is well cooked or the chewiness will negate the pleasure.

Serves four to six

1 kg/2 lb aubergines
salt
250 g/8 oz uncooked long-grain brown rice
olive oil for frying
2 tbls ground cumin
1 tbls ground coriander
2 × 396 g/14 oz cans plum tomatoes in juice
200 g/7 oz cucumber
mint to taste
garlic cloves, crushed, to taste

Cut the aubergines into thick slices lengthways, without peeling; salt generously and leave them to drain off their bitter juices in a colander for 1-2 hours, turning from time to time. Rinse the rice quickly and, while it is draining, heat a good tablespoon of olive oil in a pan and add the cumin and coriander. Once the oil and spices have released their flavour and are smelling marvellous, tip in the rice and stir well. Add the tomatoes, with their juice, squeezing each to help break them down.

Bring to the boil and simmer, very gently, covered, until the rice is cooked, when there should still be some unabsorbed tomato juice. If the mixture dries before the rice is tender, add a little water.

Rinse the aubergine slices, pat them dry, then fry to a light golden brown in olive oil. Aubergine drinks up olive oil but don't pander too much to this – use just enough to encourage the aubergine slices to soften right through and to brown only lightly. Peel the cucumber, cut in half lengthways and scoop out the seeds. Cut into half-moon shapes and stir into the rice.

Line a 1.5-1.75 litre/2½-3 pint ovenproof dish with a layer of aubergine slices, then sprinkle these with chopped mint and crushed garlic; use as much or as little as you like, but err on the generous side with the mint. Add half the rice, press down a little, make another layer of aubergine and flavour that as above, then add the remaining rice and finish with the aubergine. Press down lightly but firmly, cover with foil and bake at 180°C/350°F/Gas Mark 4 for 45 minutes. Let the timbale rest for 10 minutes, then invert on to a hot serving dish, remove the ovenproof dish and serve at once, cut into wedges with a sharp knife.

If you would like to serve a sauce with this dish, reduce a further can of tomatoes until thick and flavour with salt, pepper, garlic and more mint. This is particularly good re-heated or cold on a picnic. *Photograph, p. 115.*

FOOD FACT

A risotto is not rice containing leftovers – if anything, that is a pilaff. A true risotto is an aristocratic native of Italy's northern rice-eating districts, a descendant of the ancient soups of Venice and therefore should be so wet that it is almost impossible to eat it with a fork. It requires great care to make and is almost always served as a first course, but it can be made as a light lunch or supper dish.

RISOTTO

It is important to understand the theory of risotto, for it contradicts every other method of cooking rice. During cooking, the rice must be agitated constantly, which encourages the starch to come out of the grains. While this agitation keeps the grains from sticking together, it also makes an emulsion of the stock and butter, so you end up with cooked grains in a velvety sauce. Once you have mastered the technique, and can justify eating the huge amounts of butter and cheese needed to make a good risotto, you will be seduced by this most voluptuous of all savoury dishes.

Serves two

125 g/4 oz short-grain Italian rice (Arborio or Vialone)
6 tbls butter
30 g/1 oz onion, chopped (optional)
600 ml/1 pint boiling stock
2 tbls Parmesan or Pecorino cheese, grated

Melt 4 tablespoons of butter in a small pan and add the rice and the onion if you are using it. Stir the rice around (a wooden fork is excellent for this) until it is golden and well coated with

GLYNN'S TIP

The most important point about cooking risotto is to use the correct rice for the purpose – Italian Arborio or Vialone. These short-grain rices melt on the outside during cooking but retain a bite on the inside, partly because of their shape and partly because they have been bred to behave like that.

butter, then pour in the hot stock and start whisking. Keep whisking the rice around for 10-15 minutes (it may take up to 30 minutes if you are cooking for more than two people) until you have an unctuous sauce and the separate grains have just a faint bite in the centre. The mixture should be kept just bubbling – not too fast or the liquid will evaporate quickly. If the risotto gets too dry before the rice is ready, add a little more stock. *Don't* let the sauce evaporate entirely or cook the rice until it is soft in the middle.

Once the rice is cooked, stir in the remaining butter and the cheese and adjust the final flavouring; it is unlikely that you will need salt as the butter and reduced stock between them usually contain enough. Serve at once.

Options
Use different types of stock, especially those made with fish. I also like to reconstitute packets of Italian dried mushrooms (*porcini*) in lots of water and use them to make a wild mushroom risotto.
Saffron risotto Made as above with a little more butter and with powdered saffron or saffron strands; for special occasions add a little seafood at the last moment.
Vegetable risotto One of my favourite additions is finely grated courgettes. They love butter, cheese and rice and have an amazing affinity with chicken, so that is the stock to use.

FOOD FACT

Pilaff, pilau, pulao, pilaw – call them what you will, these Eastern dishes of rice with nuts, vegetables, fruits and meats are infinite in their variety. They are always much drier than a risotto. Use only long-grain rice and, although packaged American rice is very trustworthy, the elegant shape and princely flavour of Basmati rice will give much better results.

MAHARAJA'S BEEF PULAO

This recipe is representative of a true Indian pulao, in which the rice is cooked in the liquid already used to cook meat or other ingredients.

This is a dish for entertaining or for large families, using just one large saucepan. When you tip it out you can't believe that so much food has been sitting in a single pan. You can either mix it all together before serving, or, as I like to do, tip it out layer by layer, which gives you succulent rice studded with exotic fruit and nuts topped with a fragrant, lightly spiced meat.

Serves six generously

2 tbls oil
60 g/2 oz butter
125 g/4 oz sliced onion
1 kg/2 lb lean stewing beef, cut into large chunks
2 garlic cloves
6 peppercorns
1 tsp coriander seeds
6 cloves
6 cardamom pods (open if you wish)
2 sachets saffron powder
1.2 litres/2 pints water
375 g/12 oz rice
fruit and nuts (see below)

In a large pan, heat the oil and butter, gently brown the onions, then remove them. Add the meat, garlic and spices and cook over a fairly high heat until the meat is sealed and browning nicely. If you like, the spices can be pounded but I rather like them whole so that the dish becomes more of a biryani (see Options below). Pour on the water, bring to the boil, then turn the heat down and simmer until the meat is tender, 1-1½ hours depending on the quality of your meat. Add the rice but do not stir at all.

Add as much fruit and nuts as you would like; the best are the exotics: sliced or segmented orange, mango segments, papaya, banana, but raisins, sultanas, almonds, hazelnuts and even mundane apples, pears or grapes work well. Cover and simmer gently until the rice has absorbed all or most of the liquid. Do not stir at any time during the cooking or testing. The rice will take 20-40 minutes to become tender and you can cook it on to dry it or add more stock to make a wettish mixture. Ⓔ *Photograph, p. 115.*

Options
These are limitless – you can add as much extra garlic as you like and finely grated fresh ginger to add 'bite', or whole cumin seeds or ground cumin. Chicken makes a wonderful pulao; mutton or lamb, or a mixture of mutton or lamb and beef can be substituted for all beef.

BIRYANIS

In most respects a biryani looks the same as a pulao – but the flavour is very different. To make a real biryani, fry meat and onions in lots of butter rather than oil, then add the same sort of spice mixture as above, with the addition of a few sliced green chillies. Use one-third less water so that by the time the meat is cooked there is very little liquid left. About 30 minutes before serving, tip in 500 g/1 lb of raw rice, top that with fruit, seal well and continue cooking over gentle heat. When it is ready, a biryani is always sprinkled with rose water and served directly from the container, with the whole spices, without being stirred.

PILAFFS

The delightful pilaffs of the Middle East are made in the same way as the pulao above but dried fruits are more likely to be used, prunes, apricots and currants in particular. Nuts are best not cooked with the rice, unless you have toasted them first. It's better and more economical to strew nuts over the finished dish – lightly toasted whole almonds and roughly crushed pistachios look the best. The latter are a sign of hospitality and wealth.

CHRISTMAS PILAFF

As Christmas is a celebration with its roots in the Middle East, I think it only right we should mark this by serving some reminder of the produce of that area, especially the dried fruits and spices brought back to us by the Crusaders. This pilaff, actually from Armenia, is perfect for this, even if you don't add the final touch of apples filled with flaming spirits. Either carry this to the table on a separate platter or arrange it around the turkey and have someone strong help you carry the whole extraordinary arrangement to the table. This dish is enough for eight, which is a festive sort of number, but the recipe is simple to halve.

Serves eight

500 g/1 lb Basmati rice
chicken stock
butter
250 g/8 oz seedless raisins
250 g/8 oz dried apricots
water or orange juice
125 g/4 oz flaked or whole blanched almonds
8 small apples
8 small quinces
ground cinnamon
brandy or rum

First cook the *Basmati* rice by the absorption method, using a good chicken stock and 60 g/ 2 oz butter. Stir the seedless raisins into some butter. Add the apricots and just cover with water or orange juice. Simmer gently – don't let them get at all mushy. Lightly brown the blanched almonds. Also bake one small apple and one small quince per person. (Or slice apple, quince or pear and cook the slices until golden brown in butter.) On a warmed platter, arrange the rice and sprinkle on the raisins, apricot and nuts. Arrange the baked fruit evenly around the edge. Sprinkle with cinnamon.

Scoop out one or two apples. Fill with warmed brandy or rum and ignite, then proceed carefully to the table. For a Vesuvius effect, pile the pilaff high on a platter and make a dent in the top into which you either put a single scooped out fruit or line with foil as a receptacle for the alcohol.

Options

Mixtures of dried fruit and rice are legion and all good. The simplest way to make them is to take whatever suitable ingredients you have to hand, but ideally always include dried apricots and sauté them lightly in lots of butter. For naughty richness, sprinkle in some sugar, perhaps letting it caramelize slightly. Stir the fruits into or spread over cooked long grain rice. The correct way to cook a pilaff is to steam it for a long time, but I think this takes away a lot of the freshness of colour and flavour.

A little ground cloves might be added to the rice; I always dust pilaffs like this with ground cinnamon but you might also use the spicier nutmeg or allspice. Don't be sparing with the butter in the rice or in the fruit.

These mixtures make perfect stuffings for all poultry and white meats, but as they are so easy to make why bother stuffing them in the bird; use a stock rather than water to cook them.

KEDGEREE

A pilaff in fact, kedgeree has its roots in Indian cooking; but in the way it is usually prepared in Britain, it belongs neither to India nor Britain. Although kedgeree can be wonderful without, it is infinitely better if it is lightly spiced and, like risottos, biryanis and most other good rice dishes, it needs absolutely masses of butter. Buy naturally smoked Finnan haddock if you can, for the yellow-dyed fillets and brown-dyed whole fish neither taste nor look anything like the real thing and they dye the rice too.

Serves four to six

1 kg/2 lb Finnan haddock
1 bay leaf
125 g/4 oz butter
250 g/8 oz Basmati or long grain rice
4 hard-boiled eggs
1 tsp ground coriander
1/2 tsp ground cumin
1/2 tsp turmeric

Cover the fish well with cold water, add the bay leaf and bring slowly to the simmer. Remove the pan from the heat and, first checking by using a fork to ensure the fish comes easily away from any bones, remove the fish from the water; but reserve the water.

Melt a good knob of butter in a saucepan and cook the rice in this until it looks rather translucent. Measure the fish poaching liquid and add twice the volume of the rice to the pan. Cook until the liquid is absorbed and the rice is soft.

Meanwhile, flake the fish into generous pieces and assiduously remove every trace of skin and bone. Shell the eggs and chop them roughly and unevenly. Once the rice is cooked, melt the remaining butter and sweat the spices for a couple of minutes. Stir in the warm rice and, once evenly amalgamated, fold in the eggs and then the fish. Do this very lightly to avoid breaking up everything and thus keeping the contrast of texture and shape, which is one of the appeals of a well-made kedgeree.

Serve at once on heated plates or keep warm, covered, in a low oven until needed.

Option

There is some school of thought which encourages the addition of cream, but this shouldn't be necessary.

RICE PUDDINGS

Rice pudding belongs to the days when solid-fuel cookers were used, so that it was left in the 'cool' oven to cook at its leisure and emerge creamy and rich with a nutmeg skin that families fought over. A properly cooked, *real* rice pudding is one of the great British dishes.

Serves four

60 g/2 oz short-grain pudding rice
2 tsps butter
30 g/1 oz sugar
600 ml/1 pint creamy milk
1/2 tsp nutmeg

If you are short of time, put the rice into 600ml/1 pint of cold water, bring it up to the boil, drain and use.

Use the butter to grease a 600 ml/1 pint ovenproof dish. Put the rice in the bottom, sprinkle with sugar, then pour in the milk. Sprinkle the top with nutmeg. For best results allow the pudding to stand for at least 2 hours before cooking. Bake at the bottom of a low oven, 150°C/300°F/Gas Mark 2, for 2-2½ hours.

Options

Add raisins or currants; in order to prevent them from becoming overcooked and robbed of their sweetness, stir them in 30 minutes before the pudding is to be served.

Rose water or orange-flower water (especially the latter) added to the milk makes wonderful rice puddings. I like spiced puddings, the most fragrant addition being a couple of cardamom pods, but a cinnamon stick and a few cloves are equally effective. The most unusual additions of all are grains of gum mastic (a similar flavouring to that used for Greek *ouzo*) with either orange-flower water or cardamom – an Egyptian combination which is equally good with chicken.

King George's Rice Pudding Take the basic pudding out of the oven fairly early, while it is still wet, and mix in about 60 g/2 oz of dried fruit, some orange rind, a little orange-flower water and four egg yolks. Whisk the four egg whites fairly stiffly, fold them in and continue baking at 180°C/350°F/Gas Mark 4 for another 30-40 minutes, until the pudding is well risen and browned.

Extravagant Rice Pudding Cook the basic pudding without the nutmeg and cover the top of the dish with a foil lid or greaseproof paper to prevent a skin forming. Take it out when it is starting to stiffen and there is very little excess milk in the dish and allow the pudding to get quite cold. Whip up 150 ml/¼ pint double cream and fold it in, together with half a teaspoon of nutmeg or cinnamon. Serve in glass dishes, with a little spice sprinkled on top. If you think this sounds rich but rather plain, you are right. Flavour the cream with vanilla essence, grated orange, lemon or lime, or with high quality glacé fruit and peel, or with a liqueur.

FRAGRANT RICE PUDDING

This Indian recipe uses long-grain rice and is more complicated to make, but worth the effort.

Serves four to six

scant litre/1¾ pints milk
60 g/2 oz long-grain rice, preferably Basmati
30 g/1 oz ground almonds
1 ripe banana, mashed
3 tbls sugar
¼ tsp ground cardamom
½ sachet saffron
3 tbls pistachio nuts, shelled and roughly chopped

Bring 900 ml/1½ pints milk to the boil in a large, heavy saucepan. Stir the rice into the milk, return to the boil, then simmer over a low heat until the mixture thickens and the rice is tender. This will take 75-90 minutes; you should stir frequently to prevent the rice from sticking.

Mix the remaining milk with the almonds and add the banana, sugar, cardamom and saffron and stir to blend thoroughly. Add this mixture to the rice and continue to simmer until the pudding has thickened further (about 10 minutes). Cool, then chill thoroughly in the refrigerator. Serve the pudding in glass goblets or dishes sprinkled with the pistachio nuts. Ⓣ

GRAINS

Grains are man's best friends and among his oldest foods; our teeth remain adapted to them rather than to meat eating. To me they are invaluable for many reasons, but mainly because they are cheap and, provided they are kept cool and dark, store a very long time, thus providing a carefree storecupboard. Many (millet and buckwheat in particular) cook very quickly and combine naturally well with both meat and vegetable so you don't have to have a cookery certificate to invent something new. But most of all they are reliably delicious and enable those interested in reducing the amount of meat in their diet to serve alternative protein several times a week without radically disturbing their usual life-style or shopping habits.

BUCKWHEAT PILAFF

Strictly speaking, buckwheat does not belong with grains, being the fruit of an herbaceous plant related to rhubarb, dock and sorrel. However, as it is cooked and eaten as a cereal grain, it belongs here as far as this book is concerned. Buckwheat has been a staple in northern Europe, Asia and Russia for centuries. In western Europe, buckwheat is eaten in quantity only in northern France and Belgium.

Buckwheat can be bought roasted or unroasted. Finely ground as buckwheat flour, it is used in pancakes, or *galettes* as they are known in France, *blinis* in Russia. Coarsely ground, it is cooked essentially like rice; but there is virtually no chance of it being burnt or clumping together. In fact, it's a bad cook's dream.

For each 250 g/8 oz buckwheat (which will give about four servings), heat a little oil or butter in a medium saucepan. The better tasting the oil you use, the better the pilaff will be. Brown the buckwheat grains over a medium heat, lightly or to a rich brown, whichever you prefer, then pour over 450 ml/¾ pint hot water or stock. Let it boil for 2 minutes, then turn down the heat and simmer gently for a little longer, until all the liquid has disappeared. Put

a clean cloth over the saucepan, clamp the lid firmly on top and leave it over the lowest possible heat for 20-30 minutes. You can leave it for much longer – up to 2 hours if you like! Serve it in the same way as for rice. I prefer to leave it for only about 10 minutes so that it still has a little bite in the centre.

Options

One of the best options is 125 g/4 oz smoked streaky bacon, chopped and fried until just crisp. The buckwheat is then browned in the bacon fat. Add a little chopped onion and garlic, if you like.

Real stock always improves the dish, the more flavoursome the better. If you do not have any, soak a packet of dried mushrooms in 450 ml/¾ pint hot water and use that to cook the buckwheat, including the mushrooms.

BUCKWHEAT GALETTES

Makes about 12

250 g/8 oz buckwheat flour
250 g/8 oz plain white flour
2 tsps salt
600 ml/1 pint milk
300 ml/½ pint water
60 g/2 oz unsalted butter, melted
oil for frying
savoury filling (see method)

Sift the flours with the salt into a large bowl and make a hole in the centre. Gradually pour in the milk, beating well all the time to give a smooth batter. Allow it to stand for 30-40 minutes, then slowly beat in the water until the consistency resembles thick cream – you may need a little extra water. Add the melted butter and blend thoroughly.

Cook the galettes in the same way as for pancakes (see page 156), heating the pan and greasing lightly with oil to prevent sticking. Cook the galettes lightly on both sides (they will be cooked again when the filling has been added). Pile them on a warm plate as you make them and cover with a cloth.

Galettes can be served with a variety of fillings: thinly sliced ham or cheese, smoked salmon or other fish, sliced cooked sausage, creamed mushrooms or spinach. Fill, then fold or roll and reheat by frying in a little butter. Alternatively, place the filled galettes in a greased shallow dish with a little extra butter or oil brushed over and reheat at 180°C/350°F/Gas Mark 4.

BURGHUL

Burghul is not cracked wheat, as it is sometimes incorrectly described, but boiled wheat which has been dried to a paste and then ground. It is also called *bulghur* or, in Cyprus, *pourghourri*. Like buckwheat, burghul makes a foolproof alternative to rice in all kinds of pilaff dishes. It is so simple that anyone can prepare it, for it is already cooked, needing only to be reconstituted and heated. As with buckwheat, the opportunities for varying burghul dishes are many, beginning with the choice of oil or butter for coating the grains; deciding whether or not to brown at this stage; the choice of stock to use – or water, if you want it simple. Each variation gives a different flavour.

Serves four as a pilaff

30 g/1 oz butter
2 tbls oil
250 g/8 oz burghul
300 ml/1/2 pint hot stock or water

Heat the butter with the oil in a saucepan, then add the burghul. Stir gently until the colour is as golden-brown as you would like it. Add the hot stock or water, give it *one* stir, then turn the heat down low and simmer until all the water is absorbed; this will take only a few minutes, so don't walk away.

Turn the heat to its lowest – use a diffuser if you have one, or place the pan to one side of the electric hob – and put on the lid. Leave it to steam and soften for as long as you like.

Options

Soften a little chopped onion in the butter and oil before adding the burghul. You can also add spices; the Middle Eastern ones work best, like coriander, cumin, cloves or cardamom, but don't overdo them.

One of the most successful combinations is the Armenian tradition of topping the prepared burghul with a handful of almonds, raisins and chopped dried apricots, which have all been lightly fried in butter and finished with the lightest dusting of cinnamon.

Tiny cubes of a good melting cheese such as Gruyère or Emmental added just before serving make a tasty change, with chopped parsley or mint.

GLYNN'S TIP

If you leave burghul to stand for only a short time, you'll find that it still has a crunch in the centre, which I like, but you can leave it until it becomes soft and fluffy. I find this uninteresting unless it accompanies hot or spicy food.

TABBOULEH

A refreshing Middle Eastern salad of burghul which makes an unusual summertime starter and a very pretty addition to a buffet table.

Serves six as a first course

125 g/4 oz finely ground burghul
6 tbls olive oil
juice of at least 2 lemons
salt and pepper
250 g/8 oz parsley, chopped
125 g/4 oz mint, chopped
125 g/4 oz spring onions, chopped (optional)
salad leaves and chopped
tomato to garnish

Soak the burghul in cold water for 15 minutes. Drain in a sieve, pressing out as much excess water as you can. Put it into a large bowl and add half the olive oil and lemon juice. Season with salt and pepper. Let the burghul stand for about 1 hour, to absorb the dressing ingredients and become tender. Just before serving, stir in the chopped herbs, the spring onions (if you insist) and the remaining dressing. Test the seasoning, adding more lemon if needed. Garnish. Ⓕ

CORN BREAD

Serves four

125 g/4 oz plain flour
185 g/6 oz yellow cornmeal
2 tsps baking-powder
2 tbls soft brown sugar
1 tsp salt
2 eggs
60 g/2 oz melted butter
300 ml/1/2 pint milk

Mix together the flour, cornmeal, baking-powder, sugar and salt in a large bowl. Beat the eggs, melted butter and milk together and stir it into the dry ingredients. Blend well, then pour the mixture into a greased 23 cm/9 inch square baking-tin and bake at 200°C/400°F/Gas Mark 6 for 25-30 minutes, until golden brown. Serve hot, with butter.

POLENTA

This is a dish made from yellow cornmeal, popular throughout Italy. The cornmeal is sprinkled over salted water, then boiled gently while being stirred continuously for about 20 minutes until it comes away from the sides of the pan. This dough is turned out on to a board and shaped. Although usually fried or baked and served hot, it is sometimes eaten cold. It is a good accompaniment for rich meat, game and sausage dishes.

FOOD FACT

Corn was once used as a collective noun for bread-making grains, including wheat, but it now means only maize.

Sweet corn, or corn on the cob in its natural state, is eaten as a vegetable rather than a grain. The type of maize used for cornflour and cornmeal is gluten free and cannot be used for yeast-raised breads. Americans use cornmeal in their baking-powder spoon breads, so called because they are best eaten straight from the pan in which they are cooked, being soft and cakelike.

MILLET

Millet is the staple grain for almost a third of the world's population, particularly in China, India, Pakistan and North Africa. It is actually the generic name for a variety of small-seeded grains. Its greatest virtue is its hydration property – just 500 g/1 lb of kernels expands to feed eight people easily when cooked.

Millet flakes can commonly be found in health food shops and make a welcome addition to muesli mixtures. Millet flour is rare but is gluten-free and may be made at home in a powerful liquidizer.

To cook millet, brown it in a little oil, then pour over hot stock or water in the proportion of four parts liquid to one part millet grains. Cook over a medium heat until all the liquid has been absorbed, about 20 minutes. Fork it through to serve and flavour with fresh herbs and crushed garlic, season with salt and freshly ground black pepper. If you soften a little chopped onion, or fry some chopped bacon, at the start, you will have a more substantial dish.

MILLET PILAFF

Millet's high fat content makes it specially suited to warming winter dishes – and no pilaff is simpler and faster to make than this.

Serves four

250 g/8 oz millet grains
oil for frying
1 clove garlic, crushed (optional)
60 g/2 oz onion, chopped
500 g/1 lb boneless chicken
1 tsp ground cumin
salt and pepper
750 g/1 1/2 lb mixed vegetables (see method)
900 ml/1 1/2 pints hot water or stock

BONFIRE NIGHT BUFFET

From top, clockwise: Baked Sesame Chicken Thighs, p.88; Plum Pie with
Cinnamon Meringue, p.146; Pizza Macaroni Pie, p.34; Oven Fish Kebabs, p.76.

A FISH and FRUIT MENU
From top, clockwise: Rhubarb and Cinnamon Jelly, p.139;
Porée of Mixed Fish Fillets, p.81; Two Melon Soup, p.9.

A LIGHT SPRING LUNCHEON
From top, clockwise: Prawn, Lime and
Artichoke Macaroni, p.34; Fruit on Toast, p.153.

LUNCHING *al* FRESCO
From top, clockwise: Paprika Courgette Salad, p.59; Terrine de Bouillabaisse Christian, p.73;
Scotched Quails' Eggs, p.23; Raspberry Black Bottom Pie, p.145.

Toast the millet grains in a little oil until golden. Tip into a bowl. Cut the chicken into pieces – about 5 cm/2 inches long and 1 cm/½ inch wide. Fry the garlic and/or onion in a little more oil. Then add the chicken and brown the outside.

Add the cumin and seasoning, and stir well. Cut the vegetables into fairly large but even-sized pieces. For flavour and interest include several root vegetables and leeks, at least three vegetables in all but more if you have odds and ends to use up. Add to the pan with the hot water or stock, bring to the boil, then turn down the heat and pour in the toasted millet. Stir just once, cover, and simmer gently for 20 minutes without disturbing. At this stage the millet should be cooked and there should be no more than a little moisture left. If you like things moist, serve at once: otherwise, lower the heat to steam and dry out a little more.

OATCAKES

Oats may be bought as whole grains called jumbo oats and porridge oats, rough cut as medium or fine meal, and as flakes. Grains are used for porridge, coarse meal for oatcakes and for thickening stews. Medium oatmeal is used in gingerbreads and for coating herrings.

Makes three

250 g/8 oz fine oatmeal
¼ tsp salt
generous pinch bicarbonate of soda
½ tbls melted butter
hot water to mix

Mix the dry ingredients in a bowl, then add the fat and sufficient hot water to make a fairly stiff dough. Roll out as thinly as possible on a board

dusted with plenty of oatmeal. Use light, swift strokes and handle quickly. Roll into a circle the size of a small dinner-plate and divide into three. Bake on a hot griddle for 5 minutes, then finish off in a moderately hot oven (200°C/400°F/Gas Mark 6) for another 5-10 minutes.

MUESLI

Oats are the basis of that healthiest start to the day, muesli.

To make one serving combine 2 tablespoons of porridge oats; 1 or 2 teaspoons of chopped hazelnuts; one small unpeeled apple, grated; honey or sugar and lemon juice to taste; plus 2 tablespoons of natural yoghurt. Add as much milk as you wish.

I suggest that you try to leave out the sugar or honey and use high-fibre dried fruits for sweetness. The milk should be skimmed, but it is better not to use milk at all but to pour on fruit juice, particularly pineapple, orange or apple.

SEMOLINA

Semolina is the fine particles of hard wheat which are removed from flour in the first stages of milling.

Once used in Britain almost exclusively for making puddings, except, occasionally, as a garnish for clear soup, it is also used to make Italian gnocchi which is becoming more common thanks to a growing interest in pasta dishes.

GNOCCHI

Serves six to eight

600 ml/1 pint milk
1 tsp salt
125 g/4 oz semolina
60 g/2 oz butter
1 egg, beaten
125 g/4 oz grated cheese, Parmesan or Pecorino preferably
1 tsp made English or Dijon mustard
little grated nutmeg

Heat the milk in a saucepan with the salt, then sprinkle on the semolina and bring to the boil gradually, stirring all the time. Cook for 1 minute, then remove from the heat and beat in half the butter, the egg, half the cheese, the mustard and nutmeg. Beat very well, return to the heat and cook for another 2 minutes. Pour into a wetted Swiss roll tin and leave until cold. Cut into 2.5 cm/1 inch squares or rounds and arrange in a well-greased, shallow, ovenproof dish. Sprinkle with the remainder of the grated cheese and dots of the butter. Bake at 220°C/425°F/Gas Mark 7 for 15-20 minutes. Serve with more grated cheese and a tomato sauce.

SEMOLINA PUDDING

This pudding can be boring if it is plain or overbaked. But cook semolina in a bain marie to avoid a rubbery texture or in individual ramekins or cups and it becomes positively delicious . . . if you also flavour it nicely and serve it with something special. Michael Smith, the television cook, simmers his semolina in cream, then adds egg yolks, gelatine and orange zest, folds in whipped cream and lets the mixture set in buttered moulds. Get the basics right, and then try it his way . . . this is the basic.

Serves four to six

450 ml/¾ pint milk
pinch of salt
30 g/1 oz semolina
30 g/1 oz sugar
2 eggs, separated

Heat the milk with the salt. Sprinkle in the semolina and cook, stirring all the time, over a low heat until the grain is clear and the mixture thick – about 5 minutes. Off the heat, stir in the sugar and egg yolks. Allow to cool slightly.

Whisk the egg whites until stiff but not dry, then fold into the cool mixture. Transfer to a greased pie dish and bake at 180°C/350°F/Gas Mark 4 for 30-40 minutes until lightly browned.

Options

Flavour the mixture with vanilla essence, orange-flower water, or some finely grated orange or lemon rind. Or simply fold in an extra egg white.

• Put a layer of jam, stewed fruit or caramel on the bottom of the dish before spooning the semolina over and baking.
• Add roughly chopped plain chocolate to the mixture before baking.
• Stir 60 g/2 oz dried fruit and 1 teaspoon ground mixed spice into the semolina, before folding in the egg whites.
• Serve the pudding with warmed golden syrup drizzled over the top.

PULSES

Beans were the most important source of protein to our ancestors down the ages and feature prominently in today's healthy-eating diets, being a high-fibre, high-protein food for as little as ten per cent of the price of fish or meat. All dried beans are prepared the same way; don't be put off by the soaking time. Beans are widely available in cans which are every bit as good as those you prepare yourself.

PREPARATION PRIMER

Pulses should always be washed and picked over for debris and, in particular, small pieces of grit or stone which may chip teeth if not removed. They must then be re-hydrated. The most successful way to do that is to cover the peas or beans with cold water and leave them to soak for 8-10 hours. This gives the best results because the water encourages germination and this perceptibly sweetens the pulse. Don't soak pulses longer – say 12 hours at most – or they will break up during cooking. You may also pour boiling water over the pulses and leave for 2 hours, or cover the pulses with cold water, bring slowly to the boil and simmer for 2 minutes. Allow to cool in the water before using.

Always pour away the water in which the beans have been soaked; not only will it be dirty, it will contain a substantial proportion of the substances that cause gas to form in the human bowel.

Place the drained pulses in the pan, cover with more cold water and boil *without salt* until tender; the addition of salt will toughen the beans.

Red kidney beans must always be boiled rapidly for at least 10 minutes or toxins which they contain could prove very harmful. For this reason, never cook red kidney beans in a slow cooker or low oven without boiling first.

The cooking water may be flavoured with onions, garlic, herbs, etc. but it is more usual to discard the water and flavour the beans when they are baked after the first cooking.

> ## GLYNN'S TIP
>
> *Pressure-cooking is the perfect way to cook pulses. Ensure that the beans are covered with enough liquid (check your pressure-cooker's manual; it is usually 300 ml/½ pint per 15 minutes cooking time plus 300 ml/½ pint). Always add a few tablespoons of oil to the cooking water in your pressure-cooker to prevent foaming, which might block the safety valve.*

> ## GLYNN'S TIP
>
> *If you are worried by the forethought needed to soak and cook pulses, it makes sense to pressure-cook large quantities at a time, then cover and refrigerate, so that you can use them when you wish.*

A PULSE PRIMER

Aduki beans (sometimes adzuki) Small, smoky, red, cushion shaped, slightly sweet oriental bean much used for puddings in Thailand, China and Japan. Rather strong nutty flavour and makes a good flour, thus a most useful thickener. Simmer for 60-90 minutes or pressure-cook for 15.

Black beans *see* Kidney beans.

Black eye beans/peas Pale-cream with conspicuous black marking where each bean was attached to the pod. The flavour is slightly spicy and they are considered easy to digest. Simmer for 90-120 minutes, pressure cook for 30-50.

Borlotti *see* Kidney beans.

Broad beans Also known as fava: flattish and brown with a coarse flavour making them suitable for cooking with lots of garlic and ruggedly flavoured meats, herbs or spices. Only buy the more expensive skinned type, for the skins are over-chewy. Cook as for Black eye beans.

Butter beans Large, moon-coloured, flat beans with a bland, smooth flavour and satiny texture. Lima beans look and taste the same, and no one has convinced me that they are different. Don't stir them and break them up. Simmer for 60-90 minutes, pressure-cook for 15.

Cannellini *see* Kidney beans.

Chickpeas Also known as garbanzo: they look like shelled hazelnuts and take the longest of all to cook yet have the strongest and best flavour – peppery, spicy and slightly sweet. Simmer for 90 minutes, pressure-cook for 45.

Flageolet *see* Kidney beans.

Kidney beans A big family of different coloured beans related through their kidney shape. The flavours are different, too, and, although interchangeable, each has a special affinity or use it likes to call its own. Simmer them for 90 minutes, pressure-cook for 15.

● *Black beans* Similar to the Red kidney bean. Rich, full flavour and smooth texture, cream flesh and black skin.

● *Borlotti* (sometimes called rose cocoa) Sweetish and soft textured flesh, these vary from pale-cream to bright pink-brown and are always streaked with red and brown. Cook as for Black eye beans.

● *Cannelini* A small white bean that is particularly good with olive oil, hot with sausages and garlic or cold in garlic sausage salads.

● *Flageolet* These are young haricot (French) beans removed from the pod before they are ripe and dried carefully to keep the delicate colour and flavour. They complement duck, goose and lamb.

● *Haricot* or *Navy beans* These are used for baked beans, Boston-style Beans and the *cassoulets* of France. They are sometimes rather less kidney shaped and more cushion shaped. The flavour is creamy but bland.

● *Pinto* A rather fatter, browner cousin of the Borlotti. Cook the same way.

● *Red kidney beans* They deserve their popularity, for their colour and flavour are excellent.

Lentils Their importance as a staple is based on their high calorie and protein content, second only to soya beans. Both the red (Egyptian or Indian) lentil and the green (Continental or brown) lentil have a spicy, peppery flavour but the green one is fuller and earthier. Simmer unsoaked red lentils for 20-30 minutes, soaked ones will cook in about 15 minutes. Soaked green lentils take about 30-45 minutes, unsoaked take 1-1¼ hours to cook (15 minutes in a pressure-cooker).

Mung beans Dark, frosted olive is how I once described these and no better identification has sprung to my typewriter. They look like an unripe version of the Aduki bean. Sweet and soft when cooked, and excellent for making bean sprouts. Simmer for 60 minutes, pressure-cook for 10.

Peas Although floury, split and whole dried peas have a saving sweetness, which is why they are served traditionally with smoked meats. Whole peas need to be simmered for 2-3 hours (35 minutes in the pressure-cooker), but split peas cook in 60 minutes (10 in the pressure-cooker), hence their greater popularity.

Soya One of the world's most marvellous foods. Soya beans have the highest amount of protein per weight of any equivalent food but always retain a bite even after prolonged cooking. They are a boring, bland bean but are used to produce milk, meat stretchers and the Oriental *tofu* or bean curd. If you do want to try them, simmer for 1½-1¾ hours, 45 minutes in the pressure-cooker.

> ## FOOD FACT
>
> *All kidney beans must boil for 10 minutes during cooking: this is especially important with* red kidney *beans which otherwise may be poisonous in the extreme. Canned ones are perfectly safe to eat cold straight from the can for the processing temperature is high enough for long enough.*

Hummous

Make this dip with chickpeas which you have soaked and cooked, or with canned ones; the essential flavouring in the recipe is tahini, a paste made from sesame seeds.

Serves four to six

400 g/14 oz cooked chickpeas, drained
4 tbls lemon juice
1 or 2 garlic cloves
5-6 tbls tahini
olive oil (see method)
salt to taste
paprika, cumin, parsley, cayenne to decorate

Reserve 1-2 spoonfuls of whole chickpeas for garnish. Purée the remaining chickpeas with the lemon juice, garlic and tahini. The eventual texture should be like a thin mayonnaise. Add extra lemon juice, a little water or olive oil if necessary. Add salt to taste.

The proper way to serve hummous is not in a bowl but upon a flat plate. Scoop a small depression in the centre and fill that with good olive oil, which should also be scattered over all. Then sprinkle on sweet paprika, cumin, finely chopped parsley and a very little cayenne pepper. Top with the reserved chickpeas and serve with squares of hot pitta bread. Alternatively, use as a sauce with cold meats and fish, particularly cold chicken and duck.

Chickpea Moussaka

This is the best vegetarian version of moussaka that I know. Line a dish with aubergine slices that have been salted and drained then fried in olive oil. Strew some garlic about. Toss warm cooked chickpeas in lemon juice, more garlic, olive oil, salt and pepper, drain and stir into a thick, cheese flavoured sauce (see page 15). Layer with more prepared aubergine plus tomato slices and bake in a moderate oven (180°C/350°F/Gas Mark 4 for at least half an hour) until thoroughly heated through. Mint is an excellent herb to scatter through the top layer of sauce, or you can use the more traditional oregano. Be generous with garlic and olive oil, and make the cheese sauce really tasty by using a strong cheese. Ⓠ Ⓥ

Chickpea Stew

Either drain canned chickpeas and put into hot stock or cook dried ones as described on page 45 using stock rather than water. Add chopped tomatoes, sliced garlic and a few finely chopped root vegetables to taste, a bay leaf and a little sprinkle of dried oregano. A few minutes before serving add some small pieces of a green vegetable – sliced spinach, green beans, peas or some broccoli florets; some cooked rice can also be added. It should be well moistened with well flavoured stock and extra flavour can be added by serving a good wedge of lemon with each plateful. Ⓥ

Lentils

These are the dried seeds of a small, branching plant which formed one of the first-ever crops in the East. Richest in protein of all the pulses, they also have a high iron content, making them a valuable food staple in Third World countries. There are two main types of lentil. The red lentil, also called Egyptian or Indian, is reddish when raw, but cooks to a yellowy mush. It is used in winter soups and mixed vegetable dishes. Green or brown lentils, also known as Continental lentils, have a stronger, earthier taste than the red variety and blend well with fatty meats, smoked meats, onions and herbs. See Pulse Primer for cooking instructions.

Dhal

Fans of Indian food will know that dhal is made from cooked lentils. In fact there are over 60 types of pea, split pea and lentil that are cooked and served as dhal, most of which have no equivalent in Britain. But they are interchangeable and the most important thing is to know the different cooking techniques. The following recipes are easy to prepare and many are suitable for serving with meats and vegetables that are not curried.

Arhar dhal Add at least 125 g/4 oz of butter for each 500 g/1 lb cooked lentils plus chopped fresh red chillies, turmeric and salt. Serve garnished with fried onion rings and cumin seed. An even spicier version is made by draining the lentils when half cooked and replacing the liquid with milk; meanwhile fry lots of garlic and onion, with cloves, add some cream and saffron, stir this mixture into the dhal and simmer until cooked.

Masd-kalai In this version the lentils are cooked with aniseed and ginger.

Calcutta dhal blatt Fry chopped onion and green chillies in butter and garlic, add ground ginger and salt, mix in the cooked dhal and colour with turmeric.

Moong dhal Boil lentils with turmeric and chilli powder and strain when half done. Melt some butter in a pan and fry chopped onions, crushed garlic, sliced fresh ginger, ground coriander and whole cumin seeds. Add the dhal, fry a little longer, then add water and cook until the lentils are tender.

Hot Green Lentil Salad

Serve this as a warming starter, as a hot or cold buffet dish or as a hot or cold vegetable.

Serves six to eight as a starter

250 g/8 oz green lentils, soaked
light vegetable or chicken stock or water (to cover)
125 g/4 oz smoked German sausage
125 g/4 oz pickled cucumber or gherkin
30 g/1 oz chopped onion
1 garlic clove, crushed
8 tbls safflower or sunflower oil
4 tbls cider vinegar
2 tbls wholegrain mustard
1 tsp caraway seeds
salt and pepper

Cook the lentils in the stock or water until tender, drain and keep warm. Thinly slice the sausage and the cucumber and combine gently with the lentils. Heat together the onion, garlic, oil and vinegar for 5 minutes without boiling, then *strain* on to the lentils. Spoon on the mustard and the caraway seeds and mix it all evenly. Season to taste and serve warm or leave to cool. Ⓕ *Photograph, p. 115.*

Lentil and Vegetable Casserole

One of the most warming and satisfying dishes I know. Don't worry too much about proportions, for it tastes good whatever you do; but do use olive oil.

Serves four to six

250 g/8 oz green or brown lentils
generous 1 litre/2 pints water
1 kg/2 lb prepared mixed vegetables (see method)
olive oil to taste

Cover the lentils with cold water, bring slowly to the boil, skim then drain.

Add the water and prepared mixed vegetables. (Choose mainly root vegetables like carrots, swedes, turnips, parsnips, potatoes. Include sliced onion and garlic too, if you like; you can also put in some uncooked leftovers like tomato, red or green pepper, celery, fennel, etc. It's best not to include Brassicas like cabbage or Brussels sprouts. Cut the vegetables into neat slices or chunks, not too small or they will disintegrate during cooking.) Bring to the boil, cover and simmer gently, for at least 1½ hours, by which time the lentils will be tender.

Add any seasonings and flavourings; olive oil and dried mint are my own particular favourites, and you can add garlic now if you didn't include it with the vegetables. Simmer for another 10 minutes. Serve piping hot, with lots of fresh bread.

LENTIL and RICE PILAFF with ONIONS

Lentils and rice are often mixed together and in this Cypriot recipe olive oil is used as a flavouring. If you use stock rather than water, you won't need to use olive oil and could fry the onions in a lesser flavoured oil.

Serves four

250 g/8 oz green lentils
900 ml/1½ pints stock or water
125 g/4 oz long-grain rice
150 ml/¼ pint olive oil
250 g/8 oz onions, thinly sliced

Soak the lentils overnight, drain, then cook in the stock or water for 15 minutes. Add the rice and cook for another 15 minutes or until the liquid is absorbed. Reduce the heat to a minimum, remove the lid and cover the pan with a thick tea-cloth, and firmly replace lid. While the rice and lentils steam and fluff up, heat the oil and fry the onions until golden-brown. Tip the pilaff into a warm bowl or on to a plate and top with the onions. Serve as a vegetable.

Options

By adding sliced sausage and stirring in a few vegetables, this can become a main-course pilaff. For special occasions, stir in sliced dried apricots and walnuts.

ADUKI BURGERS

Aduki beans have a slight sweetness and are used for puddings in Japan. They have the added attraction of making a useful flour, which few beans do. Here they are the basis of a really tasty meatless burger that, like many of my bean recipes, relies for effect on a mixture of whole and puréed beans.

This quantity will make up to 12 burgers to serve between buns with sauces and mustards or to serve on platters with masses of salad. The rose-pink colour of the burger centres will be a welcome relief from the usual brown of this sort of food.

Makes about 12 burgers

375 g/12 oz uncooked aduki beans
2 tbls oil
60 g/2 oz onion, chopped
1 or 2 garlic cloves
2 eggs
4 tbls plain thick yoghurt
2 tsps ground coriander
2 tbls chopped chervil
3 tbls wholemeal flour
salt and pepper
oil and butter for frying

Soak the beans overnight or during as much of the day as you can manage. Pressure cook for about 15 minutes with just enough water to cover them plus the oil, or cook for 60-90 minutes on the top of the cooker with plenty of water and the oil. Drain well, keeping the cooking liquid as a stock for soups and sauces.

Make a purée of half the beans with the onion, garlic and eggs. Stir in the remaining beans and the rest of the ingredients and let the mixture rest, out of a refrigerator, for at least an hour so that the wholemeal flour can expand and bind the mixture. Add salt and pepper to taste.

The mixture will still be rather too soft to make into neat shapes, but who needs that anyway? Heat a light coating of oil or butter and oil and use a large spoon to dollop burger-sized portions into the pan. Cook over medium heat for about 5 minutes on each side – they will crisp and brown wonderfully. Serve with salad on half a toasted bun, with thick plain yoghurt flavoured with seed mustard and perhaps a little garlic. *Photograph, p. 115.*

Options

If you can't get fresh chervil, use good old parsley or fresh coriander leaves.

Oriental spices will give good results – use ground cumin instead of coriander, or a mixture of the two. Otherwise, leave out spices altogether and go herby – mint, fresh or dried, would be amazing, and oregano would give a Greek flavour. Ⓥ

BOSTON-STYLE BEANS

Serves four

500 g/1 lb dried weight haricot or cannellini beans, soaked and cooked
600 ml/1 pint water
½ tsp mustard powder
2 tsps salt
3 tbls dark brown sugar
3 tbls molasses
185-250 g/6-8 oz salt pork or bacon in one piece

Combine the ingredients in a heavy ovenproof casserole and push the piece of salt pork or bacon into the centre. Cover tightly and bake at 200°C/400°F/Gas Mark 6 for 1 hour, then reduce to only 125°C/250°F/Gas Mark ½ for 4 hours. Remove the lid and bake for a further hour. Stir a couple of times and add water only if the beans are really dry.

MY BAKED BEANS

I slowly perfected this recipe after years of trying to make a *cassoulet* in Britain and then deciding it wasn't possible without preserved goose or duck. It's a great dish for barbecues. Make a pot or two of beans in advance and use the barbecue to keep them hot.

Serves six

500 g/1 lb dried weight white haricot or cannellini beans or beans of your choice, soaked and cooked
2 × 396 g/14 oz cans tomatoes
1 or 2 onions, sliced
4-6 unpeeled garlic cloves
3 bay leaves
250-375 g/8-12 oz smoked bacon, cubed
250-375 g/8-12 oz garlic sausage, thickly sliced

Place all the ingredients in a large, heavy casserole and cook over a low heat. It takes 2 hours for the fat to be absorbed by the beans, for the flavours to blend, and for a thick sauce to form out of the reduced tomatoes and the beans which have broken.

CHILI BEANS and CHILI CON CARNE

Use this recipe to make chili beans if you want a meatless meal.

Serves four

oil for frying
125 g/4 oz onion, chopped
125 g/4 oz green pepper, finely chopped
1 or 2 cloves garlic, sliced
1 tbls tomato purée
500 g/1 lb cooked red kidney beans
chili powder to taste (see method)

Pour a little oil into a heavy-based pan and cook the onion, pepper, garlic and tomato purée until the onion and pepper are well softened. Stir in the beans, then flavour with chili; if you are serving the beans without the addition of meat you may find that 2 teaspoons is enough. Cook over a very low heat for 45 minutes, stirring occasionally. You might like to add a few spoons of water to encourage the broken beans to mush more and make a sauce.

For chili con carne, fry 500 g/1 lb minced pork with a little onion and garlic, then add 397 g/14 oz can of plum tomatoes. Cook with a bay leaf until the pork is tender and most of the tomato juice has been absorbed. Season lightly. Stir into the prepared chili beans and simmer together for 10 minutes. Add extra chili seasoning to taste, then simmer very gently for another 10 minutes. This is doubly good if left to cool and reheated next day.

Variations

If you are not serving chili beans to vegetarians, add pieces of salt pork or bacon for flavour. Stir in extra garlic, ground cumin or oregano if liked.

REFRIED BEANS

Refried beans or *refritos* are one of the most popular Mexican accompaniments to food. Well cooked beans are slightly mashed and then fried in pork or bacon fat. A little liquid is sometimes also added to ensure that there is a suitably thick sauce. It is a good way of using up small amounts of any kind of bean, but it looks better with the brown pinto or red kidney beans. In Mexico, *refritos* are usually left bland because they are eaten with quite spicy food. You might, however, like to add more flavourings if they are to go with something more European; so fry some onion and garlic and chopped green pepper in the fat before adding the beans.

DIPPY BEAN SALADS

Bean salads, mixtures of different beans served in a vinaigrette, are all very well but such a cliché these days. I often use beans as a first course, usually as some sort of dip. I usually use tinned beans, but you can of course use home-cooked beans. What I do is to purée one can of beans and use it as a sauce for a second can, which I usually mix with other ingredients and then dress with a vinaigrette. I make a ring of the purée and put the other mixture in the middle. It is wonderful at parties, barbecues and outdoor lunches served with hot pieces of pitta bread as scoops, or served as a first course –

everyone has to help one another and conversation naturally flows. *Photograph, p. 114.*

There are few combinations that do not work, but some look better than others:

Chickpeas Puréed with olive oil, lemon juice and garlic: serve with a mixture of *kidney beans*, crumbled Feta cheese, cubed garlic sausage, coarsely chopped parsley, dress with olive oil and lemon juice.

Red kidney beans Purée with a small can of red peppers (drained), a few teaspoons of chili seasoning, a little olive oil and red wine vinegar; serve with a mixture of drained *cannelini beans* and chopped fresh green pepper, dress lightly with vinaigrette and top with blobs of soured cream.

Cannelini beans Purée with a drained 250 g/ 8 oz can of tuna or pink salmon, a little garlic, olive oil and lemon juice; mix a second can of drained *cannelini beans* with chunks of very ripe tomato, small pitted black olives and cubes of Mozzarella cheese. Dress with olive oil and lemon juice and sprinkle with dried oregano.

Butter beans Purée with enough sharp blue cheese to be noticeable and flavour further with garlic juice and olive oil; mix a drained can of the same beans with seedless white grapes and more of the same cheese lightly crumbled. Dress with a light garlicky dressing and scatter with freshly grated lime rind.

Haricot beans Purée with toasted hazelnuts or pecans and some tomato purée adding lemon juice for 'bite'; toss a drained can of the same beans with walnut or pecan halves, cubed, cooked chicken and cubed fresh peach, pear or nectarine which has been bathed in orange juice. Dress lightly with oil and orange juice.

All these salads should be served very cold but with hot bread for dipping. Ⓥ Ⓠ

CONFETTI PIE

This pie is a real treat to eat, for the topping is one of the lightest and most delicious you will ever have eaten.

*Serves eight as a starter, four as
a main course*

*375 g/12 oz bought shortcrust pastry or
shortcrust made with 250 g/8 oz flour
(see page 129)
1 egg white, lightly beaten
2 tbls grated Parmesan cheese
2 × 400 g/15 oz cans beans (different types if
possible), drained
2 tbls olive oil
30 g/1 oz chopped fresh mint or parsley
1/2 tsp grated lemon rind
1 garlic clove, crushed (optional)
salt and white pepper
500 g/1 lb fresh Ricotta cheese
250 g/8 oz strained yoghurt
4 eggs, beaten
2 tbls grated Parmesan cheese, to garnish*

Use the pastry to line a 25 cm/10 inch pie dish at least 5 cm/2 inches deep. Bake blind for 10 minutes at 200°C/400°F/Gas Mark 6.

While it is hot, paint with the egg white and sprinkle on the Parmesan cheese. Return to the oven just long enough to set the egg white. Toss the beans in the olive oil, chopped mint or parsley, lemon rind, and garlic (if used). Season to taste and arrange evenly on the pastry. Mix the Ricotta cheese with the yoghurt, season lightly, then stir in the eggs. Ladle on to the bean mixture and sprinkle with the Parmesan. Bake at 180°C/350°F/Gas Mark 4 for 40-45 minutes until well risen and set. Cool to lukewarm before serving, or serve chilled the next day, which I think might be even better. *Photograph, p. 80.*

VEGETABLES *and* SALADS

From tongue-tingling sharpness to palate-caressing sweetness, fresh vegetables are the contemporary cook's way to dishes, alive with vitality and character.

The choice of fruits and vegetables available has never been better. The supermarkets, which not so long ago ambushed our ambitions for a varied and healthy diet, now offer us the best of produce from around the world, a true cornucopia of excitement and health. But what do most of us do? Go out shopping with the same boring old list! Shopping *without* a list is quite the simplest way to improve your diet, for the key to health is to eat the broadest possible variety of foods. It's a much more exciting way to eat, and simpler to cook too, for new fruits and vegetables don't need to be fussed about with to add interest.

Combine a new vision of fruits and vegetables with pasta, rice, pulse and grain recipes and you'll rapidly discover you've helped your budget and your health without even trying! And you'll discover how easy it is to serve vegetarian meals without appearing cranky. But take care with your cooking methods, particularly when steaming . . . and remember most vegetables can be eaten raw when young.

STEAMING

One of the best, fastest and healthiest ways of cooking vegetables is by steaming, but too few people know how to steam correctly.

Steam, given off when water reaches boiling-point, is so hot that it cooks food quickly and efficiently. However, the method creates water-vapour, which dissolves many of the salts, sugars and vitamins contained in the vegetables and they drip back into the water. So, to be worthwhile, all steaming *must* be done on plates or dishes to prevent such losses. When a vegetable, or any other food, is steamed on a plate, you collect the bonus of a puddle of dissolved vitamins and salts, invaluable nutritionally and perfect as a sauce all by itself.

I never add salt to steamed vegetables until they are cooked; steaming concentrates the natural salts so that, often, it is not necessary to add salt at all. You can, however, add other flavourings directly to the food at the start of cooking – plain or flavoured butter, herbs, chopped ginger, garlic or a little soya sauce. Remember that they will only flavour the foods with which they have direct contact.

Steaming generally takes a much shorter time than boiling, and to save more time and to make the vegetables even tastier, cut them into smallish pieces. If you prefer not to do this, at least ensure that all the ingredients are of an even size so you don't overcook one ingredient while waiting for another to catch up.

There is one honourable exception to the rule of always steaming food on a plate, and that is when you steam a whole cauliflower. Place it in a colander directly over a small amount of water in which there is some onion or other flavouring; this lets the cauliflower's juices drip into the water, giving you the basis of a delicious sauce or a liquid which can be added to a white sauce.

One last point, and an important one. Don't fall for the ploy of flavouring or seasoning the water used for steaming in the belief that this will flavour the food. That's impossible. Instead, the salt, lemon juice, sugar or herbs become more and more concentrated in the steaming liquid and make no difference to the flavour of the steamed food.

BOILING

The term 'boiling' is misleading, for a rolling boil is unnecessary and, in the case of peeled potatoes for example, it is positively harmful because it tosses them about and breaks up the surface. Simmer vegetables with care.

Rather than lots of boiling water as the cooking medium, most manufacturers of frozen vegetables recommend cooking in only a few spoonfuls, if any at all. This is a rule which you would do well to follow whether cooking frozen or fresh vegetables. It will be faster, the vegetables will be more colourful and, by using less water, fewer of the soluble goodies will have been lost.

One of my favourite techniques is to cook vegetables in a flavoured liquid which you can reduce to form a sauce. This means the vegetables are often added to cold liquid but, since you are not draining them, you don't throw away the vitamins that have been leached out. The French use this method for cooking carrots with water and butter but it is even more common in Middle Eastern countries. You don't have to use water; I cook carrots, baby turnips, swede or celeriac by first turning them in a little butter and olive oil, then simmering them in orange juice which eventually forms a thick sauce with the butter and oil. A mixture of water and wine, or cider, works well and you can use canned tomatoes for cooking aubergine, okra, onions, courgettes or kohlrabi.

> ### GLYNN'S TIP
> *It used to be recommended that large pieces of root vegetable were put into cold water so that they cooked through evenly; placing them in boiling water was said to mush up the outsides before the insides were cooked. However, I feel this is outdated thinking.*

BRAISING

When braising vegetables, the same technique is used as for meat; it is probably better understood by its other name, pot-roasting. The vegetables are cooked with very little liquid in a covered container until tender. It takes longer than other methods but gives superb results; and avoids the problem of having to cook vegetables at the last minute when you have lots of guests. See Braised Fennel page 55.

STIR-FRYING

Stir-frying is a Chinese cooking technique usually done in a wok, but a large sauté- or frying-pan may be used instead.

It involves quick cooking at maximum heat, so there is little danger of the vegetables being over-cooked and losing their goodness. There is, however, always loss of goodness through the surface area of cut vegetables when they are cut into thin strips. This loss of vitamins is particularly high if the cut vegetables are left in a bowl of water before cooking. If you have to prepare the vegetables in advance, cover them instead with plastic wrap or a damp cloth.

Main Ingredients These include meat, poultry, fish or shellfish. Remove any fat, skin and bone and (except for prawns) cut into thin strips or small cubes. If you wish, you can make up the basic sauce given below and use it as a marinade.

Secondary Ingredients Choose one or two vegetables, for example mushrooms; broccoli; French beans; *mange touts*; peas; cabbage; asparagus; red, green, yellow or white peppers; cucumber. Prepare all vegetables by cutting into 5 cm/2 inch julienne strips for fast cooking. Split stems of broccoli and other stemmed vegetables for quicker cooking.

Garnishes Choose well-flavoured vegetables that cook extremely quickly, such as alfalfa sprouts, bean sprouts, shredded spinach leaves, lettuce, Chinese leaves and other Chinese green vegetables, finely chopped garlic and ginger (mixed or used individually), finely chopped red or green pepper or spring onion (if you must). These must only be added during the very last stages of cooking, a mere 15 seconds or so before serving. You can also add a suitable sauce as flavouring.

Basic Sauce Mix together 4 tablespoons of water with 1 teaspoon of soy sauce, 1 tablespoon of cornflour, ½ teaspoon of sugar, and season with either slivers of ginger, minced garlic or finely chopped onion or shallot.

To Stir-Fry Place the wok over high heat and when hot pour in a small amount of peanut oil. Swirl the oil around the sides of the wok; if oil is added to a cold wok, the food may stick.

First fry a few slivers of garlic or fresh ginger to flavour the oil, then remove. Toss in the main ingredient and stir it around using chopsticks or a wooden fork until barely cooked.

Remove this from the wok and add the secondary ingredients, starting with those which need the most cooking time. When the vegetables are almost cooked, cover and steam, shaking the wok for about half a minute. Return the main ingredient to the wok, with the sauce if you are using it. Stir frantically for a few seconds, then add the garnish. Stir-fry for just 15 seconds and serve hot, immediately.

If your vegetables are stalky, like broccoli, add a dash of moisture with chicken stock, rice wine or dry sherry towards the end of the cooking time; the steam created raises the temperature considerably and thus ensures that the stalks are cooked.

ROASTING and BAKING

Many people now prefer to eat steamed or stir-fried vegetables with roast meat or poultry in the belief that vegetables roasted in fat are bad for their health. Only badly roasted vegetables carry risks; properly roasted vegetables are no worse for you than a slice of bread and butter. The vegetables must be turned quickly in hot fat; initially, they should be at room temperature so that they do not lower the fat temperature too much. The hot fat will quickly seal the outside of the vegetables and prevent fat from penetrating them.

Most vegetables may be baked rather than roasted, by which I mean cooked in the oven without fat. Baked beetroot, unpeeled and rubbed with a little oil, add a brilliant dash of colour to any plate in winter; parsnips and other common root vegetables, pumpkin, sweet potatoes, aubergines and courgettes may be baked with a light covering of oil, or with a basting of rich stock, or fruit juice.

NAME	SOUP	BOIL/STEAM	BRAISE/CASSEROLE	BAKE/ROAST	GRILL	SAUTE/STIR-FRY	DEEP FRY	SERVE RAW	HERBS/SPICES
ARTICHOKE: GLOBE		●	Parboil, cook in wine or stock						Parsley, tarragon
JERUSALEM	●	●		●		●	Cut as chips		Parsley, chives
ASPARAGUS	●	●							Tarragon, parsley, orange
AUBERGINE (EGGPLANT)				May be stuffed	●	●	Coat in batter		Basil, oregano
BEANS: RUNNER, FRENCH and		●	With tomatoes, onions and garlic			●		●	Dill, cumin, parsley
BROAD	●	●	●					●	Parsley, chervil
BEETROOT	●	●	●	Oil lightly		Grate, cook in butter		●	Chives, dill, nutmeg
BROCCOLI		●	In white wine	Parboil first		Parboil first		●	Coriander, cumin, orange
BRUSSELS SPROUTS	●	●				Parboil first		●	Cayenne, nutmeg, mint
CABBAGE	●	●	In stock	May be stuffed		Blanch first		●	Cinnamon, caraway, juniper

NAME	SOUP	BOIL/STEAM	BRAISE/CASSEROLE	BAKE/ROAST	GRILL	SAUTÉ/STIR-FRY	DEEP FRY	SERVE RAW	HERBS/SPICES
CARROTS	●	●	With tomatoes, onions and garlic			Julienned		●	Chives, mint, cardamom, allspice, orange
CAULIFLOWER	●	●	Blanch first			Parboil first		●	Fennel, parsley, cumin
CELERY/CELERIAC	●	●	In wine or stock	With wine or stock		Julienned	Celeriac; cut as chips		Dill weed, thyme, parsley, garlic
CHINESE LEAVES		●	Sliced, in tomato sauce			Shredded		●	Oregano
COURGETTES	●	●	Brush with oil, good with cheese or tomatoes	Blanch, may be stuffed		Slice/grate	Toss in seasoned flour	●	Tarragon, garlic, rosemary, dill, mint
CUCUMBER	●	●	In wine, or with tomatoes	May be stuffed		Cut into balls		●	Chives, dill, parsley
FENNEL	●	●	Parboil first, brush with oil or butter, cook in wine or stock	Parboil first, good baked with cheese		Blanch, then slice/quarter	Boil until tender, slice, egg and crumb	●	Tarragon, coriander
LEEKS	●	●	In white wine	Bake with tomatoes		Blanch first		●	Basil, parsley, mustard
LETTUCE	●		Hearts, in stock			In butter		●	Chervil
MANGE TOUT	●	●				In sesame oil		●	Mint
MARROW		●	With tomatoes, onions and garlic	Stuffed, wrap in foil		Cube, toss in butter			Marjoram, oregano, dill
MUSHROOMS	●	●		Stuff and bake	Brush with oil	●	Button, coat in batter (buttons)	●	Chives, parsley, nutmeg
OKRA		●	Parboil first			Egg and crumb	Coat in batter		Oregano, cayenne
ONIONS	●	●	In wine or vermouth	May be stuffed		Toss in flour; glaze	Coat in batter (rings)	●	Fennel, nutmeg, paprika
PARSNIPS	●	●	In stock	●		Parboil, toss slices in flour, cook in butter	Parboil, cut into chips	●	Tarragon, thyme, chives, cinnamon
PEAS	●	●	With lettuce, in stock					●	Mint, chervil, rosemary
PEPPERS	●		Sliced, with tomatoes	Parboil first then stuff	Remove skins	Slice and cook in oil		●	Marjoram, thyme, mint, garlic
POTATOES	●	●	Slice, cook in milk/cream/stock	Bake in skins, roast in dripping		Sliced, in balls, mashed in cakes, or grated	Chips or as croquettes		Parsley, mint, tarragon, garlic, nutmeg, horseradish
PUMPKIN	●	●	With tomatoes	Whole or in pieces, wrap in foil		Slice, toss in seasoned flour			Cinnamon, chives, allspice, ginger
SALSIFY/SCORZONERA	●	●				Blanch, fry in butter	Parboil, coat in butter		Thyme, chives, rosemary, tarragon
SPINACH	●	†				●		●	Nutmeg, chives, orange
SWEDES		●	In stock or with tomatoes	Blanch, roast in dripping		Parboil, cook in butter			Nutmeg, savory, sherry
SWEETCORN	●	●		Wrap in foil	Leave husks on				Paprika, garlic, chives, dill
SWEET POTATOES		●	Candied, in orange juice	Bake in foil					Cinnamon, nutmeg, rum
TOMATOES	●		Alone, or with other vegetables	Stuffed or halved and buttered	●	●		●	Basil, mint, oregano, marjoram, walnut oil
TURNIPS	●	●	In stock	Blanch, roast in dripping		Blanch, cook in butter		●	Parsley, chives, cinnamon, orange, mint

† Cook in own juices

SLIMMER'S VEGETABLES à la GRECQUE

A la Grecque can, and usually does, mean lightly cooked vegetables swimming in oil, but this recipe uses the barest amount and is ideal for livening up the tired-looking vegetables that we all find in the refrigerator from time to time. You can vary the selection and the amounts to suit the season or what you happen to have.

MARINADE
350 ml/12 fl oz chicken stock
7 tbls dry white wine
6 peppercorns
1 tsp fresh or ½ tsp dried thyme
6 sprigs parsley
1 bay leaf
2½ tbls lemon juice
1 tbls olive or lighter-flavoured oil
VEGETABLES
quartered onions, plus a selection of courgettes, red and green peppers, celery stalks, fennel, turnip, kohlrabi cut into slices, sticks or chunks of even size chopped parsley, to serve

For the marinade, combine all the ingredients in a medium saucepan, bring to the boil, cover and simmer for 30 minutes, then strain. Return the strained marinade to the pan and add the onions. Cover and simmer gently until they are very tender, then add the remaining vegetables and cook for a further 4-5 minutes. Pour into a shallow dish and refrigerate, covered, overnight. Serve chilled in individual small bowls, liberally sprinkled with chopped parsley. Ⓥ Ⓕ Ⓔ

VEGETABLE PUREES

If you have a food processor, this is an easy and attractive way to prepare a wide variety of vegetables, and they are easy to reheat if made in advance. The following are a few suggestions for purées and their seasonings but there are many possibilities. For a dinner party, combinations of purées with contrasting colours and flavours can be very effective, particularly if moulded or swirled into pyramid shapes.

If I am serving a large number of people (at Christmas for instance), I find purées useful, for they can be kept hot more successfully than whole vegetables. Do take the time, however, to make them really smooth by adding enough butter, milk or cream to give a rich flavour and texture, and then pass the mixture through a sieve. If you prefer a lumpy texture, make it really rugged or it will look as though you have merely been lazy!

Alabaster Once you start combining vegetables in purées, the variety of flavours expands enormously. Alabaster is a recipe from the Shaker communities of the U.S.A. whose farms were famous for their superb produce. This simple dish is typical of their cookery; it comes with admonishments that neither butter nor black pepper should be used as they would spoil the pure whiteness and satiny look which give the purée its name.

For four servings, boil 500 g/1 lb each of peeled white turnips and potatoes in separate saucepans until tender. Drain, then mash. Fold the two mixtures together and add enough double cream (up to 150 ml/¼ pint) to make the texture you prefer, or until the flavour suits you; add a little milk if the cream is very thick. Add white pepper and salt to taste.

Broad beans Purée cooked beans with a little double cream and fresh or dried savory. Season with salt and white pepper. This is particularly good with garlic and butter and olive oil instead of cream.

Carrot and swede Purée equal quantities of cooked carrot and swede with a generous knob of butter and a couple of tablespoons of cream, if you have any. Season with salt, white pepper, ground cinnamon or mace. Sweet sherry enhances a swede purée.

Cauliflower Purée cooked cauliflower with a little butter and cream, then season with grated nutmeg. This is not a purée to be kept warm but should be served immediately.

Celeriac Make a purée of cooked celeriac with up to a quarter of its weight of cooked potato, plus lemon juice and cream. Season with salt, pepper and nutmeg. You can leave out the potato and use lots of milk and butter for a whiter, smoother purée. Garlic, chopped parsley, or both, are excellent flavourings. The clean, celery-like taste makes it a perfect accompaniment for anything fatty or rich, especially game.

Leek Cook the leeks in just a little butter and purée with cream, soured cream or yoghurt. Whatever you choose, the addition of a seed or smooth mustard makes the final taste outstanding. This is one purée which is often better if slightly rough, thus avoiding the risk of having to overcook the leeks.

Parsnip Cook the parsnips in milk with a small bay leaf, and purée with some of the cooking liquid (remember to remove the bay leaf first). You can leave out the bay leaf and flavour the purée with cinnamon instead. Stir in milk or cream – this is essential for a parsnip purée or the result will be glutinous.

Peas Soften a little chopped onion in butter, add frozen peas and simmer until just cooked. Purée and season with salt, white pepper and fresh or dried mint, adding more butter or cream as necessary. Grated lemon rind or finely chopped celery leaf are good additions.

Pumpkin Purée cooked pumpkin with butter and garlic and add cream to give the final texture. Toasted flaked almonds, pine-nuts or walnuts can be stirred in at the last moment. You can add flavourings such as garlic, cumin, mace, nutmeg or cloves.

STEAMED PUREE of PARSNIPS and BASIL

Puréed vegetables, with the addition of cream and eggs, make wonderful light vegetable moulds when baked. They are ideal for special lunches or make an impressive dinner party vegetable accompaniment. This gives an example of proportions.

Serves four to five

500 g/1 lb parsnips, scrubbed but not peeled
150 ml/¼ pint single cream
4 eggs
4 tbls lemon juice
salt and pepper
dried basil

Slice the parsnips and simmer in the cream until soft. Purée, strain, then add the eggs and lemon juice. Mix well and season.

Butter a mould of about 1 litre/2 pint capacity and sprinkle the inside with basil. Spoon in the purée and stand the mould in a baking tin, containing 2.5 cm/1 inch of hot water. Cover with foil and bake at 180°C/350°F/Gas Mark 4 for about 20-30 minutes, depending on the moistness of the purée. Allow to stand for a few minutes then turn out onto a heated plate and serve with a thin tomato sauce.

Option
Carrot and Green Ginger Grate fresh ginger root into carrot purée and proceed as above.

RED PEPPER MOUSSELINES

Mousselines are lighter and more elegant versions of vegetable-purée-and-egg-recipes, because the proportion of eggs is higher.

Serves six

500 g/1 lb red peppers, sliced
60 g/2 oz onion, chopped
4 eggs, beaten
250 g/8 oz curd cheese
1-2 dsps lemon juice
garlic (optional)
6 Savoy cabbage leaves, blanched
salt
hot or sweet paprika

Cook peppers and onion gently but until really soft in 150 ml/¼ pint of water. Sieve and when cool, fold in eggs, cheese and lemon juice. Season to taste with garlic and salt. Line ramekin dishes with the blanched cabbage leaves. Fill with mixture. Sprinkle hot or sweet paprika on top.

Bake covered with foil in a tray half-filled with water (bain marie) for 30-40 minutes at 150°C/300°F/Gas Mark 2. Turn out and serve with some spicy tomato sauce poured round.

SAVOURY SORBETS

While fruit sorbets are refreshing, they are packed with sugar, so attention has turned to the making of savoury versions. In France there is an entire book devoted to making sorbets from such unlikely ingredients as prawns, aubergines and oysters. In Israel they concentrate more on herbs and vegetables of which they have an abundance. Both of these savoury sorbets are good served on their own but make more of a splash if served with seafood, particularly prawns or salmon.

AVOCADO and CUCUMBER SORBET

Serves four to six

500 g/1 lb soft, ripe avocado flesh
250 g/8 oz peeled cucumber
4 tbls fresh lime juice
1-3 tbls sugar
salt to taste

Put all the ingredients into a blender or food processor, ensuring that you have scraped as much as possible of the dark-green lining of the avocado skins into the mixture, and process until smooth. If mashing by hand, chop the avocado finely, then beat with an electric beater, or mash and whip. Make sure that the sorbet mixture is slightly sweeter than you would like the sorbet to be, as the coldness of the finished sorbet will lessen the sweetness. Spoon the mixture into a freezer container and freeze until firm. This should not need beating halfway through freezing, but if you can be bothered to do so, the finished texture will be lighter. Ⓕ

TOMATO and ORANGE SORBET

Serves four to six

2 medium or large oranges
1 medium or large lemon
1.2 litres/2 pints tomato juice
2 tsps Worcestershire sauce
2 egg whites

Peel one of the oranges and reserve the peel. Chop the peeled orange, the unpeeled orange and the lemon. Put these into the tomato juice and bring to the boil very slowly; simmer for about 5 minutes. Let the juice cool with the fruit in it. Strain, and then squeeze the fruit and add that liquid to the tomato juice.

When quite cold, stir in the Worcestershire sauce, which should give only a mild tang rather than a big bite. Freeze in a suitable container, and once it starts to set around the edges, whisk it well. If you do this several times, it will ensure an even texture.

Whisk the egg whites until they are firm but not dry and fold them into the mixture at your last whisking. This will slow down the speed at which the sorbet melts when you serve it. Return the sorbet to the freezer but remove it at least 30 minutes before serving. Ⓕ

ASPARAGUS without FEAR

Too much nonsense is talked about cooking asparagus. Although tying even-sized spears into bundles and standing them in special tall pans to cook looks impressive, it takes longer than eating them. One of the delights of eating asparagus on a hot summer's day is how little effort is required to prepare it.

Rinse the asparagus lightly and break off the bottoms wherever they decide to snap; if you have the time, you will get slightly more for your money by peeling the woody stems back to their soft centres with a very sharp knife or potato peeler – worthwhile for a couple of servings, too fiddly to do for more.

Boil water in a container in which the asparagus can lie flat – a frying-pan or a roasting-tin is ideal. Salt lightly and then lay the asparagus in it. If the asparagus is a mixture of thicknesses, it would be sensible to start cooking the thick ones slightly before the others. Once tender (you will probably have to taste-test a few!), lift them out with a fish-slice on to hot plates and serve with a suitable sauce. If they are to be eaten cold, sprinkle on a little light vinaigrette to give extra flavour and then leave them to cool.

Melted butter alone is not tasty enough to complement the bland, sweet flavour of asparagus, so sharpen it with a squeeze or two of lemon juice, or serve garlic butter, it's superb; also, you tend to use less flavoured butter than plain.

A classic flavouring for asparagus is blood orange, but try butter melted with any orange juice and a fine grating of orange rind. Don't overlook the simplicity of other flavoured butters, especially tarragon or parsley. Hollandaise sauce (see page 14) is a richer, sharper, butter-based sauce which may also be flavoured with chopped fresh herbs or with orange juice, but to make it lighter and more delicious whisk the whites of 1 or 2 eggs and fold them into a herby Hollandaise.

Cold asparagus should be served with mayonnaise and, again, an orange-and-garlic flavoured version is best. Spices may be used as well as herbs; I often sprinkle cold asparagus with coarsely ground coriander seed or toasted cumin seed. Almost any herb may be mixed into mayonnaise, especially if the mayonnaise has been lightened with a little strained yoghurt.

AUBERGINES with MINT

This unusual combination from Corsica will be enjoyed hot or cold, and served with rice it makes a simple but highly appreciated vegetarian first or main course. It is even better if its flavours are left to mature overnight. You must use a really rich olive oil and drain the aubergines by sprinkling the cubes with salt before cooking them.

Serves four

1 kg/2 lb aubergines
salt
olive oil
2-4 garlic cloves
generous handful of mint leaves
2 large tomatoes, peeled and chopped
salt and pepper
sugar (optional) to taste

Peel the aubergines, cut them into even-sized cubes and place in a colander. Sprinkle with salt and allow them to drain for about 30 minutes, rinse, then pat dry. Heat olive oil in a frying-pan and brown the aubergines lightly; cook for about 15 minutes but don't allow them to go mushy. Chop the garlic and the mint leaves (don't do this in advance or the flavour will disappear), stir these into the aubergines and cook for 2 minutes longer. Add the tomatoes and stir until amalgamated, but don't overdo it or you will spoil the appearance. Season with salt and pepper; if the oil was coarse, add a pinch or two of sugar as well. Ⓕ Ⓥ

IMAM BAYELDI

Imam Bayeldi (or The Priest Fainted) is probably the best known and most imitated aubergine dish in the world. Aubergines soak up monstrous amounts of olive oil, giving themselves a voluptuous flavour and texture. The story goes that this combination was considered so amazing by the Imam, or priest, when he first tasted it that he fainted clean away. There are thousands of versions; this is the one of the simplest I've found, served on the waterfront at Izmir in Turkey.

Serves four to six

3 large aubergines
1-2 tsps lemon juice or wine vinegar
olive oil
3 large onions, chopped
2-4 garlic cloves, crushed
375-440 g/12-14 oz tomatoes, or
440 g/14 oz can crushed tomatoes
1/2 tsp caster sugar
1/2 tsp ground cinnamon
chopped mint or parsley
toasted pine kernels (optional)

Remove the stalks from the aubergines and cut in half lengthwise. Plunge into boiling water with a little lemon juice or vinegar added and cook for 10 minutes, or until just tender. Plunge into cold water until quite cold.

Scoop out the flesh leaving a good thick shell and reserve. Pour 4 teaspoons olive oil into each shell then bake at 180°C/350°F/Gas Mark 4 for 10-15 minutes.

Meanwhile, fry the onions in a little oil with the crushed garlic until soft. Chop the tomatoes (peel if they are fresh) and add with the sugar and cinnamon. Cook for about 10 minutes, until the liquid has reduced by half, then add the chopped aubergine flesh and cook for a further 10 minutes.

Stuff the shells and serve warm or cold, sprinkled with chopped mint, parsley or lightly browned pine kernels. I never say no to extra olive oil.

JUNIPER CABBAGE

By contrast to red cabbage, the green cabbage varieties take just a few minutes to cook. Juniper cabbage is wonderful served with goose, especially with juniper-flavoured gin to beef out the sauce.

Simply quarter and slice a crisp green cabbage, removing any large pieces of core. Put into a pan containing 2.5 cm/1 inch of boiling water and cook for just 2-3 minutes, tossing from time to time. Once the cabbage is bright green and wilting, drain, salt lightly and toss in twelve well-crushed juniper berries. Stir well, cover tightly and leave for another 2-3 minutes over a very low heat, to finish cooking. Add a few spoonfuls of gin just before serving and stir in.

If you like, butter or soured cream could be stirred in just before serving.

SWEDISH SPICED RED CABBAGE

Braised red cabbage is an excellent vegetable accompaniment to ham, salt beef, game and especially roast duck. It's important that it cooks slowly and for long enough to ensure that the cabbage is very tender and the apple and onion have all but disappeared.

Serves six

300 ml/1/2 pint cold water
2 tbls molasses or black treacle
1 tbls red wine, chilli or garlic vinegar
1-2 tbls pickling spice
lard or oil for frying
1 kg/2 lb red cabbage, thinly sliced
125 g/4 oz onion, sliced
500 g/1 lb cooking apples, peeled, cored and sliced
250 g/8 oz smoked bacon, sliced or chopped
salt to taste

Put the water, molasses or treacle, wine or vinegar and spice into a saucepan and heat gently until it boils. Simmer for 10 minutes to allow the flavours to develop. Meanwhile, melt a little lard or oil in a large, heavy-bottomed saucepan or casserole and add the cabbage, onion and apple. Brown slightly, stirring from time to time, then add the bacon.

Strain the spiced liquid over the vegetables, bring to the boil, cover with a well-fitting lid and simmer very gently for 1 hour. Don't be tempted to keep lifting the lid to check during this time. Taste for seasoning, adding a little more molasses or vinegar, with 1-2 teaspoons of salt. If the cabbage looks a little dry at this stage, add a few tablespoons of water. Cover again and continue to simmer very gently for a further hour.

CIDERED CARROTS

This is a simple way to make a cheap vegetable more special. Chop, slice or make the carrots into matchsticks, then measure the space they take up in a bowl or basin. Fill the (empty) container to the same level with dry cider and pour it into a suitable pan with the carrots. Add some generous knobs of butter and cook until the carrots are tender and the liquid has reduced to a sauce consistency that you like; this can always be encouraged by the addition of further butter. For more special occasions, combine carrot and apple, or cook in a mixture of cider and cream and dust the finished carrots with a little nutmeg, cinnamon or mint. Ⓥ

BRAISED FENNEL

This is by far the most successful vegetable to braise – provided that you like the slightly liquorice flavour of fennel bulbs.

Serves four

3-4 medium fennel bulbs
150 ml/1/4 pint light stock
1-2 tbls lemon juice
salt and black pepper
30-60 g/1-2 oz butter

Slice the bulbs lengthways, in halves or quarters, and rinse. Arrange in a lightly buttered ovenproof dish. Add the stock, which shouldn't be too rich or salty because it will reduce. If you are using a chicken-stock cube, make it half-strength. Sprinkle with the lemon juice, salt and black pepper. Dot with butter, then cover.

Cook gently on the hob or in the oven (150°C/300°F/Gas Mark 2). It will take around 40 minutes to be really tender. Baste the fennel a few times during the cooking. Ⓥ

Options
Braised Endive Bought cheaply in season, crisp white Belgian endives make an elegant braised vegetable and develop a nutty flavour; I blanch them quickly first to get rid of some of their inherent bitterness and sprinkle a little crushed garlic on to them.

KOHLRABI with ORANGE and ALMONDS

Serves four

60 g/2 oz butter
1 1/2 tbls olive oil
1 tbls finely chopped onion
500 g/1 lb small kohlrabi, trimmed
300 ml/1/2 pint orange juice
flaked almonds, lightly browned, to garnish

Melt the butter in a medium pan, add the oil and soften the onions really well. Cut the unpeeled kohlrabi into quarters, or eight pieces depending on size. Add them to the saucepan and, as soon as they seem to be absorbing some of the butter and oil, add the orange juice. Simmer gently until tender (30 minutes or so). The orange juice should have reduced dramatically, combining with the butter to make a rich, syrupy-looking sauce. Serve with a scatter of lightly browned flaked almonds. Ⓥ

ORANGE MUSHROOMS

Most recipes for mushrooms are drenched with oil or butter, negating their claim to be virtually calorie free. For this recipe you *must* use a non-stick pan.

Serves two

500 g/1 lb large mushrooms
2 garlic cloves, finely chopped (optional)
4 tbls orange juice
2 tbls lemon juice
30 g/1 oz parsley, chopped

Remove the mushroom stems, and either quarter the mushrooms or leave them whole. Chop the stems finely, with the garlic if you're using it (and it is good). Heat a non-stick pan and add the chopped garlic and stems, and fry for a few minutes; add the mushroom caps and cook until you see liquid beginning to seep out. Turn the heat up and add the orange and lemon juice; let this sauce bubble and combine. Add the parsley and mix until it has soaked up the juices. Serve at once, before more liquid escapes. Ⓥ Ⓠ Ⓔ

Option
If you are not slimming or are feeling self-indulgent, you can fry the mushrooms in up to 125 g/4 oz of butter!

BAKED JACKET POTATOES

Baked potatoes are an important part of modern diets, as they are high in fibre, starch and vitamins. But *don't* wrap them in foil; it not only takes time (and wastes foil) but results in potatoes that are steamed and have soft skins. You might like them but they're not baked potatoes. The best method is to scrub baking potatoes well and pat dry, then prick a few times with a fork. Rub over very lightly with oil or butter and bake directly on the racks of the oven for 30-40 minutes, depending on their size.

Baked potatoes are one of the best snacks or fillers if you can resist the temptation to serve them with lashings of butter or soured cream; you'll need less butter if you pack them with fresh herbs or spices, or first sprinkle the cooked potato with flavoured vinegar.

Stuffed baked potatoes are a meal in themselves, and there is a better way to present them than the usual cut and squeeze technique. This is my method for serving them: trim a small piece from the bottom of the potato and stand the baked potato in the middle of the plate. Now cut across the potato three or four times, almost to the bottom, and put your filling into each cut, perhaps choosing something different for each one, or alternating. The most wicked I ever did was to alternate rolled smoked salmon sprinkled with dill and soured cream flavoured with vodka. *Photograph, p. 78.*

SWEDISH GLAZED POTATOES

Canned potatoes are excellent prepared this way; fresh ones should be small and firm, and cooked so they are still a little moist.

Serves two to four

45 g/1½ oz butter
45 g/1½ oz white sugar
500 g/1 lb cooked or canned small potatoes

Melt the butter and sugar gently in a saucepan over a medium heat. When it begins to turn brown, add the potatoes and toss continuously until a thick sauce forms around them.

PUMPKIN with ORANGE and APRICOT

Cut slices or rings of peeled pumpkin or squash about 2 cm/¾ inch thick and arrange, slightly overlapping, in an ovenproof dish. Pour in orange juice to half the depth of the vegetable, then scatter some dried apricots, whole or sliced, around the dish immersing them in the orange juice, and some flaked or whole blanched

---

FOOD FACT

Pumpkin and squash are members of a huge family of vegetables which, although still little known or understood in Britain and parts of Europe, are enjoyed enormously in most other countries. All the varieties can be treated as potato and boiled, baked, mashed or puréed. They like a good deal of butter and are excellent when flavoured with garlic, spice, or orange juice.

All types of pumpkin or squash are interchangeable in recipes, varying only slightly in moisture content or sweetness. Rather than hunting out a special type, adapt what you can get (or grow). If, however, you are lucky enough to find the Butternut, which is shaped like a large peanut, having a slight waist, it is especially good.

---

almonds (or any other nut) over the top. Sprinkle with ground coriander, salt and pepper, dot with butter and bake, uncovered, at 180°C/350°F/Gas Mark 4 for up to 45 minutes or until tender, depending on the type of squash or pumpkin. Baste after 20 minutes' cooking – not before, or you will rinse the coriander off the slices. Ⓥ

Option

Pumpkin Provencal Style Sprinkle slices of pumpkin with olive oil and cover with slightly squashed canned tomatoes, replacing the orange juice with the juice from the can. Sprinkle with chopped or finely sliced cloves of garlic, allowing at least ½ clove per person, plus a branch of fresh thyme, a little fresh rosemary and a bay leaf. Sprinkle with more olive oil and bake as above.

RATATOUILLE

This popular summer dish can be made with any proportion of the main ingredients, but the recipe I like best is the easiest to remember.

For six people, select 500 g/1 lb each of courgettes, aubergines and sweet peppers (I like a mixture of red and green). Use 250 g/8 oz onions (optional).

Cut the courgettes and aubergines into 2.5 cm/ 1 inch cubes with a piece of skin on each, which helps the pieces to keep their shape. Slice the onions, then heat 150 ml/¼ pint olive oil in a large, heavy-based pan. Add all the vegetables to the pan and turn quickly to coat each piece

---

with the oil, which is vital for the final flavour. (You could use half olive oil and half another, lighter oil, but without some of the former your Ratatouille won't be as good.)

Then add the important ingredient that pulls it all together – tomatoes. Canned plum tomatoes in their own juice are better in this dish than fresh tomatoes. Use 2 396 g/14 oz cans with their juice. Throw in some cloves of garlic, whole and still in their skins. Leave the lid off and cook gently for at least an hour. If there is still a lot of liquid, pour it off into a saucepan, reduce it over heat to just a few spoonfuls, and pour it back into the large pan. Now add seasoning. If you must have herbs, only a little basil or thyme are useful. Eat Ratatouille hot or cold, perhaps sprinkled with a drop more olive oil. Ⓥ Ⓢ Ⓔ

RATATOUILLE and EGGS

Eggs and ratatouille are found combined in a number of ways in the South of France, as well as all round the shores of the Mediterranean.

For a simple summer lunch or supper, layer a baking dish with hot ratatouille, make one deep hollow in it for each diner, break an egg or eggs into each and then bake until the eggs are just set. Dribble on some olive oil and serve with bread so you may sop up every drip of juice, oil and egg. Or make a popular version of a Provençal omelette which, like the Spanish tortilla, should never be folded but served flat. Put some warm ratatouille into the beaten eggs as soon as they are in the hot oil in the pan. Once the mixture is cooked through, serve it just like that, turn it over, or brown the top under a grill. It depends on a mixture of dexterity and size which you choose.

Clearly, variations in your vegetable mixture will make this taste different every time you make it. The most spectacular variation I've discovered, near Roquebrussane, is to stir saffron into the eggs so that when the omelette is cooked it is *jaune comme l'or* – as yellow as gold.

Sprinkled typically with parsely and garlic, and perhaps more olive oil, these omelettes should be served warm rather than hot. Best of all is to serve them cold with salad or between thick slices of bread. *Photograph, p. 79.*

GLYNN'S TIP

If you want to make Ratatouille in advance, cool the mixture as quickly as you can and then boil it hard after 24 hours. If you don't, the natural yeasts present on the skins of the vegetables will reactivate and start to ferment the mixture and you might lose the lot.

SALAD LEAVES

You may mix any of these leaves together or serve them singly, but those noted as being bitter should generally be served in small amounts or mixed with sweeter leaves. Modern salads are often served on flat individual plates and the crisper, more bitter leaves are specially suitable for this. People who enjoy good wines with their food are turning away from serving salads with dressings, conscious of the fact that vinegars have an adverse effect on the taste of wines. Instead, more use is being made of fresh herbs; generous amounts of chopped parsley tossed through or sprinkled over a salad adds colour, texture and flavour without ruining the palate, or dress just with a nut oil or with vodka. *Photograph, p. 80.*

TYPE	TASTE	TIPS/SERVING SUGGESTIONS
Chicory/ Belgian endive	Bitter	Trim off root and remove outside leaves; use whole leaves or cut into rings
Chinese leaves	Mid-bitter	Use as lettuce; keeps well in refrigerator
Cos/romaine	Mid-sweet	One of the crispest and greenest lettuce types
Curly endive/escarole	Bitter	Crisp; wash very well and pull into even pieces
Iceberg lettuce	Mid-bitter	Stays crisp but flavour sometimes bland or unpleasantly strange
Dandelion leaves	Bitter	Use only very young or blanched leaves
Lambs lettuce/mache/ corn salad	Sweet	Small leaves; cut off base and wash out grit well; dry quickly
Mesclun	Mixed	A mixture of small green leaves
Mustard and cress	Sweetish/sharp	Avoid, as over-used and boring
Nasturtium leaves	Peppery	Use whole and with restraint
Oakleaf lettuce	Sweetish	Red-edged lettuce, great in mixed salads
Orach	Peppery/sweet	Wine-red, heart-shaped leaf tasting like Rocket
Purslane	Cucumber	Fleshy leaves are used

TYPE	TASTE	TIPS/SERVING SUGGESTIONS
Radicchio	Bitter	Bright red with white veins; better in mixed salads.
Rampion		Leaves and root both used, the latter prepared like salsify
Rocket/Arugala/ Roquette	Peppery/sweet	Use with restraint; truly delicious and easy to grow
Round lettuce	Mixed	Now grown all year round and thus very variable in flavour; better torn than cut with a knife
Salad Burnet	Cucumber	Use tender leaves in the same way as watercress
Sorrel	Acidic	Use sliced but add at last minute or the cut edges oxidize and discolour. Use small amounts only
Spinach	Sweet/iron	Much sweeter and nicer than you imagine. Use whole small leaves or torn large leaves; wash extremely well.
Swiss chard/ silver beet	Stronger than spinach	Use leaves as spinach; but thick spines may be blanched and cut into matchsticks
Watercress	Peppery	Makes interesting salad by itself; leaves only are better in mixtures

VEGETABLES

TYPE	TIPS/SERVING SUGGESTIONS
Artichoke	Canned or fresh bottoms, or sliced hearts; raw bottoms when very young
Asparagus	Tips only, lightly cooked; canned not so successful
Avocado	Use sliced or cubed; toss in citrus juice to prevent discoloration
Broccoli	Florets only, raw or blanched; if yellowish they are bitter
Cabbage	All types including crisp white, young green and red, sometimes blanched first
Carrot	Use grated, sliced or in matchsticks
Celeriac	Use grated, or in matchsticks; authentic *celeri rémoulade*
Chives	I don't think these should be used in most salads (see Leeks)
Celery	Trim off stringy fibres, slice or cut into matchsticks; use leaves
Courgettes	Grate, slice or cut in matchsticks; use raw when very young
Cucumber	Used in many ways; peeled or unpeeled – matchsticks are nicer than the usual thin slices. Blanched in boiling water for a few minutes and then cooled in running water it turns a marvellous translucent green. Raw cucumber can be salted after it is sliced, drained and dried. Sprinkled with a little sugar and white wine vinegar, it makes a delicious simple salad, but must be allowed to marinate for several hours
Fennel root	Use raw or lightly blanched and thinly sliced; chop the fronds
French beans	Use lightly blanched and neatly trimmed into even sizes

TYPE	TIPS/SERVING SUGGESTIONS
Kohlrabi	Turnip-rooted cabbage; slice or grate raw or lightly blanched
Leeks	If you really must have an onion flavour, very thinly sliced leeks are better than anything else. No raw onion flavouring of any type should be used if a decent wine or a nice pudding is also being served in the same meal, for the taste of onion sticks to the palate and changes the flavour of anything eaten after it; if you enjoy raw onion, do it with something like a Ploughman's Lunch or when nothing subtle or expensive is being eaten
Mange tout	Lightly blanch after topping, tailing and stringing
Onions	Not to be used (see Leeks)
Peppers	Available in 5 colours: red, green, yellow, white and purple. The last 3 are weaker in flavour. All are better if lightly blanched first. Dress with vinaigrette and garlic while still warm
Radish	Use whole or sliced; add a few radish flowers for effect; young radish leaves can be used
Shallot	These should not be used in mixed salads (see Leeks)
Spring onions	See Leeks
Tomato	May be used in almost every way, but *please* only bother with those that have real flavour. Those sold as rock hard salad tomatoes are a contradiction in terms. Can be sliced, but it is much nicer to cut them into segments. Smarter but harder, is to peel them first and then to cut neatly, after deseeding. Well-flavoured tomatoes can stand being served directly from the refrigerator; lesser varieties should be at room temperature

FLOWERS					
TYPE	TASTE	TIPS/SERVING SUGGESTIONS	TYPE	TASTE	TIPS/SERVING SUGGESTIONS
Borage	Cucumber	Bright blue flowers; beware of hairy leaves!	Roses	Rose/smokey	Use fragrant petals from unsprayed roses; cut off white bitter bases
Marigold	Spicy	Use only a scattering from *officinalis*	Violets	Violet	Use only unsprayed; most violets from florists are sprayed and, having no smell, have no flavour
Nasturtiums	Peppery/sweetish	There is a globule of sweet syrup in the base of each flower. Use as an ingredient in a mixed salad or just with nasturtium leaves			

HERBS and SPICES

Any fresh, sweet herb can be used in a salad, but do not chop too finely or they tend to bruise and oxidize, causing a loss or change of flavours. Chopped parsley is often overlooked as a single livener of simple salads. Basil, tarragon, thyme, all varieties of mint, oregano, fresh coriander leaf and fennel leaf are delicious, either by themselves or in combination with others.

Coarsely ground spices are an unexpected salad ingredient. I use roasted black peppercorns, green peppercorns, allspice and whole coriander seeds as alternatives to ground black peppercorns. Roasted whole cumin seeds are especially good.

BASIC POTATO SALAD

Potato salad can be one of the very best or very worst of all salads. The secret lies in tossing the *warm* potatoes in dressing, then allowing them to cool and absorb the flavours. Cook the potatoes in plain water, as salted water tends to toughen the outer surfaces, and you can season the dressing to your liking.

Serves four

500 g/1 lb small new potatoes
2 tsps white wine vinegar
2 tbls olive oil
2 tbls chopped fresh dill, or 1 tbls dried dill
300 ml/½ pint soured cream
3 tsps creamed horseradish
salt to taste

Scrub but do not peel the potatoes. Cut them in half lengthways and cook in boiling water until just tender. Drain, then toss lightly in the vinegar, oil and dill. Leave to cool. Mix together the soured cream and horseradish and season with salt to taste. Stir in the potatoes, pile high on a dish and serve well chilled. Ⓥ

Option
Pink Prawn and Potato Salad Add 2 teaspoons of tomato purée to the soured cream and horseradish and stir in 125 g/4 oz peeled, cooked prawns with the potatoes.

ITALIAN SALAD

The beauty of this salad is its contrasting colours and textures.

Serves four

1 or 2 ripe but firm avocados
lemon juice
185-250 g/6-8 oz Mozzarella cheese
1 or 2 oranges (preferably navels)
1 medium fennel bulb
olive oil
1 garlic clove, crushed (optional)

Halve and peel the avocados, then slice thinly lengthways. Arrange on the bottom of a glass serving dish and sprinkle with lemon juice to prevent discoloration. Slice the Mozzarella thinly and arrange as a layer on top of the avocados. Peel the oranges, removing all the pith, then cut neat segments away from the linings and arrange these decoratively on top of the cheese. Cut the fennel in half lengthways, then slice thinly and layer over the oranges. Finally, chop the fennel fronds and scatter over the salad. Alternatively, arrange the ingredients on individual serving plates. For the dressing, sprinkle with olive oil and a little lemon juice. Serve with additional oil, flavoured with crushed garlic if you like. Ⓕ Ⓥ Ⓔ

GLYNN'S TIP

Almost all vegetables can be served as a hot salad simply by tossing them in a warm dressing of olive oil (or other good oil), a little vinegar or lemon juice and perhaps some crushed garlic. Green vegetables are very good treated this way, particularly broad beans and green beans which both love a garlicky dressing. The vinegar gives a lift to the bland, sweet, winter root vegetables; you won't believe that parsnips could taste so good!

GLYNN'S TIP

Use a warm knife when slicing Mozzarella; you will find it far easier to obtain even slices.

CAULIFLOWER PRAWN SALAD

Choose a very firm, white cauliflower and serve just the florets. The combination of raw cauliflower with cooked prawns may sound eccentric but not only does it make prawns go further, it's one of the few original variations there are in the prawn cocktail theme.

Serves four

250 g/8 oz mixed raw cauliflower and prawns, chilled
1 ripe avocado
lemon juice
4 tbls soured cream
1 tsp creamed horseradish
grated lemon rind

Mix the cauliflower and the prawns in any proportion that suits your taste or budget. Quarter and peel the avocado, then slice each quarter carefully, and as thinly as you can, into a fan shape. Cover all ingredients with a little lemon juice and arrange on four small plates of a contrasting colour. Mix the soured cream and horseradish to taste and spoon on to each dish. Scatter with finely grated lemon rind and serve well chilled. Ⓕ

Options
A little hot or sweet paprika can be added for extra colour, or lightly toasted flaked almonds sprinkled on for texture and crunch.

PAPRIKA COURGETTE SALAD

This cooked salad from Morocco is a popular party dish. If you can only get hot paprika, use a little less or the flavours will be masked.

Serves two to four

500 g/1 lb courgettes
1 heaped tsp sweet paprika
½ heaped tsp ground cumin
1 tbls lemon juice
2 tbls sunflower oil
1 or 2 garlic cloves
1 tbls olive oil
2 tbls chopped parsley

Choose even-sized courgettes. Slice them lengthways into 4 segments, then cut into chunks about 2.5 cm/1 inch long. Put into a saucepan with the paprika, cumin, lemon juice, sunflower oil and garlic. Just cover with water and simmer gently until the courgettes are barely soft.

Remove the courgettes and boil the cooking liquid until reduced to just a few tablespoons of unctuous red sauce. Toss the courgettes in this and finalize the flavour with the olive oil and parsley. Serve either warm or chilled. Ⓕ Ⓥ Ⓔ *Photograph, p. 44.*

SALADES TIEDES

Salades tièdes, or warm salads, are growing in popularity and are helping to change the image of salads from insubstantial mid-summer plates of rabbit food to more interesting and exciting dishes to be eaten at any time of the year. A warm dressing is poured over the salad, which is served immediately. It is usual for the salad to consist of the crunchier and more bitter leaves, endive, chicory, radicchio etc., as their texture will stand up to heat better than an already floppy lettuce. Sweet-tasting lambs' lettuce or *mache* and raw spinach are good as a contrast of flavours.

WARM WATERCRESS, BACON and POTATO SALAD

Watercress should be eaten as fresh as possible, when it is a veritable storehouse of flavour and vitamins; select dark-looking leaves, as these have a higher nutrient content.

Serves four

250 g/8 oz streaky bacon
2 bunches watercress
500 g/1 lb small new potatoes, boiled in their skins
2 tbls sunflower oil
2 tbls wine vinegar

Slice the bacon, leaving the rind on, into 2.5 cm/1 inch lengths. Fry until crisp, in a non-stick pan, in its own fat. Wash and dry the trimmed watercress well; divide it on to four large plates. Slice the warm or cold potatoes lengthways and arrange them on top of the watercress. Spoon out the bacon and sprinkle it on to the potatoes. Add the sunflower oil and the wine vinegar to the bacon fat, bring to the boil, scraping together the contents of the pan and spoon over the salads. Ⓕ

CHICKEN LIVER SALAD with CROUTONS

This *salade tiède* has become a classic.

Serves four as a starter

2 slices white bread, without crusts
oil and butter for frying
250 g/8 oz lambs' lettuce
1 small head radicchio
½ head curly endive
3 tbls olive oil
2 tsps wine or sherry vinegar
salt and pepper
375 g/12 oz chicken livers, trimmed
1 garlic clove, crushed

Dice the bread neatly and fry in oil until evenly browned. Drain on absorbent paper. Wash and dry the salad leaves and tear into bite-sized pieces. Make a dressing of the olive oil and vinegar, seasoned with salt and pepper, gently toss the salad in it and divide between individual plates.

Slice each liver in two or three pieces. Heat a knob of butter in a frying-pan and add the crushed garlic. Fry the livers over a fairly high heat, turning as they become brown, for 3-4 minutes. Remove with a slotted spoon and divide between the salads. Reheat the croûtons quickly in the garlic butter, scatter over the salads and serve immediately. Ⓕ

A SOUTHERN SALAD

Provided that you have juicy, fresh garlic, you might like to serve it whole and hot on top of a salad as a first course. Take 4-6 unpeeled cloves of garlic per person and boil them for 5 minutes in plain water. Drain, and simmer again in fresh water for 20-30 minutes, according to their size. A sprig of thyme and/or a strip of orange rind in the water helps the flavour. Once the garlic is squishy-soft, drain and cover with warm olive oil.

Arrange leafy salads on flat plates and squeeze over a little lemon juice. Season lightly with salt and pepper. Arrange the cloves of garlic on top of each salad, then drizzle the warm olive oil over. For a more substantial salad, add walnuts and squares or strips of crisply cooked bacon; in the former case, you could use walnut oil instead of olive oil. Ⓕ

WARM BEETROOT SALAD

Warm salads have been a part of Cypriot life for centuries. This one uses beetroot, a vegetable too often under-rated.

Serves four

500 g/1 lb raw beetroot
500 g/1 lb small potatoes
at least 10 large parsley sprigs, finely chopped
3 celery stalks with leaves, finely chopped
3 garlic cloves, finely chopped
salt and pepper
3 tbls rich olive oil
2 tbls wine vinegar

Wash the beetroot, being careful not to break the skins; don't trim the top or bottom. Boil until tender, cool, and slip off the skins. In the meantime, boil the potatoes unpeeled so that they are ready at about the same time.

Cut the beetroot and potato into thick slices or generous cubes. Layer the beetroot in a bowl first and then the potatoes. Sprinkle on the parsley, celery and garlic. Repeat until the vegetables are used up, adding salt and pepper to each layer as you go.

Heat the oil and vinegar together until warm without being really hot, pour over, and serve at once. Ⓥ *Photograph, p. 116.*

STUFFED VEGETABLES

Stuffed baked vegetables have long been a European way of making expensive meat and leftovers go further. They are used now as a way to serve filling meals with less reliance on meat as a major ingredient. Quantities for such recipes must adapt to the reality of the larder, but here is a guide. They are all much more delicious with olive oil, but a lighter safflower or sunflower oil may be substituted if you prefer it.

SPICED MEAT STUFFING

These are useful stuffings for vegetables, which can then be baked without extra liquid.

Fry a finely chopped onion in butter or oil until golden brown and beautifully tender. Add 500 g/1 lb minced lamb, beef or veal and continue frying until the meat is brown, then stir in a few tablespoons of pinenuts or whole almonds and half the quantity of currants. Flavour gently with cinnamon or with allspice.

STUFFED TOMATOES

Serves eight as a starter

10 large, ripe tomatoes
salt
2 medium onions, chopped
olive oil
125 g/4 oz fresh breadcrumbs
125 g/4 oz leftover cooked beef, veal or ham, finely chopped
salt and pepper
ground nutmeg
stock or gravy (optional)
3 or 4 egg yolks

Cut off the tops of the tomatoes and scoop out the seeds and flesh. Sprinkle the hollowed-out tomatoes with salt and turn them upside down to drain. Soften the onions in a little olive oil; add 2 of the drained tomatoes finely chopped, then the fresh breadcrumbs and meat. Season with a little salt, pepper and nutmeg, add a little stock or gravy, if you have it, and heat through. Remove from the heat and stir in the egg yolks and make a firm but pliable stuffing. Stuff the remaining 8 tomatoes and put them into an ovenproof gratin dish brushed with olive oil. Cook at 200°C/400°F/Gas Mark 6 until the stuffing is set and lightly browned (about 10-15 minutes). Serve hot or cold. Ⓕ

Options

For Lent, or for those who do not eat meat, replace the leftovers with extra onion and tomato or some other vegetable, perhaps chopped sweet peppers.

CUCUMBER-STUFFED TOMATOES

Uncooked tomato shells, with a clean, fresh-tasting filling, combine to make a wonderful summertime starter, or lunch dish.

Serves eight

8 medium tomatoes, peeled
CUCUMBER STUFFING
185 g/6 oz cottage cheese, strained
3 tbls diced celery
2 tsps chives, chopped
3 tbls mayonnaise
1 medium cucumber, peeled and grated
1 tbls chopped parsley
1/2 tsp salt
1/2 tsp white pepper
WATERCRESS DRESSING
1 bunch watercress (leaves and upper stems), chopped
8 tbls Chili Sauce
8 tbls Oil and Vinegar (see page 18)
1/2 tsp salt
freshly ground black pepper

Cut the tomatoes halfway through by making an 'X' with a paring knife – be careful not to slice down too far. Open carefully and remove the seeds without breaking off the fleshy sections. To make the filling, mix all the ingredients together. Using a teaspoon, carefully stuff the tomatoes with the mixture. Combine the ingredients for the dressing. Arrange the tomatoes on small plates with extra watercress and the watercress dressing. Ⓕ Ⓥ

TURKISH RICE-STUFFED VEGETABLES

This is one of my favourite stuffings, unusual for the inclusion of dill and allspice.

Serves four to six as a main course or six to eight as a starter

125 g/4 oz uncooked long grain rice
125 g/4 oz very finely chopped onion
8 tbls olive oil
1 tbls pine-nuts (optional)
1 tbls tomato purée
1 tbls currants
3 tbls chopped mixed mint
dill and parsley
150 ml/1/4 pint water
1 tsp ground allspice
salt and pepper
sugar to taste (optional)
1 kg/2 lb vegetables (aubergines, courgettes, tomatoes or sweet peppers)
227 g/8 oz can tomatoes

The rice must be prepared in a special way. Pour boiling water over it in a bowl and leave undisturbed until cold. Rinse very well and drain. Cook the onion in the olive oil until soft and golden brown, then add the pine-nuts (if used) and rice and gently cook for another 15 minutes. Add the purée, currants, herbs and water and simmer until the water is absorbed. Let the filling cool and then flavour with allspice, salt and pepper. The flavourings should be strong, for they are filling an ingredient which is bland and will be cooked again. If there is any bitterness, perhaps caused by the oil, add a little sugar. If you are using courgettes, choose large ones and excavate them with an apple corer, or be lazy and cut them in half; blanch them as given above. Tomatoes or aubergines are usually cut in half. Cook the scooped-out flesh in its own juices until soft and stir into the rice mixture.

Stuff the vegetables and pour any of the oil that might have escaped from the stuffing. Pour on the tomatoes and bake at 180°C/350°F/Gas Mark 4 for about an hour, depending on how mushy you like your vegetables. Turn them from time to time as you bake them. Let them cool and, when you serve them, offer more olive oil. Ⓕ Ⓥ Ⓣ

Options

Rice and Meat Stuffing Prepare 50 g/2 oz rice as above and cook a small, finely chopped onion in butter, add the rice with 150 ml/1/4 pint water and simmer until absorbed. Then add 375 g/12 oz minced cooked lamb, beef or veal and knead the mixture until the meat is smooth. Flavour with about 1 tablespoon of chopped dill, mint or parsley and 1/2 teaspoon of ground allspice.

As the rice here is rather undercooked, add a 397 g/14 oz can of tomatoes to the dish and a little water if it cooks away too soon. Otherwise, add more water to the rice in the initial stages and cook it longer.

VEGETABLE CURRY

Curried vegetables usually conjure up pictures of yesterday's leftovers in a fluorescent yellow sauce, served with a dollop of yoghurt. Pity, for with a little care and knowledge, this can become one of your most important standbys for days when time is at a premium or when you do not want to eat meat.

You should always use at least three contrasting vegetables in a curry, you'll find the root varieties give you the most texture and colour. If you haven't the range of spices to make your own curry powder and don't want to invest in acquiring them all, then buy garam masala instead of ordinary curry powder. It is also pre-mixed, but often omits turmeric which gives that bilious yellow to so many curries, and is more fragrant.

Serves four

1 kg/2 lb prepared vegetables, at least 3 kinds including some root varieties
garam masala or curry powder
oil
1-2 onions, chopped
1-2 cloves garlic, crushed
6 thin slices fresh ginger, peeled
salt
coconut cream

Simmer the prepared vegetables in water flavoured with a little garam masala (1-2 teaspoons) until half cooked. Heat a little oil in a large saucepan and fry the onions, garlic and ginger with 2 heaped teaspoons garam masala for 5 minutes. Add the drained vegetables and enough fresh water or flavoured cooking water to just cover. Season with a little salt. Simmer gently until the vegetables are tender.

To add a touch of Southern India to the curry, finish the dish by crumbling in coconut cream, which can be bought in packets, or add coconut milk from a can. Stir over a low heat, taking care not to allow the mixture to boil or it may curdle. I like to add another teaspoon of garam masala before serving, to freshen up the flavour.

LEFTOVER VEGETABLES

If you do have leftover vegetables, and would like something curried, let me suggest you try one of these delicious fritters. Incidentally, they are just as delicious cold, too.

BARAS

1-2 onions, chopped
oil and butter for frying
1-2 cloves garlic, crushed
1 heaped tsp curry powder or garam masala
500 g/1 lb cooked vegetables, a mixture or one kind
2 eggs, beaten
fresh or dried breadcrumbs

Cook the onions in a little oil or oil and butter until very soft and lightly browned. Add the garlic and curry powder or garam masala and cook for 3-4 minutes. Stir in the vegetables, mashing a little, without reducing everything to a mush. Turn into a bowl and, while the mixture is still hot, add the beaten egg to give a soft, but not sloppy mixture – you may not need all of it. Shape into small cakes. Roll in breadcrumbs (do not use coloured ones, please) and fry in hot oil. Drain on absorbent paper and serve hot, warm or cold, with a dollop of plain yoghurt.

If, like me, you do not like onions, fry the garlic and spices in hot oil then add lots of chopped fresh mint or parsley.

PIKORAS

500 g/1 lb cooked vegetables, a mixture or one kind
salt
pinch of chilli pepper
1 heaped tsp curry powder or garam masala
250 g/8 oz plain flour
2 eggs
milk
oil for frying

Cut the vegetables into thick slices or large chunks. Mix a little salt and the chilli pepper with the curry powder or garam masala and toss the vegetables in it.

Sift the flour into a bowl and make a well in the middle. Break the eggs into the bowl and slowly beat in the flour, adding enough milk to give a stiff batter.

Dip the vegetables into the batter and fry in hot oil until golden and crisp. Drain and serve hot, warm or cold.

If your vegetables have been cut small, stir them into the batter and fry spoonfuls of the mixture.

VEGETABLE GRATINS

Vegetables baked with a final crisp coating look specially warming on winter nights but they don't have to be topped with bubbling cheese. Few vegetables have a strong enough flavour to support the addition of cheese. The best topping is breadcrumbs, perhaps flavoured with a little parsley and lemon or garlic.

Serves four to six

750 g/1½ lb fresh vegetables (see Options)
300 ml/½ pint creamy white sauce or fresh tomato sauce (see pages 15 and 16)
fresh breadcrumbs for topping

Butter a shallow ovenproof dish. Prepare the vegetables and simmer in boiling water until they are just tender; they will cook further while being baked. Drain and arrange in the dish and cover with the sauce. Sprinkle with crumbs and bake at 200°C/400°F/Gas Mark 6 for 10-12 minutes, until the top is brown, but be careful not to overcook the vegetables – always a risk with gratins. Ⓥ Ⓔ

Options
Broccoli Use medium florets, discarding any parts with very thick stalks.
Leeks Cut them into 5 cm/2 inch pieces and halve lengthways unless they are very young and slender. Wash thoroughly before cooking. Leeks do not always need a sauce for a gratin. You can simply moisten them with cream or butter and sprinkle with breadcrumbs alone or mixed with cheese.

STUFFED CABBAGE in a PASTRY CASE

This was created as a special Christmas dish for vegetarians, but it is so good that it is worth cooking for non-vegetarians too. If you don't like cabbage, spinach leaves would be just as good, and even more Middle Eastern.

Serves six

1 medium green cabbage, 750 g/1½ lb
185 g/6 oz uncooked rice
4 tbls olive oil
1 small onion, chopped
60 g/2 oz seedless raisins or currants
90 g/3 oz dried apricots, sliced
salt and pepper
2 heaped tbls ground almonds
2 heaped tbls chopped fresh mint
375 g/12 oz packet frozen puff pastry
1 egg
about 15 saffron threads
150 ml/¼ pint plain yoghurt
1-2 tbls melted butter
hot paprika or chili paste to taste

Carefully detach the leaves from the cabbage, cutting away the coarse ends of the stalks. Blanch the leaves, five at a time, in plenty of boiling water for 2 minutes. Remove with a slotted spoon and refresh in cold water. Reserve 250 ml/8 fl oz of the cabbage water.

Pour very hot water over the rice and leave until the water is cold. Rinse well under running cold water and drain again. Heat the oil and cook the onion until golden brown. Add the raisins or currants, the apricots and the rice and mix well. Add the reserved cabbage water, cover, and cook until the level of the water has disappeared beneath the rice. Turn off the heat and cover tightly, using a tea towel to seal the lid. Leave to steam for 15 minutes.

While the rice stuffing is steaming, cut a narrow V-shape at the bottom of each cabbage leaf, removing the thick stem almost half way up each leaf. Dry the leaves thoroughly.

When the rice has steamed for the required time, fluff it up, season it, and add the ground almonds and mint. Roll the puff pastry out into an oblong shape (about 45 × 30 cm/18 × 12 inches). Mix the egg with the saffron threads.

Pre-heat the oven to 200°C/400°F/Gas Mark 6. Stuff the cabbage leaves by putting a tablespoon of stuffing in the centre of each, fold in both sides of the leaf and roll up. Sit the cabbage parcels on their folds while you make the others, to ensure that they don't unroll. When you have stuffed all the cabbage leaves, pile them with their folds upwards in a smaller oblong on the centre of the pastry. The pile should be about three layers high, and even (not a pyramid) with the top layer as flat and wide as the bottom. Fold over the pastry, moisten and pinch the joins so that they bond together. (If the sides don't meet, roll them a little to stretch the pastry and if you're uncertain about the bonding bit, leave the excess folded over but be sure to moisten the pastry.) Invert the whole parcel on to a baking sheet. Slash the top in an attractive pattern but don't cut right through the pastry; cut two small 'breathing holes' in the top, and paint liberally with the saffron egg. Don't throw away the leftovers, it makes beautiful scrambled eggs. Bake for 35-40 minutes at 200°C/400°F/Gas Mark 6 or 45 minutes if you know that there are thick folds of pastry underneath. Serve sliced and topped with large blobs of plain yoghurt, or with melted butter mixed with either the chili paste or some hot paprika. Ⓥ *Photograph. p. 114.*

BAKED COURGETTE FLAN

This superb recipe is the creation of Princess Marie-Blanche de Broglie, who has a cooking school in Paris and at her château in Normandy. It is typical of modern eclectic French food but like all traditional French food only works if the ingredients are good and great care is taken. This dish is supposed to be served warm rather than hot, but is wondrous cold and gets better by the day; thus it is excellent party and picnic food.

Serves at least six to eight

1 kg/2 lb courgettes, thinly sliced
1 tbls salt
2 tbls unsalted butter
4 eggs
125 g/4 oz cream or curd cheese
2 tbls grated Gruyère cheese
fresh or dried tarragon to taste
chives or spring onion to taste
salt, pepper and nutmeg
Gruyère or Parmesan cheese to finish

Sprinkle the courgettes with salt and leave to drain for 30 minutes. Rinse under running water, drain and pat dry.

Sauté the slices in butter over high heat just long enough to soften them. Beat the eggs with the cream cheese, stir in the Gruyère and flavour with tarragon and a small amount of chives or spring onion, salt, pepper and nutmeg. You will need about 1 teaspoon of dried tarragon and more if fresh.

Stir this mixture into the cooled courgettes and put into a well-buttered 20 cm/8 inches round or square baking-dish. Sprinkle on a thin crust of Gruyère and Parmesan and bake at 180°C/350°F/Gas Mark 4 for 20 minutes or until set and very lightly browned. ⑤

SPINACH and FRESH SARDINE FLAN

Yes, I know this sounds unusual, but I assure you it is a popular recipe from the Mediterranean coast and not at all difficult to make. If you can't get Swiss chard, also called silver beet, use all spinach.

Serves four to six

1 kg/2 lb spinach
1 kg/2 lb Swiss chard
3 eggs
125 g/4 oz soft curd cheese
1 large garlic clove, finely chopped
butter for greasing
freshly grated nutmeg
1 or 2 fresh sardines per person
breadcrumbs
oil or butter

Wash the spinach and chard well, drain and cook the leaves in just the water which still clings to them for 4-5 minutes until limp. Press between two plates to expel all excess water. Chop the leaves and mix together with the eggs, cheese and garlic.

Grease a gratin or ovenproof dish, add the chopped vegetables and sprinkle with nutmeg. Gut, descale and behead the sardines and arrange on top of the spinach mixture. Scatter with breadcrumbs and sprinkle with oil or dot with some knobs of butter and bake or grill until the sardines are cooked and their oil has been absorbed by the green base.

Options

This dish may also be cooked in a pastry case, baked blind and painted with egg whites before the fillings are added.

Other fish can also be used but as they will almost certainly be less oily, they should be liberally doused with olive oil – red mullet or red snapper will give the most attractive looking results.

POTATO and CREAM PIE

Vegetable pies baked in pastry into which cream is poured are common throughout Europe and were once also familiar dishes in Britain. This French potato pie will surprise you with its simple appeal.

Serves six

375 g/12 oz butter
500 g/1 lb plain flour
2 eggs
120 ml/4 fl oz milk
1 kg/2 lb potatoes (not floury)
salt and pepper
grated or ground nutmeg
1-2 tbls grated cheese (Cheddar or Emmenthal)
175 ml/6 fl oz double cream

Rub the butter into the flour to a breadcrumb consistency. Beat one of the eggs and mix it in with the milk to make a dough. Cut the dough in half and roll into two circles about 20 cm/8 inches in diameter.

Peel and slice the potatoes fairly thinly and season with salt, pepper and nutmeg. Whisk the second egg with a little water or milk and brush both circles with this wash. Cover one circle of pastry with the potatoes, leaving a border around the edge. Sprinkle with the grated cheese. Place the other circle on top and seal. Paint with egg wash and make a 2.5 cm/1 inch slit in the top to allow the steam to escape.

Cook for 30 minutes in a moderate oven (180°C/350°F/Gas Mark 4). Heat the cream until very hot (but not boiling) and slowly pour through the slit and cook for a further 5 minutes, then serve immediately.

LEEKIE PIE

500 g/1 lb trimmed leeks
1 tbls butter
500 g/1 lb shortcrust or puff pastry (see pages 129 and 133)
90 g/3 oz streaky bacon
2 large eggs (one beaten)
300 ml/1/2 pint (approx) cream or milk (see below)
freshly ground black pepper
grated or ground nutmeg

Slice the leeks thinly and wash very carefully. Drain and cook in a saucepan with no extra water until they wilt and any liquid has evaporated (tilt the pan to make sure). Stir in the butter and allow to cool.

Line a 23 cm/9 inch flan dish with half the pastry. Cut the bacon into thin strips and mix with the cooled leeks. Spread the mixture over the pastry and cover with a lid. Glaze with a little of the beaten egg and cook at 220°C/425°F/Gas Mark 7 for 30 minutes.

Heat half the cream or milk and whisk in the rest of the beaten egg. Flavour well with pepper and nutmeg, then pour slowly through the vent into the pie. If it is all readily absorbed, make up another mixture of cream and egg and add that too.

Reduce the temperature to 180°C/350°F/Gas Mark 4 and cook for a further 20-25 minutes. If you use puff pastry, turn the oven up to 220°C/425°F/Gas Mark 7 for the last few minutes, to give a nice crispness to the pastry. It doesn't matter if the middle of the pie is a little runny; if milk is used rather than cream the set will be less firm. Serve the pie warm, rather than hot.

SPANAKOPITTA

Often called Greek Spinach Pie, this dish is found all round the Eastern Mediterranean and makes perfect party food. It is particularly good cold and, although the phyllo pastry used quickly goes soft, it re-crisps in the oven very easily. The technique of draining the spinach before it is cooked stops all problems of excess liquid.

Serves four

1.25 kg/2 1/2-3 lb trimmed spinach or Swiss chard
2 or 3 tbls salt
60-90 ml/2-3 fl oz olive oil
375 g/12 oz Feta cheese, lightly crumbled
generous handful each of fresh parsley and dill (or generous amount of dried dill)
4-5 spring onions, chopped (optional)
pepper to taste (optional)
2-3 tbls burghul wheat (optional)
2-3 eggs
375-500 g/12 oz-1 lb Phyllo pastry
a little butter, olive oil or a mixture

Wash the spinach, or chard, chop or tear coarsely, add the salt and rub it into the spinach. Leave for an hour in a large colander. Rinse and squeeze well. Flavour with olive oil, the cheese and the parsley and dill, finely chopped. If you use onion ensure that it is very finely chopped.

If you have the burghul wheat, add this to the mixture; it will swell during the cooking, absorbing any excess liquid, and give a firmer pie for cutting which is useful if you expect people to eat it in their hands. Finally, mix in the eggs.

Select a rectangular ovenproof dish or roasting-tin about 36 × 25 cm/14 × 10 inches. You can use melted butter, olive oil or a mixture of the two to brush the dish or roasting-tin and the pastry. Line the dish with 6 layers of phyllo pastry, brushing each with the butter and oil mixture you have chosen. Spread the filling evenly, then top with more pastry layers treated as before with butter or oil. Score through the top 2-3 sheets with the tip of a sharp knife to make a diamond pattern. Sprinkle the top lightly with water, then bake at 180°C/350°F/Gas Mark 4 for about 45 minutes. Serve hot or cold. Ⓔ

Options
Puff pastry may be used instead of phyllo pastry and may be made ultra thin by rolling it upon itself around the rolling-pin. Cottage cheese may be used instead of Feta but this should be slightly salted first. Ⓥ

CHICKPEA and AUBERGINE PUDDING

I won't pretend that this can be run up in a few minutes, but it is worth every second you spend in preparation. Also, it happily cooks for longer than the time specified so you can wait for late guests without panic. It is such a robust and beautiful dish that it can be served on the smartest occasion.

Serves four very generously or six if you also serve lots of salad and bread

CRUST
250 g/8 oz self raising wholemeal flour
125 g/4 oz vegetarian suet
150 ml/¼ pint milk
FILLING
500 g/1 lb aubergines
salt
6 tbls olive oil
2 large garlic cloves, finely chopped
454 g/16 oz can chickpeas
75 g/2½ oz can tomato purée
1 tbls ground cumin
45 g/1½ oz butter
45 g/1½ oz flour
450 ml/¾ pint milk
90 g/3 oz strong cheese, grated

Mix the flour and suet and slowly stir in the milk to make a light dough. Roll out lightly and put one third to one side. Use the larger piece to line a 1.5 litre/2½ pint pudding basin, trying not to handle the dough too much.

Cut the aubergines into 1 cm/½ inch slices, and then each one into quarters. Sprinkle with salt, leave to drain for 20 minutes then rinse in cold water and pat dry. Fry in 3 tablespoons olive oil with half the chopped garlic until quite well cooked but without browning.

Drain the chickpeas. Heat the rest of the olive oil and stir in the tomato purée, the remaining chopped garlic and the ground cumin. Stir briskly until the cumin smells strongly and the tomato purée is bright red. Add the chickpeas and remove from the heat, stirring to coat the chickpeas evenly.

Melt the butter and cook the flour for about a minute and whisk in the milk to make a thick white sauce. Blend in the cheese and cook for a few minutes. Assemble the filling in layers. Start with a layer of aubergine, then cheese sauce then chickpeas until the ingredients have been used. Put on the pastry lid and seal well. Cover and steam for at least 2 hours. Ⓥ

Option
The dough for the above recipe is specified to be made with wholemeal flour and new vegetarian suet. Alternatively, you could use plain flour and butter, margarine or even beef suet.

FISH

Fish is everyone's best friend. It cooks quickly, is packed with protein but is lean on calories, and it tastes delicious. It is so varied that you can eat fish for days and never serve the same sort the same way twice. In return, fish and shellfish ask only that you treat them with respect.

The most common fault is to overcook fish. White fish are especially vulnerable because, having no oil in their flesh, they must always be cooked in a liquid for the best results, unless you are prepared to baste them. Cooked fish weeps, losing precious flavour and moisture the moment you take it from the heat, so never keep it waiting. Fish sauces must not be kept warm for an extended period either, because the flavour will lose its richness and delicacy and may develop bitterness.

Fishmongers will always clean fish for you, but it is as well to know what to double-check; for instance, if you wish to leave the head on, it is important to make sure that the gills are removed and that the head is cleaned out or you may get a bitter taste. All the blood lying along the backbone should be scrubbed and rinsed away, too.

GOOD COMPANIONS

Anchovy, cream, curry, egg, horseradish, lobster, mustard, leek, shallot, shrimp/prawn, tomato, white wine, vermouth, and watercress.

Herbs and spices: basil, burnet, chervil, parsley, chives, coriander (leaf and seed), dill (weed and seed), fennel (bulb and leaf), marjoram, tarragon, thyme, garlic, cumin, cinnamon, paprika, turmeric, saffron, black and green peppercorns.

FISH STOCKS and FUMETS

Collect the fish trimmings, bones and heads and wash well to remove any trace of the dark blood. Remove the gills and blood or tissues remaining in the heads. Add to the trimmings a bouquet garni of fresh herbs, crushed parsley stalks, celery tops and some peppercorns. If you want a stronger stock, add some onion, carrot and celery.

Cover with cold water and bring very slowly to the boil. *Do not use plaice bones or skin and do not simmer for more than 20 minutes or you will get a bitter taste.* Strain. To produce a *fumet*, a concentrated stock that adds flavour to cream or creamy sauces, boil the strained stock until it has reduced to about a quarter of its volume. You can freeze this in cubes. Use it to give an instant, luxurious base for sauces by adding water, wine, cream, or a mixture of these.

STEAMING

This is one of my favourite ways to prepare fish, but it is also one of the most universally misunderstood. Steaming is suitable for cooking all types and cuts of fish and has the advantage of retaining the maximum flavour and goodness.

The fish to be steamed must always rest on a plate or piece of foil. If you put it directly on to a rack or on the bottom of, say, a colander, the juices will run out and into the steaming water, so you may as well have boiled it. Thin or rolled fillets are best cooked by the closed method, where you wrap the fish loosely in buttered foil and stand it on a rack over boiling water (a

---

> ### GLYNN'S TIP
> To make a court bouillon: *heat 600 ml/ 1 pint water for about 30 minutes with a little wine, vinegar, lemon juice, a bay leaf, parsley stalks, black peppercorns and a little salt.*

---

cake-rack standing in a roasting-tin is ideal for a big fish or a number of steaks). An old-fashioned way of doing this, suitable for small portions, is to put the fish between two buttered plates or dishes and to stand them over a saucepan of boiling water. It takes a little longer for the heat to penetrate the plates but the result is the same, and you can serve the fish on the same plate, which avoids over-handling. Allow 10-15 minutes depending on the thickness of the fish.

The other method of steaming is to put the fish on a plate on the rack, or in a steamer. If you are using a roasting-tin, put a foil dome over the whole pan, so that the vapour circles the fish but cannot escape.

Either way, the fish can be flavoured with herbs and spices, a touch of flavoured butter, a sprinkle of lemon juice, wine or vermouth. Crushed garlic and chopped fresh ginger (together or separately) are especially good on steamed fish. The juices which collect in the foil or on the plate are a perfect sauce. Whisk some Boursin or butter, plain or flavoured, into it for richness and texture.

POACHING

This is one of the best ways to cook fish. Well, there are actually two ways, in a flavoured or unflavoured liquid.

The most common liquid for poaching fish is a *court bouillon*, a flavoured stock made relatively quickly. If you don't have the time to make a *court bouillon* (see this page), a vegetable stock or chicken stock cube, dissolved with twice the amount of water recommended on the packet, will do. If you can't manage either, simply add flavourings to cold water. Try white wine, marjoram, thyme or rosemary, cucumber peel,

For those in a hurry: a little of the liquid in which fish is poached can be used to make up instant potato powder. Some of the liquid may also be boiled and reduced with a little double cream to make a simple but rich sauce to serve with the poached fish.

bay leaf, celery, lemon rind, black peppercorns, some unpeeled garlic, even orange rind, or some apple peel. Heat the liquid very slowly and, by the time the water is hot, it will be well flavoured. Fish may also be poached in milk, in milk and water, in wine, wine and water or cider – with or without a few of the flavourings outlined above.

To poach the fish, remove the flavourings from the liquid and gently place the fish in the warm stock. Keep the temperature just low enough to hold the stock at a tremble. Fish fillets and steaks will cook in 10-15 minutes, depending on their thicknesss.

Once the fish is cooked it may be left in the liquid, off the heat, when it will increase in flavour. Any fish that is to be eaten cold, salmon for instance, *must* be cooled in the cooking liquid to ensure that it remains moist and tasty.

The other method is to poach fish in plain water. Wrap your fish in foil with suitable flavourings – perhaps place it on a bed of pre-cooked leeks, or with just a few dabs of flavoured butter, a spoonful of cream or a little white wine. Seal the foil very tightly and plunge into boiling water allowing the same cooking times as above.

The famous butter-based sauces – Beurre Blanc, Hollandaise and Mousseline (see page 14) – are specially suited to poached fish. Serve mayonnaise sauces only with cold fish and shellfish.

BAKING

This is an ideal way of cooking large fish, thick fillets, steaks from large fish or stuffed smaller fish. Although called baking, it is always better to cover the fish or the baking dish with foil to prevent too much loss of moisture. White fish reacts better if it has been bathed in white wine, cider or lemon juice and dotted with butter, either plain or flavoured. The seasoning advice given for steaming whole fish is relevant, too. You should baste several times during the cooking. Baking takes a little longer than most methods; allow at least 10 minutes per 2.5 cm/ 1 inch thickness of fish plus an extra 10 minutes at 180°C/350°F/Gas Mark 4.

GRILLING

Although possible for all types of fish, grilling is the method I use only for oily fish such as mackerel and herring. Grilled trout or salmon steaks sound fine but the former are usually damaged when they are turned, while the latter start dry and end drier.

Thin fillets should be grilled, without turning, on buttered foil and anything larger should be turned with blunt utensils only.

Whole fish like herrings and mackerel are grilled for about 5 minutes on each side. Flat fish like sole and plaice take about the same time and must be turned only once to avoid damaging the flesh and appearance. Grilled fish is usually basted with butter or olive oil, and is served simply with a little more of the same; horseradish and lemon wedges make good partners for oily fish.

BARBECUEING

Fish makes a marvellous addition to a barbecue, offering a main course that is neither dripping with oil and fat, nor charred. Arrange the fish on sheets of foil, in a pan, or wrap in foil with whatever flavourings you prefer, then cook the fish on the barbecue grill. Fish should never be barbecued directly on the grill. The only exceptions to this rule are thick steaks of a firm fish, such as swordfish.

SHALLOW-FRYING

This is a suitable method for cooking fillets, steaks and small whole fish, all of which are usually lightly coated with seasoned flour, with egg and breadcrumbs, or (for oily fish) oatmeal. Since butter gives the best flavour but olive oil is less likely to burn (and is more appropriate for fish from warm seas), a mixture of oil and butter is the best cooking medium. Use only moderate heat and turn over just once during cooking. Allow a total of 8-12 minutes depending on the thickness of the fish.

If you use only butter for the frying and are careful not to burn it, you can make a fast, modern sauce in the pan. Remove the fish to a warm plate and pour a few spoonfuls of wine or vermouth and a squeeze of lemon, lime or orange juice into the pan. Reduce to a syrupy consistency and add a little cream, if you have any, but not too much for, generally speaking, creamy sauces should not be served with fried food of any kind. Remove the pan from the heat and stir in several good lumps of butter until you have a nicely textured sauce. You need to train your eye here, but you can usually whisk in 90-125 g/3-4 oz butter to 150 ml/¼ pint of liquid, depending on how highly reduced and flavoured it is. It is good practice to strain such sauces as you serve them.

A la Meunière, in the style of the miller's wife, is the simplest way of finishing fried white fish and is hard to beat. Lightly coat the fish in flour (as much as would come from the miller's wife's hands) and cook it in butter. Remove it to a warm plate, and add lemon juice and extra butter to the pan. Cook until it is a little brown and pour it over the fish. Smart chefs will use only clarified butter which gives a more buttery flavour without any chance of it burning. You could of course simply put a dab of a flavoured butter (see page 18) on the fish and let that slowly melt its flavour into the flesh on the plate.

Bubbly Batter This batter recipe, which I was taught in Baltimore, is perfect for deep-fried seafood. It's actually a cheat's version of the batter containing beaten egg whites that you should use for *fritta mista*, the Italian dish of succulent mixed pieces of fish fried in batter and presented like so many golden bubbles on the plate. You will find that this batter recipe will achieve almost the same results.

Beat 2 eggs with 1 teaspoon salt and ½ teaspoon white pepper. Sift 155 g/5 oz plain flour with 1 teaspoon baking powder and add to the eggs, alternating with 250 ml/8 fl oz milk. Beat until it is really smooth. Test by dipping one piece of your fish (which should be dry) to see if the batter coats well. If it does not, beat a little of the batter into some more flour in another bowl, then beat this into the original batter – this technique avoids lumps. There will be enough batter for 500 g/1 lb fish pieces.

DEEP-FRYING

Deep-frying fish is fraught with difficulties. To do it successfully, the fat or oil must be hot enough to seal the outside before it can penetrate the flesh and increase our fat intake. Fillets should be coated with a batter (see above) or egg and breadcrumbs. Whole small fish, like herrings, sardines, sprats or whitebait, may be cooked uncoated if they have been well dried; otherwise a light tossing in seasoned flour is all they need. The cooking oil must be at 190°C/ 370°F and large amounts of fish must be divided into smaller batches, so that the oil is not cooled by plunging in too much fish at a time.

Small fish will take only 3-5 minutes; thick pieces may take as long as 10 minutes. Fried fish should be drained on absorbent paper and served with lemon wedges. Deep-fried parsley and tartare sauce are common accompaniments but help push up the fat and oil content on the plate. Instead, I like a touch of horseradish sauce.

SALT-PICKLED FISH

Salt-pickled salmon, called *gravad lax*, is usually sold at a higher price than smoked salmon but costs much less to make. Home-made, it will cost you only a few pence more than the fresh fish. Why stop at salmon? The technique works wonderfully with any oily fish; if you use pink-fleshed trout it will look like salmon but be less assertive of flavour. If you can buy a whole tuna fish you get remarkable results.

Prepare 30 g/1 oz of pickling mixture for

GLYNN'S TIP

Alternative flavourings for gravad lax: *the best alternative to dill that I have discovered is masses of sliced fresh ginger root. Mint, basil, thyme and parsley are also good, and try roasted cumin, black peppercorns or coriander seed. Don't include citrus juices in the pickle or it will lose its translucence and don't serve the pickled fish with lemon wedges. You can, however, add a little 'bite' by grating some lime, orange or lemon rind over before serving.*

---

every 500 g/1 lb of trimmed and boned fish. The pickling mixture is usually equal quantities of coarse salt and white sugar with dill weed to taste. You may vary the proportions to get a saltier or sweeter result and you can use dried dill just as successfully as fresh, but experiment by using other herbs and spices as I've suggested in my tip below. The fish must be well trimmed and filleted but unskinned (see Celebration Salmon and Salmon Trout, page 69) before weighing.

Sprinkle about a quarter of the pickle mixture in the bottom of an earthenware dish and add one piece of fish, skin side down. Sprinkle two-thirds of the remaining pickling mixture over the fish and add the other piece of fish flesh to flesh but head to tail. Strew on the remaining pickling mixture and cover with plastic wrap. Cover with a plate, or anything else that will fit flat on top of the fish, and put weights on that. Leave the fish for at least 24 hours in a cool place or 48 hours in a refrigerator. The pickling mixture will become liquid. Turn the fish every 8 hours or so, basting it well.

Serve the *gravad lax* icy cold in long, thinnish slices. I don't like to spread the slices over a plate, preferring to crumple them slightly and arrange them in a ring or nest which can then be filled with something interesting such as cold mustard-flavoured scrambled eggs; poached cucumber fingers; lightly boiled quails' eggs; or mushrooms in soured cream.

GLYNN'S TIP

To prepare a raw fish salad: *dice the fish into cubes and leave to marinate in lemon or lime juice for 4-6 hours, then exchange the marinade for a fresh one. Mix in a selection of diced fresh tropical fruit and some salad vegetables. Thin coconut milk makes a fabulous sauce.*

Never use a metal fish slice when marinating fish; the acid in the marinade will cause the metal to taint the fish.

MARINATED FISH

This method of 'cooking' fish without heat relies on the action of acid on the fish flesh. The acid will slowly turn the fish opaque and, although it will look cooked, the texture will be more like that of fresh fish. Naturally, the fish used must be *extremely* fresh, which is why I have often used deep-frozen whole tuna, but any fresh fish can be used. Cut the fish into thin slices and pour on the marinade of citrus juice only 2-3 hours before it is needed. If you cut the fish into cubes you will have to let it marinate for 4-6 hours. Serve it lightly dressed.

FISH		
TYPE/DESCRIPTION	COOKING METHODS	TIPS
ANCHOVY Tiny salt-water fish with oily flesh	Shallow-fry or grill	Available boned and marinated
BASS Bony fish with firm, white flesh. Sometimes called Salmon Bass	Poach, steam, grill, bake or barbecue in foil	Fennel is a classic accompaniment; grill on a bed of fennel stalks, or bake with sliced fennel. Sprinkle chopped fennel fronds over poached or steamed bass. Sprinkle with Pernod. Suitable for marinating and salt-pickling
BLOATER, (Yarmouth) Unsplit herring, lightly smoked and three-quarters cooked	Grill	Serve with horseradish, caper, or mustard sauce
BREAM A delicately flavoured fish with flaky white flesh. Almost always sold whole	Grill small fish; poach, bake or steam larger fish	Needs a light sauce such as Beurre Blanc. Large fish may be stuffed
BRILL A flat fish, cooked as turbot although its flesh is more fragile and its taste more delicate	Poach or steam	Suitable sauces are Hollandaise or parsley
BUCKLING Unsplit herring which have been gutted, cured and smoked	Ready-to-eat cold, or can be warmed through in the oven	Buckling makes good pâtés
CARP Fresh-water fish which can taste muddy	Best stuffed and baked or steamed	Good for quenelle mixtures, also excellent in pies. Use basil in stuffings for carp, or in sauces to accompany it

TYPE/DESCRIPTION	COOKING METHODS	TIPS
COD Good for almost all forms of cooking. Cod cheeks (throat muscles) are particularly good. Steaks, fillets or cutlets	Poach, steam, bake, grill or shallow- or deep-fry	All Béchamel and Velouté based sauces are suitable as accompaniments, particularly parsley, chive, watercress. Excellent in pies and fish cakes
COLEY Has firm, grey flesh which becomes lighter when cooked	Can be cooked in the same way as Cod (above)	Excellent in fish cakes and pies. Mask its grey colour with a tomato or herb sauce
DABS Small flat fish, similar to plaice. It has flaky white flesh	Skin and fry whole very small fish; fillet and cook larger fish as Plaice (see below)	
EELS AND ELVERS Rich, firm fatty fish, excellent when smoked	Stew in wine or bake	Often served on top of bread; dishes usually include lots of parsley and garlic
GREY GURNARD Has dry white firm flesh and large head in proportion to the body, so is expensive if buying whole fish	Bake whole; poach fillets	Excellent in bouillabaisse. Serve with Beurre Blanc or a herby tomato sauce
HADDOCK This relative of the cod has firm white flesh and is cooked and served in similar ways. Usually sold in fillets	As Cod (above)	
SMOKED HADDOCK Superior to smoked cod, particularly Finnan haddock which is the finest pale variety sold on the bone	Poach or bake	Particularly good in kedgeree. Serve baked or poached with a curry, egg or onion sauce, made with the cooking liquid
HAKE A large species belonging to the cod family. It is usually sold in steaks or larger centre cuts; its firm white flesh is delicate but can lack flavour	Shallow-fry, steam or poach steaks; bone and stuff larger cuts, then bake	Use lots of herbs in stuffings and serve with flavoursome sauces
HALIBUT A large, flat fish whose firm white flesh has excellent flavour. Usually sold in steaks	Poach, grill or bake	Serve with a delicate sauce that won't mask its superb taste, but will help to counteract a tendency to dryness, particularly when grilled
HERRING Has great nutritional value and high oil content	Grill, shallow-fry or bake (may be stuffed)	A coating of oatmeal counteracts the oiliness. Serve with a sharp sauce like gooseberry, mustard or horseradish
HUSS Member of shark family; also known as Dogfish or Rock Salmon. Has firm meaty flesh	Shallow- or deep-fry; kebab	The high pectin content of huss makes it an excellent addition to fish soup or stews, fish cakes and pies
JOHN DORY Flaky white fish with the texture of sole. Almost always served as fillets	Poach, bake – (stuff and roll fillets)	It has a tendency to dryness, so cook with liquid and serve with well-flavoured sauces – even of red wine
KIPPERS Smoked, split herrings	Brush with butter and grill. Jug method: stand kippers in a jug, pour boiling water over to cover, leave for 6 minutes. Serve with butter brushed over	The jug method is traditionally used for cooking breakfast kippers. Kippers make good pâté
MACKEREL An oily fish that must be eaten very fresh	Score skin before cooking. Grill, sprinkled with lemon juice or bake	Mackerel needs a sharp sauce to counteract oiliness, such as gooseberry, rhubarb or cranberry; bake slowly in vinegar (wine mixtures)
MONKFISH Also known as Anglerfish. The tail only is sold. Extremely firm flesh with texture of lobster	Poach, bake or grill as kebabs; barbecue in foil	Serve with sauces suitable for lobster, such as Nantua, Mornay, Hollandaise or Normandy

TYPE/DESCRIPTION	COOKING METHODS	TIPS
MULLET, RED Delicately flavoured fish with flaky white flesh. Often cooked ungutted to give a gamey taste	Small fish can be shallow-fried or grilled whole; larger fish are filleted (skin left on) or boned, stuffed and baked or steamed	Serve with sauce such as Nantua or Bordelaise. Fennel is the traditional accompaniment to baked red mullet. Never discard the liver if gutting the fish; use it for stuffing or in a sauce
MULLET, GREY Markedly inferior to Red Mullet. Often stuffed to help balance bland taste of its firm white flesh	Poach, shallow-fry or grill fillets. Stuff boned whole fish or fillets then roll and bake	Serve with strong-tasting sauce such as tomato; make stuffings with herbs and olives or anchovies
PLAICE Flat, white fish with delicate flesh	Small fish can be grilled or poached whole. Fillets can be poached, baked or grilled	Serve with light sauces such as Beurre Blanc, Parsley or Mornay. Serve fried fillets with lemon wedges. Don't use bones or trimmings for stock
SALMON Fish with oily flesh. Available as whole fish or steaks	Whole fish should be poached and served hot or cold; they may also be wrapped in foil with lemon and butter and baked or barbecued. Steaks may be poached, steamed, grilled or baked	Sauces for hot fish: Beurre Blanc, Hollandaise or fennel; for cold fish: Hollandaise or mayonnaise. Fennel and cucumber are traditional accompaniments; chervil and dill are also excellent
SARDINE Young pilchard or similar young or small fish akin to herring. It has oily, succulent flesh and is delicious eaten fresh	Scale, gut and grill or bake with tomatoes	Serve with lemon and black pepper. Use lots of parsley and serve hot or cold
SEA TROUT Also known as Salmon Trout. It has oily, pink flesh	Treat as Salmon (above)	
SKATE Has flaky white flesh. Only the wings are eaten. Poaching in acidified water eliminates any alkaline flavour. Has high pectin content, so makes a good stock	Poach, then sauté and serve with Black Butter. Dip in batter and deep-fry	Serve poached skate with tart, Lemon and Caper or Horseradish sauce. It makes excellent stock and is a good addition to soups due to its high pectin content
SMELTS Small fish with flaky white flesh and a distinctive smell and flavour reminiscent of cucumber	Deep-fry or grill; bake larger fish with almonds. Often threaded whole on to skewers	
SNAPPER Has firm white flesh. Usually sold weighing around 250 g/8 oz	Cook whole, after scaling, cleaning and scoring skin. Grill, bake or steam	Serve with a robust sauce
DOVER SOLE Superb quality flat fish with fine flavour and flaky white flesh	Grill whole *à la meunière*; poach fillets	Serve fillets with herb or lemon butter or almost any other sauce
LEMON SOLE This is not strictly a sole and has a softer texture and is of inferior quality to Dover Sole	Cook as Dover Sole (above)	
SPRATS When canned these oily fish are called Brisling	Cook as Sardines (above) or fry in a very hot, dry pan; toss in seasoned flour and deep-fry	Serve with lemon wedges, eat with fingers
TROUT, **Rainbow and Brown** Fresh-water fish	Shallow-fry. Small fish may be brushed with butter and grilled. Larger fish may be stuffed and baked, or filleted and cooked as Sole (above)	Serve whole with skin and brown curd removed. Fillets should also be skinned
TURBOT The firm white flesh of the 'king of flat fish' has an excellent flavour. Sold in steaks	Poach or steam	Serve with a fine delicate sauce such as Beurre Blanc, or Hollandaise
WHITEBAIT These are juvenile sprats and have oily flesh	Toss in seasoned flour and deep-fry	Serve with lemon wedges and deep-fried parsley
WHITING This member of the cod family has fragile, flaky white flesh and is sold either as fillets or whole fish	Fillets may be poached or grilled. Whole fish may be flattened and grilled, or stuffed and baked	Sauces and stuffings with shellfish make good partners to whiting. The flesh makes excellent quenelles

CELEBRATION SALMON and SALMON TROUT

If you are catering at home for a large number of people, perhaps for a wedding or christening, nothing looks more generous and welcoming than a whole salmon or salmon trout. Now that salmon are being farmed so successfully you can buy them during most of the year.

It is possible to bake a whole fish in foil with a stuffing, but the flesh remains more moist and tasty if it is poached and left to cool in its liquid. Although the fishmonger will have cleaned the fish for you, it is well worth taking out the bones before cooking. Use a small, sharp knife to separate the rib cage from the flesh of the cavity. Cut these out, perhaps using kitchen shears, then cut along either side of the spine so that you can open the fish out. Cut out the spine. The remaining bones will be sticking up through the flesh of both sides. These can be removed easily by pulling them out with either tweezers or pliers with pointed serrated ends. Press back the flesh to expose the ends of the bones further. Run the back of a knife across the flesh from head to tail end. Pull them out following the line in which they lie or you will tear the flesh.

Cooking method Use a fish kettle or a roasting-tin in which the fish can lie flat; you may have to cut the fish in half, but that is easily disguised later by decoration. To assist the removal of the fish from the pan when it is cooked, lay foil along the length of the pan and place the fish on top of it. Surround the salmon with masses of flavouring ingredients – parsley stalks, sliced leek (or a little onion), cucumber peel, lemon rind, black peppercorns, fresh herbs (including mint, marjoram and tarragon). Cover the fish with wine, water or a mixture of the two, then seal the pan with foil.

Place on top of the stove and turn the elements or rings beneath the pan to low. Once the liquid has boiled, turn off the heat and leave the fish undisturbed until cold. If you are nervous about this, or if the fish is particularly thick, allow the salmon to simmer for a minute or so, but no more. As long as the salmon is almost cooked at this stage, the fish will complete cooking as the hot water cools down.

Dressing the fish While the fish is still in the water, trim away the top skin, fins and other nastiness and gently scrape away the brown curd; I find it best to use a blunt, round-bladed table-knife. Once you have finished, use the side of the blade to smooth down the flesh again. Using the foil, carefully lift out the fish and turn it on to a serving-dish. Get someone to help if the fish is especially big. Dress the other side, then clean up ready for decorating.

Decorating It is effective simply to pipe a pattern of flavoured mayonnaise and/or flavoured butter on to the fish. This will neatly hide any

---

joins, tears or other damage. Butter flavoured with saffron is especially good, but neither butter nor mayonnaise is very suitable when sun or central heating is the enemy.

However, if you are like me, piping is too fiddly. Instead I use slices of cucumber to decorate the fish, which is more attractive. You start by slicing an unpeeled cucumber very thinly. Poach about half the slices just until softening, then run them under cold water; this will turn them bright green and translucent. Use these alternately with the uncooked slices to make scales all over the fish. Cover the decorated fish with aspic made following the packet instructions but using at least half white wine to water instead of all water. Remember to put a slice of stuffed olive where the eye should be before the aspic goes on. Naturally, a combination of these sensational scales and some piped butter or mayonnaise would be the best of both worlds. *Photograph, p. 113.*

AVOCADO with PRAWNS

Avocado with prawns has now overtaken tomato soup as the most popular first course in restaurants. Provided that the avocado is ripe and the pawns are served in an honest sauce, it can be very good. But why stop there? As a general rule, you serve each person with half an avocado and allow a generous 30 g/1 oz prawns per serving – so for six people a 250 g/ 8 oz packet is sufficient – but the amount of prawns can be altered according to the size of your budget or of your avocado halves.

Serves two

1 ripe avocado
1-2 tsps lemon or lime juice
60 g/2 oz peeled prawns, chilled
BASIC SAUCE
3 tbls fresh mayonnaise
1 tbls whipped cream, soured cream or strained yoghurt
1 tbls tomato ketchup
up to 1 tsp creamed horseradish, according to strength
lemon juice to taste
grated lemon or lime rind to garnish

First mix all the ingredients of the sauce together and chill well.

Make sure that the prawns are well chilled but keep the avocado at room temperature for it will then be sweeter. Cut the avocado in half, remove the stone and lightly paint all the exposed surfaces with lemon juice or lime juice. Place the halves on individual plates on a small cushion of sliced lettuce.

Mix most of the prawns into the dressing and pile lightly into the avocados. Top with the remaining prawns. Lightly grate over some lemon or lime rind and serve at once.

Options

Rich Basic Sauce For a richer dressing, use 2 tablespoons mayonnaise and 2 tablespoons cream, soured cream or strained yoghurt. These richer sauces become mysteriously marvellous by the addition of a small amount of Cognac or brandy.

Bitey Basic Sauces For a slight 'bite' (and it must be no more than that), add a few drops of Tabasco or a little Worcestershire sauce; but if you have chosen a decent brand of horseradish you will find that it has quite enough sharpness already. Squeeze in some garlic juice but do *not* use garlic powder or garlic salt. *Never* include chives, spring onions, or onion juice.

Caribbean Flavour the Rich Basic Sauce with a little dark rum instead of brandy or Cognac and use lime juice rather than lemon. Grate lime rind over the prawns.

Mint and Pernod For an extraordinary-sounding but amazingly tasty sauce, soak 1 teaspoon dried mint in 2 teaspoons of Pernod for an hour, strain, and stir into your favourite basic mixture. It improves with keeping, so make it at lunchtime for serving at dinner.

If you have fresh mint, slice about 5-6 leaves of mint per serving and toss the prawns in these. Add a little Pernod to your favourite dressing and pour over without mixing. Top with a mint sprig.

Curry and Walnuts This must be made some hours in advance so that the flavours blend fully. Use the Basic Sauce omitting the ketch-up, horseradish and lemon juice. Add 1-2 teaspoons curry paste; ½ garlic clove, crushed; 30 g/1 oz walnuts, roughly chopped; 2 teaspoons lime juice. You may like to add a little more strained yoghurt to this. Grate lime rind over the prawns before gently mixing into the sauce. The crisp crunch of hot poppadoms would make a marvellous and unexpected accompaniment to this starter.

Basil and Saffron Beautiful to look at, this sauce is redolent of hot holidays on the Mediterranean. Use the Basic Sauce omitting the ketchup and horseradish. Add the juice and some of the chopped flesh of a garlic clove; 1 sachet powdered saffron; 1-2 tablespoons roughly chopped, peeled and deseeded tomato (fresh or canned); 2 or more tablespoons shredded fresh basil. Sprinkle with coarsely chopped parsley and top with 1-2 small black olives.

Ginger and Water Chestnuts This is a sauce with an oriental twist. Toss the prawns in a few drops of sesame oil. Grate 2.5 cm/1 inch fresh ginger and squeeze through a garlic press to make at least 2 teaspoons of ginger juice. Mix the ginger juice and 1 generous tablespoon of grated or finely chopped water chestnuts with the Basic Sauce and add a touch of garlic. You may need a little salt.

This version is especially good if you cube the avocado and toss it lightly in lime or lemon juice, then make layers of the avocado, prawns and sauce (in that order) in tall glasses. Finish with avocado and garnish with some water chestnuts cut into fine julienne strips, and a few prawns.

Coriander and Orange Roughly crush 6 coriander seeds per person and toss with the prawns and a little lemon juice. Grate orange rind into the Basic Sauce to give a strong flavour and, just before serving, fold in some coarsely chopped parsley. If you have the time, garnish the avocado with some blanched matchsticks of orange rind. Ⓔ Ⓠ

RUM *and* PINEAPPLE PRAWNS

This unexpected combination of flavour will conjure up visions of Caribbean islands and warm up any winter's day. Use only fresh pineapple; it contributes to the fascinating sweet and sour effect.

Serves four

60 g/2 oz onion, chopped
1 large garlic clove, chopped
60 g/2 oz butter
2 tbls black rum
2 tsps Angostura bitters
397 g/14 oz can plum tomatoes in juice
1 heaped tsp cornflour
250 g/8 oz fresh pineapple, chopped
375 g/12 oz peeled prawns
boiled rice to serve
freshly grated lime rind to garnish

Soften the onion and garlic in the butter over gentle heat. Add 1 tablespoon of rum, the bitters and tomatoes and cook for about 10 minutes until starting to thicken slightly. Stir the cornflour into the second tablespoon of rum, add to the mixture and keep stirring until thickened. Stir in the pineapple and, once that is heated through, stir in the prawns. As soon as the prawns are warmed through serve on individual beds of rice. Grate a little lime rind over the top.

Option

If you have no Angostura bitters, change the flavour a little with a dash or two of Tabasco (but not too much).

MEDITERRANEAN PRAWNS

You'll enjoy this brightly coloured and strongly flavoured dish hot or cold; but if you are going to serve it cold, wait until the sauce is chilled before you stir in the prawns or they will lose moisture during the time the sauce cools.

Serves four

60 g/2 oz thinly sliced fresh fennel root
60 g/2 oz finely chopped onion
1 large garlic clove, chopped
1 generous tbls olive oil
30 g/1 oz butter
397 g/14 oz can plum tomatoes
60 g/2 oz black olives
2 tbls Pernod
375 g/12 oz peeled prawns
chopped parsley

Soften the fennel, onion and garlic in the oil and butter then add the contents of the can of tomatoes and cook until quite thick, at least 10-15 minutes. (To save time you could thicken this with 1 teaspoon of cornflour.) Meanwhile toss the black olives into boiling water for 5 minutes, drain and put to soak in cold water until you need them. Pitted olives are better to use, of course.

Once the tomato sauce looks good, stir in the Pernod and prawns. Serve on rice or noodles, as they would do on the coast of Provence, as soon as the prawns are hot. Garnish with the olives and plenty of chopped parsley.

PRAWNS *on* TOMATO-ORANGE MOULD

Serves four

2 oranges
1 lemon
1 litre/1¾ pints tomato juice
Worcestershire sauce to taste
Tabasco or chilli sauce to taste
salt
2 × 11 g/½ oz sachets gelatine
185-250 g/6-8 oz frozen or canned prawns
a mixture of fresh parsley, coriander, basil or oregano, to taste

Cut up the oranges and lemon, leaving the rind on, put into a pan with 900 ml/1½ pints of the tomato juice, slowly bring to the boil and simmer very gently for 5 minutes.

Strain through a colander or a large sieve, squeezing the fruit when it is cool to release all the juice. Flavour with Worcestershire sauce, Tabasco or chilli sauce and salt, remembering that the flavour will be far less sweet when cold.

Soften the gelatine in the remaining tomato juice, then dissolve over simmering water. Stir into the mixture and let it cool completely.

Arrange the prawns loosely around the base of a 1 litre/1¾ pint mould and sprinkle in the fresh herbs – parsley or coriander leaf would be the best choice. Pour in the cooled liquid and chill thoroughly until set.

Option

Set the liquid in a ring mould. Turn out when set and pile the prawns into the centre. Ⓕ Ⓣ

PRAWN MOUSSE *in* CUCUMBER JELLY

You can make either the mousse or the jelly to serve alone, but when together fluffy clouds of mousse are suspended in the jelly of dill-flavoured cucumber, giving a wonderful contrast of colour and texture. It must be made 24 hours in advance so that the flavour can develop.

Serves six

PRAWN MOUSSE
315 g/10 oz peeled cooked prawns
60 g/2 oz butter, melted
brandy or dry white vermouth to taste
lemon juice to taste
150 ml/¼ pint double cream, lightly whipped
CUCUMBER JELLY
750 g/1½ lb cucumber
dry white wine (see below)
1 tsp dried dill weed
11 g/scant ½ oz sachet powdered gelatine
salt
cucumber twists and dill sprigs to garnish

Purée the prawns in a blender or food processor. Add the melted butter and process until smooth and well mixed. Flavour with about a capful of brandy or vermouth and a couple of squeezes of lemon juice. Chill the mixture until just starting to set, then fold in the whipped cream as evenly and carefully as possible.

Lightly oil six 150 ml/¼ pint ramekins or small moulds. Spoon the mixture into the centre of these and chill well.

To make the cucumber jelly, purée the unpeeled cucumber very thoroughly in a blender or food processor, then strain through a wire sieve, assisting the process by using the back of a soup-ladle to press the mixture through. This should make about 600 ml/1 pint of liquid – add white wine to make up to this amount if necessary. Put the cucumber mixture into a saucepan with the dill and bring very slowly to the boil to extract the flavour from the herb. Strain again to remove all the dill and any small pieces of cucumber remaining. Keep straining until you have a completely smooth liquid. Make it up to 600 ml/1 pint with more wine, if you need to do so.

Heat a little of the cucumber liquid in a small saucepan and dissolve the gelatine in it.

Stir the gelatine well into the remaining liquid. Add a little salt to taste.

Allow the liquid to cool. Just before the mixture sets, ladle the jelly gently around the mousse in each ramekin. Once set, seal each ramekin in plastic wrap to avoid tainting.

Just before serving, run the tip of a sharp knife around each jelly and tip on to a small, attractive plate. Decorate simply with small twists of cucumber and sprigs of fresh dill. Serve with hot rolls or brioche or thinly-sliced brown bread and butter – no toast, please!

POTTED PRAWNS

It is more usual to speak of potted shrimps, but the authentic brown shrimps for potting are both hard to buy and the very devil to shell and de-vein. This version is simple to make and is delicious. Mace would be the spice used for shrimps, but here nutmeg is more suitable.

Makes four individual servings

60 g/2 oz chopped, peeled prawns
60 g/2 oz whole peeled prawns
½ tsp freshly ground nutmeg
125 g/4 oz clarified salted butter, melted gently

Mix the chopped and whole prawns together with the nutmeg and pack loosely into individual ramekins. Divide half the butter between the ramekins and mix gently with a fork. Allow the mixture to set a little, then cover with the remaining butter. Seal the pots with plastic wrap or foil. Refrigerate for at least 24 hours.

Serve potted prawns at room temperature on a bed of salad greens, or with brown bread and butter or hot toast. *Photograph, p. 151.*

Option
For added 'bite', colour and flavour, coarsely chop some crisp watercress leaves and blend with the prawns, allowing 1 teaspoonful per ramekin. Ⓕ Ⓣ

PRAWNS and CUCUMBER in MINT-CREAM SAUCE

This elegant dish, delicately pink and green in a rich cream sauce lightened with the tang of mint, is one of my favourite treats.

Serves six as a starter or four as a main course

375 g/12 oz cucumber
30 g/1 oz butter
¾ oz/20 g flour
milk
2 tsps dried mint
150 ml/¼ pint double cream
salt and pepper
375 g/12 oz defrosted, shelled prawns

Peel the cucumber thinly then cut in half lengthwise and scoop out the seeds. Cut across into half-moons about 1 cm/½ inch wide. Blanch in boiling water for about 4 minutes, but do not let the colour start to fade. Drain and put into cold running water, which turns the cucumber a delicious translucent green.

Melt the butter, add the flour and cook gently together for a few minutes without browning. Whisk in the milk, stir in the mint and let the sauce bubble lightly for at least 5 minutes. Then strain out the mint and stir in the cream and season to taste. Stir in the prawns and serve as soon as they are heated through. Ⓠ

MARINATED ANCHOVIES

Fresh anchovies aren't available very often which is a pity for they are usually very cheap. This Spanish recipe is simple and makes a wonderful first course for a meal where people don't mind using their fingers. It's perfect for parties and buffets, too.

As a rough guide, allow about six anchovies per person. Open the gut of each fish with the tip of a sharp knife and slice along the length of the fish. Rinse under running water, then grabbing the head, pull it towards the tail — and the bones will all come out.

Rinse the prepared fish and, if you have the time, soak them in cold water for an hour or two, which will lighten the flesh colour a little. Drain, then lay them, flesh side down, in a flat-bottomed glass or ceramic dish. Sprinkle with a little chopped garlic, parsley and salt. Pour over enough good white wine vinegar to just cover and add a few drops of olive oil. Leave the fish to marinate for 24 hours or so.

To serve, pour off the marinade (you can serve it if you wish) then turn the fish over to show the now white flesh. Sprinkle with olive oil and more parsley and serve chilled.

HOT SMOKED MACKEREL with ROASTED PEPPERCORNS

A friendly starter, or light lunch dish, where everyone helps themselves to hot smoked mackerel, a pepper-flavoured soured cream sauce and wraps it in crisp, cold lettuce leaves. You don't need to roast the black peppercorns, but the haunting flavour which results if you do makes this simple recipe really special.

Place black peppercorns in a non-stick pan, allowing about 6 peppercorns per person. Cook over a high heat until the peppercorns start to brown and pop – they'll smell a little like sharp coffee. Cool, then either crush them or put them into a pepper grinder. Flavour some soured cream (unless you are fanatics, a small

carton of about 150 ml/¼ pint should do four people) with horseradish to taste and the roasted black pepper.

Skin some mackerel, allowing ½-1 fillet per person, and pull into large pieces, removing the bones as you do so. Gently grill the mackerel pieces without letting the fat run too much. Serve quickly, with chilled lettuce leaves and the peppery, horseradish-flavoured soured cream. Encourage everyone to take some hot mackerel on to a lettuce leaf, spoon on some soured cream, then to roll it up and enjoy it! Ⓕ Ⓔ

BAKED ROLLMOPS

Scale and gut fresh herrings, reserving the roes (or milt, depending whether you have a female or male fish in your hands). Cut off the head and tail and split each fish in half, removing the bones. Rub each half with salt, pepper and mustard powder.

Grate over a small amount of nutmeg and roll each half up separately, skin side outside. Arrange the rolls neatly in a preserving jar. Cover with a mixture of two-thirds vinegar, one-third water, mixed with the pounded roe or milt.

Put a couple of fresh bay leaves on top plus any optional spices such as coriander, chili or garlic. Cover tightly and put in a very slow oven (120°C/250°F/Gas Mark ½) to cook gently for about 1 hour. If you turn the rollmops over each day, they will keep for 3-4 days unrefrigerated or 6-10 days in a refrigerator.

MUSSELS with SAFFRON RICE

This makes a substantial meal for two or a starter for four.

15 g/½ oz butter
1 sachet saffron
250 g/8 oz short grain (not pudding) rice
450 ml/¾ pint light stock or water
250 g/8 oz cooked, shelled mussels (canned are excellent)

Melt the butter in a heavy-based pan with a lid. Add the saffron and sauté the rice until translucent. Add the liquid, including the brine if using canned mussels. Cook until holes appear on the surface of the rice. Add the mussels, then cover with a cloth and the lid. Turn the heat to the lowest possible setting for 7 minutes. Fork together and serve. Ⓕ Ⓠ

SAFFRON SCALLOPS on SPINACH

Thanks to the new spirit of adventure found in supermarkets, it is now possible to serve rich, creamy sauces that have no cream in them and very little fat at all. The secret is strained Greek yoghurt, used here to give a fast, reliable and impressive finish to a boldly coloured dish. It is such a simple and fast dish that you may as well use frozen spinach, so that everything can be timed more easily.

Serves four as a starter, two as a main course

500 g/1 lb frozen leaf spinach
6 fresh scallops, with coral
30 g/1 oz chopped shallot or onion
(if onion, use less)
½ dried bay leaf
2.5 cm/1 inch square of lemon rind
1 medium-sized garlic clove
1 tbls chopped parsley stalks
1 sachet saffron powder
150 ml/¼ pint dry white wine
150 ml/¼ pint strained Greek yoghurt
2 tbls chilled butter (preferably unsalted)

Cook the spinach according to the instructions on the packet and drain well. Keep warm.

Detach the coral from the white body of the scallops. Cut the scallops in half or in thirds across the grain to give slender discs. Mix together the shallot, bay leaf, lemon rind, garlic, parsley and saffron in the bottom of a small saucepan. Put the scallops into a sieve that fits neatly over the saucepan and pour the wine through them into the pan. Bring to a rapid boil, cover and steam for 5 minutes. Remove the lid, turn the scallops gently and steam again for another 2 minutes.

Leave covered off the heat for 5 minutes while you arrange the spinach on the plates. Return the saucepan to a gentle heat and remove the scallops using a slotted spoon, dividing them evenly between the beds of spinach. Add the yoghurt to the saucepan and stir until it forms an unctuous sauce, then gradually beat in the butter. Strain the sauce and pour around the spinach. Ⓠ Ⓕ

CELERIAC SOUFFLES with CREAM SCALLOPS

This scrumptious dish isn't cheap but the blend of elegant flavours and fragrances gives unexpected combinations of luxurious textures to delight the palate. You can serve it as a stunning soufflé for two people or for four to share as a starter, cooked in individual ramekins, which are simpler to serve and looks more attractive on the table.

8 medium scallops, frozen
or fresh
150 ml/¼ pint double cream
2 tsps Pernod
salt and pepper
250 g/8 oz celeriac, peeled
4 eggs, separated

If frozen, defrost the scallops in a sieve over a bowl. Whether fresh or defrosted, the scallops should then be carefully rinsed free of remaining grit and the white cut into two or three slender discs horizontally. Try not to damage the bright arc of coral. Measure 150 ml/¼ pint of water (you can add the juices formed by defrosting the scallops). Bring it to the boil, add the scallops and boil for just 1 minute. Drain quickly, but save all the cooking liquid. Butter four 9 cm (3½ inch) ramekins lavishly and distribute the scallops and corals evenly. Spoon 1 tablespoon of cream into each, then ½ teaspoon of Pernod, which should go around the scallops and not over them. Season lightly and then leave in a cool place.

Add the rest of the cream to the cooking liquid. Thinly slice the celeriac and cook it in this liquid until it is really tender. Take out the celeriac and purée it. Reduce the cooking liquid over heat until only about 3 tablespoons of bubbly-thick sauce are left. Add to the celeriac purée, mix well and salt lightly. Whisk in 3 egg yolks and keep the mixture at a tepid temperature. You can do this by putting the dish over a bowl of hot water without any direct heat underneath. Then, whisk the 4 egg whites until stiff but not dry, and fold lightly into the warm celeriac mixture. Divide evenly between the prepared ramekins, then stand them in a roasting tin. Pour boiling water into the tin until halfway up the sides of the ramekins. Bake at 180°C/350°F/Gas Mark 4. A single soufflé should bake for 24 minutes; individual ramekins take only 10 minutes. Don't worry if the mixture is higher than the sides of the ramekins before they go into the oven. The soufflés will not rise a great deal, and anyway it looks good if it tumbles down the sides a little.

Option
Use 60 g/2 oz prawns instead of scallops per serving.

GLYNN'S TIP
In a restaurant the Caviare Packages would be called something en surprise, *revealing that one ingredient is hidden inside another — and thus taking away the surprise! When you are serving the dish, tell your guests nothing and allow them to be surprised by the gorgeous effect of cutting through the snow-white outside to the treasures within.*

CAVIARE PACKAGES in VODKA SOURED CREAM

This recipe can be used to stretch a small amount of the better types of sturgeon caviare, Sweden's beautiful golden *löjrom*, or the big eggs of American salmon (which I think look and taste like fishy tapioca). This method also stops lumpfish roe from sharing their colour and makes an inexpensive dish look grand.
Serves four to eight depending on the amount of caviare you include in each package.

4-8 lettuce leaves
caviare according to your purse, but at least 30 g/1 oz
5 tbls vodka
little chopped shallot
11 g/½ oz sachet gelatine powder
450 ml/¾ pint soured cream, at room temperature
2 tsps horseradish cream

Blanch the lettuce leaves for a few seconds in boiling water, then plunge them into very cold water. Drain flat on paper towel, and cut out any thick stalks. Divide the caviare evenly between the leaves and fold into neat, even packages.

Put the vodka and shallot into a small bowl and sprinkle in the gelatine. When it has softened, set the bowl over barely simmering water and stir gently until the gelatine has dissolved. Cool it a little while you discreetly flavour the soured cream with horseradish. As each proprietary brand is different, be cautious about the quantity which you add. Strain the gelatine liquid into the soured cream and stir the mixture very well. Half-fill six suitably sized small moulds with this mixture and let them set firmly in the refrigerator. Put a package of caviare in each and fill the containers with the remaining vodka-soured cream. Chill for at least 4 hours.

To enhance the shimmering whiteness, turn the moulds out on to coloured plates each lined with a blanched lettuce or Savoy cabbage leaf. Ⓕ Ⓢ *Photograph, p. 77.*

FISH MOUSSELINES

These warm mousses are very fashionable and expensive in restaurants but not too difficult to make at home. The problem with most mousselines is that the flavour is usually pounded, creamed and steamed out of the basic ingredient, so you must choose a well-flavoured white fish such as haddock or a combination of fish like coley and cod, plaice or sole.

Serves four to six

250 g/8 oz raw white fish trimmed, skinned and boned
pinch of grated nutmeg
1/2 tsp finely chopped onion
a little garlic juice
1 tsp lemon juice
2 egg whites
180 ml/7 1/2 fl oz double cream, chilled
salt and white pepper
chopped fresh herbs (optional)
sprigs of fresh herbs to garnish
serving sauce (see below)

Ensure that the fish is completely free of skin or bone and any discoloured flesh. Using a mortar and pestle or a food processor, make a paste of the fish with the nutmeg, onion, garlic and lemon juice. Blend in the egg whites and then chill the mixture for at least 45 minutes.

Make sure that the cream is very cold and then whisk it into the fish mixture. It is best to do this by hand to put plenty of air into the structure. Add a little salt and white pepper. Herbs can be included but it is usual to leave these mousselines absolutely white.

Prepare the moulds or timbales by buttering them generously; if you use moulds which hold about 75 ml/3 fl oz you will have extra mousselines which are useful in case they don't all turn out properly or you drop one!

Arrange a suitable fresh herb sprig at the bottom of each mould – a frond of dill or fennel; a sprig of tarragon or thyme. Stand the moulds in a roasting-tin and ladle the mousseline mixture into them. Pour boiling water around the moulds until it comes halfway up the sides. Cover the whole tin with a dome of foil and seal tightly. Cook at 160°C/325°F/Gas Mark 3 for 25 minutes. The mousselines are done when you can insert a fine-bladed knife cleanly.

Remove the moulds from the oven and take each one carefully from the roasting-tin. Let them stand, uncovered, for at least 5 minutes during which time any excess liquid will be absorbed. Have some warm plates ready; run a sharp knife around the inside of each mousseline, put the plate on top of each and invert quickly.

Surround each mousseline with a sauce and decorate with a little of the same herb that you used at the base of the mould. You can take your time serving these, for both the mousseline and the sauce should be warm rather than hot.

Serve with a simple, cream sauce (see page 14). Ⓕ Ⓢ

TERRINE DE BOUILLABAISSE CHRISTIAN

I know that this is not a real *bouillabaisse* mixture of fish but it is based on a splendid dish of this name served to me by Christian Millo of the Auberge de la Madone at Peillons behind Nice. Provided that you can get the red-skinned *rouget* – red mullet – it is the prettiest terrine you have ever seen, and when served with saffron-flavoured mayonnaise it makes a spectacular first course or buffet dish.

Serves six as a main course or twelve as a starter

185 g/6 oz red mullet fillets
185 g/6 oz red snapper fillets
375 g/12 oz monkfish
250 g/8 oz cod steak
2 tbls good quality olive oil
3 celery sticks, trimmed and sliced
185 g/6 oz onion, thickly sliced
125 g/4 oz fennel bulb, sliced vertically
1 bouquet garni
1 tsp finely grated orange rind
1 unpeeled garlic clove (more if liked)
250 g/8 oz tomatoes, peeled, halved and de-seeded
900 ml/1 1/2 pints fish stock or wine and water
2 × 11 g/1/2 oz sachets gelatine
3 tbls finely chopped parsley
saffron and garlic mayonnaise to serve

Trim the fish, taking care that the monkfish has no sign of any membrane or discoloured flesh. Cut the monkfish and cod into 5 cm/2 inch-long pieces. Heat the oil in a large pan and add the fish, celery, onion, fennel, bouquet garni, orange rind, garlic and tomatoes. Add the fish stock or a mixture of water and wine and bring it very gently to just under the boil and let it 'smile', that is, barely move, for about 20 minutes. Strain very carefully, trying not to break up the fish pieces, then reduce the stock over higher heat until just 600 ml/1 pint remains. Pour off a few spoonfuls of the stock and sprinkle the gelatine into it. Stir until the gelatine is dissolved, then return this liquid to the stock and mix well.

Layer the fish and chopped parsley in the bottom of a 1.2 litre/2 pint terrine or loaf-tin, ensuring that the pink skins of the mullets are face down, so that you will see it when the dish is turned out. The fish should fill about half the terrine. Pour in enough of the stock to cover the fish and let it begin to set. Remove and discard the onion, garlic and bouquet garni from the strained vegetable mixture. Then add the tomato, fennel and celery to the terrine. Pour in the remaining stock. Cover and chill overnight.

Serve sliced, with mayonnaise into which you have stirred some saffron powder and a little chopped garlic.

Options
Serve with chopped watercress added to mayonnaise.

For a clearer terrine the stock may be clarified but if you do this, ensure that the fish is cold or the stock will cloud again.

Add a sachet of saffron powder to the stock after it has been reduced, and set the fish in it; this looks wonderful and can then more genuinely be called a Terrine de Bouillabaisse. Ⓢ Ⓕ *Photograph p. 44.*

SPINACH and FISH TERRINE

Serves six

440-500 g/14-16 oz boneless white fish
220-250 g/7-8 oz undyed boneless smoked fish
300 ml/1/2 pint dry white wine
30 g/1 oz onion, finely sliced or chopped
15 g/1/2 oz parsley stalks
1 dried or 2 fresh bay leaves
3 generous strips fresh lemon rind
125 g/4 oz spinach, cooked and drained
2 egg whites
11 g/scant 1/2 oz sachet gelatine
salt and pepper
ground nutmeg
lemon juice to taste

Clean the fish well, removing skin, gristle and bones. The smoked fish can be a kipper but this is difficult to bone properly. A finnan haddock gives excellent results; and the white fish can be as simple as cod or ling.

Put the white wine into a saucepan with the onion, parsley stalks, bay leaf and lemon rind. Use this to gently cook the white fish, then remove and set aside. Add the smoked fish to the liquid, cook and drain. Strain the cooking liquid and measure it. You should have 150 ml/ 1/4 pint. If it is more, reduce over high heat; if less, make up with water or wine.

Put the white fish, spinach and the egg whites into a blender or food processor. Work until it is a really smooth paste. Dissolve the gelatine in the cooking liquid over low heat and add to the mixture. Taste and season with salt, pepper, ground nutmeg and lemon juice, being careful not to overdo it with the last two.

Using a suitably small loaf tin, oil it lightly and put in about two-thirds of the spinach-fish mixture. Flake the smoked fish and arrange it in strips running the length of the tin. Add the rest of the mixture, smoothing the top. Chill well until set, dip very briefly into warm water and turn out. Slice very thinly with a sharp knife dipped in hot water. Serve with a chilled tomato sauce (see page 16).

FRESH FISH CAKES

Use the freshest cod and undyed smoked haddock, such as Arbroath smokies or a finnan haddock, and you'll change your mind about fish cakes being boring. There's plenty of opportunity to make the recipe your own way by adding different herbs and spices or by combining fish and shellfish, and by serving with interesting sauces.

Makes eight to ten fish cakes

375 g/12 oz cod fillet
185 g/6 oz naturally smoked haddock fillet
milk or water as needed (see below)
salt and pepper
500 g/1 lb potatoes
2 tbls coarsely chopped parsley
1 egg, separated
30 g/1 oz butter
fresh white breadcrumbs for coating

Cover the fish with milk or milk and water (the amount will depend on the size of your fillets). Add a little seasoning and poach until *only just cooked.*

Peel and boil the potatoes (or do the reverse). Dry over a low heat for a few minutes, mash then beat in the parsley, egg yolk and butter. Do not add salt but flavour lightly with a little pepper; the smoked fish will provide enough salt.

Skin and lightly flake the fish and stir gently into the potatoes, leaving plenty of identifiable chunks. Chill for 30 minutes for easier handling and improved flavour. Roll the mixture into a sausage about 23 cm/9 inches long and cut into slices about 2.5 cm/1 inch thick. Beat the egg white with a pinch of salt and brush the cakes all over. Roll the cakes in fresh white breadcrumbs and, if you can, chill again.

Fry in very hot oil about 1 cm/½ inch deep; so you don't make tide marks around the cakes; turn carefully once only. Drain on absorbent paper and serve very hot accompanied by small wedges of lemon.

Options

Provided that you remember that fish cakes are supposed to taste of fish and not pepper or anything else too spicy, you can exchange the parsley for mint or sorrel, chop up some peeled tomato, or add a very little finely chopped onion. It is specially worth adding a bay leaf, lemon and parsley stalks and black peppercorns when the fish is being poached and then to let the fish cool in that liquid. Tinned shellfish, especially clams or smoked oysters, are very good added to the mixture.

Brown breadcrumbs give added crunch to the outside of the cakes, as do oat flakes. You can cheat with instant potato. I usually make it up with milk rather than water, or spoon in some milk powder. Made up with fish poaching liquid it tastes marvellously real.

STORECUPBOARD FISH CAKES

Instant mashed potato and canned pink salmon can make terrific fish cakes in no time at all.

Makes 8-10 cakes

300 ml/½ pint milk or water
150 ml/¼ pint dry white wine
1 bay leaf
1 slice of onion or celery stalk
black peppercorns
125 g/4 oz dried potato powder
1 egg, separated
30 g/1 oz butter
2 tbls chopped parsley
a little grated lemon rind
439 g/15½ oz can pink salmon
1 tsp tomato purée
1 tsp anchovy essence (optional)
salt and pepper
fresh or dried white breadcrumbs for coating
butter for frying

In a saucepan mix the milk or water with the wine, bay leaf, onion or celery, and peppercorns. Bring to simmering point and set aside for 15-20 minutes. Strain and use to make up the potato mixture. Beat in the egg yolk, butter, parsley and lemon rind.

Drain the can of salmon and remove all the skin and bones. Mash half the fish with the tomato purée, anchovy essence (if used) and a little salt and pepper. Mix the mashed potato and fish mixture lightly, then fold in the rest of the fish, leaving as many chunks as possible. Chill for 30 minutes if you have the time. Roll the mixture into a sausage about 22.5 cm/9 inches long and cut into slices about 2.5 cm/1 inch thick. Beat the egg white with a pinch of salt and brush it all over the cakes. Roll the cakes in the breadcrumbs and chill until you are ready to cook them. Heat the butter in a frying-pan and fry the fish cakes until golden on both sides.

Options

Canned tuna fish can also be used but the paler types, often called 'chicken of the sea', give the best results. These cakes are also very good with a little garlic added and fried in olive oil.

REALLY GOOD FISH LOAF

Far superior to the usual fish loaf, this recipe is light, moist and looks spectacular with three contrasting layers, but you can simplify the recipe by making it all as one mixture. Use the very best ingredients available, taking special care to buy good white bread for the breadcrumbs. If the mixture makes more than you think you need, you can freeze leftovers very successfully.

Serves four or more

375 g/12 oz cod fillet
150 ml/¼ pint milk or single cream
1 bay leaf
6 peppercorns
3 eggs
60 g/2 oz fresh white breadcrumbs
30 g/1 oz butter, melted
salt and pepper
freshly grated nutmeg (optional)
1 tbls chopped parsley
185 g/6 oz smoked salmon 'off-cuts'
60 g/2 oz watercress
1 tbls lemon juice

Poach the cod in the milk or cream with the bay leaf and peppercorns until barely cooked. Strain off the liquid and reserve. Skin and flake the fish and mix with 5 tablespoons of the cooking liquid, 2 eggs, all but 2 tablespoons of the breadcrumbs and half the butter. Season to your taste; I like to add some freshly grated nutmeg. Halve the cod mixture and mix the parsley into one half.

Chop the smoked salmon and the watercress and mix with the remaining egg, breadcrumbs and butter, plus the lemon juice and remaining cooking liquid. Season lightly if necessary (remember that the salmon is salted and the watercress is peppery).

Butter a 1 kg/2 lb loaf-tin, terrine or deep ovenproof dish. Spoon in all the salmon mixture and level off neatly. Spoon in the plain cod mixture followed by the parsley-flavoured cod.

Place in a roasting-tin and add enough hot water to come halfway up the sides of the loaf-tin. Cover with a lid of foil and cook at 180°C/350°F/Gas Mark 4 until firm to the touch and just beginning to brown, about 10 minutes. Allow the loaf to cool for at least 5 minutes before turning out.

Options

Brown breadcrumbs give a good flavour but tend to blur the definition of the layers; perhaps use them just for the salmon layer. You could use canned pink salmon to replace either fish layer. Also, whole canned baby clams, smoked oysters or Danish mussels would be super surprises to find in the mixture, especially if the shellfish are tossed in parsley and garlic before adding. Ⓕ Ⓣ

CHUNKY FISH PIE with CHEESE SCONE TOPPING

With sweetcorn, leeks and celery leaves for colour and flavour, and a topping of cheese scone mixture, this is a million miles away from the usual fish pie. Scone-topped pies are usually called 'Cobblers', but as this is my mother's recipe I have never dared!

Serves six

45 g/1½ oz onion, finely chopped
1 small celery stick, sliced
45 g/1½ oz butter
30 g/1 oz flour
450 ml/¾ pint hot milk
1 bay leaf
1 kg/2 lb mixed white fish, skinned, boned and cut into large cubes
90 g/3 oz leeks, thinly sliced
198 g/7 oz can corn kernels, drained
a few celery leaves, chopped
salt and pepper
chopped parsley
4-6 eggs, raw or hard-boiled (optional)
FOR THE TOPPING
250 g/8 oz plain flour
1½ tsp baking powder
warm milk to mix
30 g/1 oz cheese, grated

To make the white sauce, sauté the onion and celery in the butter. Add the flour and cook for a minute or so. Stir in the hot milk and bay leaf. Bring to the boil and cook for several minutes. Place the fish cubes into a deep baking-dish and add thinly sliced leeks, the corn, some chopped celery leaf, salt, pepper and a handful of parsley. If using eggs, make hollows in the mixture and carefully place the eggs in each. Avoid breaking the yolks of the raw eggs. Pour over the sauce.

Make the topping by mixing the flour with the baking powder and adding warm milk to mix. Shape the mixture on a floured board and cut into pieces with a sharp knife. Arrange the scones on top of the pie and sprinkle with the grated cheese. Bake at 200°C/400°F/Gas Mark 6 for 20 minutes, then reduce the temperature to 180°C/350°F/Gas Mark 4 and cook for another 20 minutes.

FOOD FACT

True koulibiac is a Russian pie of fresh salmon baked in a yeast-raised crust with rice and eggs, finished with as much butter as you can put into it. The expense of both salmon and butter contradicts the dish's peasant origins.

GLYNN'S TIP

For a really rich golden look to the New Koulibiac, paint the raw pastry with yellow food colouring (see page 134), or mix a little saffron into the beaten egg used for glazing, which also adds a fascinating flavour.

NEW KOULIBIAC with GREEN MARBLING

This is an adaptation of Prue Leith's famous *Saumon en Croûte*. It is a combination of fish, a rich stuffing of almonds and spinach plus a few extra touches of the East – currants and pine-kernels.

Serves six greedy people or twelve at a buffet

1.5 kg/3 lb mixed fish fillets (see below)
salt and pepper
500 g/1 lb puff pastry
beaten egg to glaze
SPINACH STUFFING
125 g/4 oz fresh white breadcrumbs
60 g/2 oz ground almonds
125 g/4 oz raw spinach, well washed and chopped
¼ tsp lemon rind
1 egg
30 g/1 oz butter
salt and pepper
30 g/1 oz currants
1 tsp ground cumin
2 tsps pine-kernels
soured cream, flavoured butter or mayonnaise to serve

Choose at least two kinds of fish which will make thinnish fillets, such as lemon sole and pink trout. If you can include something as attractive as red mullet, a more expensive sole, or some shellfish, it will be even better.

Skin the fillets (but not if red mullet) and trim them of any discoloured flesh or bones. Season very lightly. Roll out slightly less than half the pastry to make a rectangle about 30.5 cm × 22.5 cm/12 inches × 9 inches, and cut into a stylized fish shape. Bake on a wetted baking-sheet for 10 minutes at 200°C/400°F/Gas Mark 6 until risen, golden brown and crisp through. If your pastry is fairly thick, it may need an extra 2-3 minutes' baking upside down, to ensure a really crisp base. Set aside to cool.

Make up the stuffing by mixing all the ingredients together. Spoon one third of the stuffing on to the pastry base (you won't be able to spread it, but as the fish cook, the stuffing will absorb their juices and expand to fill any gaps). Then layer the fish and the rest of the stuffing at random, contrasting the colours, sprinkling in the currants, cumin and pine-kernels as you go.

Roll out the remaining pastry until it is big enough to cover the filling and tuck under the base. Seal the edges well with a little water. Use pastry trimmings to add eyes and fins to the fish shape, and press a teaspoon over the pastry to create the 'scales'. Paint with beaten egg and bake at 200°C/400°F/Gas Mark 6 for 10 minutes. Reduce to 180°C/350°F/Gas Mark 4 and bake for a further 20 minutes.

Serve hot with dollops of soured cream or a flavoured butter (see page 18). Garlic and parsley butter is equally good. Or serve it cold with a flavoured mayonnaise. Ⓕ Ⓢ
Photograph, p. 80.

Options
Watercress stuffing Use the stuffing mixture given in the recipe but substitute watercress for the spinach.

BAKED COD STEAKS with SMOKED OYSTERS

This recipe gives maximum flavour and effect for minimum effort.

Serves four

300 ml/½ pint milk
herbs for flavouring (bay leaf, parsley stalk, onion, etc.)
30 g/1 oz butter
20 g/¾ oz flour
125 g/3½ oz can smoked oysters or mussels
4 cod steaks, 185-250 g/6-8 oz each
grated rind of 1 lemon
salt and pepper
chopped parsley to garnish

Heat the milk with a bay leaf, some parsley stalk, a slice of onion and some black peppercorns. Take off the heat, cover and allow the flavours to infuse for 5-10 minutes, then strain. Cook the butter and flour together gently for a few minutes and whisk in the flavoured milk, then stir in the oil from the can of smoked oysters or mussels.

Put the cod steaks into a shallow ovenproof dish that only leaves a little room to spare, and lay the smoked oysters or mussels round the fish. Pour the sauce over and sprinkle with grated lemon rind. Cover with foil and cook for 20-30 minutes, depending on the thickness of the fish, at 190°C/375°F/Gas Mark 5.

Carefully remove the fish steaks to a warm plate. Stir the sauce well but avoid breaking up the smoked oysters or mussels; correct the seasoning if necessary, then pour it around the cod steaks. Sprinkle with parsley, or a mixture of additional lemon rind and parsley, and serve immediately.

LEEK-FILLED PLAICE FILLETS in CREAM SAUCE

Serve this dish as a special meal for two. The quantities can be increased but the reduced sauce takes some time to prepare and would interrupt a meal.

Serves two generously

*4 plaice fillets, 125-155 g/4-5 oz each, skinned
4 tsps seed mustard
125 g/4 oz leeks, very thinly sliced
60 g/2 oz butter
salt and pepper
4 tbls dry white wine
5 tbls double or whipping cream*

Lay the fish with the less attractive sides up. Spread with the mustard. Cook the leeks in a pan with no added water until they are soft but still nicely green. Cool a little, then mix in the butter. Spread the leeks on to the fillets, leaving the last inch or so of the pointed end uncovered. Season and roll up, starting from the wide end, and place them seam side down in an ovenproof dish. Pour over the wine, cover with foil and seal. Cook at 180°C/350°F/Gas Mark 4 for 20-25 minutes depending on the size of the fillets.

When cooked, pour off the liquid into a small saucepan, cover the fish again and keep warm. Rapidly reduce the cooking liquid over high heat to a third of its original volume, then add the cream and continue heating until reduced to a coating consistency or to the thickness you like best.

Arrange the fish on hot plates, slice each roll two or three times almost through to reveal the green filling, pour cream into the slits so that it puddles around the fish, and serve at once with some prepared vegetables. Ⓢ Ⓕ

SKATE WINGS with ORANGE BUTTER SAUCE

The classic accompaniment to skate wing is the so-called black butter which should be a nutty golden brown. It is so easy to overcook and make it literally black (and thus unpleasant) that I think you will much prefer the certainty and the flavour of my version.

Starter for six to eight and a main course for four

*2 medium to large skate wings
250 g/8 oz long grain rice
rind and juice of 1 large orange
60 g/2 oz butter
150 ml/1/4 pint double cream
2 egg yolks
salt and pepper
chopped parsley
slices of orange or lemon (optional)*

Simmer the wings for about 15 minutes in a flavoured liquid (such as a court bouillon (see page 64) of wine and water). Cook the rice and keep hot. Remove flesh from the bones of the wings, and cut into bite-sized pieces. Pare the orange rind very thinly, cut into julienne strips and blanch in boiling water for 5 minutes. Drain and run cold water through them to set and intensify the colour. Melt the butter, add the cream and bring to boil.

Beat the egg yolks until smooth; continue beating them into the butter and cream then heat over a double saucepan until the mixture is thick and custardy. Stir constantly as it will curdle if it gets too hot. Add the orange juice and rind, season, add the skate and heat through, turning it over gently rather than stirring, which will spoil the texture.

Place the skate, with its sauce, in a ring of rice and decorate with lots of chopped parsley, and perhaps some slices of orange or lemon. Hot bread, flavoured with herbs, garlic (or both) would be an excellent accompaniment.

APPLE and CIDER BRAISED TROUT

It is common to cook mackerel and other oily fish slowly in a sharp liquid, and delicious it is, too. But here delicately coloured and flavoured pink trout are cooked equally slowly *over* a bed of Cox's Orange Pippin apples with cider, cider vinegar and lemon. It is one of the few fish dishes that is prepared to wait for guests; once it is cooked, you can turn the oven down even further and keep the dish warm until ready to serve.

Serves four

*4 pink fleshed trout
300 ml/1/2 pint dry cider
4 tbls cider vinegar
60 g/2 oz onion, very finely chopped
375 g/12 oz Cox's Orange Pippin apples
4 × 5 cm/2 inch strips lemon rind
2 bay leaves
black peppercorns
lightly cooked spinach to serve*

Ask the fishmonger to gut the fish and remove the spine and the gills. Leave the heads on unless you are squeamish. Mix together the cider and cider vinegar and bathe the fish in this. Leave to marinate for an hour if you can, but just leaving them in the liquid while you prepare the rest of the ingredients will improve the flavour enough.

Sprinkle the onion over the bottom of a shallow casserole or ovenproof dish in which the trout can lie side by side. Peel and core the apples and cut them into even segments – do not slice them. Add the lemon rind, bay leaves and some black peppercorns. Lay the trout on

this and pour on the cider and cider vinegar mixture.

Cover tightly with foil and bake at 120°C/250°F/Gas Mark 1/2 for 45 minutes, basting a couple of times. Quickly scrape away the top skin of each fish for the sake of appearance and serve on a bed of lightly cooked spinach, first basting with the pan juices. If you are feeling wicked, you could reverse the no-fat, low-calorie appeal of this dish by topping it with a dollop of soured cream. Ⓕ

TROUT with CELERIAC STUFFING

*4 medium trout
125 g/4 oz celeriac root, grated
30 g/1 oz roasted hazelnuts, roughly chopped
1 small garlic clove, crushed
lemon juice to taste
salt and pepper*

Make sure that the trout are well cleaned and that all the dark blood along the backbone is scrubbed away.

Mix together the celeriac, hazelnuts and garlic and season with the lemon juice, salt and pepper. Divide the stuffing between the fish and lay them in an ovenproof dish; cover with foil or wrap each fish individually. Bake in a moderate oven (180°C/350°F/Gas Mark 4) for 15 minutes.

Option
Wrap the fish in vine leaves and poach gently in fish stock or wine and water for 15 minutes.

OVEN FISH KEBABS

Now, this *is* a good idea – kebabs which aren't threaded on to sticks or skewers, and which can't be dried out by a high flame. Instead, they are baked in foil, staying moist and succulent. Bake them all with the same flavourings or give each line of cubed fish a different colour and appeal, and serve some of each to everyone. Whatever you do, make sure that you cut the fish into generous-sized pieces or it will look mean when it shrinks during cooking, as fish inevitably does.

Skin and trim 750 g/1 1/2 lb cod fillet and cut into even chunks.

Line a roasting-tin with a large piece of lightly oiled foil – make it big enough to fold over and be sealed when the fish is added. Lay the fish in four straight lines and add the flavourings of your choice. *Photograph, p. 41.*

Here are some which I like.

Tangy Citrus Add the grated rind of a lemon and an orange plus their juice and a few dots of butter; this is good with a little fresh or dried thyme and garlic.

A SUMMER DINNER PARTY
From top, clockwise: Caviare Packages in Vodka Soured Cream, p.72;
Lamb with Green Olives, p.118; Hot Summer Fruit Gratins, p.148.

STYLISH FAST FOOD
From top, clockwise: Stuffed Jacket Potatoes, p.56; Olive-oil fried eggs with mixed spice dip, pp.22 and 23;
Chili Beef and Avocado, p.108; Monkey Bread with Flavoured Butters, pp.163 and 18.

THE CONTEMPORARY PICNIC
From top, clockwise: Monkey Bread, p. 163; Chicken Awsat, p. 86;
Continental Fruit Pie, p. 144; Flat Saffron Omelette with Ratatouille, p. 56.

A VEGETARIAN and FISH BUFFET

From top, clockwise: New Koulibiac with Green Marbling, p.75; Pineapple Truffle Loaf, p.144;
Confetti Pie, p.49, alongside Gremolata Vegetables and Wholewheat Pasta, p.32; Contemporary Salad Leaves, p.57.

Celery and Carrot Include about 250 g/8 oz of finely julienned celery and carrot tossed in 50 g/2 oz butter with a little lemon juice.

Spinach-wrapped Flavour with either of the above mixtures and then wrap each cube of fish in a lightly blanched spinach leaf.

Fresh Ginger Grate on fresh ginger and sprinkle with a little sesame seed oil and toasted sesame seeds; serve with a light soya sauce.

Spicy Tomato Mix 250 g/8 oz of chopped tomatoes with 2 teaspoons turmeric powder, 2 teaspoons of hot paprika and as much chopped garlic as you like.

Fold the foil over and seal well. Cook at 220°C/425°F/Gas Mark 7 for 10-12 minutes. Serve on a bed of rice with a crisp green vegetable or a salad.

SPICED TOMATO FISH CASSEROLE

A casserole of fish is a contradiction in terms, for fish must never be cooked for a long time. But I use the term deliberately to show that it is possible to obtain excellent results by letting fish sit with flavourings for a long time. You can use just one type of fish for this but a mixture looks attractive and gives a better flavour. At least a quarter of the weight should be mackerel (with heads removed, cleaned and cut into large chunks, or just halved if they are small). I also like the contrasted texture and appearance of pieces of skate wing. Huss or dog fish is particularly good and easy to work with because it is boneless; try its more expensive cousin the monkfish, too. Cod, coley and other white fish will do well as long as they are cut into generous pieces.

Serves six

1 kg/2 lb prepared mixed fish (see above)
125 g/4 oz onion, sliced
125 g/4 oz red pepper, sliced
2-3 garlic cloves, sliced (optional)
1-2 tbls vegetable oil
2 tsps sweet paprika
2 tsps ground cumin
1 tsp ground turmeric
1 tsp ground cinnamon
2 tsps freshly grated orange rind
2-3 tbls orange juice
397 g/14 oz can plum tomatoes
salt and pepper

Lay the prepared fish in a shallow glass or ceramic dish.

Cook the onion, pepper and garlic (if used) in a little oil until soft but not brown. Stir in the spices and orange rind and heat for a few minutes until the spices begin to release their fragrances.

Tip the mixture on to the prepared fish and swish out the pan with orange juice, adding that to the fish. Mix well, then leave to marinate for a few hours in a cool place, or overnight in the refrigerator.

When ready to serve, sieve the contents of the can of tomatoes to remove all the seeds, then add half a can of water. Heat this in a large pan and season to taste. Now add the fish with its marinade and simmer very gently for 10-15 minutes at the most.

Serve at once on a bed of plainly cooked brown rice, or with potatoes boiled in their skins and quartered. Ⓣ Ⓢ Ⓕ

POREE of MIXED FISH FILLETS

Leeks form the foundation of good cooking throughout the Bordeaux wine region. La Rochelle, on the coast of the Charente, is one of France's finest fishing ports. There you will find Serge, one of the country's finest fish restaurants, where I ate a dish like this. Here it is adapted to the fish which we can find easily, and the simplicity of its ingredients and technique is belied by the superb appearance and flavour. Red mullet, so essential for colour, is always cheaper if bought frozen, and just as good for such a recipe.

Serves four generously

4 pink trout fillets (about 250 g/8 oz)
4 plaice fillets (about 375 g/12 oz)
4 red mullet fillets (about 250 g/8 oz)
2 tbls dry white vermouth
4 tbls white wine (preferably sweet)
freshly ground black pepper
250 g/8 oz medium sized leeks, well washed and trimmed
15 g/1/2 oz butter
150 ml/1/4 pint double cream, at room temperature

Skin the trout and plaice fillets but leave the red skin on the mullet fillets, making sure that all the scales are removed. Mix the vermouth, 2 tablespoons of wine and a little pepper together as a marinade and brush it over the fillets. Roll them up, ensuring that the mullet skin is on the outside and the plaice is rolled flesh side outwards. Put the rolled fish into a dish and pour over any remaining marinade; leave for at least 1 hour.

Meanwhile, cut four pieces of leek approximately as long as the average roll of fish (probably something like 5 cm/2 inches). Braise these until just tender in the rest of the wine. Slice the remaining leek very finely and sauté in the butter until soft but still bright green. Choose an ovenproof dish with a lid into which you estimate that the leeks and fish will fit neatly without much extra space. Make a bed of the chopped, sautéed leeks; pack in the rolled

fish and the leek pieces in a decorative way in a single layer. Pour over the marinade and the braising liquid from the leeks. Cover and cook at 180°C/350°F/Gas Mark 4 for 20 minutes.

Remove the cover and pour in the cream, cover and return the dish to the oven for just long enough to warm the cream through; 5 minutes should be sufficient.

Give each person a rolled fillet of trout, plaice and red mullet plus a chunk of leek. Scoop out the leeks from the bottom and pour the sauce over the fish. *Photograph, p. 42.*

Options

If you have no vermouth, use Cognac, which is more authentic in the Charente anyway. If you can't find red mullet, just use plaice and trout.

GLYNN'S TIP

Flat fish (especially sole) must always be rolled with the flesh side outwards because there is a strong ligament which pulls the flesh into a curve when it is cooked and if rolled incorrectly it will unroll.

POULTRY *and* GAME BIRDS

Once feast-day luxuries, wild and farmed table birds perfectly combine
their low-calorie appeal with every type of vegetable, fruit, herb or spice.

The only possible reason for wanting to live in the bad-old, good-old days is the huge variety of birds which used to be eaten but which are not now. I love the wildness of birds, of buying mallard and teal with their feathers on, and actually enjoy finding shot in my pheasant.

For me there is no better culinary sight than of a golden roasted turkey or goose brought proudly to the table. What greater pleasure is there than chewing on the bones of quails roasted in vine leaves, or better value than pigeon, perhaps braised with chestnuts and whole garlic cloves.

And the choice improves almost daily. Baby turkeys, the perfect replacement for the capons the EEC does not allow, are available fresh and frozen all year round; there are turkey steaks, chops, fillet and escalopes. Chickens can be free range, corn fed or black-legged and there seem just as many different cuts. What's more, chicken and turkey are considered the healthiest of all meats. Their high protein content and low saturated fat level make them the ideal base for healthier eating. And if you remove the skin the fat content is reduced dramatically – by up to 60 per cent.

To most people game birds should have lived free and have been caught by hunters in open seasons, but this is no longer so. For economy and, surprisingly, conservation, many of these birds are now farmed as youngsters and only released into the wild for a few months before the hunting season begins. This helps explain why supermarkets now regularly stock game birds – in many, pigeons seem available all year round, even if deep-frozen.

This greater availability means more people are looking for a change from the accepted way of serving game. And so they should for game chips, bread sauce, bacon and fried breadcrumbs are about the worst possible accompaniments, and any claims they make to being 'traditional' are suspect to say the least. Even if the claims

are correct this is not to say that tradition is right and it certainly isn't always the best.

Breadcrumbs, for instance, only emerged fried during the mid-19th century when iron ranges replaced open fires and made cooking in fat in shallow pans a possibility. Frying was a fashion. The same goes for bread sauce, which has no counterpart in other cuisines, despite the fact that most sauces were once thickened with bread. This bland mixture became fashionable later in the 19th century when pasteurisation and then refrigeration made milk safe to drink for the first time – another gimmick which became 'traditional' but which had no business doing so.

You'll enjoy game birds far more if you plan accompaniments to them as if they were any other meat, with a complement of vegetables or a salad. Autumn and winter root vegetables, particularly celeriac, are the best, and the bird's somewhat sweet flavour is better enhanced by the sharpness of a rowan berry jelly or perfume of a quince jelly than the insipid sweetness of redcurrant jelly; even a fresh, hot unsweetened apple sauce is better than that. More robust is red cabbage cooked with apple or chestnuts but don't douse it with vinegar or you will spoil your wines.

The ability to roast a bird so that it is golden outside and succulent inside is the first cooking technique that most people attempt to perfect – and find that such a seemingly simple task is fraught with difficulties. It's not if you remember that you are *not* spit-roasting. A spit-roasted bird is always marvellous, for the juices in the flesh flow from side to side as it turns and very few escape. When you roast a bird in a pan on its back, juices are dribbling away all the time – and basting doesn't help a jot, for the fat and juices merely run off the skin. The rule is to cook the birds on their sides. The fatty duck and goose are the exceptions and may be cooked on their backs, basting themselves as they cook. Otherwise you should follow these rules:

A BIRD ROASTER'S PRIMER

● Check that a frozen bird is completely defrosted and that there are no ice-crystals inside. Salmonella, which not only causes food poisoning but can actually kill the young, old and sick, lives on the bones of poultry and unless the bones are cooked through the warmth of the oven actually encourages the bacteria to multiply. Properly cooked poultry is always safe. Game birds and duck are not infected and may be served pink; indeed, they are better thus.

● Take the trouble to remove any feathers or stubs that remain on the skin. If they burn they will add an unpleasant flavour. If you don't want the trouble of plucking game, simply remove the skin and feathers in one.

● Cut away the bottom joint of the leg if it is still there (the one without flesh on it).

● Ease back the skin over the front of any bird to be carved, and cut out the wishbone. You can put the bone back in place during cooking but having it easily removable saves trouble when it comes to carving.

● Cut away all trussing, which is only needed for spit-roasting. It looks neater but means that you often overcook the breast while trying to cook the bunched up flesh of the thigh and side. Legs left free will cook as fast as the breast.

● Don't put stuffing into the body cavity. It does not flavour the flesh in any way and may prevent the heat getting through to the bones to cook them. Most stuffings, especially those which include bread, actually draw juices from the breast. Add a few items that will make steam and moisten the bird: quartered onion, sliced lemons and oranges, apples.

● If you like to carve slices of meat and stuffing together, and flavour the flesh at the same time, lift the skin away from the breast and spread a stuffing containing butter, oil or fat between the skin and the flesh. Re-shape the breast and roast in the usual way. Alternatively, remove the wishbone and put the stuffing into the loose pocket of skin at the neck end and secure that to the back of the bird with a toothpick or two, not too tightly or the skin will split when the stuffing swells during cooking.

● Never roast a bird, particularly a turkey, on its back. Cook them on their sides so that the juices stay in the breast. Turn regularly from side to side during cooking.

● Once a bird is cooked it should be left to stand for 5-20 minutes, according to size, allowing the juices to settle into the flesh. The flesh itself relaxes and becomes more tender and easier to carve. Leave the bird on its side and turn half way through the resting time or, even better, tip it on to its breast.

● Without the wishbone in the way you can carve directly through the stuffing under the skin to the flesh and place beautifully contrasted slices on to the plates. For a big bird such as a turkey it will be faster and keep the flesh hotter if, with a sharp knife, you remove a whole side of the breast at a time – cut along the centre breast bone and then following the line of the rib cage cut right down to the wing. Put the breast on to a suitable warmed platter, then at the table cut it across into slices as though a loaf of bread. Cut off the drumstick and cut slices from that for those who like darker meat.

BRAISING/CASSEROLING

I have recently developed a braising technique which is very effective for poultry and game birds. The tough leg portions cook in the liquid while the breast gently steams. This method also helps you serve faster.

First remove the parson's nose and wishbone. Remove the legs and cut them in half at the joint. Cut off the back, leaving the heart-shaped breast portion whole.

Prepare a selection of vegetables and brown them in oil and butter. Brown the legs and back of the bird and arrange on top of the vegetables in a casserole. Brown the breasts. Add sufficient liquid (wine, stock, water) barely to cover the vegetables, season and bring slowly to the boil. Stand the breast portion on top so that it braises in the steam, cover and cook gently for up to 40 minutes. Remove the breast and legs and keep warm. Sieve the rest of the pan contents, reduce a little over high heat and check the seasoning. Serve the breast sliced, with the leg portions and the sauce (which you can thicken if you wish) poured over.

POULTRY		
BIRD	COOKING METHODS	TIPS
ROASTING CHICKEN Oven-ready bird; that is, cleaned, plucked, drawn and trussed, with or without giblets, available fresh or frozen	Roasting: 190°C/375°F/Gas Mark 5, 20 mins per 500 g/1 lb + 10-20 mins depending on size. Roast on side, not back Casseroling/Braising: on top of stove or in oven 170°C/325°F/Gas Mark 3; 2¼-2¾ hours for whole bird, 1-1½ hours, jointed	Remove giblets before roasting, use (ex. liver) to make stock/gravy. Put half lemon and herbs inside bird for flavour; stuff between flesh and skin or in neck cavity. Never stuff main cavity. 1.5 kg/3 lb bird serves 4; 2 kg/4 lb bird serves 5-6
POUSSIN Baby chicken, 4-6 weeks old	Roasting: 180°C/350°F/Gas Mark 4 for 60-70 mins depending on size Grilling: cut through backbone and flatten, brush with butter/oil and season; moderate heat 20-25 mins, turn halfway through cooking	Around 500 g/1 lb in weight – serves 1
DOUBLE POUSSIN Baby chicken 6-8 weeks	Roasting: 180°C/350°F/Gas Mark 4 for 70-90 mins depending on size. Grilling: as above, allow 30-35 minutes	Around 1 kg/2 lb in weight – serves 2
BROILER Bird around 10 weeks old, often frozen	Sauté: joint, toss in seasoned flour, brown in oil/butter then continue cooking over moderate heat 25-30 mins, turning often	1-1.25 kg/2-2½ lb – serves 3
SPRING CHICKEN Young bird, 8 weeks old, usually sold fresh	Roasting and grilling: as Double Poussin (above)	1-1.25 kg/2-2½ lb – serves 3
TURKEY Usually killed at 16-20 weeks, sold fresh or frozen	Roasting: allow 12-15 mins per 500 g/1 lb (see text on p. 98)	Hen birds are usually more succulent
BABY TURKEY Young bird	Roasting: as Chicken (above) Braising: allow 15 mins per 500 g/1 lb + 15 mins	Around 2.5 kg/5 lb – serves 6
BOILING FOWL Old bird, sold after their egg-laying period, anything from 8 months	Boiling: 2½-3½ hours, depending on size and age Casseroling: similar time as for boiling	Cooked flesh is ideal for pies, croquettes and curries. Brushing breast with lemon before boiling keeps it white. Needs long, slow cooking. 1.75-2.75 kg/3½-5½ lb bird serves 4-6
CORN-FED CHICKEN Both French and Irish varieties available, usually fresh not frozen	As Roasting Chicken (above)	Has more flavour than a roasting bird but tends to be fatty
POULET NOIR Black feathered black-legged variety of chicken with distinctive gamey flavour; fresh oven-ready	As Roasting Chicken (above)	Has more flavour than a roasting bird

POULTRY (continued)

BIRD	COOKING METHODS	TIPS
DUCK Usually killed at 9-12 weeks at average weight 3 kg/6 lb. Called a duckling until acquiring its second feathers at around 8 weeks old. Young birds have soft yellow beaks, soft leg skin and pliable feet	Roasting: 190°C/375°F/Gas Mark 5 for 30 mins per 500 g/1 lb Casseroling: (jointed) after initial browning, at 180°C/350°F/Gas Mark 4 for 1-1¼ hours	Prick all over to release fat; roast on a rack, rub skin with salt and pepper. Serve with a sharp fruit sauce – cherry, orange or cranberry. Allow 500 g/1 lb per person
GOOSE Highly prized bird with excellent flavour but very fatty. Usual weight around 3-5 kg/6-10 lb. Young birds have soft yellow feet, downy legs and pliable yellow bill	Roasting: 12-15 mins per 500 g/1 lb at 180°C/350°F/Gas Mark 4	Prick all over to release fat; roast on a rack; collect fat in bowl. Serve with giblet gravy, see page 99 Don't discard the fat – excellent for cooking Allow 500-750 g/1-1½ lb per person
GUINEA FOWL Birds are farmed, and should be hung to give a gamey flavour. Vary in size from about 1 kg/2 lb (chicks) to 1.75 kg/3½ lb. Look for smooth pliable feet and a white plump breast	Roasting, braising or casseroling: as Chicken (above)	Tendency to dryness so ideal for braising or casseroles. A small bird will feed 2, a larger one 3 or 4 if casseroled

Note: The parson's nose, which contains the preen gland, should be removed before cooking any bird in liquid, otherwise there is a danger, particularly with slow cooking, that the chemical from this gland will seep out and taint the whole bird; ducks and geese are especially prone to this.

GAME BIRDS

BIRD	COOKING METHODS	TIPS
GROUSE Look for young birds with downy breasts and pointed wing feathers. Hens are superior to cocks in flavour	Roasting (young birds) 200°C/400°F/Gas Mark 6 for 30-45 mins, depending on size Casseroling or pies (older birds): 180°C/350°F/Gas Mark 4 for 1¼-1½ hours	Should be hung for minimum of 3 days, up to 14 days for a gamey flavour Serve 1 young roast bird per person; an older casseroled bird serves 2
PARTRIDGE English Grey or French Red-legged varieties. Young birds have pointed wing feathers, pliable breast bones and feet	Roasting (young birds): as Grouse (above) Casseroling or pies (older birds): 180°C/350°F/Gas Mark 4 for 1½ hours; jointed, 1 hour Grilling: split, medium heat for 20 mins	Should be hung for 3 days. In France, young birds (under 6 months) are sold as Perdreau, older birds as Perdrix. A young roasted bird serves 1, an older casseroled bird serves 2
PHEASANT Often sold as brace of cock and hen; hens are smaller but plumper	Roasting: 200°C/400°F/Gas Mark 6 for 20 mins per 500 g/1 lb Casseroling: jointed, as Partridge (above) Grilling: split, 25-30 mins, turning frequently	Should be hung for a minimum of 3 days, up to 3 weeks in very cold weather Roasted birds serves 2-3 people, casseroled birds 3-4 people
PIGEON Can be very tough; best casseroled	Roasting (young birds): 220°C/425°F/Gas Mark 7, 20 mins per 500 g/1 lb Casseroling: 170°C/325°F/Gas Mark 3 for 1½ hours	If serving breasts only, allow 3 per person, otherwise 1 bird per person
QUAIL Unlike some game birds, they are not served rare	Roasting: 220°C/425°F/Gas Mark 7 for 20-25 mins Casseroling: 190°C/375°F/Gas Mark 5 for 35-40 mins Grilling: 20 mins under low heat	Serve on a croûte of fried bread; 1 bird per person. Baste frequently with butter
WILD DUCK **(mallard, widgeon, teal)** Often have fishy or muddy taste, due to their marshland habitat	Roasting: 220°C/425°F/Gas Mark 7 for 20 mins (teal) or 30 mins (mallard and widgeon) Casseroling (mallard and widgeon): 180°C/350°F/Gas Mark 4 for 1 hour	Eat fresh or hang for 1-3 days only. A teal serves 1 person, mallard and widgeon serve 2-3 people Fill body cavity with orange or lemon slices
SNIPE Tiny birds, cooked undrawn	Roasting: 220°C/425°F/Gas Mark 7 for 20 mins	Traditionally served on a piece of toast, with its beak pushed through its body. May also be served on a skewer
WOODCOCK Roasted undrawn	Roasting: as Snipe (above)	Can be served whole, as for Snipe or split and served on toast as a starter

DUCK

Ducks are easy to cook because you don't have to do anything much but time them. Rubbing the skin with garlic always works magic and, even though a duck does not need to be cooked on its side, it is worth putting some sliced onion, orange or lemon inside the bird. Cook the duck on a rack to keep it above the fat, or simply pour the fat off as the bird cooks. Cut off the parson's nose, for the nasty-tasting preen gland there has a habit of imparting a bitter flavour to the pan juices.

Sauces for ducks need not be complicated. The most popular is an orange sauce which is better for being simple:

Pour juices from inside the roasted duck into the roasting-tin and set the bird aside to rest before carving. Pour off most of the fat from the pan juices and for four people squeeze in the juice of 2 good-sized, ripe, sweet oranges plus a little lemon juice and boil rapidly until a syrupy sauce results. Carve the duck, pouring any juices which have escaped from it into the roasting-tin; boil and strain again before serving. You can cut matchsticks of the orange peel, blanch in boiling water until soft, throw into cold water to keep their colour, and either add to the sauce or strew them artlessly over the carved duck. If the pan juices are slightly pale, add 2 tablespoons of sugar to the pan before adding the orange juice and boil until it caramelizes, then proceed. If the sauce is too fatty and too sweet, a drop or two of vinegar points it beautifully.

Duck breasts are a delicious alternative to steak. Trim each breast nicely of any fat which overhangs the edges of the flesh. Remove every scrap of feather or down which remains and with a very sharp knife cut a criss-cross pattern through the skin and fat almost to the flesh. Heat a non-stick or heavy-based frying-pan. Add some butter for flavour if you like, but you run the risk of it burning and spoiling your chances of making a sauce in the pan. Put the duck, skin side down, in the very hot pan and move gently from side to side to prevent it sticking until the fat runs. The skin will quickly brown and may even burn in places. Cook for 7 minutes for medium pink duck breast, 10 for cooked through. Turn the duck and pour off all the fat. Cook for the same length of time on the second side. Remove the breast and set aside in a warm place for 10 minutes during which it will relax and tenderize. Meanwhile, cook a little fruit in the pan, segments of apple and orange for instance. Remove the fruit, pour in some red or white wine or fruit juice and boil like mad, scraping up any sediment. When reduced to a syrup, remove from the heat and stir in some knobs of butter until the sauce is thick and smooth. Slice the duck breast diagonally into thin slices. Arrange on the plate with the fruit, pour over the sauce – and enjoy.

SUPREMELY GOOD HEALTH

It's common knowledge, or should be, that white meats are healthier than red as a form of protein, being low in cholesterol. Traditionally, turkey was eaten only a few times a year and chicken was always roasted but today's producers are introducing new cuts of poultry for faster cooking. Some are cuts of dark meat suitable for both grilling and casseroles (which take less time to cook than the tougher cuts of red meat) but the most useful are the white-meat cuts, especially the suprêmes (boneless breasts). Most of the following recipes which use supremes of chicken are suitable for escalopes or other cuts of white turkey. Most of the recipes for breasts of duck are also adaptable to both chicken or turkey cuts.

There is currently some confusion about the word *magret*, which is being used to describe boneless sûpremes of duck. But a true magret comes only from a duck which has been fattened to produce *foie gras de canard*, which perversely produces a thinner breast with less fat than is usual on an ordinary duck.

POULTRY SALADS

Salads made with cold poultry are both attractive and good to eat. Serve big chunks of flesh, a well-flavoured mayonnaise and one or two additional ingredients.

The most popular poultry salad in the world is renamed every time there is a Royal anniversary – it was once Coronation Chicken but I've seen it as Royal Wedding, Anniversary, and Christening Chicken. It has a curry and mango-chutney mayonnaise and can be very tasty.

Always cut cold poultry into large chunks or pull it into long, thick, generous strands. Most of the sauces based on mayonnaise are suitable for use in poultry salads (see page 17) and, as far as ingredients go, you add everything to the salad that you would put on to a plate with poultry.

Try cold chicken, turkey, duck or goose with the following:

● Mayonnaise flavoured with curry paste, mango and mango-chutney.
● Green pepper and chillies with sliced mango or papaya.
● Sliced avocado, orange segments and garlic in a chili-sauce mayonnaise.
● Sliced pears bathed in tarragon vinegar in a garlic mayonnaise.
● Fresh peaches or nectarines in mayonnaise with peach chutney, cumin, coriander and garlic.
● Cold cooked pasta with saffron and chopped basil or mint leaves.

> ### GLYNN'S TIP
> *Slices of turkey breast meat, often called escalopes, are the healthiest flesh, other than fish, available. They can be grilled or fried and as they are so low in cholesterol a smear of butter for the latter doesn't hurt at all. They don't like too much heat or they shrivel and dry; too little heat means they steam and stew in their own juices. Cook them as you would a piece of expensive steak. Eat them like veal, with just lemon juice or a little unsweetened pickle and lots of vegetables.*

● Sliced apple, orange and walnuts in yoghurt mayonnaise.
● Tomato, black olives and Mozzarella cheese, sprinkled with oregano.
● Toasted almonds and orange segments.
● Poached cucumber segments and water-melon cubes in orange mayonnaise.
● Cubed cooked potato, celery, nuts.
● Blanched strips of red, green and yellow peppers, garlic mayonnaise.

TURKEY and STRAWBERRY SALAD

This is one of my latest recipes which makes a delightful summer dish.

Serves four

MARINADE
raspberry or strawberry vinegar
350 g/12 oz turkey breast
150 ml/¼ pint strained yoghurt
150 ml/¼ pint mayonnaise
cranberry sauce, to colour and flavour
cardamom seeds, crushed (4-6 pods)
175 g/6 oz ripe strawberries, sliced

Marinate the turkey breast in the vinegar. Cook lightly, then pull turkey into generous strips. Mix the strained yoghurt with the mayonnaise and colour and flavour this mixture with the cranberry sauce. Add the cardamom seeds and the sliced strawberries and mix.

Serve in a Minted Rice Mould (see page 36). *Photograph, p. 113.*

POTTED CHICKEN LIVERS

This basic recipe uses bacon and butter mixed but you can vary the flavour and the texture by using just one or the other or by substituting only chicken fat.
A high proportion of fat is necessary to keep the pâté moist but easy to serve; if you like a softer texture, cut down on the proportion of bacon.

Makes 1 kg/2 lb or 16-24 servings; you can easily reduce or increase the quantities

375 g/12 oz very fatty smoked bacon, derinded
250 g/8 oz onion, finely chopped
125 g/4 oz unsalted butter
2 dry or 4 fresh bay leaves
1 tsp dried thyme
1 tsp dried rosemary
1-2 garlic cloves, crushed (optional)
500 g/1 lb chicken livers
medium sherry or Cognac to taste
pepper to taste
melted butter to cover
sprigs of herbs, peppercorns and chilis to garnish

Dice the de-rinded bacon and cook uncovered in a saucepan over a medium heat until the fat is running well, but do not let the bacon become crisp. Add the onion, butter and herbs and continue cooking uncovered until the onion is really soft. Add some garlic to this mixture if you like.

Pick over the chicken livers to ensure that there are no bright green bitter gall bladders attached and cut away any portions of liver that have been stained with green. Increase the heat, add the livers and turn constantly until they are cooked through but their juices are still slightly pink.

Let the mixture cool a little, remove the bay leaves and work in a blender or food processor to the consistency of your choice. You can reduce it all to a very smooth purée, leave it a little coarse or even make half smooth and half coarse and mix the two together. Add a few capfuls of medium sherry or Cognac to balance the flavour

---

GLYNN'S TIP

Your pâté will turn sour very quickly if the onion in Potted Chicken Livers is even slightly undercooked. Potted Chicken Livers keep very well for at least a week and after a few days the saltpetre in the bacon will have turned the pâté a delightful pink colour when cut, so its always worth making it in advance. It still keeps well after cutting, provided you do not leave it out of the refrigerator.

---

and perhaps some pepper, but don't add salt for the bacon has more than enough.

Turn the pâté into a serving bowl and press plastic wrap onto the surface while it cooks, to prevent an unsightly crust from forming. When cool, cover with a layer of melted butter and decorate with a few herbs, peppercorns, dried chilies and the like.

Options

If you are serving the pâté as a first course, forget the hassle of making toast and serve a scoop of pâté on a base of mixed salad leaves. Dress this with a very light mixture of oil and lemon juice, or just with oil. Alternatively try my favourite presentation for such dishes: a spoonful of vodka and a sprinkle of freshly grated lime rind. Eaten with a knife and fork, it is a much more elegant way to enjoy pâté.

Add 2 tablespoons of roasted black or green peppercorns to the onion and herb mixture.

Add 60-125 g/2-4 oz of toasted walnuts, almonds, pecan nuts or hazelnuts to the finished pâté or stir in untoasted but chopped pistachio nuts. The rich flavour is further enhanced by the addition of a few spoonfuls of walnut or hazelnut oil. Ⓕ Ⓠ Ⓔ

CHICKEN AWSAT

This stunning chicken pâté in a loaf is based on a recipe from Claudia Roden and makes any picnic into a party. It is also perfect as the centre-piece of a light lunch with salad. It is at its best if made a few days in advance.

Makes about 16 slices

1 medium-sized, good quality wholemeal or white unsliced loaf
90 g/3 oz unsalted butter
250 g/8 oz chicken livers, trimmed
1 tsp ground cinnamon
1/2 tsp ground allspice
salt and pepper
1.5 kg/3 lb free-range chicken, boiled
6 tbls Cognac (or more)
3 tbls chopped parsley
2 tsps dried mint
60 g/2 oz chopped pistachios, almonds, or a mixture
lemon juice to taste

Cut a thick slice from the top of the loaf and reserve. Excavate most of the crumb from the loaf as neatly as possible, making even, sharp corners and leaving as thin a crust as you can manage. Do not take the crumb from the lid at this stage.

Melt the butter and cook the livers with the cinnamon and allspice. When cooked, flavour lightly with salt and pepper.

Divide the cooked chicken into dark and light meat. Pull the breasts into long, thick pieces and reserve. Using a blender or food

processor, purée the livers and their cooking liquid with the dark meat and any remaining white meat. Stir in the Cognac, parsley, mint, chopped nuts, and lemon juice to taste.

Layer the mixture in the bread shell, placing the chicken strips lengthways in either a random or regular pattern according to your inclination. I usually give the breast meat a little extra flavour by sprinkling with Cognac. Once you have used up all the fillings, spread the cut edge of the bread with pâté to seal and a thick layer of parsley. Put the lid on top. If it doesn't fit, scoop out some of the crumb from the crust until it sits neatly. Cover tightly with plastic wrap and chill thoroughly for at least 4 hours but preferably 24 hours to allow the flavours, especially the mint, to develop.

Serve thinly sliced by itself on beautiful plates. Add salad only if it is to be a main course. Ⓕ Ⓣ *Photograph, p. 79.*

Options

You can, of course, use a few pounds of turkey meat, a roast or boiled duck or a couple of pheasants. The better the birds, the better will be the result.

For subtlety, use vodka instead of Cognac; for economy, use sherry or a very dry vermouth. I don't think whisky works – although it might with a stronger flavoured meat like grouse.

PARTRIDGE PATE with PISTACHIOS and ALMONDS

This is one of the most expensive pâtés to make if you have to buy your bird, but the expense is justified as you get far more, and better tasting, pâté than with other recipes. Also, the older the bird, the tastier the dish. I made this originally for a Christmas menu and it was the first time I was able to afford to give everyone partridge – so perhaps it wasn't that expensive!

Serves six to twelve as a grand starter or buffet dish

1 partridge, dressed
200 ml/7 fl oz dry white vermouth
60 g/2oz onion, chopped
125 g/4 oz bacon, de-rinded and cubed
1/2 blade mace
1 bay leaf
1/2 tsp ground cinnamon
6 black peppercorns
2 tbls brandy
125 g/4 oz belly of pork, chopped
185 g/6 oz chicken livers
30 g/1 oz pistachio nuts, shelled
30 g/1 oz ground almonds
1 pkt vine leaves, blanched and drained

Put the partridge into a small saucepan and pour over the vermouth. Add the onion, bacon cubes and spices; bring to the boil and simmer, covered, for about an hour or until the bird is tender and the bacon melting.

Cool the partridge in the stock, then remove the breasts in one piece, sprinkle them with brandy, and leave to marinate. Remove all the rest of the flesh from the bird and combine with the solids from the cooking liquid. Return the bones to the strained cooking liquid and reduce over a medium heat until just 2-3 tablespoons remain.

In the food processor, finely chop the belly of pork, then add the partridge and bacon mixture, together with the chicken livers, and process. Stir into this mixture half the pistachio nuts, the ground almonds and the reduced stock.

Lightly oil a 500 g/1 lb loaf-tin and line with some of the vine leaves. Layer half the mixture on the bottom, then pull the breasts into three (the fillet and the remainder divided in two, lengthways) and arrange on top, sprinkled with the whole pistachio nuts. Finish with the remaining mixture, cover with vine leaves, then put a dome of foil over the tin and secure firmly. Place in a bain-marie or baking-tin half filled with very hot water and cook at 180°C/350°F/Gas Mark 4 for 40-45 minutes. Allow to cool in the bain-marie. Chill overnight before turning out and serving in slices. Ⓕ Ⓣ

MOUSSELINES of CHICKEN and APPLE with APPLE WINE and CREAM SAUCE

Jill Foster, who helped to give birth to this book, won a major competition with this recipe; but only after working with me for many months did she reveal that she had based it on a recipe of mine that she had discovered before we met!

Serves six as a starter

125 g/4 oz Bramley apple, peeled and cored
1 tbls lemon juice
375 g/12 oz chicken breasts, boned and skinned
1 whole egg
2 egg whites
1 tbls finely chopped shallot
1 tsp finely chopped garlic
pinch of nutmeg
300 ml/1/2 pint double cream, chilled
SAUCE
300 ml/1/2 pint white wine
300 ml/1/2 pint chicken stock
300 ml/1/2 pint double cream
pinch of nutmeg
salt and pepper

Put the sliced apple with the lemon juice into a saucepan and cook over a gentle heat, until very soft. Reduce to a purée in a food processor.

Put the roughly chopped chicken breast into a food processor and reduce to a paste.

Add the apple purée, egg and egg whites, shallot, garlic and nutmeg and process for a few seconds. Chill the mixture thoroughly. Whip the cream lightly and gently fold into the cold chicken mixture. Butter six timbale moulds and divide the mixture between them, levelling off the tops, then stand them in a roasting tin, or similar. Half fill the tin with hot water, cover with a foil lid and bake at 170°C/325°F/Gas Mark 3, for 30 minutes.

While the mousselines are cooking, make the sauce. Put the wine and stock in a pan and reduce by rapid boiling until about 150 ml/1/4 pint remains. Add the cream, nutmeg and a little salt and pepper. Continue to boil gently, stirring frequently, until the mixture thickens slightly. Test for seasoning and adjust if necessary.

Remove the timbales from the oven, take off the foil lid and allow to cool for 5 minutes. Invert the mousselines out on to warmed plates and serve with a puddle of apple wine and cream sauce, attractively decorated with feathery fronds of fennel.

ORIENTAL CHICKEN

Once you have cut everything up, which takes time but can be done while the chicken is marinating, you can cook this in minutes even if you don't have a wok.

Serves four

750 g/11/2 lb boneless chicken meat
2.5 cm/1 inch fresh root ginger
2 rings of canned pineapple
3 tbls soya sauce
3 tbls pale dry sherry (or rice wine)
3 tbls syrup from the pineapple
125 g/4 oz carrots, cut into julienne strips
125 g/4 oz leeks, cut into julienne strips
60 g/2 oz green pepper, cut into julienne strips

Cut the chicken meat into 1 cm/1/2 inch strips, and cut the peeled ginger root into the finest matchsticks you can manage, making about 1 tablespoon in all. Cut the pineapple rings into 1 cm/1/2 inch segments.

Mix the chicken, ginger and pineapple together then marinate in a mixture of the soya, sherry and syrup for up to 2 hours at room temperature.

Blanch the finely cut vegetables in boiling water just long enough to brighten their colour and make them a little limp. Drain and cover. Drain the marinade from the chicken and pineapple and reserve. Cook the chicken and pineapple in a wok if you have one, or stir in a heavy pan over quite high heat – if it is too low the chicken will not be sealed and will lose too much of its liquid, which toughens it. Once the chicken is cooked, add the reserved marinade and the vegetables, toss lightly to mix well and heat through. Serve with rice.

STIR-FRIED CHICKEN STRIPS

The Chinese technique of stir-frying must be one of the quickest of all cooking methods – although the time you gain in cooking is generally lost in the lengthy preparation, for everything must be properly sliced and to hand before you start. But the results are well up to dinner party standards.

Serves four

750 g/11/2 lb boneless chicken breasts
2 tsps cornflour
4 spring onions (including 2.5 cm/1 inch of green tops)
1/2 large green pepper
4 tbls groundnut or sunflower oil
2 tbls walnuts, coarsely chopped
2 tbls chili paste (optional)
1/2 tsp salt
pinch of sugar
4-6 tbls chicken stock

Slice the chicken breasts into uniform strips no more than 5 mm/1/4 inch thick; if the breasts are very thick, you may need to slice them in half through the middle first. Put them in a bowl, dredge them with the cornflour, and then toss them in it. Slice the spring onions into very fine rounds. Slice the pepper into strips the same size as the chicken.

Heat a wok (if you have one) or a heavy saucepan or frying-pan over a high heat. When hot, add the oil (it should sizzle). Before the oil starts to smoke, add the spring onions, green pepper and walnuts, and stir-fry for 1 minute. Add the chili paste (if used), the salt and sugar; reduce the heat to low and stir rapidly for 1 minute. Add the chicken and turn the heat back up to high; stir-fry for 2 minutes or until the chicken loses its pinkness. Add the stock (which should not be too strong in flavour) and blend well for 1 minute. Remove from the heat and serve instantly with rice. Ⓢ Ⓣ

QUICK TURKEY CHILI

If you are going to serve leftover turkey or chicken hot, it must be re-flavoured before being put into a sauce. In this recipe it sits with chopped onion and garlic for an hour or so to absorb their flavours and it is moistened by oil.

Serves two

2 tbls tomato purée
oil for frying
90 g/3 oz onion, finely chopped
1 small garlic clove, finely chopped
1-2 tbls ground chili powder
1 tsp ground cumin
250 g/8 oz cooked turkey, in large cubes
396-454 g/14-16 oz canned red kidney beans,
undrained
salt and pepper

Stir the tomato purée in very hot oil until it thickens, then add the onion, garlic, chili powder and cumin and cook until the onion is soft. Stir the poultry cubes into the hot mixture, take it from the heat and leave for at least 2 hours.

Reheat, then add the beans and heat through very thoroughly. It is even better to cook it gently for 30 minutes or more so that the onions dissolve away completely. Add salt and pepper to taste and serve.

BARBECUED CHICKEN BITS

Either served as a messy but chatty first course, buffet, barbecue or picnic dish, chicken bits (wings, thighs or drumsticks) are great baked in a Barbecue Sauce. Use the recipe on page 16 as a guide – it covers 3-4 dozen wings with the tips cut off and divided at the remaining joint.

Finely chopped green pepper is a very good addition to such sauces; you can replace the bottled tomato sauce with canned tomatoes for a lighter flavour, or use half and half; I also like to add very finely chopped ginger. If you can't make up your mind then make several versions and let people dip and choose as they like from pots kept hot on the back of the barbecue.

GLYNN'S TIP

Use chicken wings (unskinned) instead of thighs, but cut off the tips and last joints which can be used for stock if you like. These are simple to make in large quantities baked in large roasting tins instead of on a rack. If your butcher or supermarket doesn't sell them, look in the nearest freezer centre.

CHICKEN and PINEAPPLE KEBABS

This favourite combination of flavours is always welcome at a barbecue, but how about serving kebabs as a first course? If you don't have a suitable grill for cooking them, lay them in a roasting-tin and bake them in a very hot oven.

Makes 8 kebabs as a starter or 4 as a main course
16-24 smaller ones as part of a selection at a barbecue

750 g/1½ lb chicken meat, boned
439 g/15½ oz can pineapple chunks in syrup
4 tbls dry sherry or Montilla
2 tsps minced fresh ginger
8 tbls soy sauce
8 tbls pineapple juice (from the can)

Cut the meat across the grain into 1 cm/½ inch wide strips, then into even-sized cubes. Thread the chicken and pineapple on to skewers, beginning and ending with a pineapple chunk and with two chicken and one pineapple chunk alternately in between. Arrange the skewers in a shallow dish, mix the remaining ingredients together and pour them over. Marinate at room temperature for 2 hours, basting from time to time. Grill, at about 8 cm/3 inches from the heat, for 2 minutes each side. Serve hot or cold. Ⓕ

Options

Squares of red and green pepper make an obvious but colourful and delicious ingredient to thread on to the skewers. Less usual are fresh mint and bay leaves.

CITRUS-HERB CHICKEN WINGS

Another party and picnic goody, these chicken nibbles are also an excellent way (served hot or cold) to start off an informal dinner for family or friends. No one can be starchy while eating with fingers!

Serves four to eight

4 large or 8 small chicken wings
4 tbls fresh lemon juice
4 tbls fresh lime juice
¼ tsp salt
plenty of black pepper
1 generous tsp ground ginger
½ tsp sweet paprika
1 or 2 garlic cloves, finely chopped
3 tbls chopped parsley
½ tsp dried tarragon
1 tsp dried dill weed

Oil an ovenproof dish large enough to take the chicken wings side by side in one layer. Rinse

the chicken, pat dry and arrange in the dish. Stir the fruit juices together and pour them over the chicken, then mix the seasoning, spices and herbs and sprinkle evenly over the wings. Cover the dish with foil and refrigerate for 2-4 hours. Heat the oven to 190°C/375°F/Gas Mark 5 and bake for 25 minutes. Remove the foil and bake for a further 20 minutes. Let the chicken cool, then refrigerate or freeze until needed. Ⓕ

Option

If you would rather serve the chicken wings hot, include a few generous knobs of butter when you are baking them.

Instead of tarragon and dill, use only thyme, a delicious combination with garlic, citrus and butter.

You could use thighs instead of wings as more substantial picnic fare.

BAKED SESAME CHICKEN THIGHS

The increasing availability of specialized Chinese ingredients in supermarkets gives you access to sesame oil, one of the most fascinating of the nut oils, but which must be used with great discretion. It is often painted on to cooked whole poultry to give the mysteriously exciting finish that only restaurants used to be able to create. Here it is used a little more generously in a dish that is ideal as a first course when you don't mind getting your fingers dirty. It is equally good served cold.

Serves four as a starter

4 large or 8 small chicken thighs
(see Tip)
8 tbls soy sauce
2 tbls sharp orange marmalade
2 tbls pale dry sherry or rice wine
2.5 cm/1 inch peeled fresh ginger, chopped
1 tbls sesame oil
¼ tsp ground ginger
2 large garlic cloves, minced or finely chopped
2 tbls sesame seeds (or more)

Take off all the skin from the thighs. Mix together the soy sauce, marmalade, sherry or rice wine, fresh ginger, oil, ground ginger and the garlic. Marinate the thighs in this mixture for 2 hours at room temperature, basting and turning from time to time. Place on a rack, sprinkle generously with sesame seeds and bake at 220°C/425°F/Gas Mark 7. After 15 minutes, baste the chicken and turn the oven down to 190°C/375°F/Gas Mark 5 for 10 minutes.

Serve from one large platter, or make it elegant by serving on individual plates with a small salad sprinkled with a dressing that contains just a touch of sesame oil.
Photograph, p. 41.

TANDOORI CHICKEN

Traditionally, tandoori chicken is cooked in a tall, narrow-topped oven of clay – the tandoori. But as it is now almost as popular as fish and chips these days, authenticity only goes as far as the flavouring. It is a simple mixture with only the mustard oil and the colouring being unusual. If you can't get powdered colouring from Indian shops, use liquid ones with great restraint, but see the note below. If preferred you can leave it out altogether, for it is only for presentation rather than flavour.
I'm sure there are many variations but this recipe came from Pat Chapman who set up the Curry Club, so that's more than good enough for me!

Serves four

4 large chicken pieces (preferably quarters)
3 tbls lemon or lime juice
2 tsps salt
6 garlic cloves
150ml/1/4 pint (approx) plain yoghurt
2 tbls mustard oil
1 1/2 tsps hot or sweet paprika
1 1/2 tsps ground coriander
1 1/2 tsps ground cumin
1 tsp ground ginger
little orange or red food colouring

Skin the chicken pieces and gash them all over with short but deep slashes. Rub over with the citrus juice and 1 teaspoon salt and leave for half an hour or so.
Squeeze or finely chop the garlic into the yoghurt. Stir in the oil, spices and colouring. Coat the chicken pieces evenly, cover and leave in a cool place (not the refrigerator if possible) for 24 hours, turning from time to time.
Heat the oven to 220°C/425°F/Gas Mark 7. Stand a grilling rack in a roasting-tin. One by one, remove the chicken pieces from the marinade and let the excess drip back. Lay the pieces on the rack. Bake for about 30 minutes depending on how big (and how cold) they are. To give the slightly charred finish of real tandoori cooking, place beneath a grill for a few minutes.
Serve with a salad and wedges of lemon to squeeze over. Ⓔ

Option
The tandoori marinade may be used for turkey, duck or pigeons but also for turkey pieces and for chicken wings or thighs. It makes spectacularly good hot or cold party or buffet food and picnic or lunch box snacks. Multiply the recipe as many times as you like.

CHICKEN TONNATO

This is a cheaper, cheat's version of Italy's famous *Vitello Tonnato*, an amazing dish of sliced, braised veal in a tuna-flavoured mayonnaise. It tastes equally good with escalopes of turkey breast.

Serves four

2 celery sticks, sliced
1 large carrot, sliced
125 g/4 oz finely chopped onion
1 garlic clove, crushed (optional)
1 bay leaf
a few peppercorns
strips of lemon rind
4 chicken supremes (boned chicken breasts)
250 ml/8 fl oz water or white wine
250 ml/8 fl oz thick mayonnaise
185-250 g/6-8 oz canned tuna fish, drained
toasted flaked almonds to garnish

Mix the celery, carrot and onion (plus the garlic if used) and make a bed of them on the base of a small ovenproof dish. Add the bay leaf, a scatter of peppercorns and the lemon rind and lay the supremes on top. Pour over the water or white wine and cover with foil. Bake at 180°C/350°F/Gas Mark 4 for 30 minutes. Remove the chicken pieces and cool completely. Strain the cooking liquid.
Dilute the mayonnaise with enough of the strained stock to make a fairly thin sauce.
In a blender or food processor, make a coarse purée of the drained tuna fish and whisk into the sauce. Slice each cooked supreme thickly into three or four pieces, using a slanting action. Arrange on a flat platter, then pour the sauce over. Cover and chill for 24 hours. Just before serving, scatter on some toasted, flaked almonds. Ⓣ Ⓢ

SUMMER FRUIT CHICKEN

This startling combination began as a joke but now sits somewhere between cliché and classic. Select tasty red-fleshed strawberries; the white-fleshed ones have very little real strawberry flavour.

Serves four

12 big, firm, ripe strawberries
2 tbls unsalted butter
4 chicken supremes (boned breasts) or turkey escalopes
60 g/2 oz spring onions, finely chopped
small garlic clove
4 tbls strawberry vinegar or white wine vinegar
5 tbls chicken stock
300 ml/1/2 pint double or whipping cream
2 tbls tomato purée
Cognac or vodka to taste

Rinse the strawberries in running water only if absolutely necessary, then quickly pat dry. Leave the green calyx on. Melt the butter in a frying-pan. Fry the supremes gently for about 3 minutes on each side, but take care not to overcook or they will toughen. Remove the chicken and keep warm. Add the chopped onions and garlic to the pan and cook for 2-3 minutes. Pour in the vinegar, increase the heat and cook until the liquid becomes syrupy. Add the chicken stock, cream and tomato purée, stir until blended, then simmer for 5 minutes until starting to thicken.
Return the chicken to the pan and simmer until the sauce has become a good coating consistency (this should take about 5 minutes). Remove the chicken with a slotted spoon on to a warm serving dish. Quickly strain the onion and garlic from the sauce. Wipe out the pan so that there is no debris left and return the sauce. Check the seasoning, perhaps adding a little Cognac or vodka, then add the strawberries to the sauce and warm over a gentle heat for 1 minute, gently swirling the pan – don't stir, or the fruit will break up. Pour the sauce over the chicken and serve at once. Ⓠ Ⓢ

Options
Use raspberry vinegar and raspberries; cherry vinegar and black or red cherries; blackcurrant vinegar and blackcurrants. You can, in fact, mix these up with any other summer fruit. Blackberries are specially good like this.

CARIBBEAN PINEAPPLE CHICKEN

Rum and raisins flavour this combination of chicken joints (boneless or not, as you please) and fresh pineapple.

Serves four

4-8 chicken joints, skinned
4 tbls fresh lime juice
2 tbls butter
2 tbls vegetable oil
2 tbls raisins (large stoned ones, if possible)
2 tbls dark rum (or more)
dash of Tabasco sauce
2 or 3 large red, ripe tomatoes, skinned and chopped
½ pineapple, peeled and cubed

Marinate the chicken joints in the lime juice for at least 4 hours. Heat the butter and oil and fry the joints (drained and patted dry) until nicely browned all over, then reduce the heat and fry gently for another 10 minutes. Add the raisins, rum, Tabasco and tomatoes, cover the pan and cook very gently for 20 minutes. Check occasionally to make sure it isn't getting too dry; if so, add a little more chopped tomato.

Five minutes before serving, add the cubed fresh pineapple and butter and cook on until the fruit is heated through well, which sweetens the flavour somewhat.

Taste the sauce and add a little more rum or some lime juice if necessary to get the flavour just to your liking. Serve with rice which has been flavoured with saffron or turmeric.

Option
Instead of adding the pineapple pieces, you can fry them an attractive golden brown in 1 tbls butter and sprinkle them over the chicken when it is served. Ⓔ Ⓠ

BREAST of CHICKEN with TARRAGON

The success of this recipe lies in the affinity of tarragon for chicken and for courgettes, and of courgettes for chicken. To that, you could also add the affinity that cream has for both!
The greatest affinity this recipe has with the cook is that it is happy to be made in advance and reheated and combined just before serving.

Serves four

750 g/1½ lb even-sized courgettes
600 ml/1 pint dry white wine
2 tbls finely-chopped fresh tarragon or 3 tsps dried tarragon
300 ml/½ pint double cream
4 chicken supremes (boned breasts)
salt and pepper

Cut the courgettes diagonally into long, thick slices, put them into a colander, sprinkle with salt and leave for 1 hour. Put the wine and tarragon into a saucepan and boil steadily until reduced to half the original volume, then strain. At the same time, simmer the cream until it has reduced by half.

Carefully pull off the fillet from beneath each supreme and cut the rest of each breast into three even strips lengthways. Put the reduced, tarragon-flavoured wine into a pan and add the chicken. Cook very gently for 5 minutes. Take care not to overcook the chicken, or it will shrivel and become tough. Take the pan off the heat, but leave the chicken in the liquid.

Rinse and drain the courgettes and cook in boiling water for 3 minutes, or until they just begin to soften. (If your courgettes are small and young, they may take only a minute or two.) Drain, then add to the reduced cream.

At this stage the chicken and courgette mixtures can both be covered with plastic film and left to stand until required. To serve, heat both separately in their pans over very gentle heat. Take the chicken from the pan using a slotted spoon and add to the courgette mixture. Stir in enough of the tarragon wine to make the sauce into the consistency you like, then check the seasoning and add salt and pepper as necessary.

This is good served on a bed of plain rice, or with plain boiled potatoes, or even with a baked potato. I have served the chicken with a salad of chicory and diced beetroot in a simple walnut-oil dressing. It would be delicious with almost any light salad, but I would omit the dressing if serving wine with the dish.

CHICKEN SUPREMES with CELERIAC and GRAPES

Pretty colours and contrasted textures make these the epitome of modern eating – fat-free and exciting.

Serves four

4 chicken supremes (boned breasts) or turkey escalopes, 125-185 g/4-6 oz each
2 tsps dry white vermouth
12 large fresh spinach leaves
250 g/8 oz seedless Muscatel grapes
90 g/3 oz grated raw celeriac
1 fresh lime
plain thick yoghurt

Skin the breasts and cut out any pieces of the wingbone which may be left attached. Brush the breasts with the vermouth. Blanch the spinach leaves until wilting, then plunge into cold water. Halve the grapes and, if you have the time, peel them also.

Cut out the spines of the spinach leaves and

arrange in four overlapping pairs, smooth side down. Arrange a bed of the celeriac in the centre of each pair of leaves and grate lime rind directly over the top. Divide the grapes over the beds of celeriac, cover with the prepared breasts, again smooth side down. Cover each parcel with one of the remaining spinach leaves, turn back the lower leaves to make neat parcels, and turn over.

Arrange the parcels on a flat, thin heatproof plate or dish, cover, and steam for about 25 minutes. The easiest way to do this is to stand the dish on a rack in a roasting-tin of boiling water on top of a cooker and to cover the whole pan with a dome of foil.

Serve with a dollop of yoghurt into which you have mixed some of the juice from the lime. Ⓢ

Options
You may like to add yoghurt to the celeriac to make a wetter topping to the chicken, or to spread a little softened butter on the spinach before the celeriac to give a richer flavour.

BAKED CHICKEN SUPREME with COURGETTE CRUST

A marvellous example of the modern way of cooking without using butter or animal fat. The small amount of olive oil is essential for flavour, although you could substitute sunflower or safflower oil. Increase the ingredients in proportion for extra servings.

Serves one

125-185 g/4-6 oz red or green pepper, celery and carrot, cut into thin matchsticks
onion, garlic or ginger juice (see below)
1 chicken supreme (boneless, skinless breast)
salt and pepper
olive oil
125 g/4 oz courgettes
lime or lemon juice (optional)

Blanch the matchsticks of mixed vegetables for a few minutes in boiling water and drain. Flavour lightly with onion, garlic or fresh green ginger juice, made by pressing the vegetables through a garlic crusher.

Make a bed of the vegetables in an ovenproof dish and put the supreme on it. Season, and smear with a little olive oil. Grate the courgettes coarsely and flavour lightly with more of the onion, garlic or ginger juice. Shape this courgette mixture over the chicken to make a complete coating. Bake at 180°C/350°F/Gas Mark 4 for about 25 minutes or until the supreme is cooked through.

DUCK BREASTS with FRESH PEAR and CUMIN

Boneless supremes of duck are increasingly available and make a superb main course. An added advantage is that the duck *must* be cooked in advance and left to sit for 10 minutes or longer, which tenderizes it.

Serves two

2 duck breasts, boned
Poire William
1 tsp ground cumin
1 small garlic clove, crushed
1 tsp whole cumin seeds
1 fresh pear (Williams are best)
60 g/2 oz onion, chopped
300 ml/1/2 pint white wine
125 g/4 oz butter

Slash through the fat of the skin side of the duck breasts, making a lattice pattern. Rub in on both sides 2 capfuls of Poire William, the ground cumin and garlic, and leave to marinate at room temperature for at least an hour.

Heat a non-stick pan and toss in the cumin seeds; keep stirring until they have toasted nicely. Immediately remove them from the pan and keep to one side.

Peel the pear, cut it in half lengthways, remove the core and, using a thin, sharp knife, slice thinly from just inside the stalk end to the bottom, leaving the slices joined at the stalk end. Push gently to make a fan shape. Lay in a shallow, heatproof dish, pour a capful of Poire William over each half and leave to marinate.

Heat a heavy pan until really hot and put in the duck breasts skin side down. Cook for 7-10 minutes without turning, depending on how well cooked you like duck. Drain off most of the fat and turn the duck over to cook for an equal amount of time.

Put the breasts on to a warmed plate and leave in a warm place (not an oven) for 10-15 minutes, during which time they will colour evenly and tenderize. Put the pear, still in the dish, under a medium grill to cook through. Into the pan put the onion, white wine and a little Poire William to taste, and simmer at

gentle heat until reduced to about 6 tablespoons. Cut up the butter into chunks and stir in, off the heat. Keep warm over very low heat until you are ready to serve.

Put a duck breast on to the side of a warm plate, and place the hot fanned pear to one side. Pour the sauce through a sieve over the pear to coat it and flood the plate around the duck. Sprinkle the dish with the toasted cumin seeds, using rather more on the pear than on the sauce. Ⓢ *Photograph, p. 149.*

Options

Pear and Pernod Marinate the breasts in 4 tablespoons of Pernod and 4 tablespoons of water or white wine. Spoon an extra 2 tablespoons of Pernod over the prepared pears. Make a sauce by heating the marinade in the pan and whisking in some cold butter.
Mustard, Blackcurrants and Mint For each duck breast, squeeze a little garlic into the pan, and 2 capfuls of vodka. When bubbling, add 2 teaspoons of Dijon or seed mustard and 1 tablespoon of fresh or de-frosted blackcurrants. Serve soon after the blackcurrants are heated through, decorated with some fresh mint leaves.

CARAMELIZED APPLE and CHICKEN CASSEROLE

Yes, this is another chicken and apple recipe but this is probably the simplest to cook; the caramel colour and flavour add a lot of interest without the need to add cream (unless, of course, you just happen to have some).

Serves four to six

1.5-2 kg/3-4 lb roasting chicken, jointed
300 ml/1/2 pint dry cider
1 tsp grated lemon rind
butter or oil for frying
250 g/8 oz Bramley apples, thinly sliced
60-125 g/2-4 oz onion, thinly sliced
1 tbls white or golden granulated sugar

Marinate the chicken joints in the cider and lemon rind for at least 2 hours. Drain and pat dry. Brown the pieces lightly in butter or oil.

Put the apple and onion into a heavy saucepan or casserole and pour on a little of the cider to stop the apple from turning brown. Arrange the chicken pieces on top.

Put the sugar into a small saucepan and cook over a moderate heat until it turns a rich brown. Pour in the remaining cider and stir until the caramel has dissolved. Pour this liquid over the chicken, cover and cook gently for about 1 hour, or until tender. The casserole may be cooked in a low oven (150°C/300°F/Gas Mark 2).

Option

For a special occasion you could reduce the

cooking liquid, add cream and reduce still further or stir in either fromage blanc or a strained thick plain yoghurt.

WARM PIGEON and PEAR SALAD

Serves four as a starter

Cut the 4 breasts from 2 pigeons and skin them. Peel a ripe pear, cut it in half and core it; then slice into matchsticks. Leave the pear to steep in a little tarragon vinegar for at least 30 minutes. Put 8 tablespoons of oil into a pan (safflower or sunflower oils are best and the addition of a little walnut or hazelnut oil would be excellent). Add a good nut of butter for extra flavour and a few slivers of garlic if you like it. Cook the breasts gently for about 4 minutes on each side so that they are still a little pink in the middle; remove and leave to set before slicing. Put the pears into the cooking liquid to warm through.

Slice the pigeon breasts thinly, lengthways, and lay them over salads arranged on individual flat plates. The salad should be of leaves of varying types, colours and textures such as endive, watercress, crisp lettuce and chicory. Pile the warmed pears neatly in the middle of each arrangement.

Add a little more of the tarragon vinegar in which the pears were steeped to the pan until the dressing is sharp enough for you. Bring to the boil to emulsify it slightly and spoon this dressing carefully over the pigeon breasts and the pears before sprinkling the remainder over the salad itself. Serve at once. Ⓕ

Option

Some walnut halves or some cloves of unpeeled garlic, which have been boiled until very tender, might also be added.

> ### GLYNN'S TIP
>
> *It is fashionable to serve only the breast of pigeon, but these shrink alarmingly if taken from the carcass before cooking. Better to cook on the bone and then slice off once they have rested and set.*
>
> *The simplest way to cook pigeons for one or two is to cut them down the back and open them out flat. They can then be grilled. The back and leg flesh of any bird is scanty and tends to be bitter, so cut them off and leave the heart-shaped breast on the bone.*

GARLIC-BRAISED PIGEONS with CHESTNUTS

Almost all my favourite autumnal flavours are combined in this dish, which has the distinction of *not* using bacon as a base; you'll find that dried chestnuts give a wonderful smoky flavour.

The legs and the backs of the pigeons are casseroled in wine while the breasts braise above them, so all the flavour possible is retained.

Serves four

4 pigeons
butter or butter and oil for frying
60 g/2 oz onion, finely sliced
125 g/4 oz celeriac, cubed
8 whole garlic cloves (unpeeled)
60 g/2 oz dried chestnuts
300 ml/1/2 pint robust red wine
salt

Remove the legs of the pigeons and then, cutting along the base of the rib cage, separate the backs from the breasts. Brown the breasts in butter, or a mixture of butter and oil, and remove them from the pan. Brown the legs and backs and set aside. Add the onion and cook gently until golden.

Lay the pigeon backs on the bottom of a heavy-based saucepan into which they will just fit. Scatter over the onion, celeriac, whole garlic cloves and the dried chestnuts.

Arrange the eight pigeon legs in a layer and finally place the pigeon breasts on top, flesh side up. De-glaze the original pan with the red wine and pour this liquid over the pigeons. Salt lightly, cover tightly and simmer for 40-45 minutes.

Serve each guest a whole breast and two legs surrounded by celeriac and chestnuts; the garlic will be soft enough to squash into the juices. I like to serve root vegetables with these pigeons – swede, turnip, carrot or more celeriac – and plain boiled or steamed potatoes garnished with lots of parsley. Ⓢ

ROAST PARTRIDGE with YOUNG CABBAGE

Partridge is one of the sweetest of game birds but is now one of the rarest. The classic way to present them was to cook an old bird with cabbage, discard the carcass and serve the flavoured cabbage with a young roast partridge. Who has the budget to do that nowadays? But the combination of partridge and cabbage is so good that I have developed this recipe; it combines the best of traditional and modern techniques, and gives you a much better flavour and more of the bird to enjoy.

Serves four

2 young partridges
4 tbls walnut oil
3 tbls butter
60 g/2 oz leek, shallot or onion, chopped
60 g/2 oz carrot, chopped
300 ml/1/2 pint light red wine
2 ripe pears
oil and butter for grilling
375 g/12 oz young cabbage, thinly sliced
30 g/1 oz extra butter to finish the sauce

Take the legs from each partridge and divide them into two. Chop off the claws if they are still attached. Cut the backs off the birds but leave the wings. The separated breasts will look like two plump, winged hearts.

Heat 2 tablespoons of oil and 2 tablespoons of butter and brown the legs and backs, then remove. Cook the leek and carrot until they, too, have some colour. Add the red wine; return the legs and backs and cook gently until the legs are tender (about 35 minutes, depending on the age of the birds). Strain and reserve the cooking liquid. Reserve the leg pieces but discard the backs and the vegetables.

Roast the breasts at 190°C/375°F/Gas Mark 5 for 20 minutes. When cooked, put them to rest for 10 minutes in a warm place. Meanwhile, halve and core the pear, peel it and cut it into a fan shape. Dribble over a little extra oil and dot with butter. Place the halves under the grill to warm through. Heat the remaining 2 tablespoons of walnut oil and 1 tablespoon butter in a large pan and when very hot stir in the cabbage and keep stirring until wilted but still crisp and green. Heat the legs in the reserved liquid.

To serve, make shallow mounds of cabbage in the centre of four large, hot plates. Put the partridge breasts on top and arrange the pieces of leg on the cabbage. Whisk the extra butter into the sauce to thicken it and pour it on to the cabbage. Place a pear half on each plate and serve at once. Ⓢ

BAKED PHEASANT in GIN and JUNIPER CREAM

When serving four people with pheasant on special occasions, I find it simpler and more reliable to carve two smaller hen birds than one large cock. By removing the skin and cooking the birds under foil so that they steam-bake, you can serve a creamy sauce, something you'd never do had they been roasted.

Serves four

2 hen pheasants, dressed but untrussed
2 large garlic cloves, halved
150 ml/1/4 pint gin
6 juniper berries, lightly crushed
1 lemon, halved
2 tbls butter
150 ml/1/4 pint double or soured cream

Remove the skin from the birds and rub all over with the cut garlic cloves. Put a garlic half inside each one. Heat the gin a little, ignite and pour just a few spoonfuls over each bird. Quickly add the juniper berries to the remaining warm gin and set both the birds and the gin in a warm place for an hour or so for the flavours to develop.

Put half a lemon inside each bird and smear the breasts with the butter. Place the birds on their sides in a roasting-tin and cover with a dome of foil sealed tightly around the edges. Roast at 220°C/425°F/Gas Mark 7 for 30 minutes, turning after 15 minutes and basting with half the juniper-infused gin. Remove the foil, turn the birds on their backs and baste with the remaining gin before cooking for a further 10 minutes. Turn the birds on to their breasts on a warm plate and allow to stand for at least 10 minutes. Meanwhile, put the roasting-tin over direct heat and reduce the juices until brown and syrupy. Stir in the double or soured cream.

To serve, cut the whole breasts off the carcasses, or simply cut the birds in half with kitchen shears. Strain the sauce over the birds and serve with colourful vegetables; a pilaf of toasted barley adds the right earthy note. Ⓢ

ROAST GROUSE with RASPBERRIES

Allow half a grouse per person. Remove the skin of each bird altogether. Put about 2 teaspoonfuls of fresh or de-frosted raspberries into each bird. Lay the birds on their sides in a roasting-tin and drape thin slices of smoked streaky bacon over the breasts, leaving the legs exposed.

Roast at 200°C/400°F/Gas Mark 6 for 15 minutes; turn the birds on to the other side for another 15 minutes, transferring the bacon.

Remove the tin from the oven and stand the birds on the front of their breasts for at least 15 minutes in a warm place (not the oven). This gives even, pink flesh; if you want the flesh a little darker, allow 3-4 minutes extra on each side in the oven.

Now de-glaze the pan by heating it on top of the stove until the cooking juices are boiling. Add 2 teaspoons of raspberry vinegar or *framboise eau-de-vie* per bird little by little and scrape up all the brown bits. Let it cook for 2 minutes before testing to see if more flavouring is needed. Just before serving, scatter in half a dozen raspberries per person and let them just heat through without cooking, and do not crush them by stirring.

To serve, use rugged kitchen scissors or poultry shears (an excellent Christmas gift for a cook) to cut along the backs of the birds, then through the breast bone to make two attractive halves. I take the legs off and serve them as a second helping. Arrange the breasts neatly towards the edges of warmed plates, spoon the gravy and raspberries to one side of the birds and arrange the raspberries from inside the birds on the other side. Put the bacon on the opposite side of each plate. Serve a garlicky purée of celeriac, or *haricots verts* (which go marvellously with raspberries and raspberry vinegar), thinly sliced parsnips or turnips. Swedes, lightly buttered and topped with a prepared mustard, also contrast well.

This dish looks and tastes even better with several slices of Chestnut Polenta (see below) made with raspberry vinegar or *eau-de-vie*. Most people eat only half a grouse but if the birds are small or appetites large, cook one per person. Ⓕ

Options

Smear butter on to the birds rather than using bacon and put a teaspoonful in each bird, too.

CHESTNUT POLENTA

Real *polenta* is a speciality of the Veneto region around Venice. It is a mush of fairly coarse cornmeal which is baked in the oven or sliced and deep-fried. This chestnut version may be adapted to any game bird or meat you are cooking by changing the flavouring liquid.

Serves four to six

250 g/8 oz can unsweetened chestnut purée
2 tbls fruit juice, liqueur, vinegar, brandy or black rum for flavouring
2 tsps cornflour or arrowroot
2 large eggs

Mash up the chestnut purée with the flavouring liquid; if using orange or lemon juice, grate in some rind too. Orange liqueurs are excellent additions but you can also use brandies or black rum (especially good with goose). The sharper

eaux-de-vie, unsweetened, are all interchangeable. Test and taste – the liquid must not dominate or the chestnut flavour will be lost during cooking.

Beat in the cornflour or arrowroot and the eggs. Butter a small ovenproof dish in which the polenta will lie no more than 2 cm/¾ inch thick. Score the top into a pattern with a fork and bake at 180°C/350°F/Gas Mark 4 for about 30 minutes, until firm. Serve sliced and warm, close to, or sitting in, the gravy or cooking juice of the accompanying dish.

MALLARD with TURNIPS and KUMQUATS

You'll need two mallards to serve four people but when they are out of season one large domestic duck will do. Turnips are a classic accompaniment to duck but here they are tossed in caramel. Their rich brown colour, the yellow of the peppers, the bright orange of the kumquats, the gold of the roast duck and the sumptuous orange sauce look like autumn on the plate and would also make a marvellous treat on Christmas Day.

Serves four

2 mallards, dressed
1 garlic clove, halved
185 g/6 oz yellow peppers
3 tbls caster sugar
300 ml/½ pint orange juice
250 g/8 oz baby turnips, sliced thinly
125 g/4 oz kumquats

Cut the tails off the ducks to remove the preen gland and pull out any remaining stubs of feather or down. Rub the skins with the garlic.

Slice the peppers into half from top to bottom and then cut across into even straight strips. Blanch them in boiling water until they are just starting to go limp. Heat 2 tablespoons sugar in a saucepan until golden-brown in colour. Carefully add 2 tablespoons orange juice. Toss the sliced turnips in the caramel, then arrange on the bottom of a roasting-tin. Spread the peppers over and place the ducks on top. Heat half the remaining orange juice and pour over the ducks. Roast at 200°C/400°F/Gas Mark 6 for 30 minutes.

Meanwhile, quarter the kumquats lengthways and remove the pips. Place with the remaining orange juice and sugar in a saucepan and cook gently, uncovered, until the kumquats are a little transparent and the syrup has almost evaporated.

When the ducks are cooked, pour the juices from their body cavities back into the pan. Place the ducks, peppers and turnip mixture on to a hot platter and keep warm. Pour off the excess fat from the roasting-tin and boil the juices

until they are rich and dark and form a good sauce consistency.

Halve each duck with kitchen shears, cutting down either side of the backbone for speed. Place on hot plates; put a mound of the vegetables at one end, some of the kumquat at the other and pour the sauce between the two on the breast side. Serve with crisp green vegetables and small roasted potatoes. Ⓢ *Photograph, p. 150.*

SPICY BAKED CHICKEN

Whenever I managed one of my rare breaks from BBC-TV *Breakfast Time* for more than a few days, my spot was often taken over by the beautiful international film star and mistress of Indian food, Madhur Jaffrey. This is one of the most popular of the recipes she demonstrated. It is a marvellous buffet, party and picnic dish and is suitable for cooking all sorts of poultry and poultry portions. The paste should sit on the pieces for at least 3 hours before cooking; if you want to leave it for longer, overnight perhaps, then cover with plastic film and put it into the refrigerator.

Serves four

1 tbls ground cumin seeds
1½ tbls paprika
½ tsp cayenne pepper
1 tbls ground turmeric
1-1½ tsps ground black pepper
2½ tsps salt, or to taste
2-3 cloves of garlic, mashed to a paste
6 tbls lemon juice
4-8 chicken pieces
3 tbls vegetable oil

Mix the cumin, paprika, cayenne, turmeric, black pepper, salt, garlic and lemon juice in a bowl until well blended. Rub the mixture over the chicken pieces, pushing it into any cracks and openings you find and also along the bone of the drumsticks. Arrange the pieces in a shallow baking tray, skin-side down, and allow to stand for at least 3 hours (see note above).

Brush the chicken pieces with the oil. Bake for 20 minutes at 200°C/400°F/Gas Mark 6 then turn over and bake for a further 20-25 minutes, or until the chicken is tender. Baste every 10 minutes with the cooking juices.

When the chicken is cooked, remove and keep warm on a serving dish. Skim off any excess fat from the cooking juices and pour the remainder into a small saucepan. Boil rapidly until the liquid is reduced and is a little syrupy. Pour the sauce over the chicken pieces and serve at once. Ⓔ

CASSEROLED SAFFRON APRICOT CHICKEN

This recipe was developed for pressure-cooking, but works just as well using a casserole, or a saucepan with a well-fitting lid.

Serves four to six

1.5-2 kg/3-4 lb roasting chicken
397 g/14 oz can plum tomatoes in juice
60 g/2 oz finely chopped onion
250 g/8 oz dried apricots
3 tbls lemon juice
2 tsps ground cinnamon
2 sachets saffron powder
2 tsps orange-flower water
salt and pepper
30 g/1 oz butter
3 tbls flaked almonds
2 tbls currants
extra lemon juice and ground cinnamon to finish

Untruss the chicken if necessary, remove any lumps of excess fat and cut off the parson's nose. Tip the contents of the can of tomatoes into a measuring jug, mash with a fork to break them up, then make up the quantity of 450 ml/ ¾ pint with water. Pour half of this mixture into a pressure-cooker, a flame-proof casserole or a saucepan large enough to take the chicken. Stir in the chopped onion and 185 g/6 oz of the dried apricots.

Into the remaining tomatoes stir the lemon juice, ground cinnamon and saffron powder. Sit the chicken in the pressure-cooker, casserole or saucepan, pour the tomato liquid over and bring to the boil. Close and seal the pressure-cooker and cook under pressure allowing 10 minutes to 500 g/1 lb. To braise in the casserole or saucepan, turn down the heat and simmer gently, covered, allowing 25 minutes to 500 g/ 1 lb.

When the chicken is cooked, take it out and keep warm, covered, while you make the sauce. Remove any pieces of skin or bone from the cooking liquid and tip the remainder into a food processor or blender and purée. Pour the purée through a sieve into a clean saucepan, stir in the orange-flower water and season to taste with salt and pepper.

Melt the butter in a pan, slice the remaining dried apricots and add to the pan with the almonds and currants. Toss them in the butter until they are warmed through, then add a little lemon juice and ground cinnamon. Divide the chicken into portions and serve on a large dish with the apricots and almonds scattered over the top and a little sauce poured around. Offer the remaining sauce separately. Accompany with rice or with a Burghul Pilaff (see page 40).

CHICKEN with CELERY, LEMON and JUNIPER

This is a homely recipe that can easily be converted into something special.

Serves two generously

1.25 kg/2½ lb roasting chicken
oil or butter for frying
60 g/2 oz sliced onion
1 large celery stick
2 thick slices of lemon
6 lightly crushed juniper berries
1 bay leaf
1 or 2 whole garlic cloves
white wine (see method)
salt and pepper

Remove excess fat from the inside of the chicken and cut off the parson's nose. Remove any trussing strings. Brown lightly all over in a little oil, butter or a mixture of both. Remove from the pan and pat off excess oil or butter with absorbent paper.

Put the onion, celery, lemon, juniper berries, bay leaf and garlic into a heavy-based saucepan with a tight-fitting lid that is just large enough to take the chicken. If the fit is too tight, some of the flavourings can be put inside the bird. Place the chicken on top and pour in enough white wine to reach just to the top of the wing joint (most of the bird should be out of the liquid). Season lightly, cover tightly, bring to the boil, then reduce to a steady, low simmer. Cook for about 25 minutes per 500 g/1 lb or until cooked. (If a leg moves easily, the chicken is done, but with this method of cooking the bird will not dry out easily, so, if in doubt, cook for another 10-15 minutes.)

Remove the bird from the pan and cover lightly with foil. Strain the pan juice and return to the pan. The purist would reduce this sauce over heat, adjust the flavouring and serve but, for a touch of luxury, reduce some double cream until it is thick and add to the reduced pan juices or mix the reduced juices with a generous quantity of strained plain yoghurt off the heat. Ⓢ

GLYNN'S TIP

The recipe for Turkey in a Cranberry Overcoat (page 98) is a version of a recipe I created for use with pheasant.

Adapt the proportions according to the size of your bird and enjoy the pleasure of serving game without the hassle of carving a carcass at table or the untidiness of bones left on the plate.

POUSSINS with TOMATO, SAFFRON and CORIANDER

This is a superb way of enjoying small chickens as a main course. The bright colours look marvellous and the unexpected combination of flavours is memorable.

Serves four

4 poussins (baby chickens)
1 sachet powdered saffron
250 g/8 oz canned whole or chopped tomatoes
30 g/1 oz fresh coriander leaf and stalk
2 large garlic cloves
60 g/2 oz butter
salt and pepper

Trim any loose skin from the birds, remove any feathers and cut off the parson's nose from each one. Dissolve the saffron in a little of the juice from the tomatoes and paint the birds all over with that. Fold the coriander a few times and cut roughly. Put most of it into the cavities of the birds, and place them in a small roasting-tin with the remaining coriander and tomatoes. The tin should be just big enough to take them.

Chop the garlic finely and sprinkle or squeeze the juice over the birds. Dot with the butter and season very lightly with salt and pepper. Turn the birds on to their sides and cover the dish with foil.

Roast at 180°C/350°F/Gas Mark 4 for about 30 minutes or until the birds are cooked through, turning them on to their other sides half way through the cooking time.

Serve on plain rice or chopped potatoes that have been boiled in their skins. Ⓢ

CASSEROLED PHEASANT with CRANBERRY SAUERKRAUT

A festive-looking way to ensure that one pheasant will serve four people generously.

Serves four

1 pheasant, dressed
125 g/4 oz smoked streaky bacon
60 g/2 oz shallots or onion, chopped
875 g/1¾ lb sauerkraut
125 g/4 oz fresh or frozen cranberries
300 ml/½ pint cider or dry white wine

Choose a heavy flameproof casserole with a lid, which is large enough to take the bird and the sauerkraut. Remove any feather stubs and trussing from the bird and brown it a little in the casserole and set aside. Cut the bacon into thin strips and cook with the shallots or onion until they have browned a little. Drain the sauerkraut well (probably unnecessary for canned sauerkraut) and add it to the bacon and shallots. Toss well, then add 90 g/3 oz of the cranberries and mix again.

Smooth the mixture into an even layer and make a slight depression in the top. Put the remaining cranberries inside the pheasant and place it on top of the sauerkraut. Pour over the cider or wine and bring it to the boil over a high heat; cover, and reduce the heat to a gentle simmer for 35 minutes. Remove the bird and pour the berries and juices inside it into the pan. Keep the bird warm tipped on its breast. Turn up the heat under the sauerkraut until only a few drops of liquid remain. Joint or slice the bird and serve on beds of sauerkraut. Ⓢ *Photograph, p. 150.*

Options

Hearty eaters can be kept happy with a single pheasant by the addition of thick slices of smoked or garlic sausage to the sauerkraut.

Slices of peeled and cored apples cooked lightly in garlic butter make a good accompaniment with plainly boiled or steamed potatoes.

BRAISED GUINEA FOWL with CRAB APPLE SAUCE

Let me give you the most important variation first – if you can't get guinea fowl, a free-range or corn-fed chicken does very nicely indeed. This is an autumn recipe, of course, and is a useful way to use crab apples for something other than jelly!

1.5 kg/3 lb (approx) guinea fowl or roasting chicken
60 g/2 oz chopped carrot
60 g/2 oz chopped celery
60 g/2 oz chopped onion
1 garlic clove, crushed (optional)
oil for frying
375 g/12 oz crab apples, roughly chopped
300 ml/½ pint stock, cider, wine or water
salt and pepper
butter to finish sauce

Remove all excess fat from the guinea fowl and cut off the parson's nose. Put the chopped vegetables and garlic (if used) in the bottom of a saucepan or flameproof casserole which is just large enough to hold the bird. Heat a little oil in a frying pan and brown the bird on all sides, making sure it is a golden brown colour.

Sit the bird on top of the vegetables in the saucepan or casserole, spread the crab apples around and pour the chosen liquid over. Season lightly with salt and pepper. Bring to the boil, reduce the heat so that the liquid is just simmering, cover the pan and cook for about 45 minutes or until the bird is tender. When it is ready (its legs will move loosely when it is cooked) take it out of the pan and keep warm, covered with foil, while you make the sauce.

Tip the contents of the pan into a sieve standing over a clean saucepan and force the purée through using the back of a wooden spoon or ladle. Warm the sauce gently; if it is too thick, add a little more stock, cider, wine or water. Finally, beat in small lumps of butter to give the sauce a good shine and sweeten the flavour. Taste and adjust the seasoning. Joint or carve the bird and serve with a little of the sauce, handing the rest separately in a warmed sauceboat.

Options

Instead of using vegetables to flavour the apples, use a cinnamon stick and a few cloves or allspice berries; you may have to stir a little honey or brown sugar into the purée at the end. If you have plenty of crab apples, put some whole into the bird during the cooking and serve them on the purée for contrasted colour and flavour.

Instead of crab apples you can use ripe damsons or red fleshed plums. Finish with a little Cognac or brandy.

STRETCHED DUCK with FLAGEOLETS

The proportion of bones to flesh on a duck is such that even a large bird, say 2.5 kg/5 lb, won't feed six. However, here's a way of giving everyone lots of duck flavour, by making use of the affinity which duck fat has with flageolet beans. I *know* it's bursting with fat, but if you serve it with a green salad, and finish with an exotic fresh-fruit salad made with juice rather than syrup, little harm will have been done. But you will have fed six people very well with just one duck; that's almost a miracle.

Drain 2 × 397 g/14 oz cans of flageolets and mix them with 90 g/3 oz cubed salt pork or cubed garlic sausage. Put a quartered onion and a couple of crushed garlic cloves into the cavity of the duck and rub garlic all over the skin. Put the duck on the beans in a roasting pan and roast at 200°C/400°F/Gas Mark 6 to the preferred degree of pinkness (allow about 20 minutes per 500 g/1 lb). Drain out the juices from inside the bird and reserve. While the duck is resting before carving, purée half the flageolets with the cooking juices in a blender, then stir in the whole beans and reheat, seasoning to taste.

This is also a marvellous way to cook goose and you will need only one extra can of flageolets for a goose between 4.5 kg-5.5 kg/ 10-12 lb. Be extra generous with the garlic.

ROAST CHICKEN with BLACK PUDDING and APPLE

I always thought that this classic French idea was too dreadful even to contemplate, let alone eat! How wrong I was. It is one of the best chicken dishes I've eaten and really wonderful cold. But do use Cox's Orange Pippin apples, as their sweetness is an important part of the balance of flavours. Spinach is the best possible accompaniment.

Serves four to six

2 large Cox's Orange Pippin apples
250 g/8 oz black pudding, skinned and sliced
1 garlic clove, chopped
2-3 tbls Calvados, Cognac or marc
pinch of ground allspice or cloves (optional)
1.5-2 kg/3-4 lb roasting chicken
small glass white wine, cider or light beer
1 small onion, sliced
1 bay leaf

Peel and thinly slice 1 apple. Mix together the black pudding, garlic, apple and spirit of your choice. If the black pudding is a little bland, add extra spirit or some ground allspice or a little ground cloves (you can taste the black pudding as it is thoroughly cooked when it is sold).

Lift the skin over the breast of the chicken and push the stuffing evenly between the skin and the breast flesh. Smooth the breast back into an even shape. Peel and slice the remaining apple. Lay the slices evenly on the bottom of a roasting tin or ovenproof dish and sit the chicken on top. Pour on the white wine, cider or beer and put the sliced onion and the bay leaf inside the bird. Roast the chicken the way you like best – I would use a moderately hot oven (190°C/375°F/Gas Mark 5) at 25 minutes per 500 g/1 lb with the chicken laid on its side and turned from time to time.

While the bird rests after cooking, laid on its breast, drain excess fat from the pan and put the apple and juices from inside the bird (not the onion or bay leaf) through a sieve to make a purée to be served as a sauce. Sweeten with a little butter if you like.

Options

Cooked whole chestnuts may be added to the black pudding with a little ground cinnamon, too.

At Christmas time you can increase the proportions of this stuffing to use for a turkey, or even better, for goose. If you do this, put the stuffing into the neck skin rather than between the skin and breast to avoid it becoming too greasy.

MINTED ROAST CHICKEN with AVOCADO

Serves four

1.75 kg/3½ lb roasting chicken
1 large bunch of mint
juice and rind of 1 lemon
a little butter
1 ripe avocado
150 ml/¼ pint double cream

Lay a large sheet of foil on a flat surface and sit the chicken in the middle of it. Ease the skin away from the flesh of the breast and insert mint leaves between the flesh and skin. Stuff any remaining mint inside the cavity of the bird. Sprinkle lemon juice over the chicken and put the rind in the cavity. Press pats of butter over the top of the bird, then wrap loosely in the foil, leaving room for steam.

Cook for 1-1½ hours at 180°C/350°F/Gas Mark 4 until the chicken is done. Peel and slice the avocado and place in a saucepan with the cooking juices from the chicken. Heat gently, gradually adding the cream. Cook the sauce for about 5 minutes, stirring without breaking the avocado slices. Divide the chicken into four portions and serve with hot avocado and the sauce.

STIFADO – CHICKEN STEW

A national standby in Greece, stifados are essentially a stew of any meat with masses of onions, red wine and olive oil, and finished with oregano. I think that chicken makes the best version. It is essential that the flavours of any stifado are allowed to mature for a day or more before being eaten.

Serves four to six

1 kg/2 lb small, evenly sized onions
1.75-2 kg/3½-4 lb roasting chicken, jointed
4 garlic cloves, chopped
1 or 2 bay leaves
salt and pepper
½-1 tsp dried oregano
150 ml/¼ pint olive oil
150 ml/¼ pint red wine
1-2 tbls red wine vinegar

Peel the onions carefully and put half of them in the bottom of a large, flameproof casserole. Lay the chicken pieces on top, and sprinkle with the chopped garlic and bay leaves. Flavour with salt, pepper and some oregano (½ teaspoon is plenty at this stage). Cover with the rest of the onions and pour over the oil and red wine and just a spoonful of the vinegar.

Cook very gently, covered, at 150°C/300°F/Gas Mark 2, or on top of the stove; try to ensure that the onions do not break up. It will take about 1-1½ hours for the chicken to be tender. Cool the casserole quickly by standing the pan in cold running water, then leave it for several hours, or overnight, before gently reheating and serving. About 10 minutes before serving, check the flavouring and add more oregano or vinegar if required. Ⓣ

Options

Although not authentic, it is popular to add the contents of a large can (397 g/14 oz) of tomatoes in their own juice, which gives a richer, thicker sauce.

THE BOILED CHICKEN

It sounds boring, but this remains one of the most satisfying dishes there is. A boiling fowl gives a stronger, richer result but is hard to get and takes very much longer to cook; a nice tender roasting chicken gives excellent results in a third of the time.

Serves four to six

1.75-2 kg/3½-4 lb boiling fowl or chicken
½ lemon
1 onion, sliced
1 carrot, sliced
1 stick celery, sliced
1 bouquet garni
1 tbls flour
30 g/1 oz butter
300 ml/½ pint milk
salt and pepper
handful finely chopped parsley

Prepare the bird by washing out with cold water and cutting off the parson's nose. Trim the legs, tuck the wings under the body, then rub the breast with the cut side of the lemon. Put the lemon inside the body cavity. Choose a large saucepan or casserole with a well-fitting lid and put the bird in it, with the vegetables, bouquet garni and sufficient water to just cover and simmer over a very low heat – or transfer to an oven 150°C/300°F/Gas Mark 2 for about 3-3½ hours until tender, depending on size and age of bird. (A roasting chicken will cook much faster, about 1¼ hours.)

When cooked, transfer the bird to a dish and keep warm while making the sauce. Strain the cooking liquid into a bowl or jug and skim off the excess fat which will rise to the surface.

Melt the butter in a saucepan and stir in the flour, cook for 2 minutes but don't let it brown. Off the heat, stir in 300 ml/½ pint of the strained cooking liquid and the milk. Return to the heat and bring to the boil, stirring continuously, until smooth, then stir in the finely chopped parsley. Simmer the sauce over a gentle heat for 5 minutes, stirring occasionally.

To serve, divide the bird into portions, arrange on a serving dish and coat with some of the sauce. Offer the remaining sauce separately.

Options

Omit the parsley from the sauce but add two hard-boiled eggs; stir the finely chopped whites into the sauce and garnish the completed dish with rows of sieved yolk.

If you don't like thickened sauce, boil up some of the cooking liquid to reduce it a little, then flavour it with pinches of mustard powder and add masses of chopped parsley just before serving. In this case I serve the chicken in wide soup or pudding bowls so there's really lots of the liquid to enjoy. Even better is to have a variety of boiled vegetables also in the bowl – potatoes, carrots, parsnip, quartered cabbage – thus making a traditional Boiled Chicken Dinner.

CHICKEN and LEEK with SMOKED OYSTERS

This wonderful steamed savoury pudding is made in a large pudding-basin so that the contents can be served in generous-looking pieces.

Serves four to six

315 g/10 oz self raising flour
155 g/5 oz beef suet, shredded, butter or margarine
175-200 ml/6-7 fl oz milk
500 g/1 lb boneless chicken breast
12-15 large spinach leaves
100 g/4 oz can smoked oysters, drained (oil reserved)
90 g/3 oz lean back bacon cut into strips
1 tbls plain flour
300 ml/½ pint dry cider
freshly ground black pepper
125 g/4 oz leeks, thickly sliced and washed

Mix the flour and suet or fat together and stir in the milk to make a firm dough. Use just over two-thirds of the dough to line a 1.75 litre/3 pint capacity pudding-basin. Cut the chicken flesh into large cubes, 2.5 cm/1 inch square.

Blanch the spinach leaves by tossing them into boiling water for a few seconds and then

---

> ### GLYNN'S TIP
>
> *To speed up the process of removing fat from a hot stock, drop a couple of ice-cubes into the stock and the fat will adhere to them as they float to the top. Alternatively, dab the top gently with pieces of kitchen paper which will absorb the fat but leave the stock behind.*

plunging them into cold water. Cut out the stems, and wrap a smoked oyster in each leaf.

Cook the bacon gently in a pan until the fat runs. Pour in the oil from the can of oysters, add flour and cook, stirring, for a couple of minutes over a medium heat. Take the pan off the heat, stir in the cider and continue cooking until a smooth sauce has formed. *Do not add salt, which will come from the bacon,* but add some black pepper.

Pack the basin evenly with cubes of chicken, rounds of leeks and spinach-wrapped oysters. Pour on the sauce and give the bowl a gentle shake or two to encourage the contents to settle. Put on the pastry top, seal, cover and steam for at least 2 hours – up to an extra 45 minutes won't do any harm as long as the water doesn't evaporate. Ⓢ *Photograph, p. 116.*

CHICKEN, AVOCADO and COCONUT PIE

I first cooked this Creole-influenced dish in front of hundreds of people at the Ideal Home Exhibition while broadcasting with Gloria Hunniford on Radio 2. Thousands of listeners wrote in for the recipe and almost all of them wrote again to say how much they'd enjoyed it. Who said the British don't like new flavours and exotic ideas? The thyme, a basic ingredient of Creole cooking, bridges the flavour gap between the coconut and the avocado.

Serves four

30 g/1 oz butter
30 g/1 oz plain flour
300 ml/½ pint chicken stock
300 ml/½ pint milk or cream
60 g/2 oz thinly sliced onion
¼ tsp dried thyme
60 g/2 oz block cream of coconut, grated
250-375 g/8-12 oz firm avocado
juice of 1 lime or 3 tbls lemon juice
4 small chicken supremes (boned breasts)
2 ripe, firm bananas
freshly ground allspice
salt and pepper
375 g/12 oz puff pastry
beaten egg to glaze

Melt the butter in a small pan, add the flour and cook for 2 minutes without allowing it to brown. Stir in the stock and milk or cream off the heat, add the onion and thyme; return to the heat and bring to the boil, stirring all the time. Simmer for 5 minutes. Strain the sauce, stir in the grated cream of coconut and allow it to cool. Put a small pie-funnel in the middle of a suitably sized pie dish. Peel and slice the avocado and use it to line the base of the dish. Squeeze over half the lime or lemon juice.

Remove the skin from the chicken supremes.

Cut them almost in half lengthways. Cut each banana into two lengthways, then cut each piece across its centre. Put two pieces in each supreme, return to its original shape and slice each stuffed supreme diagonally into three even pieces. Arrange in the pie dish and sprinkle with the remaining lime or lemon juice. Add a generous amount of freshly ground or grated allspice. Pour the sauce over evenly, and season lightly with salt and pepper.

Roll out the pastry, cover the dish and decorate, simply or elaborately, and glaze with beaten egg. Chill the pie while you heat the oven to 200°C/400°F/Gas Mark 6. Bake for 20 minutes, then reduce the heat to 190°C/375°F/Gas Mark 5 for a further 20-25 minutes.

I think you'll find this is enough on the plate by itself but you may like to add rice or, if you like Caribbean food, sweet potato. Follow with a salad. Ⓢ

ROAST GOOSE with GIN and LIME SAUCE

To balance the rich, sweet taste of goose fat, I've added a citrus flavour from the East – fresh, green lime. To make the slices of goose look more interesting, use the goose fat to cook a Swiss rösti in the proper way but flavoured, untraditionally, with apple and more lime.

Serves six to eight

4-5.5 kg/9-12 lb oven-ready goose
300 ml/½ pint dry white wine
300 ml/½ pint water
1 bay leaf
1 whole garlic bulb or allow one clove per person
6 juniper berries, crushed
salt
150 ml/¼ pint gin
juice of 1 lime

The day before cooking, remove all excess fat from the goose (usually just inside the vent). Slice the giblets into small pieces, including the neck. Brown the giblets with a tiny piece of goose fat then add the wine, water, bay leaf, the whole head of garlic and juniper berries. Cover and simmer gently for an hour or so until the liquid has reduced by half then strain. Remove the garlic, wrap in foil and discard the giblets and herbs. Once the liquid has cooled, skim well, then cover and refrigerate with the garlic.

Next day, rub a little salt into the skin of the goose, unwrap the garlic head (do not skin), and place inside the bird, then stand it on a rack in a deep roasting tin. Calculate the cooking time at 12 minutes per 500 g/1 lb at 180°C/350°F/Gas Mark 4 plus an extra 15 minutes to allow the bird to rest before carving. Pour off the fat during cooking and reserve.

Before you sit down to your feast, remove the

cooked goose from the oven, and transfer it to a heated dish and cover lightly with foil. Pour off the excess fat and add the juicy brown bits from the bottom of the pan to the stock you have previously made. Add the gin plus the lime juice to taste. Simmer over medium heat to reduce. To serve, slice along the breast, serve with a wedge of rösti, sauce, and a cooked clove of garlic.

APPLE and LIME RÖSTI

Rösti is a Swiss dish of grated potato and onion which is made into a crisply coated pancake, traditionally cooked in goose fat. Here I have incorporated apple and sharpened the mixture. This dish can be prepared the night before but is best if made no longer than an hour or so before you cook it.

Serves six to eight

1.25 kg/2½ lb waxy potatoes
375 g/12 oz Bramley cooking apples, cored but not peeled
grated rind and juice of 2 limes
1 garlic clove, crushed
salt to taste
goose fat or butter, melted

Cook the potatoes in their skins until only just starting to soften – they must not be cooked through. Cool, peel, then grate coarsely into a bowl. Coarsely grate in the apples and immediately pour in the lime juice. Add the finely grated rind of just 1 lime then the garlic and salt. Blend everything together with your hands. Cover closely until it is time to cook the mixture.

Half an hour or so before you sit down pour the goose fat or butter into a large frying pan to a depth of 6 mm/¼ inch. Heat the fat to a high temperature then remove it from the heat and add the Rösti. Press down evenly. Put it back over a medium heat and let the base gently turn a crisp golden brown. If it is a non-stick pan it is easy to turn the Rösti over by sliding it on to a plate and flipping it back into the pan. If it is not a non-stick pan this is a little tricky and it is better to dribble some more goose fat or butter over the top and to brown it under the grill.

Serve in wedges sprinkled with the grated rind of the second lime.

GLYNN'S TIP

Rösti is better made with goose fat but any fat or oil with flavour is worth using; use walnut oil and include some walnuts; use olive oil and mix garlic into the potatoes.

A FRUIT STUFFING for GOOSE

This is one of the few stuffings I recommend that can be placed inside a bird. It is acceptable because it doesn't go in at the start of cooking and it does not fill the cavity. But it is too wet to go into the neck as a stuffing. Make a gravy with the giblets as well.

Cook equal weights of sharp dried apricots and stoned prunes in orange juice until soft but not cooked right through. For each 375 g/12 oz fruit (which is about right for 4 people) add 1 teaspoon of ground cinnamon and scant teaspoon of ground ginger plus a bay leaf. Add a clove of garlic, too, if you like. Put the mixture into the goose when it is about three-quarters cooked, so that it absorbs some of the fat and liquid inside the bird. Spoon the mixture out and keep it warm while the bird is resting.

This is ideal for ducks, too, as well as chickens and turkeys.

BABY TURKEY BREASTS in a CRANBERRY and PECAN OVERCOAT

Baby turkeys, weighing 2.75-3 kg/6-7 lb, have replaced capons, which are no longer allowed under Common Market regulations. They are available fresh and frozen year-round from national supermarket chains and are ideal for special occasions. With the hard work done in advance and carving so simple, this recipe could be the key to letting you join the Christmas celebrations, rather than simply cooking for them.

Serves six, with some left over

3 kg/6½ lb dressed baby turkey with giblets, fresh or frozen
8 tbls gin
125 g/4 oz onion, coarsely chopped
1 bay leaf
stick of celery
sprig of thyme
1.2 litres (2 pints) boiling water
1 clove garlic
125 g/4 oz fresh wholewheat breadcrumbs
250 g/8 oz fresh or frozen cranberries
2 tsps dried mint
salt
60 g/2 oz or more pecan nuts
60 g/2 oz butter

Remove the giblets from the turkey and pull off the skin. With a very sharp knife remove both sides of breast meat in single pieces. This is very simple to do if you start by cutting either side of the thin breast keel and then cut around the rib cage with the blade of the knife angled into the bone.

Trim neatly and put into a shallow flat dish. Pour over 6 tablespoons of the gin and cover. Leave at room temperature for 4 hours, basting and turning from time to time.

Remove all the dark meat from the carcass, legs and wings and put to one side with the heart and the liver. Chop the carcass and brown it well together with the gizzard and chopped neck in a heavy saucepan. Add half the onion, the bay leaf, celery and thyme and pour on 1.2 litres/2 pints of boiling water. Cook gently for several hours, drain, then return the liquid to the pan and continue cooking, uncovered, until reduced to 300 ml/½ pint of rich turkey stock.

Purée the remaining onion with the garlic and then purée the dark turkey meat. You may have to do this in small amounts – it is nicer to leave some of it coarse and some fine. Then make the fresh breadcrumbs in a food processor or blender and tip in half the cranberries. Process only long enough to chop them, ideally leaving some of them only halved – do not reduce them to a purée. Add the bread and cranberry mixture to the onion, garlic and turkey, sprinkle on the mint and pour on any of the gin marinade that has not been absorbed. Knead and squeeze everthing together with your bare hands until thoroughly mixed.

Divide the mixture into two on a baking sheet or in a shallow roasting pan. Squash the two portions out until there is an area equivalent to the size of the turkey breasts in the middle of each; the mixture should be about 6 mm/¼ inch thick. Put on the turkey breasts, salted very lightly. Work the mixture over the breasts and sides evenly, making sure it is not too thick over the narrow tip of the breast. Smooth the surface and twist the narrow end to make each shape like a thick comma or like the two ying and yang signs. Press pecan halves into the mixtures; 60 g/2 oz is enough for an undivided line down the centre of each, but if you have more you can make whatever pattern you like.

Leave the prepared breasts in a cool place, (but not the refrigerator) for at least an hour – the longer the better. They must be at room temperature when you cook them, which takes 45 minutes at 180°C/350°F/Gas Mark 4 plus 10-15 minutes standing time.

To make the sauce, heat the turkey stock and tip in the remaining cranberries. Cook until they are just popping then liquidize and strain through a fine sieve.

When you are ready to serve, reheat the sauce to simmering point, then take from the heat. Stir in the remaining gin and about ½ teaspoon of salt according to taste and then stir in the butter in 4 portions. Keep warm but do not boil.

Serve the turkey sliced and with a generous amount of sauce on the plate. If you think it needs garnishing, some fresh mint looks nice on the sauce. *Photograph, p. 151.*

THE CHRISTMAS TURKEY

When roasting a large turkey, always have someone else on hand to close the oven door as quickly as possible when taking out the bird to turn it, or you lose so much heat your timing will be ruined.

First put the bird, untrussed and on its side, into an oven preheated to 220°C/425°F/Gas Mark 7 for 10 minutes, then turn it over and cook for the same time. Then reduce the oven to 180°C/350°F/Gas Mark 4 and cook for 12-15 minutes per 500 g/1 lb weight, turning every 30 minutes. Provided that the bird is at room temperature when you start cooking and you open and close the oven quickly, 12 minutes per 500 g/1 lb cooks most birds beautifully. Big birds take a little less, if anything. If you divide the number of pounds by 5 you will get an estimate of the cooking time. Even a 10 kg/20 lb bird takes only 4 hours.

If you follow the above instructions I guarantee a succulent turkey no matter how big it is, but here are a few extra points I've gathered over the years for the Christmas turkey:

• Covering the turkey with bacon is not necessary if it is roasted on its side – and, anyway, the flavour of bacon is intrusive. Anoint the side with butter if you like, which helps to flavour the juices. Once the bird is well browned, cover it with a loose dome of foil. Do not seal the pan with foil for this steams the bird and spoils the flavour.

GLYNN'S TIP

To turn a big bird from side to side takes care and strength. I use very thick oven gloves and someone else to steady the pan. Put one hand inside the cavity – and grab the pointed end firmly. Put the other hand under the breast end that is lying in the pan and turn the bird in several stages. Don't worry in the least if the skin tears, which it sometimes does; the stuffing is protecting the flesh. If the flesh is exposed, this is one of the few times when it is worth basting with cooking juices. Put foil loosely over the top and all will be well.

To test if the turkey is cooked, stick a skewer through the leg and through the thickest part of the breast at a slight downwards angle. If the juices which run out are clear, the turkey is cooked; if there is the slightest tint of pink, cook a little more.

● Ignore recipes that cook a bird for a long time at a slow temperature, for this will guarantee either a dry bird or one that is seething with salmonella, or both. Most important, never re-heat a cooked bird.

● Make sure you know how heavy your bird is with its stuffings and write the weight down in order to calculate the cooking time before you start.

● Have the bird at room temperature before you start cooking. Ⓔ Ⓢ

GIBLET GRAVY

Ideally, make giblet gravy a day before serving. Using a large pan, brown the giblets from the bird in a little oil or butter, remove, and lightly brown about half their weight of sliced onion. Return the giblets to the pan with a few pieces of thinly peeled orange zest, a couple of bay leaves, some peppercorns and a crushed clove of garlic, if you like it. Cover with at least 600 ml/ 1 pint of red or pseudo-port wine, red wine and water, or with chicken stock, and, once boiling, scrape up the bottom of the saucepan to release the brown debris which will colour and flavour the liquid. Simmer for an hour or more until the liquid has reduced by half.

Remove from the heat, leave the giblets in the liquid, cool, cover and stand overnight. Next day remove the fat from the surface and strain off the liquid.

To complete the gravy, remove the cooked turkey from the roasting-tin, pour off most of the fat from the tin, and boil up the rest of the juices, again scraping up the debris and brownings. When brown and thick, strain this into the giblet sauce and heat through. Adjust seasoning before serving. If you like a sweet gravy, stir in a little redcurrant or cranberry jelly.

If you want a thickened gravy, add a teaspoon or so of cornflour slaked with some of the cold stock.

Ensure that your family or guests don't ruin your efforts by swamping everything on the plates with gravy. And, whatever you do, don't use gravy granules or anything of that type.

A CONTEMPORARY TURKEY

Did you really enjoy your last Christmas turkey dinner? Just think about it. Turkey with gravy, bland bread sauce and bread stuffing, bacon rolls and sausages, roast potatoes, plus mashed potatoes.

No matter how well it is cooked, it can hardly look or taste like a celebration of anything other than fat and starch.

Next year, follow the Americans (for roast turkey originated there) and don't hide behind 'tradition'. Look at the huge variety of veget- ables available at Christmas and enjoy a real celebration on your plate:

● Orange-fleshed sweet potatoes, boiled in their skins in thick slices.

● A purée of celeriac root, made with lots of milk to keep it white, with parsley stirred in just before serving.

● Beetroot cooked in orange juice and butter.

● Sliced leeks cooked in their own liquid and finished with a few spoonfuls of seed mustard.

Make a gravy by all means but also serve Cranberry Relish (page 179) or piping hot cranberry sauce with orange juice or Cognac or vodka or gin stirred in.

MEAT

From sizzling roasts to the elegance of sweetbreads in a cream sauce, here is a range of flavours and textures to complement every season, and everyone's favourite vegetables and salads.

Glistening beef fat, golden pork crackling, the sweetness of new season's lamb or veal, robust kidneys and tasty liver – the pleasure of meat eating is endless. But isn't meat eating bad for you? Of course it isn't. As part of a varied diet, meat of all kinds is very important but it is perhaps better to eat somewhat less of it than we used to, eat leaner cuts and to think more carefully about what we serve in the same meal. For instance, if you like roast meat with roast vegetables and a pan sauce, and why not, you shouldn't really serve cheese in the same meal or a pudding with lots of cream; indeed, if you eat large portions you probably shouldn't eat any other dairy or animal products the same day. If you enjoy a periodic blow out – such as a roast followed by a cheese course followed by something like my orange-caramel steamed pudding, go right ahead. Enjoy it thoroughly, but *don't* do it every day.

Kidneys, liver, sweetbreads and the like are excellent alternatives to the traditional meat cuts. They're generally far cheaper, cook quickly and are particularly good for you; for example, it's recommended you eat liver at least once a week. If you find liver too strong-flavoured, soak it in milk for a few hours or overnight.

As with cakes and biscuits, don't let do-gooders and diet hysterics stop you eating red meat if you enjoy it, but include it as part of a varied diet and enjoy the benefits of good flavour and good health.

BRAISING

The meat is first browned all over then placed on a bed of chopped vegetables, with a small amount of liquid to keep it moist. Browning the vegetables first and using wine or stock as liquid give added flavour to less tasty joints of meat. Once cooked, the vegetables can be puréed or sieved to enrich the sauce.

Suitable cuts: beef – rib, brisket, silverside, flank, shin (my personal favourite, it has lots of flavour and doesn't break up during cooking); lamb – fillet, breast; pork – leg steaks, loin (chump) steaks; veal – leg, shoulder, fillet, breast, neck-end of loin.

Method Brown the meat all over to seal then brown chopped root vegetables. Stand the meat on the vegetables with wine/stock/water to barely cover them. Cover and cook at 170°C/325°F/Gas Mark 3 allowing 45 minutes per 500 g/1 lb, minimum cooking time 3 hours.

GRILLING

Only suitable for tender cuts of meat, which should be well basted to prevent drying out. Season well before grilling but NEVER add salt as this encourages loss of juices and makes the meat tough. Position the meat on a rack about 7.5 cm/3 inches from the heat source.

FRYING

Suitable for tender cuts; there is less likelihood of the meat drying out than with grilling, but take care not to over-cook or the meat will toughen. Season as for grilling and remember to fry the best side first, while the cooking fat is clean. Use only enough fat to moisten the pan, and keep the heat high. If you have a non-stick pan, use no fat unless you want to add a knob of butter for flavour.

ROASTING

Preparation Weigh the joint and calculate the cooking time (see chart). Heat the oven. Sprinkle the joint with a little freshly-ground black pepper; I prefer not to salt meat at this stage as it draws out the meat juices. Rub the flesh with a cut clove of garlic, or make a few incisions in the fat and insert thin slivers. Fresh herbs may also be inserted in this way, although they tend to burn during roasting so are best buried beneath the fat. Place the meat onto a rack in a roasting tin, which allows circulation of air around the joint and assists even cooking. A couple of slices of onion (there is no need to peel it) and a bay leaf in the bottom of the tin add flavour to the cooking juices and the gravy made from them.

If the joint is very lean, as is sometimes the case with beef and almost always with veal, it is a good idea to include 1-2 tablespoons of dripping in the roasting tin and to baste the joint with this regularly during cooking; meat with a covering of fat need not be basted.

Shape and thickness of meat dictates how long it will take to cook so use the following cooking times as a general guide only. If you are concerned about judging whether meat is cooked, it may be a good idea to invest in a meat thermometer; this should register 60°C/140°F for rare meat, 70°C/155°F for medium, 80°C/170°F for well done, when inserted in the thickest part of the joint.

POT-ROASTING

Suitable for small joints which would otherwise shrink excessively, or for cuts requiring slower cooking to tenderize the meat.

Suitable cuts: beef – brisket, silverside, topside; lamb – stuffed and rolled breast; veal – all joints, particularly small ones.

Method Heat a little oil or dripping in a pan and brown the joint rapidly on all sides. Place in a suitable casserole or pan, cover and cook slowly, at 150°C/300°F/Gas Mark 2 allowing 35 minutes per 500 g/lb plus 35 minutes over, minimum cooking time 90 minutes after initial browning.

GOOD COMPANIONS

Beef: Yorkshire pudding, unthickened meat juices, English mustard and horseradish. Onions, carrots, celery, tomato (in stews/casseroles), parsnips, potatoes (especially roasted) and mushrooms. Olives, bacon (streaky), garlic (crushed or whole; unpeeled in casseroles). Orange peel (in stews), prunes, honey, brown sugar, and tomato purée (in casseroles/stews). Red wine, Madeira, brown ale/stout, Cognac and Worcestershire sauce. Aniseed (especially in stews), bay, caraway (especially in goulash), cardamom, cumin, coriander, curry paste, chili, fennel, ginger, marjoram, parsley and thyme.

Pork: Apples and gooseberries (in sauces), prunes and dried apricots. Haricot and butter beans (especially with gammon/ham). Cabbage (green and red), celeriac, leeks, garlic, tomatoes, mushrooms, onions (whole baby ones, in stews/casseroles, with sage in stuffing), red and green peppers and celery. Orange and lemon (especially in sauces for pork and gammon), white wine and cider.
Bay (under crackling), cloves, dill (weed and seed), fennel, marjoram, oregano, sage, rosemary, thyme (especially with bacon), caraway, cardamom, cayenne, cinnamon, mustard, juniper berries and black peppercorns.

Lamb: Garlic (under the skin or served whole, onions (cooked until very soft as a sauce for cutlets), peas (whole or puréed, flavoured with mint), baby spring vegetables (carrots, courgettes, sweetcorn and potatoes), mushrooms and tomatoes. Prunes and apricots (fresh or dried with mint). Capers (with cold lamb). Orange. Laverbread. Sweet mincemeat. Sharp fruit jellies: crab apple, quince, medlar, redcurrant and rowanberry.
Herb jellies and mint jelly – rather than mint sauce, which properly belongs to mutton.
Basil, chives (especially in savoury butter), marjoram, parsley, rosemary, tarragon, thyme, caraway seeds (good in hotpots), cinnamon, cumin, coriander, dill and mace.

Veal: Bacon (especially smoked). Cheese (especially Gruyère). Orange and lemon. Mushrooms, tomatoes, celery, fennel, peppers and baby onions. White wine, Marsala and sherry. Soured cream. Hot and sweet paprika, caraway, tarragon, parsley, lemon pepper, rosemary and dill. Tuna – in cold mayonnaise.

Game: Bacon (streaky). Onions, mushrooms (especially flat, field variety), beetroot, celery, celeriac (especially with garlic in a purée), cabbage (green, red and white), parsnips, swede and turnips. Chestnuts, oranges and raspberries. Garlic cloves (especially whole; unpeeled in casseroles/stews). Chocolate (to finish sauces – in very small amounts), olives and raisins. Redcurrant, rowanberry, cranberry, medlar and quince. Red wine, Madeira, sherry, cider and white wine (especially for rabbit). Bay, juniper, paprika, parsley, nutmeg, rosemary, sage and thyme.

BEEF		
CUTS/DESCRIPTION	COOKING METHODS	TIPS
SIRLOIN From ribs, next to the rump; sold on or off the bone	High temp roasting: 220°C/425°F/Gas Mark 7 15 mins per 500 g/lb + 15 mins over : rare 20 mins per 500 g/lb + 20 mins over: medium 25 mins per 500 g/lb + 25 mins over: well done Slow roasting: 180°C/350°F/Gas Mark 4 30-35 mins per 500 g/lb + 30 mins over Note: for large joints (over 5 kg/10 lb), very thin joints and those cooked on the bone, reduce cooking times by 5 mins per 500 g/lb	Fine-grained, prime quality meat with thin covering of fat
RIB Fairly large joint when on bone, also sold boned and rolled **FORERIB (MINIBONE ROAST)** Cut from next to sirloin, bone cut short	High temp roasting: as Sirloin (above) Slow roasting: as Sirloin (above)	
TOPSIDE (US Rump Roast) Boneless joint from top of leg	Slow roasting: as Sirloin (above) Pot-roasting: after initial sealing and browning in frying-pan – 150°C/300°F/Gas Mark 2, allow 40-45 mins per 500 g/lb (minimum 3 hours)	Unless very high quality, best suited to pot-roasting – gives a tender flavoursome result
BACK AND TOP RIB OR MIDDLE RIB From between forerib and shoulder, sold boneless and trimmed	Pot-roasting: as Topside (above) Braising with vegetables: after initial sealing and browning in frying pan – 170°C/325°F/Gas Mark 3, allow 45 mins per 500 g/lb (minimum 3 hours)	Economical, flavoursome joint
BRISKET From belly area under ribs; usually sold off the bone	Pot roasting: as Topside (above) Braising with vegetables: as Middle Rib (above)	Coarse-grained can be fatty but has lots of flavour
SALTED BRISKET	Boiling: 30 mins per 500 g/lb + 30 mins over (minimum 1½ hours), time from point water starts to simmer	Good pressed and served cold
SILVERSIDE (US Top Round) From outer leg – chunky, boneless	Pot-roasting: as Topside (above) Braising with vegetables: as Middle Rib (above)	Coarse-grained, must have long slow cooking
SALT SILVERSIDE	Boiling: as Brisket (above)	Traditional joint for boiled beef and carrots. Soak for 1-2 hours before cooking

BEEF

CUTS/DESCRIPTION	COOKING METHODS	TIPS
AITCHBONE Connects rump to silverside. Once a large joint with big bone and lots of fat, now usually sold trimmed and boneless	Slow roasting: as Topside (above) Pot-roasting: as Topside (above)	Lots of flavour Sometimes salted
FLANK (THICK and THIN) Belly area under the forerib and loin, adjoins brisket	Braising with vegetables: as Middle Rib (above) Casseroling: after frying to brown meat and veg., 140°C/275°F/Gas Mark 1, 2½-3 hours	Coarse-grained, fattier than brisket
LEG AND SHIN	Stewing: don't fry meat; cover with cold water or stock, bring to simmer and allow 3½-4 hours minimum (140°C/275°F/Gas Mark 1 in oven)	Sinewy, muscular, lean meat. Long slow cooking essential to break down tough fibres. Full of flavour
CHUCK OR BLADE From shoulder area	Casseroling: as Flank (above) – allow 2 hours minimum	Lean meat, good flavour, needs slow cooking in moisture. Good for pies and puddings

STEAKS

CUTS/DESCRIPTION	COOKING METHODS	CUTS/DESCRIPTION	COOKING METHODS
FILLET Very lean, tenderest and most expensive steak; 'centre' or 'eye' choicest part. **Châteaubriand:** Cut from centre of fillet, around 375 g/12 oz weight **Tournedos:** Rounds weighing about 155 g/5 oz **Filets Mignon:** Steaks cut from thin end of fillet, weight about 90 g/3 oz	Grilling (see chart) Frying (open): 4-7 mins (1.25 cm/½ in thick)	**ENTRECOTE** Literally, 'between ribs'; often cut from sirloin or rump, fat trimmed off	Grilling (see chart) Frying (open): 5-7 mins Sautéing with wine: 7-10 mins
RUMP Cut from next to sirloin; more flavour, a choice cut, 'point' best part	Grilling (see chart) Frying (open): 5-7 mins Frying (covered): 7-10 mins	**FORERIB** 1.25 cm/½ in thick cut from forerib	Grilling (see chart) Frying (open): 7-10 mins Frying (covered) with wine and herbs: 10-12 mins
SIRLOIN Thick cut from top known as a Porterhouse (min. 1.25 cm/½ in thick)	Grilling (see chart) Frying (open): 7-10 mins Frying (covered) with vegetables: 10-12 mins	**BUTTOCK** Slices of rump or topside Flattened, stuffed and rolled known as beef olives	Braising with vegetables: seal and brown first, then transfer to oven in covered pot 170°C/325°F/Gas Mark 3 for 1½ hours
Thin cut (sometimes also beaten flat) known as Minute steak (6 mm/¼ in thick)	Frying (open): 2-3 mins each side		

NEWER CUTS

Beef à la mode: Round side of silverside, rolled and larded with strips of pork fat.

Continental roast: Top ribs, fat, skin and gristle removed, trussed with pork fat.

Contre Filet: Chump end of sirloin steak with thin pork fat tied round it.

French roast: Centre cut of topside, 7.5-10 cm/3-4 in wide, with thin pork fat tied round it.

Rôti de luxe: Corner cut of topside, all fat, skin and gristle removed, three sides covered with strips of pork fat.

Rôti de romsteck: Rump steak, gristle removed, with thin pork fat adjoined to its natural fat.

Rôti de tranche: Topside, rump or silverside, rolled and trussed with thin beef fat.

HOW TO CHOOSE
Look for cherry red flesh with some marbling or intracellular fat to give juicy meat and help prevent shrinkage during cooking. The fat – not too much of it – should be dry, creamy coloured and flaky.

GRILLING STEAK (BROILING)

US guidelines:

Thickness	Distance from Heat	Very Rare	Rare	Medium Rare	Medium	Well Done
2.5 cm/1 in	5 cm/2 in	3	4	5	6	7
3.75 cm/1½ in	7.5 cm/3 in	6	7	8	9	10-12
5 cm/2 in	10 cm/4 in	14	15	16	17	18-19

British guidelines:

Thickness	Rare	Medium	Well done
1.25 cm/½ in	4	6	8
1.75 cm/¾ in	5	9-10	12-15
2.5 cm/1 in	6-7	10	15
3.75 cm/1½ in	10	12-14	18-20

Note: For steaks on the bone, increase distance from heat by 2.5 cm/1 in and increase cooking time by 4 mins.

CHARCOAL GRILLING TIMES (BROILING)

		Very Rare	Rare	Medium Rare	Medium	Well Done
2.5 cm/1 in		3	4-5	6	7-8	9-10
3.75-4.5 cm/1½-1¾ in	fire: hot 10 cm/4 in from heat	4	5-6	7-8	9-10	12-15
5 cm/2 in		6-7	8-9	10-12	14-16	18-20
6.25 cm/2½ in	fire: moderate 12.5 cm/5 in	10-12	13-15	16-18	20-22	23-25

PORK

CUTS/DESCRIPTION	COOKING METHODS	TIPS
LOIN With or without bone, with or without rind (essential for crackling), sometimes includes the kidney	Roasting: 190°C/375°F/Gas Mark 5, 35 mins per 500 g/lb + 35 mins For crackling, increase to 220°C/425°F/Gas Mark 7 last 20 mins	
LOIN CHOPS With or without bone	Grilling: 12-15 mins Frying (open): 15-18 mins Frying (covered): 20-25 mins	Baste often Keep moist
CHUMP END Joint from end of loin, includes small bone and rind	Roasting: as Loin (above)	
LOIN CHUMP STEAKS Slices 1.25 cm/½ in thick, trimmed	Grilling: 15 mins Frying (covered): 15-20 mins Braising: After browning, 170°C/325°F/Gas Mark 3, 45 mins per 500 g/lb minimum 1¾ hrs	Baste often No waste
FILLET TENDERLOINS Prime lean meat in long boneless strips	Stuffed and roasted as Loin (above) With stuffing, *en croûte* Sliced, beaten flat, fried and finished with rich sauce	 Expensive but economical
LEG Sold as half-legs and quarter-leg cuts. Three-cuts: Fillet, Middle cut (leanest), Knuckle end	Roasting	Prime meat, little bone Insert bay leaves under crackling
LEG STEAKS Lean, no bone or rind – 1.25-1.85 cm/½-¾ in thick	Braising: As Loin chump steaks Frying (covered): 15-20 mins	
SHOULDER JOINT Flavoursome, often boned or part boned Neck-end fattier joint Cubed meat used for casseroles and pies	Roasting: As Loin (above)	
SHOULDER STEAKS Lean, need slow cooking	Grilling, slowly: 18-20 mins Frying gently (covered): 18-20 mins	Baste often
SHOULDER (SPARE RIB) CHOPS Can be fatty, but have good flavour. Ideal for barbecues	Grilling: 20 mins	Marinate first and baste with marinade while cooking

PORK

CUTS/DESCRIPTION	COOKING METHODS	TIPS
HAND AND SPRING (US Picnic/Arm) Divides into: HAND – boneless, good flavour, ideal cut up for casseroles and pies SHOULDER HAND JOINT – large bone KNUCKLE END HAND – lean, with one, economical	Roasting: As Loin (above) as Hand Casseroling: 140°C/275°F/Gas Mark 1 for 2 hours (timed from moment water/stock simmers)	
BELLY (US SPARE RIBS) Thin joint of streaky meat and bone, may be boned, stuffed and rolled Ribs removed in one piece with meat between – marinate	Roasting: As Loin (above) Grilling: 20 mins	Baste often
STREAKY THICK END JOINT Lean end; 3 ribs, sometimes salted	Boiling (from simmering point): 30 mins per 500 g/lb + 30 mins over (minimum 1½ hours)	
STREAKY RASHERS 6 mm/¼ in slices without bone	Slow roasting on rack: 40 mins Frying, slowly: 20 mins Casseroling (cut up): as hand knuckle end above	
GAMMON/HAM Gammon is a leg removed from a whole side of cured pork. A ham is a leg from a fresh side of pork and subsequently cured	Boiling: Place in cold water to cover, bring to the boil then reduce to a simmer, allowing 25 mins per 500 g/lb + 25 mins over for joints up to 5 kg/10 lb over 5 kg/10 lb, allow 15-20 mins per 500 g/lb + 15 mins over. (Time the cooking from the moment the water starts to boil.) Baking: Boil for half time above, drain, wrap in foil and bake in a heated oven (180°C/350°F/Gas Mark 4) until 30 mins before end of cooking time. Increase heat to 220°C/425°F/Gas Mark 7, remove joint, glaze and return to the oven to finish. Alternatively, calculate the cooking time, bake in a heated oven (170°C/325°F/Gas Mark 3) 30 mins before end of cooking time, increase heat to 220°C/425°F/Gas Mark 7. Apply the glaze and return to oven to finish.	Skim occasionally when boiling

NEWER CUTS OF PORK

Escalopes: Slices from the leg, rind and fat removed, flesh beaten out to 3 mm/⅛ inch thickness.

Boneless loin: Two boneless loins, trimmed of fat, on top of each other with tails opposite – tied.

Double loin steaks: Boneless, weight around 185 g /6 oz

VARIETIES OF GAMMON/HAM

COOKED HAMS:
Wiltshire: A mild cured ham with characteristic straw coloured meat.

York: The finest of hams; the name is said to derive from York Minster, the building of which provided the oak sawdust for the first smoking fires.

Jambon de Paris: French equivalent of York ham, also known as Jambon Blanc. Mild tasting, pale pink in colour, sometimes studded with green peppercorns.

Bradenham or Chippenham cure: Processed in molasses, rather than brine, giving a consequent black skin and deep red meat.

AMERICAN SPECIALITY HAMS:
Smithfield: Authentically, comes only from peanut-fed hogs raised in the peanut belt of North Carolina and Virginia and is smoked and processed in Smithfield, Virginia. It has deep brownish red firm flesh and a smoky, salty flavour.

Virginia: Authentically, Virginia hams come only from hogs fattened on peanuts or those having been allowed to forage for acorns and nuts. It has a salty flavour.

RAW HAMS:
Bayonne: Dry salted, cured in brine with red wine added. It is smoked with herbs, often over hay.

Parma: From pigs fed on the whey discarded when making Parmesan cheese. It is dry, salted, but not smoked.

Westphalia: From pigs fed on acorns from the Westphalian oak forests. It is dry salted and cured in brine before being cold-smoked over beech and ash fires to which juniper berries are added.

Raw hams are served very thinly sliced with lots of freshly ground black pepper over them; often accompanied by melon or figs.

HOW TO CHOOSE
Age is not important as all animals are slaughtered very young and are therefore tender with little fat. Flesh should be pale pink and moist, fat white and moist, but not slimy, rind thin and hair-free.

LAMB

CUTS/DESCRIPTION	COOKING METHODS	TIPS
LOIN (WHOLE OR HALF) Backbone jointed for easy carving, or may be boned and stuffed Also divided and sold as Loin Chops	Roasting: 180°C/350°F/Gas Mark 4: 30 mins per 500 g/1 lb + 30 mins over Grilling: 10-15 mins Frying (covered): 12-15 mins	Lean meat with a thin covering of fat. Baste often
LOIN CHUMP CHOPS From end of loin	As Loin Chops (above)	Bony, but economical
LEG Most popular joint. Sold as whole leg or as half-legs FILLET (sometimes boned) KNUCKLE	Roasting: As Loin (above) Pot-roasting: After initial frying: 150°C/300°F/Gas Mark 2: 35 mins per 500 g/1 lb (minimum 1¾ hours) Braising: After initial browning: 170°C/325°F/Gas Mark 3: 40 mins per 500 g/1 lb (minimum 1½ hours)	Prime lean meat, very thin fat and skin. Roast on bed of mint or with mint stuffed under skin. Garlic is good, too
SLICES OF LEG Cube for kebabs	Grilling or frying	Can be tough
SHOULDER Joint with most flavour but lots of bone and fat, so often boned and stuffed. Also sold as half-shoulders	Roasting: As Loin (above) Pot-roasting: As Leg (above)	
BLADE AND KNUCKLE (more bone) Meat also cubed for kebabs, curries etc.	Roasting: As Loin (above) Braising: As Leg (above)	
BEST END NECK 5-6 cutlets, sold whole or cut between ribs as Best-end-neck chops	Roasting (2 tied as 'crown roast' or 'guard of honour'): As Loin (above) Grilling: 6-10 mins, depending on size Frying (open): 6-8 mins Frying (covered): 8-10 mins	Baste often
BREAST Thin strips of very fatty meat with some rib bones; most successful when boned, stuffed and rolled	Pot-roasting or braising: As Leg (above)	
NECK (MIDDLE AND SCRAG END) Very bony but good flavour	Hot pot and casseroles: 140°C/275°F/Gas Mark 1 for 2 hours from time water simmers	A modern classic
NECK FILLET Boned strips of tender, lean meat; ideal to cube for kebabs, curries etc.	Fry slices in non-stick pan	

NEWER CUTS

Brochette: Neck fillet, super-trimmed to leave prime lean meat.

French cutlets: Best-end-neck chops trimmed of meat to one width of eye of meat, dressed with frills.

Noisettes: Loin, minus chump chops, boned and trimmed, rolled and tied then cut into 1.85 cm/¾ in steaks.

Gigot: Leg of lamb with knuckle joint removed.

Saddle: Pair of loins with tail split and each side wrapped around a skewered kidney. Joint laced with pork fat and decorated.

HOW TO CHOOSE
Young animals have pale pink flesh; in older ones it becomes light red. Look for red staining on the ribs, indicating youth, and for bluey cartilage at the knuckle end of the leg bone.

VEAL

CUTS/DESCRIPTION	COOKING METHODS	TIPS
LEG Prime roasting joint, sold on the bone or boned for stuffing. Meat cut from the leg may be used for casseroles	Slow roasting: 180°C/350°F/Gas Mark 4: 30 mins per 500 g/lb + 30 mins Pot roasting: After initial browning, 150°C/300°F/Gas Mark 2: 35 mins per 500 g/lb + 35 mins (minimum 1½ hours) Braising: After initial browning, 170°C/325°F/Gas Mark 3: 40 mins per 500 g/lb	With minimal fat content veal tends to be dry; gentle moist cooking is essential

VEAL		
CUTS/DESCRIPTION	**METHODS OF COOKING**	**TIPS**
SHOULDER Usually sold boned, rolled and tied; may be stuffed. Meat cut from the shoulder is suitable for use in pies and stews	Pot-roasting: As Leg (above) Braising: As Leg (above) Stewing: After initial browning, 140°C/275°F/Gas Mark 1 for 1½-2 hours	Rosemary is excellent flavouring
FILLET (CUSHION) Very lean, expensive cut from the leg; often sliced thinly then beaten flat, stuffed and rolled for 'olives'	Frying: 6-10 mins Braising: After initial browning, as Leg (above), minimum 1 hour	Take care not to allow meat to dry out; serve with a sauce
ESCALOP (SCHNITZEL) Thin slices from the topside, beaten flat	Frying: 6-10 mins Frying (covered): 10-15 mins	
BREAST Thin cuts which are usually sold boned and rolled, often stuffed. Rolled breast may be cooked, as veal mould	Pot-roasting: As Leg (above) Braising: As Leg (above)	
FRICANDEAU Leg, shoulder or breast, trimmed, rolled and wrapped in a layer of thin pork fat	Slow roasting: As Leg (above) Pot roasting: As Leg (above)	Not suitable for unrolling and stuffing
LOIN Roasting joint, on or off the bone. May be stuffed and rolled	Pot-roasting: As Leg (above)	
LOIN CHOPS Divided loin; rump end chops are known as Chump Chops	Frying (covered): 15-20 mins	
CUTLETS From the neck end of the loin	Frying (covered): 12-15 mins Braising: As Leg (above)	

NEWER CUTS	
	HOW TO CHOOSE
Noisettes: Loin, boned and trimmed of fat and gristle, rolled then tied and cut into 6 mm/¼ in steaks.	Flesh should be pale pink, fine-textured, soft but not wet. There is very little fat; it should be creamy white or faintly pink.

A GOOD PORK PATE

When you wish to feed a crowd, nothing is as successful as a good pâté. It is all the better for being made in advance, allowing the flavour to develop.
Allow 60 g/2 oz per person if the pâté is part of a mixed buffet or served at a drinks party, and about 125 g/4 oz per person if the pâté is among two or three main dishes.

Makes about 1.5 kg/3 lb

500 g/1 lb trimmed belly of pork
375 g/12 oz fatty bacon
500 g/1 lb chicken or pork livers
250 g/8 oz onions, coarsely chopped
2 or 3 garlic cloves
1 tsp dried thyme
½ tsp ground nutmeg
½ tsp ground allspice
½ tsp black pepper
2-3 tbls Cognac
45 g/1½ oz dry white breadcrumbs
125 g/4 oz sliced streaky bacon

Mince or chop the belly of pork coarsely and the bacon finely, then mix together. Make a purée of the liver, onions, garlic, thyme, spices and Cognac in a blender and stir it into the pork and bacon. Mix in the breadcrumbs.

Extra flavour can be obtained by leaving the uncooked pâté in a cool place overnight but if you intend to do so, leave out the onions, for they will discolour and sour the mixture. Finely chop or process them separately and add just before cooking.

Pour the mixture into a 1.7 litre/3 pint capacity ovenproof dish or terrine and arrange the strips of bacon across the mixture, tucking the ends well down the sides. Stand in a roasting-tin, add boiling water as a bain marie, and bake at 180°C/350°F/Gas Mark 4 for 1¾ hours. If you can let it stand in a cool place for several days before serving, so much the better. Ⓕ

Options
Apart from leaving out the breadcrumbs to make a softer pâté, you can adapt the recipe by changing the texture of the belly of pork and the bacon to make it coarser or finer. Rosemary is a good alternative to thyme and a few pinches of ground cloves always enhance a pork dish; or add 6 crushed juniper berries and some grated orange rind.

A little red or white wine can add some savouriness – pour about 150 ml/¼ pint of wine over the pâté just before baking.

GLYNN'S TIP
The dried breadcrumbs give the pork pâté a firm texture for slicing without having to press it. It also means that the juices are retained in the pâté rather than being squeezed out to the edges. Some authorities say that bacon should not be used in pâté, but there is an important reason for doing so: the traces of saltpetre used to cure the bacon keep the baked pâté rather pink, which makes it far more attractive. Using chicken livers instead of pork liver also gives a pinker result.

POTTED HARE

This is a classic way to make highly flavoured hare go further as you can use the legs for this dish. Save the tender saddle for roasting or sautéeing; perhaps serve it in slivers scattered on top of an interesting mixed salad as a modern first course.

Makes about 375 g/12 oz

60 g/2 oz onion, chopped
1 garlic clove, crushed
1 tbls oil
60 g/2 oz smoked bacon
90 g/3 oz lean belly of pork
250 g/8 oz hare on the bone
150 ml/¼ pint red wine
1 tbls pickling spice
4 juniper berries
2 bay leaves
5 cm/2 inches orange rind
125 g/4 oz unsalted butter
freshly ground black pepper
1-2 tbls Cognac

Brown the onion and garlic lightly in the oil. Cut the bacon and belly of pork into smallish pieces and fry them for about 3 minutes until the fat is beginning to run. Remove these ingredients and brown the hare lightly.

Return the onion mixture to the pan, add the wine, pickling spice, juniper berries, bay leaves and orange rind. Cover and simmer until the meat is falling from the bones (which may take up to an hour), adding more liquid to the pan if necessary during the cooking time.

Remove the hare and, while you take the flesh from the bones, reduce the cooking liquid until syrupy. Put the hare flesh and everything from the saucepan into a food processor or blender, add the butter and process until you have an even texture; you can make the mixture as smooth or rough as you like. Try only adding half the hare at first and make a very smooth paste, which will ensure that the whole spices do not remain, and then process the remaining hare to give some texture.

Let the mixture cool and then finish the seasoning. You probably won't need salt but pepper is always good with game. Stir in as much Cognac as you like, spoon the mixture into a suitable container, cover tightly and leave for at least 24 hours before serving. Ⓕ

SALAD *of* SWEETBREADS *and* FOUR PEPPERS

The herbs and spices used to flavour a quality dry white vermouth are a reliable shortcut to well-flavoured sauces for the adventurous but busy cook. But even the driest vermouths have an underlying sweetness and so must be used with discretion.

Serves four as a main course, six to eight as a starter.

750 g/1½ lb lambs' sweetbreads
salt
1 lemon
salt
½ red pepper
½ green pepper
½ white pepper
½ yellow pepper
300 ml/½ pint double cream
150 ml/¼ pint dry white vermouth (Chambery is best)
1 tbls chopped parsley

Soak the sweetbreads in plenty of cold water for at least 4 hours, changing the water at least four times. As the water gets clearer, add a little salt to encourage the final traces of blood to float free.

Put the sweetbreads into cold water in a saucepan, add a squeeze of juice from the lemon and bring slowly to the boil. Simmer for just 3 minutes, then drain and cool under running cold water. Pull off any large lumps of membrane , but leave on the thin coating which holds the sweetbreads in shape. Drain well and sprinkle with a little lemon juice and salt.

Cut a 5 cm/2 inch strip of rind from the lemon, remove all traces of white pith, then chop the rind finely and set aside.

Cut the peppers into fine, even, straight strips. Throw them into fast-boiling water and blanch for 30 seconds so that the colour brightens. Plunge immediately into cold water, then drain well.

Put the cream and vermouth into a small saucepan and reduce over medium heat until half the original volume and thick enough to coat the back of a spoon. Add the sweetbreads to the pan, lower the heat and warm through very gently. Spoon on to warmed plates. Sprinkle on the parsley and grate the lemon peel finely directly on to the plates. Arrange the pepper strips around the edge of the plate in a trellis pattern and serve at once. Ⓕ

WARM SALAD *of* SADDLE *of* HARE *or* VENISON

A marvellous way to make a small amount of the most expensive cut of hare or venison go a long way – served hot and topping a salad of mixed leaves, whole garlic cloves and walnuts. The garlic is cooked until it is a paste; squash it as you eat it and dip the pieces of venison or hare into it.

Serves four

250 g/8 oz saddle of hare or venison
13 large garlic cloves
2 tbls sunflower oil
125-250 g/4-8 oz mixed salad leaves (see method)
2 tbls walnut oil
60 g/2 oz walnut halves
2 tbls lemon juice
8 tsp white wine vinegar

Take the fillets from the saddle of hare and trim off all the membrane; if using venison do the same. Cut 1 garlic clove in half and rub it over the meat.

Simmer the remaining 12 whole, unpeeled garlic cloves in a little water until they are very soft, almost translucent-looking, which may take as long as 45 minutes. Sauté the fillets in the sunflower oil for about 5 minutes and then put to one side to rest for 5 minutes in a warm place.

Select mostly salad leaves which are slightly tougher and more bitter, and which will not wilt when warmed, such as red radicchio, curly endive, watercress leaves, Belgian endive, oak-leaf lettuce. Some sweet lambs' lettuce and some cos lettuce are both worthwhile additions. Essentially, you should go for contrast of colour and texture. The leaves should be washed, well dried and torn into medium-sized pieces. Arrange in low mounds on flat plates and keep cool.

Add the walnut oil to the pan and lightly brown the walnut halves. Slice the fillets thinly and arrange on top of the salads. Quickly add the garlic cloves, lemon juice and vinegar to the pan. Heat through, then spoon this dressing evenly over the hare and salad, and serve. Ⓕ Ⓢ
Photograph, p. 150.

CHILI BEEF and AVOCADO

For those who don't like to eat much meat but love lots of flavour, the avocado balances the spiciness of the chili and makes the minced beef go very much further.

Serves four

500 g/1 lb good quality minced beef
1-2 garlic cloves, crushed
2 tbls tomato purée
2 tbls chili powder
salt and freshly ground black pepper (optional)
300 ml/½ pint water
2 ripe avocados
1 fresh lime
4 tbls thick strained yoghurt

Warm a thick frying-pan or non-stick pan and add the beef. Cook over a medium heat, stirring from time to time until all excess liquid has been steamed away and much of the meat has browned. Add a garlic clove – or more if you like. Stir well, then push to one side and add the tomato purée. Let it fry for a minute to thicken and redden it, then stir it evenly into the meat. Sprinkle in the chili (make sure it is a mixture of spices including cumin and not just cayenne pepper, which is often sold as chilli pepper), then add the water. Cook gently, uncovered, until the meat is tender and most of the liquid has evaporated; this will take 30-45 minutes.

Halve and peel the avocados and remove the stones. Lay each half flat with the cut side down and cut into thin, diagonal slices. Arrange each slice in a curve on warm plates. Put a little mixed salad also on the plate, then divide the chili beef. Top the beef with a spoonful of yoghurt. Grate a little of the lime rind over each plate and then squeeze the juice on to the avocado. *Photograph, p. 78.*

Option
The chili sauce is also wonderful spooned over sliced baked potatoes.

LAMB CHOPS on TOAST

It's always difficult to know what to do to make lamb chops interesting. This idea came to me one night when the cupboard was almost bare but there was a little mint struggling in the garden. Wholemeal bread is very much better than white, but if you do not have any, cook the dish anyway. If you cannot buy double lamb chops from your butcher or supermarket, put two single chops together and pretend!

Serves one

1 medium-thick slice of good wholemeal bread
seed mustard (Moutarde de Meaux, Dijon, or similar)
fresh mint leaves, or a sprinkle of dried mint
1 double lamb chop

Preferably using a mustard that is mixed with wine, smear the bread all over and cover with mint leaves, or a sprinkling of dried mint; be generous for the flavour diminishes during cooking.

Put the double lamb chop (two fairly thin undivided chops rather than an extra thick chop) on top of the bread and curl its ends inwards – trim them, if you have to. Put the whole thing on a baking sheet and cook in the oven at 180°C/350°F/Gas Mark 4 for 10 minutes. Turn the chop over (just the chop, not the bread) and cook for another 10 minutes. After this time the lamb will have pink flesh, but if you like it particularly well done leave it in for a few more minutes.

The juices from the meat will have soaked into the bread and the edges of the bread will have toasted and crisped deliciously from the combination of fat and oven heat. ⓠ

KIDNEYS in MUSTARD SAUCE

Serves four as a starter, two as a main course

6 lambs' kidneys
salt and pepper
3 tbls butter
1 tbls oil
185 g/6 oz leeks, thinly sliced
113 g/4 oz can baby corn, drained
1 shallot, finely chopped
5 tbls white wine
5 tbls double cream
2 tsps Dijon mustard
lemon juice
2 tbls chopped parsley
2 slices toast, with crusts removed and each cut into 4 triangles

Skin the kidneys, remove the core and membranes and cut into thin slices. Sprinkle with pepper. Heat 1 tablespoon of butter with the oil and fry the kidneys rapidly to brown evenly. Remove and keep warm.

Melt the remaining butter in a saucepan and toss the leeks to coat them. Season with salt and more black pepper, then arrange the drained corn on top. Cover the pan and simmer gently for 10 minutes. Add the shallot to the frying-pan and cook until softened. Pour in the wine and reduce for 2-3 minutes over high heat. Take the pan off the heat, stir in the cream and mustard and mix well. Return to the heat and boil until the sauce thickens. Return the kidneys to the pan, reduce the heat and simmer for 2-3 minutes to warm through. Season with salt, pepper, a squeeze of lemon juice and stir in the chopped parsley.

Pile the kidneys and sauce in the centre of warmed plates with the triangles of toast and a border of the leeks and baby corn. Ⓕ

AMONTILLADO KIDNEYS

Serves two

6 lambs' kidneys
3 tbls butter
1 tbls olive oil
60 g/2 oz stoned black olives
90 g/3 oz mushrooms, thinly sliced
salt and pepper
120 ml/4 fl oz Amontillado sherry
4 tbls brandy
4 tbls double cream
lemon juice to taste
1 tbls chopped parsley

Skin and core the kidneys, then cut into thin slices. Heat 1 tablespoon of butter with the oil in a pan and fry the kidneys over a high heat. Remove and keep warm.

Blanch the olives for 2 minutes and drain. Heat the remaining butter in a second pan and sauté the mushrooms for 3-4 minutes; add the olives, season with salt and pepper and keep warm.

Deglaze the kidney pan with the sherry, add the brandy and cream and reduce over high heat until the liquid is half the original volume. Return the kidneys to the pan with the mushrooms, lower the heat and simmer for 1 minute. Season with salt, pepper and a squeeze of lemon juice. Serve immediately, sprinkled with chopped parsley.

CHINESE-MARINATED BELLY of PORK

I think this is the favourite pork dish I have created, something I have served in restaurants where I have cooked it for a cold starter with a mixed salad and as a hot main course. It is economical and great for midweek meals, informal parties, barbecues and picnics – good and tasty whatever the time of day or year.

Serves four or more as a main course; eight as a first course

1 kg/2-2¼ lb lean belly of pork (with some bone)
3 tbls soy sauce
2 tbls dry sherry or lemon juice
2 tbls chilli sauce
1 tsp ground allspice
1 tsp ground cinnamon
½ tsp ground cloves
1 garlic clove, crushed

Remove the bones from the pork and score through the fat deeply so that the flesh is exposed. Put the pork into a shallow dish just large enough to hold it.

Mix the remaining ingredients together and pour the mixture over the pork, making sure it penetrates the slashed fat. Turn the meat over then leave to marinate for 12 hours in a cool place, or up to 24 hours in a refrigerator. Turn the pork over during this time, if possible.

Cook the pork on a rack in a roasting tin at 220°C/425°F/Gas Mark 7 for 10 minutes. Reduce the heat to 170°C/325°F/Gas Mark 3 and cook for a further 30 minutes per 500 g/1 lb (35 minutes per 500 g/1 lb if it was marinated in the refrigerator). Do not baste the meat while it is cooking.

Let the cooked pork rest for 10-15 minutes before slicing. Serve with a little of the defatted pan juices if you like.

To make a larger quantity of sauce, add a little water to the defatted pan juices, heat and strain. To serve cold, let the meat cool on the rack then chill.

Note: Do not marinate longer than the given times; shorter times give quite good results – 4 hours at room temperature is fine.

I once boiled up the bones from the belly of pork to make a small amount of stock, combined that with the cooking juices from the pork and used the mixture to poach some gooseberries, which made a stunning sauce. Flavour it if you like with a little more of the same flavourings in which the pork marinated. Alternatively, make the sauce with apples or pears.

Ketchup Meat Loaf

This is marvellous family food but, like all simple food, you should buy the best ingredients you can afford. This can make twelve servings as part of a hot buffet but four to six hungry members of a family will demolish it at one sitting on a cold night.

Serves four to six

1 kg/2 lb good minced beef (chuck steak for preference)
¾ tsp salt
90-125 g/3-4 oz fine breadcrumbs
1 garlic clove, crushed
60 g/2 oz celery, finely chopped
60 g/2 oz onion, finely chopped (or more)
5 generous tbls tomato ketchup
1 tbls Worcestershire sauce
1 tsp dried thyme
plenty of freshly ground pepper
2 large eggs

Mix all the ingredients together very well, using your hands, then shape it into a loaf or put into a large loaf tin. Bake at 180°C/350°F/Gas Mark 4 for 60-75 minutes.

Serve hot with tomato or mushroom sauce (see pages 15 and 16), cold with salad, or in buns or pitta bread with salad, pickles and mustard.

'Ice' the loaf, by topping with mashed potato flavoured with herbs or, better still, with mustard and butter. Replace in the oven for 10 minutes, or until the top is nicely browned.

Option
Fruited Meat Loaf Use 750 g/1½ lb of minced beef with 250 g/8 oz of minced pork and add 90 g/3 oz of raisins. Season with a brown fruit sauce, rather than tomato ketchup, with a half teaspoon of dried sage and 2 tablespoons of chopped fresh parsley replacing the thyme.

Hamburgers

If you want real hamburgers, you don't need a recipe. A hamburger is simply coarsely minced beef (chuck steak is the best) made into a patty with the least possible handling and no seasoning other than a little salt on the outside. It must not be squashed into shape but very lightly shaped. It is then either grilled, or cooked in a pan with virtually no fat, and served on a toasted hot bun with a choice of salad leaves, pickles, sauces and mustards.

If you have meat that is of inferior quality or has a high fat content, it may be lightly flavoured with a small amount of very finely chopped onion (no more than 1-2 tablespoons for 1 kg/2 lb of meat) or garlic. You might try very finely chopped celery, also. It is common in America to form the meat round a chip of ice with a pat of butter, which keeps the inside moist and safe from overcooking. Overcooking is what makes hamburgers tough.

Approximate cooking times are:
Grilled Cook at high heat. A 2.5 cm/1 inch thick hamburger (at room temperature) will take 3-5 minutes on each side. Turn only once.
Chargrilled On a really hot barbecue, a 2.5 cm/1 inch thick hamburger will be cooked through but still pinkish in 6-7 minutes per side, depending on the prevailing wind!

Remember that the bun *must* be toasted; in the old days it was also buttered.

Minced Meat Plate Pie

This good, mid-week, standby recipe is tasty and economical and easy to make, especially if you use ready-made pastry. Any leftover pie is ideal for lunch boxes. Make it for a picnic, as it travels well.

Serves four

375 g/12 oz shortcrust pastry
125-185 g/4-6 oz onions, chopped
oil for frying
500 g/1 lb good quality lean minced beef
salt and freshly ground black pepper
Worcestershire sauce
2 tsps fine or medium oatmeal
milk or beaten egg to glaze

Roll out the pastry and use half of it to line a fairly deep dinner-plate.

Fry the onions in oil until softened and lightly browned, then add the beef and cook until most of the liquid has evaporated and the meat smells beefy; if some of it should brown, so much the better. Season generously with salt, pepper and a good shake of Worcestershire sauce, then stir in the oatmeal (which is a simple way to thicken the mince) and let the mixture cool.

Once cool, taste the mixture and adjust the seasoning. Put the filling on to the pastry base and cover with the remaining pastry. Seal the edges well and make a few small slashes over the top. Brush with a little beaten egg or milk to glaze, then bake at 180-200°C/375-400°F/Gas Mark 5 or 6 for 20-30 minutes, until the pastry is well cooked and the meat heated through. Serve hot or cold. Ⓔ

Cornish Pasties

As a famous supermarket chain discovered when they attempted to market pasties containing carrots, you simply cannot muck about with such a famous food and still call it a pastie. This recipe was given to me in Cornwall by a woman who demands she remains anonymous – because she makes pasties to a different recipe according to whether they are for family and friends or for the pub down the road. This is the family one.

Makes one pastie

185 g/6 oz made shortcrust pastry (see page 129)
60 g/2 oz chuck or rump steak
125 g/4 oz raw potato
60 g/2 oz onion (optional)
30 g/1 oz swede if in season
salt and pepper

The pastry should ideally be made with lard or beef dripping. Roll out the pastry to the size of a largish bread and butter plate, then trim neatly.

It is important that the meat and vegetables are not minced or finely chopped but are cut into thin, fairly evenly sized flakes. You can jumble them together or layer them directly onto the pastry as you cut them. The order is up to you but I like the meat layered between the vegetables. Use plenty of salt and black pepper.

If you are not very adept at crimping, simply fold the pastry over and seal it well with a fold. Crimpers can either do this with the seam on the side, or turn the pastie halfway over and seal and crimp it across the top.

Pasties should be started in a hot oven – 220°C/425°F/Gas Mark 7 for 15 minutes to begin browning and then the heat reduced to 180°C/350°F/Gas Mark 4 or less for another 30-45 minutes. The time will depend on how thickly you have sliced your meat and potato, thus you will have to experiment a little.

PARTY PIE

This is ideal for feeding large numbers of people when you have a restricted budget. The ingredients aren't expensive but they're full of interesting flavour and texture. The real bonus is that it tastes better 24 hours after being made. Take the time to paint the pastry and you'll have a party-piece that everyone will remember.

Serves eight

250 g/8 oz chicken livers
60 g/2 oz onion, chopped
2 garlic cloves
1 tsp ground allspice
½ tsp ground nutmeg
1 tsp dried thyme
½ tsp dried rosemary
6 juniper berries, crushed
3 tbls brandy or port
375 g/12 oz belly of pork, de-rinded and boned
250 g/8 oz smoked lean bacon
500 g/1 lb ready-made puff pastry (or see page 133)
6-8 large eggs
freshly ground black pepper
250 g/8 oz large mushrooms
beaten egg, to glaze

Purée the livers, onion, garlic, spices, herbs and brandy or port in a blender or food processor.

Cut the pork into chunks and slice the bacon into strips or chunks and add them to the purée in the processor. Make an even-textured mixture which is not too smooth. If you don't have a processor, mince or finely chop the meats and stir them into the purée.

Use an ovenproof casserole or baking-dish with a rim that is at least 7.5 cm/3 inches deep and line it with two-thirds of the pastry. Stand a pie-funnel in the middle, then add half the meat mixture. Level the top and carefully break in the eggs, arranging them so that they join and cover the whole surface – if they don't, add one or two more. Pepper the eggs generously, then cover with the remaining meat, sprinkling rather than spreading so you don't break the egg yolks. Slice the mushrooms thickly and arrange on top. Make an extra rim with the pastry trimmings, cover with the remaining pastry, and seal very firmly.

Cut one or two vents in the top and paint the pastry, if you like, with undiluted food colourings. Let it dry before glazing with beaten egg. Bake at 220°C/425°F/Gas Mark 7 for 20 minutes, then reduce the heat to 180°C/350°F/Gas Mark 4 and cook for another 60 minutes. Serve cold. Ⓔ

BACON and EGG PIE

The most popular pie I know, this is good served hot or cold, and is quite the best thing imaginable for eating in the open air. Although a standby in Australia and New Zealand, it seems to have its roots in the West Country.

Serves four to six

375 g/12 oz ready-made puff pastry (or see page 133)
250 g/8 oz smoked streaky bacon
6 large eggs
salt and freshly ground black pepper
beaten egg to glaze

Choose a pie dish about 20-23 cm/8-9 inches in diameter and line with half the pastry. Cut the bacon into uneven pieces, about the size of half of your thumb, and fry gently until the fat is running freely. Drain well, then arrange on the base of the pastry. Break the eggs into the bacon, putting five around the edge and one in the middle. Tilt the dish gently to ensure that the egg whites all meet. There's probably enough salt in the bacon but add a little extra if you must, then grind in some black pepper.

Roll out the remaining pastry and use it for the pie crust, glaze with a little beaten egg if you have another one, then bake for 25 minutes in a preheated oven (200°C/400°F/Gas Mark 6). Reduce the heat to 160°C/325°F/Gas Mark 3 and bake for a further 15 minutes.

Options

Any vegetable that has an assertive flavour or contrasted texture can be added to make this your own. Diced green pepper is not a cliché here but a genuine contribution, so are leftover cooked peas, some pre-cooked onion, a little garlic or fried potatoes.

STUFFED KIDNEY CUSHIONS

Serves six as a starter

6 lambs' kidneys
125 g/4 oz mushrooms, very finely chopped
1 tbls butter
1 tbls sherry, wine or brandy
2 tsps Dijon or strong mustard
1 garlic clove, crushed
1 tsp dried oregano
1 tbls dried white breadcrumbs
salt and pepper
250 g/8 oz frozen puff pastry
beaten egg or milk, to glaze

Skin the kidneys and, using sharp scissors, cut out the fat and membrane in each one and make the pocket as large as possible.

Put the mushrooms into a small saucepan with the butter, alcohol, mustard, garlic, and oregano. Cook for 2-3 minutes until the mixture is thick and only very slightly liquid. Stir in the breadcrumbs, season to taste with salt and pepper, then cool.

Roll out the pastry thinly and divide into six even-sized rectangles.

Stuff the kidneys with the cooled stuffing. Put each kidney on to a piece of pastry. Wet the edges; fold in the short sides first, then the long sides. The pastry won't meet – you should have covered the kidney but be able to see the stuffing through the gap in the pastry. Brush with beaten egg or milk to glaze.

Bake at 220°C/425°F/Gas Mark 7 for 20 minutes. Serve hot. Ⓕ

MARINATED LAMB FILLET with SPINACH in PHYLLO

Marinating the meat and preparing the spinach parcels for this Greek dish can be a put-off but neither stage is difficult. A little patience is all that is needed to make a success of this unusual recipe.

Serves four

750 g/1½ lb lamb fillet
grated rind and juice of 1 lemon
1 or 2 garlic cloves, crushed
1 tbls fresh mint or 1 tsp dried mint
salt and pepper
250 g/8 oz fresh spinach leaves
4 phyllo pastry sheets
1 tbls butter, melted
2 tbls olive oil

Trim the lamb, cut into four pieces and score on both sides to allow the marinade to penetrate. Mix the lemon juice and rind, garlic, mint and seasoning. Put the meat into a shallow dish and pour the marinade over. Leave for 2-4 hours at room temperature, turning the meat once or twice.

Blanch the spinach leaves in boiling water for a few seconds until they wilt, then plunge immediately into iced water, drain, and dry on kitchen paper. Wrap each piece of marinated lamb in three or four spinach leaves, making neat parcels.

Put a sheet of phyllo pastry on a board and brush with the melted butter and oil mixed together. Put a spinach parcel on top and roll it up loosely, tucking in the ends neatly. Wrap the other three parcels in a similar way, then brush all four with the remaining oil and butter.

Bake at 180°C/350°F/Gas Mark 4 for 30-40 minutes, depending on whether you like your lamb pink or cooked through. Let the parcels rest before cutting into thick slices to serve fanned out on the plate. Ⓣ Ⓢ

110

Options
Thick Greek yoghurt can be added to the marinade.
Apricot Lamb Chop 60 g/2 oz dried apricots and simmer them in 4 tablespoons of lemon juice for a few minutes until they soften. Put a spoonful of this mixture on top of the lamb fillet before wrapping up in the spinach leaves.

SWEETBREADS with LETTUCE and ARTICHOKES

A thoroughly modern recipe with a delightful fresh, pale colour and an unexpectedly good combination of braised lettuce and artichokes.

Serves four

500 g/1 lb lambs' sweetbreads
salt and pepper
1 lemon
2 tbls butter
60 g/2 oz shallot, finely chopped
1 celery stick, finely chopped
1 bay leaf
1 sprig fresh thyme
150 ml/¼ pint white wine or chicken stock
4 small lettuce hearts
397 g/14 oz can artichoke hearts, drained and rinsed
1 tbls brandy
6 tbls double cream

Soak the sweetbreads for at least 4 hours in cold water, changing it every hour and adding a little salt to draw out all traces of blood. Put them into a saucepan with a slice of lemon, cover with cold water and bring to the boil. Simmer for 3 minutes, drain and cool under running cold water. Remove large pieces of membrane and fat but not the thin transparent skin which holds the sweetbreads in shape.

Melt half the butter in a saucepan, add the shallot and celery and cook gently until they soften. Add the bay leaf and thyme and arrange the sweetbreads on top. Pour the wine or stock over, bring to the boil, then lower the heat, cover and simmer very gently for 20 minutes.

Wash the lettuce hearts but do not dry them. Slice in half lengthwise and arrange half in the bottom of a saucepan. Arrange the artichokes over the lettuce in an even layer, season with salt, pepper and a squeeze of lemon juice. Put the remaining lettuce on top, cover the pan and simmer very gently for 20 minutes.

Remove the sweetbreads and strain the cooking liquor into a clean pan. Add the brandy and reduce over a high heat until syrupy. Add the cream and continue boiling for 2-3 minutes to reduce slightly. Carefully return the sweetbreads to the pan without breaking them up, lower the heat and warm through gently.

Arrange the lettuce and artichokes on warmed plates to form a ring. Using a slotted spoon, take the sweetbreads from the sauce and pile in the middle of the plates. Quickly whisk the remaining butter into the sauce to give it a shine, then pour it over the sweetbreads and serve immediately. Ⓕ Ⓢ

SWEETBREADS with CHESTNUTS & MUSHROOMS

A salad of very young spinach leaves and curly endive with no dressing on it is the perfect accompaniment to this rich dish. On celebratory days you could serve this in smaller portions as a first course.

Serves four as a main course, six to eight as a starter

500 g/1 lb lambs' sweetbreads
salt and pepper
lemon juice
60 g/2 oz dried mushrooms
60 g/2 oz dried chestnuts
30 g/1 oz butter
2 shallots, finely chopped
1 tbls plain flour
150 ml/¼ pint dry white vermouth
150 ml/¼ pint double cream

Soak the sweetbreads for at least 4 hours in cold water, changing it every hour and adding a little salt to encourage the final traces of blood to float free. Put the sweetbreads into a saucepan with a squeeze of lemon juice and bring slowly to the boil, simmer for just 3 minutes, then drain and run under cold water to cool. Remove any large lumps of membrane or fat, but not the thin transparent skin which keeps the sweetbreads in shape. Drain well and sprinkle with lemon juice.

Rinse the dried mushrooms free of grit, then put them into a small saucepan with the chestnuts. Cover with warm water and allow them to soak for 30 minutes. Bring slowly to the boil and simmer very gently for 20-30 minutes, until both are tender and there is only a little liquid remaining in the pan, then cool.

Melt the butter in a saucepan and cook the shallot until softened but not brown. Add the flour and cook for 2 minutes, then stir in the vermouth. Bring to the boil, stirring continuously, until thick and smooth, add the mushrooms and chestnuts with any remaining liquid, cream and seasoning. Cook for 2-3 minutes, until the sauce has a good consistency, then stir in the sweetbreads, lower the heat and simmer to warm them through gently. Ⓕ Ⓢ Ⓣ

KIDNEYS, LIVER and BACON with GARLIC

This is an extraordinarily different way to serve kidneys or bacon, cooked at a very low temperature with masses of garlic to give a voluptuous new experience, doubly enhanced by being served on crisp slices of garlic toast. It's essential to soak the kidneys and liver in milk beforehand, to ensure a mild flavour.

Serves four

250 g/8 oz lambs' liver
250 g/8 oz lambs' kidneys
milk for soaking
250 g/8 oz lean smoked bacon
1 tbls olive oil
90 g/3 oz butter
4 garlic cloves, peeled and thinly sliced
salt and pepper
5 tbls double cream
2 tbls parsley, chopped
TO SERVE
French bread
garlic butter

Cut the liver and kidneys into thin strips, 5 mm/¼ inch wide, place in a bowl and cover with milk. Leave to soak for at least 1 hour. Cut the bacon into strips of a similar size.

Heat the oil with 1 tablespoon of the butter in a pan and fry the bacon until it just starts to crisp. Drain the liver and kidneys, roughly pat dry with kitchen paper, then add the meat to the bacon and fry quickly until just beginning to brown. Turn the heat as low as you can, add the remaining butter and garlic, season with salt and pepper, then cover and cook very gently for 30 minutes.

Cut the bread at a slight angle into 2.5 cm/1 inch slices. Spread with garlic butter, put on to a baking-sheet and bake for 10 minutes at 200°C/400°F/Gas Mark 6, until brown and crisp. Keep warm.

Add the cream to the saucepan, increase the heat and reduce for 2-3 minutes until the sauce has a good consistency. Check the seasoning and stir in the parsley. Serve the mixture piled on to the garlic toasts. Ⓢ

GLYNN'S TIP

Calves' sweetbreads are rated much more highly than lambs' and cost much more, but the culinary difference is minimal. They are also much less common, so I should use the frozen lambs' ones from New Zealand.

MARINADES for LAMB KEBABS

The following marinades will each coat 500 g/ 1 lb cubed leg or neck fillet of lamb.

ORIENTAL MARINADE
4 tbls soy sauce
3 tbls lemon juice
2 tbls oil
1 tbls minced or grated fresh ginger
1 or 2 garlic cloves, crushed (optional)
SPICY MARINADE
1 tbls oil
4 tbls lemon juice
1 heaped tsp ground coriander
1 heaped tsp ground cumin
1 garlic clove, crushed (optional)
1 tbls minced onion (optional)

Mix all the ingredients together and leave the meat in the marinade at room temperature for 2 hours, turning as often as you can. Transfer the lamb to skewers with fresh bay leaves between the cubes, or alternate with pieces of pepper, whole mushrooms, whole cherry tomatoes or cooked baby new potatoes in their skins.

When the meat is cooked, add a little more fresh lemon juice to the remaining marinade, warm them together, then pour over the kebabs to serve.

LAMB STEAKS NICOISE

Boneless lamb steaks are far better value than chops and much more interesting to eat, especially when they are cooked in a delicious sauce such as this.

Serves four

oil for frying
4 boneless lamb steaks, 185 g/6 oz each
397 g/14 oz can plum tomatoes, crushed
125 g/4 oz celery, chopped
1 or 2 garlic cloves, crushed
60 g/2 oz stuffed green olives
3 anchovy fillets, chopped
1 heaped tsp dried basil
salt and pepper

Heat the oil and fry the steaks quickly on both sides to brown, then set aside. Mix the remaining ingredients and transfer to a casserole or ovenproof dish. Sit the lamb on top and season with a little more pepper. Cover and cook at 180°C/350°F/Gas Mark 4 for 30 minutes. Remove the lid, turn the lamb steaks over, sprinkle with a little pepper and return to the oven, uncovered, for another 15 minutes. Make full use of the oven and bake some potatoes at the same time to serve with the lamb.

LAMB STEAKS with ORANGE and ROSEMARY

A very simple way to serve lamb steaks. If you leave them marinating longer than 4 hours before cooking, keep them covered in the refrigerator, but bring them to room temperature before cooking.

Serves two

2 lamb steaks, boned, 185 g/6 oz each
whole-grain mustard
1 tbls fresh rosemary or 1 tsp dried rosemary
juice of 2 oranges
juice of 1 lemon
1 small garlic clove, crushed
5 tbls white wine
salt and pepper
1 tbls butter
watercress or fresh rosemary to garnish

Spread the steaks on both sides with the mustard and put them side by side in a shallow dish. Sprinkle with the rosemary and add the citrus juices, garlic, white wine and seasoning. Leave the meat to marinate at room temperature for 4 hours. Thirty minutes before you plan to cook the steaks, drain off the marinade into a small saucepan. Boil over medium heat until it is reduced and syrupy. Heat a non-stick frying-pan and cook the steaks quickly over high heat for 3-4 minutes on each side, depending on how pink you like your meat. Keep them warm, covered on a plate.

Strain the reduced sauce into a clean pan and over low heat beat in the butter a little at a time to give a shine and thicken it a little. Make a puddle of sauce on two heated plates, arrange the steaks on top and garnish with one or two watercress leaves, or a tiny sprig of fresh rosemary. Ⓣ Ⓢ

VEAL ESCALOPES in MUSTARD CREAM SAUCE

This quick and easy recipe is bound to impress! If the veal hasn't already been flattened, put it between two sheets of wet greaseproof paper and beat it with a rolling-pin.

Serves four

60 g/2 oz unsalted butter
2 tbls oil
2 tbls finely chopped shallot
4 veal escalopes, 125-185 g/4-6 oz each
salt and freshly ground black pepper
100 ml/3½ fl oz dry white wine
2 tbls Dijon mustard
150 ml/¼ pint double or whipping cream
1 large ripe tomato, peeled, cored and finely diced

Heat the butter and oil, add the shallots and cook gently for 5 minutes to soften without browning. Season the meat with salt and pepper on both sides and cook over moderate heat for 2-3 minutes on each side. (Don't overcook the meat; don't worry if it doesn't brown.) Remove the escalopes and keep warm, covered.

Pour the wine into the pan and bring to the boil, scraping up the pan sediment. Reduce until only 2 or 3 tablespoons of liquid remain, then whisk in the mustard and cream. Boil for 2 minutes, check the seasoning and spoon the sauce over the veal escalopes. Sprinkle with chopped tomato and serve immediately. Ⓠ Ⓢ

Option
Use thick yoghurt instead of cream.

ESCALOPES with WILD MUSHROOMS

Sauté 125 g/4 oz wild mushrooms in 30 g/1 oz butter. Cook the veal as above and keep warm. Make the sauce but omit the mustard and instead stir in the cooked mushrooms, seasoning with salt, pepper and lemon juice. Serve the veal topped with the sauce, decorated with chopped parsley.

This recipe is equally successful using slices of turkey breast – these should be cooked for 5 minutes on each side.

LIVER MARSALA with PARSLEY GNOCCHI

Even those who are not normally fans of liver will like this dish with its rich sweetness.

Serves four

500 g/1 lb lambs' liver
125 g/4 oz lean smoked bacon
2 tbls seasoned flour
30 g/1 oz butter
1 tbls olive oil
1 tsp sweet paprika
200 ml/⅓ pint Marsala
150 ml/¼ pint water
375 g/12 oz gnocchi
generous knob of butter
3-4 tbls chopped parsley
150 ml/¼ pint soured cream or strained yoghurt

Cut the liver and bacon into really thin strips no wider than 5 mm/¼ inch. Toss the liver in the seasoned flour to coat lightly. Heat the butter and oil in a frying-pan and fry the bacon strips until just crisp, then remove. Add the liver to the pan and toss over a high heat to brown all over but do not overcook. Remove to a plate. Stir the remaining seasoned flour into the pan

FAMILY CELEBRATION BUFFET
From top, clockwise: Turkey and Strawberry Salad in Minted Rice Mould, pp.85 and 36;
Celebration Salmon, p.69; Macaroon Bases with Fresh Fruit, p.140.

THE CONTEMPORARY VEGETARIAN

From top, clockwise: Chilled Dried Fruit Salad, p.138; Stuffed Cabbage in
a Pastry Case, p.61; Dippy Bean Salad, p.49.

GOING with the GRAIN
From top, clockwise: Aduki Burgers, p.48; Aubergine and Brown Rice Timbale with
Tomato Sauce, pp.36 and 16; Hot Green Lentil Salad, p.47; Maharaja's Beef Pulao, p.37.

WINTER TRADITIONS RECREATED
From top, clockwise: Honeyed-Almond Stuffed Apples with Apricot Coulis, p.148; Chicken and
Leek with Smoked Oysters, p.96; Warm Beetroot Salad, p.59.

with the paprika and scrape up the sediment from the bottom. Pour in the Marsala and water and stir while bringing to the boil. Boil for 4-5 minutes, to cook the flour and thicken the sauce a little.

Meanwhile, cook the gnocchi as directed on the packet. Drain well. Add a knob of butter to the pan and all but half a tablespoon of the parsley and toss the gnocchi to coat thoroughly. Transfer to a heated serving dish and keep warm.

Return the liver and bacon to the pan and heat through gently in the sauce. Swirl in the soured cream or yoghurt to give a marbled effect, check the seasoning, then pour into the middle of the gnocchi on the serving dish. Sprinkle with the reserved chopped parsley and serve at once. ⓦ

LIVER with VERMOUTH and RUBY GRAPEFRUIT

An unusual combination you may think, but try it and see how good it is. The grapefruit must be of the superior pink-fleshed variety, which has a subtle spiciness to complement its delightful colouring. If you're feeling extravagant, and fancy an even more aromatic sauce, try using Campari instead of red vermouth.

Serves four

500 g/1 lb lambs' liver, thinly sliced
seasoned flour for coating
1 tbls olive oil
30 g/1 oz butter
200 ml/1/3 pint red vermouth
1/2 tsp allspice, coarsely ground
1 ruby grapefruit, segmented and free from all pith
salt and pepper

Toss the liver in seasoned flour to coat very lightly. Heat the oil and butter in a pan and fry the liver over a medium heat until drops of blood appear; turn over and fry the other side. Remove to a plate and keep warm, covered.

Pour the vermouth into the pan, add the allspice and bring to the boil, scraping to loosen the pan sediment. Reduce until very slightly syrupy, lower the heat and add the grapefruit segments. Simmer gently to warm the fruit through and check the seasoning. Serve the liver with the segments alongside and a little sauce strained over the top.

RABBIT with FENNEL in YOGHURT SAUCE

I suppose this could be called a blanquette, for everything is pale: but take my word, this is a hundred times better than a classic blanquette, and probably one of the best recipes in the book.

Serves four

60 g/2 oz butter
250 g/8 oz fennel, thinly sliced (reserve green fronds)
1 garlic clove, crushed
500 g/1 lb rabbit meat, diced
150 ml/1/4 pint dry white wine
4 tbls dry white vermouth
salt and pepper
strained Greek yoghurt

Melt the butter in a heavy pan and stir in the fennel and garlic. Add the rabbit and stir until well coated with butter. Do not brown. Pour in the wine and vermouth, season lightly and simmer for about 45 minutes or until the rabbit is tender.

Remove the pan from the heat and stir in as much yoghurt as you need to make a thick white sauce. Chop the fennel fronds finely and scatter on top. Marvellous with jacket potatoes.

RABBIT in SOURED CREAM and MUSTARD

The combination of soured cream and a strong mustard counteracts the sweetness of rabbit.

The mustard prevents the cream from separating, but if you find it tastes too strong cook it a little longer and the 'bite' will disappear. If you don't like specks in sauces, use a mustard that does not have seeds in it.

Serves four

750 g/1 1/2 lb boneless rabbit, diced
flour for dusting
salt and pepper
oil and butter for frying
450 ml/3/4 pint chicken stock, white wine, or a combination of both
few sprigs of fresh thyme
4 tbls seed mustard
150 ml/1/4 pint soured cream

Toss the rabbit lightly in flour, then season with salt and pepper. Using a flameproof casserole or saucepan, brown the rabbit in equal quantities of oil and butter; be generous, for there is no fat on the rabbit meat. Add the stock and/or wine and the thyme, cover and simmer for about 45 minutes.

At least 15 minutes before serving, remove the thyme, stir in the mustard and bring to the boil, and cook uncovered until less than half the

original amount of liquid remains. Stir in the soured cream and simmer over a very low heat to reduce a little more if necessary. Just before serving, check the flavour – you may need to add a touch more mustard. This dish can be kept hot and continues to improve in flavour, but don't be tempted to heat it to boiling point.

This dish goes wonderfully with baked potatoes, which always taste good with soured cream.

RABBIT STEWED in CIDER

A most appealing dish in winter, which includes turnips simmered in the same pan.

Serves four

1 large rabbit
oil for frying
6 medium onions, sliced
3 shallots, sliced
1 garlic clove, chopped
1 tsp plain flour
750 ml/1 1/4 pints dry cider
1 clove
salt and pepper
1 kg/2 lb turnips

Cut the rabbit into serving portions and brown in hot oil in a large heavy-based saucepan. Add the onions, shallots and garlic and continue to cook, turning the rabbit until it is brown all over. Sprinkle with the flour and cook for 2-3 minutes; add the cider, clove and salt and pepper. Bring to the boil, cover and simmer gently for 45 minutes.

While the rabbit is cooking, peel the turnips, cut into two, then into dice. Put them into boiling water and cook for 10 minutes, drain, and add to the rabbit. Continue to simmer for a further 15 minutes. Arrange the rabbit and turnips on a hot serving dish and serve at once.

FOOD FACT

Soured cream is made from single cream and therefore is lower in fat than double cream. It thickens and enriches sauces wonderfully and will not curdle when heated, provided the sauce is not acidic – but best not try.

Double cream rarely curdles in a sauce but single cream is notorious for so doing, even when there is thickening present. Don't confuse commercial soured cream with cream that is 'off'; the former is controlled and safe, the latter is not and should not be eaten.

VEAL with RED PEPPERS and LEEKS

This recipe was an attempt to create a better and more modern version of that French favourite, a *blanquette de veau* (veal in white sauce). This is not only more contemporary in content, but is also much simpler to achieve.

Serves four to six

1 kg/2 lb pie veal
60 g/2 oz butter
125 g/4 oz onion, sliced
1 garlic clove, crushed
1 tbls tomato purée
200 ml/⅓ pint white wine
200 ml/⅓ pint water
185 g/6 oz red pepper
125 g/4 oz leek
thick plain yoghurt to serve

Cut the meat into generous chunks (about 4 cm/1½ inches) and brown in the butter. Add the onion and garlic and cook for 3-4 minutes until softened and lightly browned. Stir in the tomato purée so that it coats the meat, and cook for 2 minutes. Pour in the wine (reserving a couple of tablespoons) and water, bring to the boil, then cover and simmer for 45 minutes, so that the meat is tender and the liquid thickens.

Cut the vegetables into fine julienne strips of even length. Toss them in the remaining wine with a knob of butter in a small pan for 3-4 minutes, until they just begin to soften.

Top each serving with a generous tablespoon of plain thick yoghurt and then scatter the vegetables over that; it's the opposite of what you would expect to do and all the more wonderful because of that. ⓢ

OSSO BUCCO

One of the best of all casserole dishes for its colour and sweetness, and for the fun of picking out the marrow in the bones. Many non-Italian recipes leave out the topping of gremolata, but this is what lifts it out of the ordinary.

Serves four

veal knuckle, full of marrow
cut into 7.5 cm/3 inch pieces
(allow approx. 375 g/12 oz per person)
seasoned flour
60 g/2 oz butter
300 ml/½ pint white wine
500 g/1 lb tomatoes, peeled, seeded and chopped
125 g/4 oz celery, finely chopped
125 g/4 oz onion, finely chopped
125 g/4 oz carrot, finely chopped
1 tsp dried sage
1 tsp dried rosemary
300 ml/½ pint chicken stock

Toss the meat in seasoned flour. Heat the butter and brown the veal all over, then pour in the wine and cook for 10 minutes. Add the vegetables and herbs with half the chicken stock. Bring to the boil, reduce the heat, cover and simmer very gently for 1 hour.

Uncover the pan and continue cooking until the meat is meltingly tender, adding more chicken stock if necessary. Remove the veal, using a slotted spoon, and arrange on a heated serving dish. Bring the sauce to the boil, check the seasoning and add more stock if necessary. Strain over the meat and serve sprinkled with

GREMOLATA
5-6 tbls chopped parsley
1 garlic clove, crushed and chopped
grated rind of ½ lemon

Mix the parsley, garlic and lemon rind together. Sprinkle over the veal and sauce.

LAMB PAPRIKAS

This is the sort of stew which is frequently incorrectly called a goulash. A goulash is actually more of a soup and should never have soured cream served with it. As with all stew-type dishes, it is important that the chunks of meat are generous – at least 2.5 cm/1 inch cubes – or the end result will look frugal.

Serves four

1 tbls oil
250 g/8 oz onions, finely sliced
1 kg/2 lb lamb, boned and cut into 2.5 cm/1 inch cubes
2 tbls seasoned flour
396 g/14 oz can plum tomatoes in juice
3 heaped tsps sweet paprika
2 heaped tsps hot paprika
185 g/6 oz red or green pepper
150 ml/¼ pint soured cream

In a large saucepan or flameproof casserole, heat the oil and soften the onion over a low heat without allowing it to brown. Toss the meat in the seasoned flour to coat lightly, then add to the pan and seal. Add the tomatoes and half the paprikas, mixed together. Bring to the boil then lower the heat, cover and simmer gently for about 1 hour, until the meat is very tender. If there seems to be too much liquid in the pan, remove the lid for the last period of cooking and allow it to reduce.

Cut the pepper into neat, even-sized chunks and add to the casserole with the remaining paprikas. Continue simmering for 15 minutes, until the pepper is soft but not overcooked. Serve with rice, or treat the dish as a kind of goulash and add some cubed cooked potatoes for the last period of cooking. Top each serving with a dollop of soured cream and the finest dusting of paprika.

Option
This dish is equally successful using cubed veal or pork.

LAMB with GREEN OLIVES

Nowadays, in Provence, stews are likely to be made from lamb with tomatoes and garlic. But before the tomato arrived in Provence, the cooks of that region relied on locally grown olives, herbs and often strips of orange rind to flavour mutton stews. This is a typical, authentic Provencal recipe, with a gentle restrained use of herbs and garlic which balances perfectly the richness of the meat. But you must brown the lamb and the onions well, separately, or the dish will look and taste bland.

Serves four to six

1 kg/2 lb lean lamb or mutton
2 tbls olive oil
2 tbls butter
125 g/4 oz finely chopped onion
2 tsps flour
200 ml/⅓ pint dry white or rosé wine
1 garlic clove, peeled
1 strip orange rind (optional)
1 bay leaf
small sprig of thyme
salt and pepper
125 g/4 oz green olives (Salonenque, ideally)
125 g/4 oz fresh mushrooms (optional)

Cut the meat into generous bite-sized pieces. Heat the oil and butter in a large saucepan or flameproof casserole and brown the meat on all sides. Work in batches in order that the pan temperature doesn't drop too low otherwise you will be stewing the meat rather than sealing it. Remove the lamb as it is browned, then cook the onion in the olive oil and butter until they are soft and brown. Stir in the flour and cook until coloured a light golden brown. Add the white wine, stir until boiling and smooth then return the meat to the pan together with 300 ml/½ pint hot water, the garlic, orange rind, bay leaf and thyme. Season lightly with salt and pepper; bring to the boil then lower the heat, cover and simmer gently for 45 minutes, longer for mutton.

Meanwhile, blanch the olives briefly, stone them if necessary and leave soaking in cold water. Ten minutes before serving, take the bay leaf, thyme, orange rind and garlic out of the casserole and add the drained olives together with the sliced mushrooms if you are including them. Serve very hot, on a bed of noodles buttered or tossed in olive oil. *Photograph, p. 77.*

SPICY LAMB STEW with PRUNES

The sweetness of the lamb is enhanced by the spicy-sweet flavours in the sauce. It reheats very well, so it's worth making a large amount.

Serves six

60 g/2 oz butter
2 tbls olive oil
1 tsp ground cinnamon
1 tsp ground ginger
1 tsp turmeric
1.5 kg/3 lb lamb, boned and cut into 2.5 cm/1 inch cubes
450 ml/3/4 pint water
2 heaped tbls chopped parsley
2 tbls chopped celery leaves
250 g/8 oz onions, finely sliced
2 celery sticks, finely chopped
250 g/8 oz no-need-to-soak stoned prunes
2 tbls honey
salt and pepper
2 tbls sesame seeds, toasted

In a large saucepan or flameproof casserole heat the butter and oil, add the cinnamon, ginger and turmeric and stir well over a low heat. Add the lamb, stir to coat thoroughly, and cook for 10-15 minutes until the meat is lightly browned. Stir in the water, parsley and celery leaves, cover and simmer for 1 hour.

Add the onions, celery, prunes and honey, season and continue simmering for a further hour. Stir occasionally and remove the lid for the last 20 minutes to allow the liquid to reduce.

Serve with pasta or rice and sprinkle each serving with toasted sesame seeds.

Option
This recipe is equally delicious using cubes of rabbit and is a particularly suitable way of cooking the sometimes tough Chinese rabbit which is readily available frozen.

FOOD FACT

True hot-pot was made from mutton and flavoured with a little spicy-hot sauce. Kidneys were added for extra flavour, and oysters, too, in the days when they were the food of the poor. Nowadays, mutton is all but impossible to buy and oysters are outside the scope of most pockets, but you can't expect to make a worthwhile dish with lamb, potatoes and onions alone, as is often suggested. You must compensate for the rich flavour of the mutton.

WINDY CITY LAMB CASSEROLE

This dish takes several hours to cook at a low oven temperature, so it's ideal if you have an Aga-type cooker, or a slow cooker. If not, make full use of the oven space by making meringues, or stewing fruit at the same time. Perhaps make a double quantity and freeze half for later – or have a party. It's a dish that tastes best reheated, so cook it the day before you need it.

Serves six

500 g/1 lb haricot or lima beans, soaked overnight
12 small lamb neck chops
oil for frying
250 g/8 oz onion, sliced
3 or 4 garlic cloves, chopped
3 bay leaves
1 tbls fresh or 1 tsp dried thyme
300 ml/1/2 pint red or white wine
396 g/14 oz can plum tomatoes in juice
1-2 tsps made mustard

Simmer the soaked beans in unsalted water for 60-90 minutes, or until tender, then drain and transfer to a casserole. Trim the fat from the chops and brown them by frying in a little oil. Add to the beans, with the onion, garlic, bay leaves and thyme. Gently stir them all together, gradually adding the wine and tomatoes. Cover, and cook very gently on the hob at the lowest possible heat on a diffuser; or in the oven at 140°C/275°F/Gas Mark 1; or in a slow cooker.

It will take 3-4 hours for the meat to tenderize and for some of the beans to become a mushy sauce. If there seems too much liquid when the meat is tender, take off the lid and cook until it evaporates. If it seems dry, add a little more wine and cook for a little longer. Stir in the mustard just before serving. Ⓣ

A MODERN IRISH STEW

Sadly, mutton is no longer available to give this dish its authentic flavour. To compensate, the cooking liquid should be Guinness, but any stout will do. Choose big potatoes and onions and make the slices thick and generous.

Serves four

185 g/6 oz streaky bacon
2 celery sticks, chopped
750 g/11/2 lb large onions, thickly sliced
1-1.5 kg/2-3 lb large potatoes, quartered
1.25 kg/21/2 lb neck of lamb on the bone
1 tbls seasoned flour (optional)
450 ml/3/4 pint stout (large can)
salt and pepper

Cut the bacon into strips and cook in a frying-pan until the fat is running.

Fry the celery and a third of the onions in a frying-pan until brown, then remove. Trim off as much fat as possible from the lamb and brown on both sides in the frying-pan. If you like a thicker gravy, toss the meat in seasoned flour first.

Mix the raw onion with the cooked bacon, cooked onion and celery. Layer in an ovenproof casserole with the meat and potatoes, ending with potatoes. Pour in the stout, season, cover and simmer for 2 hours. If you like the potatoes to brown a little, remove the lid for the last 20 minutes of the cooking time.

A MODERN LANCASHIRE HOT-POT

Sad to say, most people have no idea just how good a real hot-pot can be. I've given a large quantity suitable for family occasions, but it can be halved.

Serves eight

2 bay leaves
1 kg/2 lb potatoes, finely sliced
salt and pepper
250 g/8 oz onions, finely chopped
5 tbls oil
1 kg/2 lb best end or neck of lamb chops
30 g/1 oz plain flour
600 ml/1 pint water or 300 ml/1/2 pint water with 300 ml/1/2 pint strong beer
11/2 tbls Worcestershire sauce
1 tsp anchovy sauce
6 lambs' kidneys

Put the bay leaves at the bottom of a large, deep casserole and arrange just over half the thinly sliced potatoes on top. Season well. Brown the onions in 2 tablespoons of the oil in a frying-pan, then remove with a slotted spoon and set aside. Trim as much fat as possible from the chops, flour them lightly and brown them in the pan using the remaining oil. Pour the oil from the pan and add the water or beer and water mixture. Scrape up the sediment from the bottom of the pan, stir in the Worcestershire sauce, anchovy sauce and seasoning.

Remove any white skin or membrane from the kidneys, then cut across into slices. Layer the chops over the potatoes, packing them tightly together. Put the slices of kidney on each chop and a little cooked onion on top. Season, then add the final layer of potatoes, arranging them attractively. Pour the stock over the top, cover with foil or a lid and bake at 220°C/425°F/Gas Mark 7 for 30 minutes. Turn the oven down to 160°C/325°F/Gas Mark 3 and cook for a further 90 minutes, taking the lid or foil off for the last 45 minutes, so that the potatoes will turn nicely brown.

GAMMON with CARROT and PARSNIP SAUCE

The beautiful colours and simple home-cooked flavours of this dish make a perfect example of what most people think of as warming winter food. This piece of gammon will feed four and the amount of sauce will be very generous, so you could cook a larger piece (at least 1.75 kg/ 3½ lb for six) but still make the same quantity of sauce.

Serves four generously

1.25 kg/2½ lb lean gammon
2 dried bay leaves
250 g/8 oz onions, chopped
12 black peppercorns
250 g/8 oz carrots
250 g/8 oz parsnips
30 g/1 oz butter
150 ml/¼ pint milk

Put the gammon into cold water and bring slowly to the boil. Pour off that water and start all over again. This time add one of the bay leaves, the onion and peppercorns and then cook at a gentle simmer for 30 minutes per 500 g/ 1 lb plus an extra 30 minutes.

About 30 minutes before the gammon is cooked, peel and slice the carrots and parsnips and put them into a saucepan with 300 ml/ ½ pint of the water from the gammon. Then add further water just to cover the vegetables and the second bay leaf. Cook until tender – up to 20-25 minutes. Cool slightly, remove the bay leaf and sieve the vegetables or purée in a blender with 150 ml/¼ pint of the cooking water. Transfer to a saucepan to reheat gently and stir in the butter and milk. Add extra milk if needed to get a nicely flowing sauce, which should be of a consistency somewhere between double and single cream.

Slice the gammon and serve with generous amounts of sauce, but do not obscure the meat as its pinkness is important to the presentation. The best accompaniment would be boiled potatoes tossed in chopped parsley.

Option

The traditional accompaniment for boiled bacon was pease pudding boiled in a cloth at the same time. It's a bind to make this from the start but you can make something worthwhile using tinned pease pudding. Mix 450 g/1 lb of prepared pease pudding with 3 eggs and a tablespoon of butter. Line a bowl with 4 strips of clingfilm, add the pudding and seal. Wrap in more cling film and then in several layers of foil. Cook with the meat – it will float when done, but needs to cook for at least 45 minutes.

BACON with GARLIC-ORANGE SAUCE

Boiled bacon is a boon and not to be ignored at any time of year. The long, slow cooking reduces the effect of the garlic so that each clove becomes sweet and unctuous, with a texture not unlike mayonnaise.

Serves four to six

1.5 kg/3 lb boneless smoked bacon joint, rolled
1 litre/1¾ pints orange juice
2 tsps pickling spice
whole cloves (optional)
1 cinnamon stick
8-12 garlic cloves, unpeeled
2 bay leaves
rind of 1 orange, cut into very thin julienne strips
2 tbls chopped parsley

Put the bacon into a saucepan, cover with cold water and bring to the boil. Simmer for 2 minutes, then drain. Return the bacon to the pan, pour over the orange juice with enough water so that the joint is covered by about 2.5 cm/1 inch of liquid. Add the pickling spices, garlic cloves and bay leaves. Add extra cloves to make the number from the pickling spice up to six, if necessary. Bring to the boil, then lower the heat, cover and simmer gently, allowing 25 minutes to 500 g/1 lb plus 25 minutes. During the last 20 minutes' cooking time, strain off 300 ml/½ pint of the liquor into a saucepan, add the orange strips together with all the garlic cloves taken from the bacon pan. Poach gently while the bacon finishes cooking and while you slice the meat.

Stir the parsley into the sauce. Arrange the meat with the sauce poured over, so that the garlic and parsley are on top with the orange sauce spread over the plate.

GLYNN'S TIP

If making the spiced meatballs on the day you are going to eat them, start by making the sauce, then make the meatballs while it cooks. You can also make the meatballs well in advance and refrigerate until needed.

LIGHTLY SPICED MEATBALLS in SAUCE

These intriguingly flavoured meatballs are based on a Scandinavian classic but rely on Eastern spices for flavouring. The recipe makes about 36 balls of 2.5 cm/1 inch diameter, but it is an easy recipe to divide or to multiply.

You can do all the hard work with an old-fashioned mincer and sieve, but you'll find this recipe easy if you have a food processor.

Serves four generously

MEATBALLS
45 g/1½ oz wholemeal bread with crusts removed
7 g/¼ oz parsley
90 g/3 oz onion, chopped
1 garlic clove, crushed
1 tsp salt
1 tsp coriander seeds or ground coriander
500 g/1 lb lean minced pork
½ beaten egg
salt and freshly ground black pepper
oil for frying
SAUCE
30 g/1 oz butter
60 g/2 oz chopped onion
500 g/1 lb fresh tomatoes, peeled and de-seeded, or
397 g/14 oz can plum tomatoes
½ tsp ground turmeric
1 generous tsp ground cumin

Make a paste of the bread, parsley, onion, garlic, salt and coriander seeds in a food processor, stopping to scrape down the mixture from time to time. Add the pork and process until smoothly mixed but with some texture left. Turn into a bowl and mix gently with the egg, a little salt and plenty of black pepper from the mill. With wet hands, form the mixture into 2.5 cm/1 inch balls and let them set in the refrigerator for at least half an hour. If, however, you are able to leave them for a whole day or overnight, the flavour will be much improved.

Combine the butter, onions and prepared tomatoes and cook over low heat for 1-1½ hours until thick. You can also used canned tomatoes which have been sieved. When the sauce is almost cooked, add the spices. Make a smooth purée of the sauce in a food processor or by putting through a sieve.

Brown the meatballs in a little oil in a large saucepan and cook, turning evenly, for a good 15 minutes until well browned and cooked through. Drain off any excess oil, add the tomato sauce and cook for another 20-30 minutes to allow the flavours to blend, but do not boil hard. Serve over rice or buttered plain noodles.

SPARE-RIBS with PLUM-SAUCE GLAZE

Spare-ribs come in different guises – rib bones with just a little flesh on them, sometimes called Chinese or American spare-ribs; or the British type which are generally sold as thin cuts from the shoulder that look like a chop; or strips of belly of pork called spare-ribs. This recipe uses any of the British cuts, which (just to confuse the matter further) might also be called shoulder or blade steaks. In any case, for two people you will need four thinnish cuts of meat, making a total weight of 500 g/1 lb. (As the pork must be grilled to finish, it is sometimes difficult to cook the recipe easily for more than two people.)

Although the method sounds unusual, it is close to the traditional Chinese style of cooking.

Put the spare-ribs into a pot of cold water with sliced onion, a garlic clove and a bay leaf. Bring to the boil, simmer for 15 minutes, then drain.

Mix together 3 tablespoons of plum jam, ½ teaspoon of ground ginger and 1 tablespoon of wine vinegar, cider or wine. Put the prepared meat on to the rack of a grill-pan and paint generously with half the jam mixture. Grill at a high heat for 10 minutes without letting the jam burn. Turn several times, basting three or four times.

Let the pork cool a little before serving. It can be gently reheated, when it is even better.

SPICY RED PORK and BEAN CASSEROLE

This is a great dish for informal parties: it is easy to make, will wait for hours and can be re-heated as many times as you like. Serve it with crusty fresh bread, with pitta bread, rice or jacket potatoes. Stretch the meat by adding more beans and tomatoes (adjust the seasoning), or include sliced mushrooms.

Serves four

500 g/1 lb rindless streaky pork rashers
184 g/6½ oz can sweet red peppers, drained
425 g/15½ oz can red kidney beans, drained
396 g/14 oz can plum tomatoes, chopped
2 tbls tomato purée
1 tbls sweet paprika
½-1 tsp chili powder
3 tbls sweet sherry or red wine

Cut the pork into 1 cm/½ inch pieces. Chop the red peppers roughly and mix thoroughly with the rest of the ingredients in an ovenproof casserole. Cover and cook at 150°C/300°F/Gas Mark 3, for 2-2½ hours, stirring once or twice to make sure it isn't sticking or getting dry; if it seems too dry, add a little water. Ⓔ

PORK with CELERIAC

The richness of the pork is complemented by the clean flavour of celeriac and brightened by the orange and parsley; the dish has the happy and unusual characteristic of being at once warming but also fresh-tasting.

Serves four

oil for frying
750 g/1½ lb lean pork, cubed
250 g/8 oz onion, thinly sliced
2 tsps ground coriander
2 fresh or 1 dried bay leaf
375 g/12 oz celeriac, peeled and cubed
396 g/14 oz can plum tomatoes
2 tbls chopped parsley
2 tsps ground coriander
2 tsps grated orange rind

Heat a little oil in a large saucepan and fry the pork until sealed, add the onion, coriander and bay leaves, and continue cooking for 5 minutes until brown and fragrant. Stir in the celeriac and tomatoes, bring to the boil, then cover tightly and simmer very gently for 1½-2 hours.

When the pork is cooked, mix together the parsley, coriander and orange rind, stir into the pork and serve at once.

CASSEROLED PORK with PEPPERS

This Mediterranean-inspired recipe is both colourful and flavoursome and makes a welcome change from many pork stews, which can be both pale and bland. Don't cook the peppers for too long, or you will lose their bright colour – 15 minutes is all they need.

Serves six

1.5 kg/3 lb lean pork, cubed
olive oil for frying
90 g/3 oz carrot, finely chopped
60 g/2 oz celery, finely chopped
2 unpeeled garlic cloves, lightly crushed
300 ml/½ pint dry white wine or cider
300 ml/½ pint chicken stock
salt and pepper
3 sweet peppers (green or red or a mixture of both)
397 g/14 oz can plum tomatoes, drained
chopped parsley to finish

Make sure that the meat is in good-sized cubes (at least 2.5 cm/1 inch) or it will shrink to unappetizing bullets when cooked. Heat the oil in a frying-pan and brown the pork all over – do it in batches, or the pan temperature will drop and the meat will stew rather than fry. Put the pork into an ovenproof casserole with the carrot, celery, garlic, wine or cider and stock, season lightly and bring to the boil. Reduce the heat, cover and simmer gently for 2 hours or until the pork is tender.

Cut the peppers into neat, even-sized pieces (not rings, please) and add to the casserole with the whole tomatoes. Stir very gently, then continue simmering, uncovered, for another 15 minutes. Stir in lots of chopped parsley and serve with rice or potatoes. Ⓢ

A BEEF STEW PRIMER

Daube, carbonnade, casserole – whatever you call it, beef cooked in a liquid is a *stew*. I use the word 'stew' as often as possible as a reminder that the basic British stew is one of the most difficult dishes to cook properly because it *is* so basic. In many books, the ingredients are simply meat, onions, flour, water, salt and pepper. This can actually make a dish well worth eating, but only if you follow the rules rigidly. If not, it is boredom on a plate. Once you can make a good, basic British stew, you will then be able to cook any of the recipes with fancy names.

The single, most important, rule is that both the onions and the meat must be well browned, to give colour and a rich flavour to the sauce and also to seal in all the meat juices.

The best way to brown meat and onions is not in the casserole or saucepan in which it will be stewed but in a frying-pan. The large surface area enables the moisture created to be easily evaporated so that the meat can brown. In tall pots, the meat steams and actually loses the moisture which should be sealed inside. Brown the meat first and remove it from the pan; then brown the onions, return the meat, add the liquid and scrape up any pan juices and sediment before turning the mixture into your ovenproof casserole with the seasonings of your choice.

Always cut meat into generous pieces; it shrinks during cooking and can easily look mean.

Chuck steak is one of the most popular meats for stewing and gives excellent flavour. Flank is very good, too, but tends to dissolve away into shreds and must be cut into really big pieces. Shin is usually the cheapest but is the most reliable and always keeps its shape. I think it is a waste of money to stew sirloin or other steaks.

Never boil your stew but let it cook barely bubbling. This gives the most tender and moist results and ensures that you won't end up with shreds of meat.

Once you have mastered the basic stew, try replacing plain water with beef stock or red wine, or a mixture. The following recipes give good reliable results using various cooking liquids. With all stews, you can make them heartier or stretch them by adding nicely shaped root vegetables towards the end of cooking. Adding them at the start means they will be flabby and tasteless.

BEEF with STOCK

Serves four to six

1 kg/2 lb stewing beef, cut into 5 cm/2 inch cubes
125 g/4 oz smoked bacon, blanched and cut into
small pieces
250 g/8 oz onion, chopped
1 tbls flour
1 beef stock cube dissolved in 750 ml/1¼ pints water
freshly ground black pepper
bouquet garni (optional)
1 garlic clove, crushed (optional)
1 tbls Worcestershire sauce

Prepare as for Beef Cooked in Wine (see next recipe) seasoning with lots of freshly ground black pepper; the bacon (or salt pork) does not strictly belong in this sort of recipe but helps the savouriness immensely; so do the bouquet garni and garlic. Fifteen minutes before the end of cooking time, add 1 tablespoon Worcestershire sauce and continue cooking, uncovered.

Options

The most common additions to beef and stock stews are root vegetables, which add both nutrition and colour. Make the effort to cut them into matchsticks or even cubes for presentation's sake and add towards the end of cooking time so that they just cook through; their savouriness will still be added to the liquid by then.

Beef and Mushroom Use old, full flavoured, open mushrooms instead of the bland button type. Slice the large mushrooms after peeling and stir into the stew a few minutes before serving so they do not shrink. This is even more important if you are using wild mushrooms. Dried mushrooms should be rinsed well and put into the stew to hydrate and flavour the liquid for at least 1 hour; they give the richest and best flavour and colour. If you are making a beef and mushroom pie, layer the mushrooms thickly on top of the meat before you add the pastry so that when it is cut you get a heavenly waft of mushroom.

Oysters and Mussels Although fresh oysters and mussels were traditionally used to flavour British beef pies, they are too rare and expensive to use these days. I have had tremendous success, however, using drained smoked oysters and the marvellous Danish mussels preserved in brine. Add them to a stew some 20 minutes before serving but do not stir much or they will break up. They are actually far better used in a pie, where they are not stirred.

Steak and Kidney Use three parts beef to one part kidney, i.e. 750 g/1½ lb beef to 250 g/8 oz trimmed kidney. Ox kidney is the most popular; it should be well trimmed of tubes, fat or gristle and browned with the meat. A combination of beef steak, kidney and mushrooms is one of the most satisfying combinations of all.

BEEF COOKED in WINE

Serves four to six

2 tbls oil
250 g/8 oz smoked bacon, blanched and cut into
5 cm/2 inch strips
1 kg/2 lb stewing beef, cut into 5 cm/2 inch cubes
250 g/8 oz onion, sliced
1 tbls flour
70 cl/1¼ pint bottle red wine
salt and pepper
1 garlic clove, crushed
bouquet garni

Heat the oil in a large frying-pan, cook the bacon until brown but not crisp and put it into a flameproof or ovenproof casserole or large saucepan. Fry the beef in batches to brown it well all over and put with the bacon. Lower the heat and fry the onion until softened and golden. Stir in the flour and cook for 2 minutes. Pour in the wine, bring to the boil, stirring continuously, until smooth and slightly thickened. Pour over the meat and bacon, season generously and add the garlic and the bouquet garni. Bring back to the boil, cover and cook over a very low heat for 2 hours or more, depending on the quality of the meat. If you prefer, you can cook it in a low oven (150°C/300°F/Gas Mark 2) until the meat is tender. Remove the bouquet garni and serve.

BEEF COOKED in BEER

You need slightly different rules when beef is cooked in beer. The classic recipe is called a carbonnade and comes from Belgium. To counteract the bitterness of the beer, a much higher proportion of onion is used and sugar must be added in the final stages. The result is a marvellously rich flavour with just enough mystery about it to get you extra marks. Make sure you use beer or stout rather than lager.

Serves four to six

1 kg/2 lb stewing beef, cut into 5 cm/2 inch cubes
2 tbls seasoned flour
60 g/2 oz butter
300 ml/½ pint water
750 g/1½ lb onions, chopped
450 ml/¾ pint canned beer
salt and pepper
2 tbls red wine vinegar
bouquet garni
1-2 tbls brown sugar

Toss the meat in the seasoned flour to coat lightly. Melt half the butter in a frying pan and fry the cubes of meat until brown. Transfer to a saucepan or flameproof casserole. Pour half the water into the frying pan to remove the sediment and add to the meat.

Melt the remaining butter in the frying pan and fry the onions over medium heat until brown. Add the onions to the meat and deglaze the pan as before with the remaining water. Season with 1 teaspoon salt, ½ teaspoon ground black pepper and the red wine vinegar, then add the bouquet garni and the beer. Put the saucepan or casserole on the heat, bring to the boil, cover and simmer very gently for 2 hours. Add 1-2 tablespoons brown sugar to taste and continue cooking for a further 30 minutes. Remove the bouquet garni and serve.

DAUBE PROVENÇAL

Clearly a variation on the French red wine stew, this is by far the tastiest of them all. I actually collected this recipe while researching for a book; note how few herbs are used in genuine Provençal cooking. The garlic? Well, if it is genuine South of France garlic, it is so sweet that one bulb isn't considered much at all. Strong garlic should be used with very much more restraint.

Serves four to six

1 kg/2 lb stewing beef, cut into 5 cm/2 inch cubes
½ tsp salt
¼ tsp pepper
1½ tbls white wine vinegar
1½ tbls olive oil
185 g/6 oz belly pork, cut into 1 cm/½ inch cubes
60 g/2 oz smoked back bacon, in 1 cm/
½ inch strips
1 bulb garlic, whole and unpeeled
3 strips pared orange rind
3 whole cloves
1 sprig thyme
1-2 bay leaves
300 ml/½ pint red wine

Put the meat into a bowl with the seasoning, vinegar and oil; stir and leave to marinate at room temperature for at least 1 hour.

Fry the pork and bacon over high heat for 4-5 minutes until the fat runs. Take the meat from the marinade, pat dry on kitchen paper and fry in batches to a good brown all over. When all the meat has been browned, return to the pan with the whole garlic bulb, orange rind, cloves, thyme and bay leaves. Stir over the heat for 2 minutes, then pour in the wine. Bring to the boil, cover and simmer very gently over a low heat for 3-4 hours or until meltingly tender.

As long as the saucepan has a well-fitting lid, there should be enough liquid to provide a syrupy sauce. Check during cooking to make sure that the meat isn't becoming dry; if so, add a little more wine. Remove the orange rind, thyme and bay leaves before serving.

Option

This is specially good with the added richness of dried mushrooms. I have also used it as the basis for pies with both smoked oysters and mussels.

A REAL GOULASH

If the finished dish looks like a soup, that's the way it should be. Genuine goulash *is* a soup. The dishes called 'goulash' which are served with soured cream are actually Paprikas. This is a substantial dish, with a hearty flavour and appearance, and does well in my home as a main course for informal entertaining.

Serves four to six

375 g/12 oz onion, finely chopped
oil or beef dripping for frying
750 g/1½ lb shin of beef
1 tbls sweet paprika
750 g/1½ lb peeled potatoes
185 g/6 oz chopped red pepper
salt and pepper

Brown the onions well in oil or beef dripping. Cut the meat into large pieces (at least 5 cm/2 inch each) and stir into the onions but do not brown the meat. Pour in enough water to just cover the meat and sprinkle in the paprika. Cook very gently until the meat is almost tender. Cut the potatoes into large pieces and add to the saucepan with the chopped pepper. Add more water to cover the mixture, and salt and pepper to taste, and simmer until the potatoes are cooked but still firm. Serve in deep bowls so that you can first spoon up the soup and then the meat and potatoes. Ⓔ

Options

Although it is correct to use only sweet paprika, you can use other types and flavours, or mix hot and sweet paprikas to make a taste that suits you. It is also acceptable to stir a little more paprika or chopped pepper into the soup just before serving to freshen the flavour and appearance.

CREOLE BEEF

This recipe is from the Seychelles and is part of their tradition of Creole cooking, something easily identified by the common use of thyme and vinegar in combination. The addition of tomatoes makes the dish really individual and avoids the need to brown the meat; but it is better if you do.
This is a rather liquid sort of stew and needs to be served with lots of rice or boiled potatoes.

Serves four to six

1 kg/2 lb stewing beef
375 g/12 oz onions, finely chopped
2 large garlic cloves, finely chopped
1 tbls chopped parsley stalk
1 tsp dried thyme or 2 tsps fresh
1 tbls vinegar
470-500 g/15-16 oz can plum tomatoes in own juice
about 600 ml/1 pint boiling water
salt and pepper

Cut the meat into generous even cubes. Mix the onion and garlic with the parsley and thyme. Toss the meat in this with the vinegar and leave to marinate about 30 minutes.

Tip the meat and its marinade into a saucepan and simmer for 10 minutes, then add the tomatoes and all their juices plus the water and salt and pepper. Stir well and simmer very gently until cooked, about 1½ hours or more.

Option

Before adding the meat, stir 1 tablespoon flour into 2 tablespoons hot fat and add twelve peeled pickling type onions. Let them colour lightly without burning them or the flour. Then proceed as above.

FRAGRANT BEEF

This is a dish for those who like the appeal of fragrant spices. It is finished and thickened with coconut cream, which makes it something like a light curry.

Serves four to six

900 g/2 lb stewing beef in large chunks
oil for frying
250 g/8 oz onion, finely chopped
2 tsps granulated sugar
8 whole, unpeeled garlic cloves
1 fresh lime, quartered
1 cinnamon stick
8 cardamom pods
6 whole cloves
2 sachets saffron powder (or to taste)
600 ml/1 pint boiling water
125 g/4 oz (solid) coconut cream

Brown the meat in a little oil and remove from the pan. Cook the onions until very soft, then sprinkle in the sugar and cook until it has caramelized and the onions are a good golden brown. Stir in the garlic cloves, lime, cinnamon, cardamom, cloves and saffron and when their fragrance is noticeable, add the meat and water.

Simmer gently only half covered until the meat is tender, about 1-1½ hours depending on the quality of the meat used. Remove the cinnamon stick, and if you have the patience, remove the other whole spices, too, but this is not essential. Break up the coconut cream and stir into the liquid, but do not let it boil. Taste and assess the thickness of the sauce. You may need to add up to 50 per cent more coconut, but beware of smothering the subtle flavours of the spices.

You will have noticed that black pepper is not added to this dish as it actually goes bitter when cooked for extended periods. If you would like just a little 'bite' and a lot more fragrance, stir in freshly ground black pepper a few minutes before serving.

BOILED SALT *or* CORNED BEEF

Once meat has been in brine for more than a few days it toughens and the only way to cook it is by boiling, except of course that actual boiling is the worst thing you can do. It often takes much longer than you expect, the meat shrinks far more than you want, but in the end it can become one of the most satisfying plates in the world. Because beef is also fairly expensive, you should take special care to cook it well and serve it nicely. This recipe is actually for a Boiled Beef Dinner, traditionally meaning vegetables were added to the saucepan for the last 45 minutes and the meat and vegetables served together with some of the stock. If you have a pan large enough, this is ideal. But you may have to take out the fully cooked beef and then cook the vegetables, which is a faster way for they can cook at a higher heat than the meat.

Serves four

1.5 kg/3 lb (at least) salt silverside, topside or brisket
1 onion, stuck with 6 cloves
1 tsp black peppercorns
2-3 carrots
any other root vegetable except potatoes (see method)
2-3 dry bay leaves (important)
few cloves of garlic
1-2 thin strips orange or lemon peel

When you buy the meat, ask how long it has been in brine. If more than three or four days it is worth getting rid of some of the salt by putting the meat into cold water, bringing slowly to the boil, discarding the water and starting again. Even if it hasn't been brined long it is always worth tasting the water when it first comes to the boil – if it seems very salty start again. Skim off any foam and scum then add all the flavourings. They will not be served or eaten so do not need to be cut up attractively. Cover the pan, set it at the lowest simmer possible and leave for 30 minutes per 500 kg/1 lb plus 30 minutes – but be prepared to cook it even longer. I always cook well in advance for the meat gets extra moist and flavoursome if allowed to cool in its cooking liquid.

For four people, cook at least 1 kg/2 lb mixed root vegetables, cut into nice shapes in stock from the pan or a mixture of stock and water. When all is ready, strain 300 ml/½ pint stock into a small saucepan and bring to the boil. Flavour lightly with about 2 teaspoons made mustard, then stir in 2-3 tablespoons coarsely chopped parsley. Do not boil but heat just until the parsley turns a bright green. Pass this with the sliced meat and vegetables.

Option

The sauces used for boiled bacon would be excellent and unexpected with this.

SPICED SALT BEEF

Spiced beef is a great and ancient British favourite now seen mainly at Christmas-time. It takes a long time to make from fresh but if you start with salted meat it takes only four or five days. Spiced salt beef is a wonderful enlivener of the palate on Boxing Day and, although I think it is more astonishing when served hot, it is equally a remarkably good cold cut, too. The recipe can be halved, of course.

Serves six to eight

2.3 kg/5 lb salt silverside in neat shape
90 g/3 oz muscovado sugar
2 tsps black peppercorns
1 tsp ground mace
1 tsp ground nutmeg
1 tsp dry mustard powder
1 tsp ground coriander
1/2 tsp ground cloves
6 dried bay leaves
3-6 garlic cloves
2 cinnamon sticks
185 g/6 oz muscovado sugar
300 ml/1/2 pint port wine
4 × 5 cm/2 inch strips orange peel
2-3 onions, quartered
chopped fresh parsley

Although the spice and sugar will tend to balance out any residual saltiness in most cases, I think it better always to place the meat in cold water and bring it slowly to the boil to rid it of excess salt before you start this recipe. Then you are ensured against a disaster. Drain the meat quickly and let it cool as fast as you can.

Crush the sugar and peppercorns together in a mortar or in a robust bowl and mix in all the ground spices. Crumble in the bay leaves, crush and chop the garlic and add, break up and add the cinnamon sticks.

Stand the beef on a plate or in a dish. Sprinkle on the spice mixture, turn the meat until well covered and then press the mixture firmly onto all the surface. Wrap the whole container, not just the meat, in several layers of foil and leave in the refrigerator at least three and up to six days, turning from time to time.

Put the meat and spices into a large saucepan and add the second amount of sugar and the port, which does not have to be the expensive type but may be the Cyprus Ruby wine or British Ruby wine – you could also use a sweet sherry I suppose, but I never have. Cover the mixture with cold water. Add the orange peel and onion and bring slowly to the boil. Simmer so the water barely moves for at least 30 minutes per 500 g/1 lb plus 30 minutes. It may take as long as 4 hours.

It is good to let the cooked meat stand in the hot stock for an hour or so before serving as this will gently continue the tenderising and ensure the spiciness has penetrated all the meat.

Serve sliced generously with a ladleful of the cooking liquid into which you have stirred chopped parsley and, if you like, a little grated orange rind.

To serve it cold, let it cool completely in the liquid.

Options
Halfway through the cooking, taste the liquid for a balance of flavour. You might find it needs a little more sweetness and then you can add a spoonful of sugar. Otherwise, I think clove is the most useful addition, but in very small quantities.

CASSEROLED VENISON with BEETROOT

This dish, with its fabulous colour and earthy combination of flavours, uses a relatively small amount of venison.

Serves four

500 g/1 lb stewing venison, cut into large cubes
oil for frying
125 g/4 oz onion, sliced
1 tsp allspice berries, lightly crushed
3 cloves
2 large garlic cloves, sliced
185 g/6 oz raw beetroot, grated
1 tbls plain flour
300 ml/1/2 pint robust red wine
2-3 tbls port

Brown the venison in a little oil. Remove it from the pan and brown the onion well with the spices and garlic. Add the beetroot and continue cooking over a high heat for another 3 minutes, so that a little of the beetroot is browned too. Add the flour and cook for 2 minutes, then pour in the wine, stirring well to de-glaze the bottom of the saucepan. Return the venison to the pan, then cover and simmer gently until the meat is tender, which might take up to 50 minutes. Stir in the port just before serving.

Options
Instead of oil, you can use beef dripping or 125 g/4 oz smoked bacon cut into strips. And if you have no port, stir in redcurrant jelly or a cream sherry to taste. Orange rind would also make an added refinement and is an excellent flavouring for game. Ⓔ

PORK FILLET with SPINACH and ORANGE

Serves four

750 g/1 1/2 lb pork fillet (tenderloin)
500 g/1 lb leaf spinach, cooked and chopped (or defrosted and well drained)
2 navel oranges
1 garlic clove, crushed
salt and freshly ground black pepper
150 ml/1/4 pint red or white wine, orange juice or water
1 tbls sugar

Trim off any untidy bits from the pork and all the fat. Mix the drained spinach with the finely grated rind of one of the oranges and the crushed garlic; spread this mixture over the bottom of an ovenproof dish or small roasting-tin and arrange the pork on top. Squeeze the juice from the grated orange into a measuring jug. Cut four even slices from the other orange and set aside. Squeeze the end pieces from this orange into the jug, then make up the juice to 150 ml/1/4 pint with water and pour over the pork. Season. Bake, uncovered, at 180°C/350°F/Gas Mark 4 for 1 hour, turning the pork over halfway through.

While the pork is baking, cook the orange slices. Choose a pan into which they will all fit in one layer and pour in 150 ml/1/4 pint wine (red or white), orange juice or water. Add 1 tablespoon of sugar, stir until dissolved, then increase the heat and allow the syrup to bubble for 2-3 minutes. Lower the orange slices into the pan and cook over a moderate heat for 10 minutes, or until the skin becomes translucent. Allow the fruit to cool in the thick syrup.

When the pork is cooked, remove it from the tin and let it rest for a few minutes before slicing, at an angle, into medallions about 1 cm/1/2 inch thick. Stir the spinach mixture, check the seasoning and put a portion on to four warmed plates. Arrange the pork slices around the spinach, decorate with a slice of the cooked orange and spoon over the syrup.

PORK FILLET with LEEKS and APRICOTS

Serves four

750 g/1 1/2 lb pork fillet (tenderloin)
500 g/1 lb leeks, washed and trimmed
125 g/4 oz dried apricots
150 ml/1/4 pint dry vermouth, white wine or orange juice
salt and freshly ground black pepper
30 g/1 oz butter
30 g/1 oz pine nuts
1/4 tsp ground cumin

Trim off any untidy bits from the pork and remove all fat. Reserve one leek and slice the remainder fairly thinly. Spread the sliced leeks over the base of an ovenproof dish or small roasting-tin. Put 90 g/3 oz of the apricots into a small saucepan with the vermouth, wine or orange juice and bring slowly to the boil. Simmer for 2 minutes, then pour over the leeks, spreading the apricots evenly. Arrange the pork on top and season with salt and pepper. Bake, uncovered, in a preheated moderate oven 180°C/350°F/Gas Mark 4, for 1 hour, turning the pork over halfway though cooking, again seasoning with salt and pepper.

When the pork is almost cooked, slice the reserved leek into julienne strips about 5 cm/2 inches long. Cut the remaining dried apricots into strips. Melt the butter in a pan and cook the apricots and pine nuts for 3-4 minutes, until they are golden brown, then toss in the leeks and continue cooking for another 2-3 minutes until they soften a little. Season with salt, pepper and ground cumin.

Allow the cooked pork to rest for a few minutes before slicing, at a slight angle, into medallions about 1 cm/½ inch thick. While it is standing, put the leek and apricots from the baking dish into a blender or food processor and purée the mixture. Taste and adjust the seasoning, adding a little more ground cumin if you like. Put a circle of purée on to four warmed plates, arrange the slices of pork around the edge and scatter the sautéed apricots, leeks and pine nuts over the top. Ⓢ

PORK FILLET with CHESTNUTS

This casserole has a nice rustic look about it – just the dish for a cold winter's evening. It can be made using slightly cheaper boneless leg steaks, and you could try replacing the red wine with a good strong cider.

Serves four

375 g/12 oz peeled chestnuts
2 tbls oil
625 g/1¼ lb pork fillet, trimmed
200 ml/⅓ pint dry red wine
200 ml/⅓ pint good meat stock
3 medium onions, cut into 8 segments
2 medium carrots, cut into 1 cm/½ inch chunks
2 garlic cloves, crushed
salt and pepper
250 g/8 oz leeks

If the chestnuts are fresh, steam for 15-20 minutes until they soften. Canned ones may be used as they are, but rinse in cold water first.

Heat the oil in a large saucepan or flameproof casserole and brown the pork well on all sides. Add the wine, stock, onions, carrot and garlic,

season well and bring to the boil. Cover, reduce the heat and simmer very gently for 30 minutes.

Wash and trim the leeks and cut into 1 cm/½ inch slices. Add the leeks and chestnuts to the pork and continue simmering for a further 40 minutes, until the pork and vegetables are tender.

Remove the pork from the casserole, strain off the cooking liquid into a saucepan and reduce over a high heat until syrupy. Cut the pork into medallions, arrange in a circle on a heated serving dish, pile the vegetables in the centre and pour the sauce over.

PORK FILLET with PRUNES

The classic version of this dish from the Touraine region of France calls for the prunes to be simmered separately, the pork medallions being fried in butter. The liquor from the prunes is used to deglaze the frying pan, it is then reduced and finally enriched with cream to make the sauce. The following recipe uses no cream, but still retains the strong, rich flavour of the original.

Serves four

1 heaped tbls granulated sugar
150 ml/¼ pint white wine or water
60 g/2 oz onion, sliced
250 g/8 oz cooking apple, peeled, cored and sliced
125 g/4 oz ready-to-eat stoned prunes
salt and pepper
2 fresh or 1 dried bay leaf
750-875 g/1½-1¾ lb pork fillet

Heat the sugar in a roasting tin over a medium heat until it caramelizes to a good rich brown. Turn down the heat and pour in the wine or water – take care and stand back, as it will splutter alarmingly. Stir until the caramel dissolves, then add the onion, apple and prunes. Season well with salt and pepper, add the bay leaf then sit the pork on top. Cook at 190°C/375°F/Gas Mark 5, allowing 40 minutes per 500 g/1 lb meat. Baste the pork with the juices two or three times during cooking.

When the pork is cooked, let it rest for a few minutes while you make the sauce. Reserve a few of the prunes and push the rest of the pan contents through a sieve, or blend them, to give a smooth sauce. Check the seasoning, put into a saucepan and keep warm over a low heat. Slice the pork at a slight angle into medallions about 1 cm/½ inch thick. Spoon a little sauce onto heated plates, arrange the pork on top and garnish with the reserved prunes.

VENISON with COGNAC and GARLIC SAUCE

Many restaurant chefs no longer marinate game for days on end, believing that the natural flavour should be retained. Cuts such as venison fillet don't need to marinate for tenderness, but a few hours in a savoury liquid adds a little piquancy. If the amount of meat seems small, remember that it is trimmed and very rich; it can be increased by 30-60 g/1-2 oz per serving if you wish. The garlic butter can be bought ready-made in many supermarkets.

Serves four

500 g/1 lb venison fillet, trimmed
8 tbls red wine mixed with Cognac (see method)
½ garlic clove, chopped
1 tsp finely grated orange rind
4 juniper berries, crushed
butter for frying
4 tbls Cognac
150 ml/¼ pint double cream
2 tbls garlic butter (see Tip below)

Cut the fillet into 4 even-sized pieces, and trim off all the fat and membrane. Mix the wine and Cognac in whatever proportions suit you and add the garlic, orange rind and juniper berries. Spoon it over the meat and leave at room temperature for a few hours, turning from time to time. Scrape all the flavourings from the meat; strain and reserve the marinade.

Sauté the fillet pieces for 5-7 minutes in butter over a medium heat, which will cook them medium-pink. Remove to a warm plate to allow the venison to rest and set. De-glaze the pan with the marinade, then add the Cognac and cream and reduce quickly to a coating consistency. Remove from the heat and whisk in the garlic butter in lumps.

Slice the fillets to reveal the pink centres and serve on a pool of the sauce. These are marvellous accompanied by either the sharp taste of pickled damsons or the sweeter flavour of sweet-spiced prunes (see page 180).

GLYNN'S TIP

To make the garlic butter for the Venison with Cognac and Garlic Sauce, crush 3-4 cloves garlic and mix with 125 g/4 oz butter.

KLEFTIKO – CYPRIOT ROASTED LAMB

Many butchers and supermarkets sell ready-cut pieces of shoulder (with the bone in), weighing about 375 g/12 oz, which are ideal for this dish. Otherwise, buy a shoulder and ask the butcher to saw it into 4-6 pieces; make sure that he saws, rather than chops, the joint, or you'll end up with nasty splinters of bone.

Serves four to six

1 shoulder of lamb, cut into 4-6 pieces, or pieces of lamb weighing about 375 g/12 oz
juice of 1 large lemon
5 tbls olive or peanut oil
1 large onion, chopped
2 bay leaves
2-3 tsps dried oregano
lemon wedges to serve

Trim the fat from the lamb and put the pieces of meat into a deep roasting-tin with the other ingredients, then just cover with cold water. Cover the pan with foil and cook at 200°C/400°F/Gas Mark 6 for 30 minutes. Lower the heat to 140°C/275°F/Gas Mark 1 and continue cooking for another 2 hours. Don't be tempted to lift the foil during this time.

Ideally, the *kleftiko* should be left to cool in the cooking liquid for several hours, preferably overnight. You can carry on cooking without waiting, but the flavour won't be so good.

To serve, pour off the cooking liquid and roast, uncovered, at 200°C/400°F/Gas Mark 6, until the meat is light-brown – about 20 minutes. Serve the *kleftiko* with roast potatoes, a salad and, most important, lots of lemon wedges to be squeezed over the meat.

BAKED LIVER with LEMON and JUNIPER

If you like liver, you'll love this dish. It is baked in a whole piece, rather than being sliced, and makes a far more impressive dish to serve, carved at the table. The sharpness of the sauce is a perfect partner to the richness of the liver.

Serves four

500 g/1 lb lambs' liver, in one piece
rind and juice of 1 lemon
10 juniper berries, crushed
150 ml/¼ pint cider or white wine
60 g/2 oz onion, finely chopped
125 g/4 oz celery, finely chopped
1 apple, peeled, cored and chopped
2 tbls oil
salt and pepper
sugar to taste
chopped celery leaves, to garnish

Remove any visible tubes or pieces of gristle from the liver and place it in a shallow dish. Grate the lemon rind over the top, add the juniper berries and pour over the lemon juice and cider or wine. Leave to marinate for at least 1 hour.

Put the chopped onion, celery and apple into the bottom of an ovenproof casserole. Heat the oil in a frying-pan, take the liver from the marinade, pat it dry using kitchen paper, then brown quickly on both sides.

Put the liver on top of the vegetables and pour the marinade over. Cover the dish and bake at 180°C/350°F/Gas Mark 4 for 35-45 minutes, depending on the thickness of the piece of liver and how well-done you like it. Remove the liver to a plate and keep it warm while you make the sauce.

Strain the pan contents through a fine sieve into a clean saucepan, pressing the vegetables with the back of a spoon to extract as much juice as possible. Season with plenty of salt and pepper and just a touch of sugar if you find it too sharp for your taste. Garnish. Slice the liver at the table and offer the sauce separately. Ⓢ

BRAISED LIVER on LEEK and FLAGEOLET PUREE

The savoury sauce of leeks and delicate green beans which accompanies this dish is made my favourite way – puréeing the ingredients upon which the meat is cooked, preserving all the goodness and flavours. If you have large appetites, increase the liver to 185 g/6 oz each.

Serves four

60 g/2 oz butter
500 g/1 lb lambs' liver, thinly sliced
375 g/12 oz leeks, thinly sliced
2 garlic cloves, crushed
397 g/14 oz can flageolet beans, drained
salt and pepper
1 orange
4 tbls white wine or water

Melt half the butter in a flameproof casserole and fry the liver quickly to brown lightly on both sides. Set aside. Add the remaining butter to the pan and cook the leeks and garlic over a medium heat until softened. Stir in the beans

---

> ### GLYNN'S TIP
>
> *It is always worth soaking liver in milk for a few hours before using. The milk absorbs any strong flavours; doubly important if you buy strongly-flavoured pork liver.*

---

and season well. Arrange the liver on top of the leeks and grate the orange rind over the top. Add the wine or water, cover and cook at 180°C/350°F/Gas Mark 4 for 20 minutes.

Remove the segments from the orange, making sure they are free from all pith. Put the cooked liver on to a plate and keep warm, covered. Purée the leeks and beans in a liquidiser or food processor until smooth. Reheat and check the seasoning. Place a spoonful of purée on to warmed plates with the liver alongside, and decorate with the orange segments. Ⓢ

CELERIAC STUFFED BEST END with VEGETABLE PUREE

Rack or best end of lamb, simply roasted with a little garlic or herbs, is one of the sweetest cuts. To make it more substantial, I stuff flavoured grated celeriac between the skin and the meat, which is equally good raw or cooked.

Serves six

2 best ends or racks of lamb, each comprising 6 chops, chined (cut through rib bones)
250 g/8 oz peeled celeriac
2 tbls lemon juice
1 or 2 garlic cloves, crushed
1 heaped tbls Dijon mustard
olive oil
white or red wine for the sauce

Put the racks, fat side down, on a board. Cut down the inside of the spine, through the separation made by the butcher and around the eye of the meat. Continue cutting around the meat and back, inside the skin and fat. Now the skin, though still attached to the spine, will be separate from most of the meat, making a pocket which can be stuffed.

Grate the celeriac into the lemon juice, add the garlic and mustard and mix well. Push the stuffing between the eye meat and the fat and secure the rack into roughly its original shape using toothpicks or cocktail sticks. Turn the meat over, score the fat into a diamond pattern and rub with a little olive oil. Roast at 180°C/350°F/Gas Mark 4 for 35-45 minutes, depending on how pink you like your lamb.

Let the meat rest for at least 10 minutes; remove the toothpicks or cocktail sticks and cut off the chined spine. With the juices left in the pan after you have poured off most of the fat, pour in a little white or red wine and boil to make a small amount of syrupy sauce. Quickly cut each rack into individual stuffed cutlets, between bones. If there are any juices from carving, add them to the sauce, boil again and serve beside the neatly arranged cutlets. Serve with Pumpkin and Apricot Purée (over page).

PUMPKIN & APRICOT PUREE

750 g/1½ lb pumpkin
60 g/2 oz butter
½ tsp ground allspice
30 g/1 oz dried apricots, chopped
1 tbls pine kernels (fried golden brown in a little butter)

Peel and cube the pumpkin, then cook in boiling salted water for about 15 minutes until tender. Drain, and purée with the butter and allspice. Pour back into the saucepan, stir in the apricots and heat gently for 5 minutes. Serve topped with the pine kernels.

STUFFED SHOULDER of LAMB

A shoulder of lamb can be a rather fatty joint and is tricky to carve. Boned, trimmed of fat and given a tasty stuffing, it is a different matter entirely. It is then moist, tender, full of flavour and simple to slice, hot or cold. I put together this recipe as a dish to celebrate Easter; the flavourings of fruit mincemeat and orange suggest the Holy Land.

Serves six

1.75 kg/3½ lb shoulder of lamb, boned
125 g/4 oz fresh breadcrumbs
185 g/6 oz fruit mincemeat
2 oranges
grated rind of 1 lemon
2 tbls brandy or lemon juice
1 egg, beaten
150 ml/¼ pint red wine
150 ml/¼ pint orange juice
salt and pepper
2 tbls chopped parsley

Trim any fat from the boned shoulder, inside and out. Mix together the breadcrumbs, mincemeat, grated rind of both oranges and lemon, brandy or lemon juice and beaten egg.

If it seems a little dry, add some juice from one orange to moisten. Stuff the lamb and sew it up loosely, or secure with toothpicks or cocktail sticks. Roast the lamb, standing on a rack in a roasting tin, allowing 30 minutes per 500 g/1 lb plus 30 minutes over, at 180°C/350°F/Gas Mark 4.

Peel one orange and carefully remove the segments, free from all pith. When the meat is cooked, let it rest while you make an unthickened gravy by boiling the pan juices with the wine and orange juice until well reduced and syrupy. Season the gravy well, stir in the chopped parsley and the orange segments and serve a little of the sauce spooned over each serving of sliced lamb.

SPINACH, ALMOND and MINT STUFFED LAMB

Here are some Middle Eastern flavours with which to stuff a boned leg or shoulder of lamb. If you can't find a friendly butcher to bone it for you, it is worth taking the time to do it yourself, as it makes the carving so much easier. Make sure that the small oval piece of bone that floats over the joint is removed, or it will get in the way of the carving-knife.

Serves four to six, depending on the size of the leg or shoulder of lamb (allow about 250 g/8 oz per person)

1 leg or shoulder of lamb, boned
500 g/1 lb fresh young spinach leaves, washed and chopped
salt
1 handful fresh mint, chopped
90 g/3 oz ground almonds
1 tbls wine vinegar (or sherry)
white wine for basting
2 slices of white bread, with crusts removed
1 garlic clove, chopped
handful of fresh parsley
juice of 2 oranges

Trim all the fat from the lamb. Layer the chopped spinach with a little salt in a colander or sieve. Leave to drain for 2 hours, then squeeze dry. Put the spinach into a bowl with the chopped mint, ground almonds and vinegar, and mix well. Stuff the leg with the spinach mixture, fold the flaps under and secure with toothpicks or cocktail sticks. Put the meat in a roasting-tin, and cook at 190°C/375°F/Gas Mark 5 for 45 minutes, basting once or twice with a little white wine.

Put the bread, garlic and parsley in a blender or food processor and chop; or make breadcrumbs, crush the garlic, chop the parsley and mix together. Moisten with the juice of half an orange. Spread this mixture over the top of the lamb and return to the oven for a further 15-35 minutes, depending on the size of the joint and how pink you like your meat.

Remove the cooked meat to a warm dish and, while it is resting, pour the remaining orange juice into the roasting-tin. Mix in any topping which has fallen off the meat, bring to the boil and reduce to a syrupy gravy. Check the seasoning and spoon over the sliced meat.

TARRAGON CREAM LAMB

I couldn't resist including this recipe, which was my standby for years before food became my career. It's a little old-fashioned and naughty to serve meat in cream, but as the meat is relatively fatless, you could defend your choice by serving this dish as part of an otherwise healthier meal.

Remove the skin and score the lamb as for the above recipe. Rub a generous teaspoon of dried tarragon into the cuts, then marinate in half a bottle of dry white wine with some sliced onion and a couple of bay leaves. Cook as for next recipe, removing the foil halfway through cooking and at the same time pouring most of the juices into a saucepan. While the meat continues to cook, reduce these juices to a quarter their original volume, then stir in at least 150 ml/¼ pint double cream and 1 teaspoon of dried tarragon. Continue simmering the sauce to extract maximum flavour and achieve a good creamy consistency. When the meat is cooked, let it rest and add the remaining cooking juices to the sauce. Keep the sauce bubbling and reducing while you slice the lamb, then adjust the seasoning and strain before serving.

HONEY, SOYA and FRESH GINGER LAMB

Roasting at this low temperature helps to prevent shrinkage of the meat; marinating and scoring means that it cooks much faster. This is a celebration dish when a plain roasted leg of lamb isn't festive enough.

Serves four to six, depending on the size of leg (allow about 250 g/8 oz per person)

1 leg of lamb
30 g/1 oz fresh ginger, peeled
2 tbls honey
3 tbls lemon juice
4 tbls soy sauce

Slice all the skin off the lamb, together with as much fat as possible. (Save it for roasting potatoes, unless you are concerned about cholesterol levels, in which case, throw it away.) Cut really deep scores in a criss-cross pattern on all sides of the meat. Cut the ginger into thin slices, then into matchsticks. Stuff them evenly into the cuts all over the lamb, then stand it in a roasting-tin. Mix the honey, lemon juice and soy sauce and pour it over the meat. Leave to marinate for 4 hours at room temperature. Spoon the liquid over the meat as often as you can during this time.

Cover the meat and the roasting-tin with foil and cook at 160°C/325°F/Gas Mark 3. Calculate the cooking time, allowing 15 minutes per 500 g/1 lb plus 15 minutes over (5 minutes more per 500 g/1 lb if you don't like your lamb pink).

Take off the foil lid 15 minutes before the end of cooking and remove all the pieces of ginger. Baste the meat well and return to the oven to finish cooking. Allow the lamb to rest for 10 minutes before carving and serve with a little of the strained sauce poured over. Ⓢ

LOIN of PORK with RED CABBAGE and CHESTNUTS

Although hundreds of miles apart, Denmark and the Limousin in central France share a passion for pork and red cabbage. In Denmark, roast loin with crackling is always served with red cabbage, boiled potatoes or small potatoes coated with caramel. In the Limousin red cabbage and chestnuts are a classic accompaniment. My version combines the best of both ideas, and takes advantage of the high quality of the red cabbage and chestnuts available in cans.

A perfect meal to serve when entertaining; you could buy and cook a larger joint without needing to increase the amount of cabbage and chestnuts.

Serves four to six

1-1.25 kg/2-2½ lb loin of pork, chined and scored
3 fresh or 2 dry bay leaves
500 g/1 lb jar or can of red cabbage
4 crushed juniper berries
150 ml/¼ pint red wine
125 g/4 oz canned whole chestnuts, drained

Ensure that the butcher has chined the loin (that is, sawn through the ribs at the spine end so that you can carve the meat easily when it is cooked). Insert a sharp-pointed knife under some of the scoring made for crackling and insert the bay leaves, which give a remarkable extra fragrance to roasted pork. Rub the rind with oil and a little salt, the French way, or pour over some boiling water and pat it dry, the Danish way.

Roast at 180°C/350°F/Gas Mark 4 for 30 minutes per 500 g/1 lb plus 30 minutes, but do not baste. Allow the joint to rest for a good 10 minutes before removing the chine bone and the crackling.

Meanwhile, drain the red cabbage, rinse quickly in running water and drain again. Add the juniper berries and wine to the cabbage in a saucepan and boil uncovered until the wine has been absorbed. Keep warm and stir in the chestnuts just before serving, trying not to break them up too much.

Slice the pork thickly and serve with crackling. Hot apple sauce would go very well. Ⓔ Ⓢ

LOIN of PORK with PEARS

Choose under-ripe cooking pears for this dish and you'll find they retain lots of flavour, even after cooking.

Serves four

1 tbls white sugar
150 ml/¼ pint cider or water
250 g/8 oz peeled, cored and sliced pears
60 g/2 oz onion, sliced
salt and pepper
1 dried bay leaf
½ tsp ground allspice
1 kg/2 lb loin of pork, trimmed

Heat the sugar in a roasting-tin over a medium heat until it turns to a good brown caramel. Add the cider or water (stand back so you are not splattered with hot sugar) and stir until the caramel dissolves. Add the pears, onion and seasonings, then put the pork on top (making sure that the bay leaf is underneath). Cook in a preheated moderately hot oven (190°C/375°F/Gas Mark 5), allowing 30 minutes per 500 g/1lb plus 30 minutes.

When the pork is cooked, take it out and let it rest while you make the sauce. Drain off any excess fat, discard the bay leaf, put the contents of the roasting-tin into a food processor or blender and purée until smooth. Check the seasoning, slice the pork and offer the sauce separately.

Options

You could of course make this with apples or, wonderfully, with quinces. Any version would be further enhanced by being accompanied by a peeled half apple or pear, sliced into a fan and lightly grilled with a brushing of melted butter.

PASTRY

Provided the basic rules are followed, pastry-making is not difficult and, like all other skills, improves with experience. In this chapter I cover the pastries I consider to be basic, together with a number of variations and one or two recipes.

There is no denying that some cooks make much better pastry than others. Great skill can be used to fashion wondrous concoctions — moulds of choux balls in a towering, caramel-veiled *croquembouche* or layers of paper-thin puff pastry in a *mille feuille*. Pastry-making is a specialist side of cooking, but we do not all need to be great *pâtissiers* to use pastry regularly, especially now that such good pastry can be bought, chilled or frozen; nor do pastry dishes need to be complicated or calorie-laden. Some of the best modern first courses and puddings combine pastry with fish, fruit or vegetables. (I am always looking for new ways to use puff-pastry *mille feuilles* as first courses.)

Don't forget the trick of painting pastry (see page 134). In the Middle Ages it was done with red sandalwood, blue woad, herb juice and golden saffron. It's easier and cheaper now.

PASTRY-MAKER'S PRIMER

● With one or two exceptions, pastry-making should be *cool* and *quick*. All the ingredients, utensils, and especially your hands, should be cold; all the mixing and rolling should be done speedily.
● Use plain flour for the short (crumbly) type of pastry and strong (bread) flour for layered pastry

– rough puff, for example. Salt should always be included when sifting the flour; allow ½ teaspoon to each 250 g/8 oz flour.
● Use only your fingertips when rubbing fat into flour, and lift the mixture high out of the bowl as you do so. This keeps the butter cool and incorporates air into the mixture.
● Roll pastry in one direction only, moving it around on a *lightly* floured board to achieve the required shape. *Never* turn pastry over during rolling. Use light, short, sharp movements; heavy-handed rolling means heavy pastry.
● Allow rolled pastry to relax in a cool place for a few minutes before you cut it to shape. This allows the gluten in the flour which has been over-stretched by the rolling to relax back to its real length. By doing this you dramatically reduce the chances of your pastry shrinking during cooking. It is usual to let pastry relax after the pie has been made, too, but the most important time is immediately after rolling (ensure that the underside of the pastry is not sticking to the board — throw some flour under it if there is the slightest chance that stickiness will prevent the pastry from shrinking).

SHORTCRUST PASTRY

For a richer pastry, use all butter instead of butter and lard.

Makes a 20 cm/8 inch single pie crust

185 g/6 oz plain flour
salt
60 g/2 oz butter
30 g/1 oz lard

Sift the flour with a generous pinch of salt. Rub the fats into the flour (start by cutting them

into chunks, then use the fingertips) until you have the texture of breadcrumbs. Add a bare 2 tablespoons of very cold water and stir the mixture with a knife until it sticks together in lumps. If the mixture looks very dry and is reluctant to form lumps, add a little more water, but take care not to add too much or the pastry will be sticky and difficult to roll out.

Use one hand to gather the pastry together in the bowl, then knead *lightly* for just a few seconds so that the dough is smooth.

Roll out immediately, or, if you have time, leave it to rest for a few minutes in a cool place. (If you put it in the refrigerator, be sure to cover it with plastic wrap.) Use as required. As a general rule, shortcrust pastry should be baked at 200°C/400°F/Gas Mark 6, until lightly browned.

FOOD PROCESSOR or MIXER SHORTCRUST PASTRY

The rubbing-in stage of any shortcrust pastry-making can be carried out successfully in a food processor, or by using a mixer. However, the addition of water and the formation of dough is a little more tricky because it is easy to over-mix and end up with tough pastry as a result. Another common pitfall is the addition of too much liquid, making the dough both sticky and tough.

Food processors generate a lot of heat, and the mixture quickly becomes warm, which melts the butter, so it is extremely important to work *very* quickly. Once the breadcrumb stage has been reached, stop the processor *immediately*. Turn the crumbs over lightly to dissipate any accumulated heat, close the processor lid and, once started, dribble in the given amount of water as quickly as possible. It will look as though you need more, but watch carefully. Instantaneously the crumbs will lump together around the spindle. Turn off the processor the moment this starts to happen. Over-processing at this stage is the greatest cause of imperfect pastry. Gently gather together the pastry, knead just once or twice by hand and then let it rest a good 20 minutes, as above. Once mastered, this method is a very easy way to make pastry.

GLYNN'S TIP

For a lighter, flakier food processor shortcrust, add the butter in large pieces and stop the initial process when there are still large flakes and crumbs.

RICH SHORTCRUST PASTRY

This richer pastry, made with egg yolk, is one of my favourites; the flavour options which follow may be used for the simpler shortcrust pastries, too.

Makes a 20 cm/8 inch single pie crust

185 g/6 oz plain flour
salt
125 g/4 oz butter
1 egg yolk

Follow the same rubbing-in procedure as for shortcrust pastry, but mix to a dough using the egg yolk lightly beaten with a scant tablespoon of cold water. Don't add the egg all at once; you may only need part of it depending on the type of flour used, kitchen temperature and the size of the egg.

Options

Rich Cheese Shortcrust Add to the flour 60-90 g/2-3 oz finely grated hard cheese with a bare teaspoon mustard powder and ½ teaspoon cayenne pepper.

Rich Herb Shortcrust Add several tablespoons of fresh herbs or several teaspoons of a dried one. Mint is very good, and so is tarragon, but you could use any that complement the filling.

Rich Sweet Shortcrust Stir 30 g/1 oz caster sugar into the flour and add a few drops of vanilla essence to the egg yolk before mixing.

Lemon, Orange and Lime Shortcrust Add the equivalent of 1 teaspoon of finely grated lemon, orange or lime rind. This must be grated directly on to the flour to ensure that as much of the flavourful citrus oil as possible is included. It is especially good for apple or pear pie crusts.

Almond Shortcrust Add 30 g/1 oz ground almonds with 1 tablespoon caster sugar to the flour and a few drops of almond essence to the egg yolk before beating.

Toasted Almond Pastry Add 45 g/1½ oz finely chopped toasted almonds, or toast 45 g /1½ oz ground almonds in a small pan over a medium heat until evenly browned. Stir into the flour, with 1 tablespoon of caster sugar.

SHORTCRUST PASTRY with OIL

It is possible to make shortcrust pastry using oil rather than fats, although it does not remain fresh for long and does not freeze successfully. I'd also add that oil is usually rather heavy and boring, so unless you are serving someone who cannot eat dairy foods I would use fats instead.

Makes a 20 cm/8 inch single pie crust

4 tbls oil
2 tbls water
185 g/6 oz plain flour
salt

Beat the oil and water together in a bowl to form an emulsion, then sift the flour with a generous pinch of salt; stir with a knife until a dough is formed. Knead lightly, then roll out immediately on a floured board and bake as soon as possible.

WHOLEMEAL PASTRY

You probably don't need me to tell you that wholemeal pastry can be among the most uninspired, heavy and tasteless foods.

The sensible thing to do is not to make a completely wholemeal flour pastry but to use any of the shortcrust recipes and replace up to 50 per cent of the white flour with wholemeal flour, which makes a deliciously nutty pastry – provided, that is, that you use at least 50 per cent butter and not all oil. In addition, I often use wholemeal flour when rolling out white-flour shortcrust pastry, which adds a subtle nutty flavour; it's good with both savoury and sweet pies.

You may well find you need more water than usual and you must definitely let the pastry rest at least 30 minutes, or longer, if you have a high proportion of wholemeal, for only this will give the wholemeal pastry some elasticity, making it faster and easier to roll.

PATE SUCREE

This very short (crumbly) sweet French pastry is used for Continental flans and tarts. It retains a good shape during baking, being less liable to rise or shrink than shortcrust pastry.

In contrast to the previous recipes, the ingredients for Pâte Sucrée should be warm, with the butter softened and cut into small pieces. Once made, the dough should be thoroughly chilled before rolling out.

Pâte Sucrée should be baked at 190°C/375°F/ Gas Mark 5, unless the recipe states otherwise. It is important not to overcook Pâte Sucrée, as it quickly acquires a burnt taste even if slightly over-browned. Remember this, especially when making tarts and flans which require baking blind; take care to protect the edge with foil during the second baking.

Makes a 20 cm/8 inch single pie crust

185 g/6 oz plain flour
salt
90 g/3 oz butter, softened
3 egg yolks
few drops vanilla essence
90 g/3 oz caster sugar

Sift the flour with a generous pinch of salt on to a large board, scrubbed table or marble slab. Make a large well in the centre and into it put the butter (cut into small pieces), the egg yolks, vanilla essence and caster sugar. Using a 'pecking' motion with the index-finger and thumb of one hand, blend the mixture together until it resembles scrambled eggs.

Using a palette knife, scoop up the flour over the mixture and cut it in until roughly amalgamated. Quickly form into a ball and knead sufficiently to give a smooth dough. Cover with plastic wrap and chill for at least an hour before rolling.

Options

Almond Pâte Sucrée (Pâte Frolle) – Use 60 g/ 2 oz caster sugar, 90 g/3 oz ground almonds, 155 g/5 oz butter, 185 g/6 oz flour, 2 egg yolks and a few drops of almond essence. It is particularly important that this dough is not over-handled, or the oil in the almonds will be released, making the pastry hard when baked.

Valentine Pastry – Pâte Sucrée and Pâte Frolle will make bases for hundreds of elegant sweet courses. This is the best, which costs a fortune in Michelin-rated restaurants. Shape two thin heart shapes per person about 10 cm/4 inches long and fairly wide; bake them at 190°C/375°F/Gas Mark 5 until the edges are only just starting to colour. To serve, spread one shape with thickly whipped double cream (or with clotted cream) and nestle perfect strawberries into it, pointed side up. Cover with the other pastry heart and sprinkle on a little icing sugar. Flood the plate with raspberry purée flavoured with rose water; draw patterns by dropping on cream and pulling it with the end of a pointed knife. Add a tiny rosebud or other flavour and serve chilled. What a beautiful Valentine!

Processor Pâte Sucrée – It is possible to make Pâte Sucrée in a food processor, putting all the ingredients into the machine and using short bursts until a dough is formed. Stop immediately this happens, or it will become warm and sticky and very difficult to handle. The butter in this case should not be soft, but cold and cut into small pieces.

TULIPES GLACEES

Makes about 14

185 g/6 oz plain flour
125 g/4 oz icing sugar
2 egg yolks
3 egg whites

Sift the flour and sugar together into a bowl. Beat the egg yolks together lightly, and also the whites, separately. Add to the flour mixture and mix well.

Line a baking sheet with Bakewell non-stick paper and on it trace 4 circles, about 12 cm/4½ inch in diameter, then turn the paper over (if your baking sheet is small, it is probably best to make only 2 at a time). Pour a tablespoon of batter onto each circle and with the back of a spoon spread to fill the outline you have drawn. Bake at 180°C/350°F/Gas Mark 4 for 5 minutes or until the edges are just turning brown. Have ready 4 small, straight-sided glasses, inverted and covered with foil. Take the tray from the oven, allow the biscuits to cool for just half a minute then carefully lift from the paper using a palette knife and place over the glasses. Use your fingers to scallop the edges of the 'tulips'. Allow the tulips to cool before removing them to a tray to get quite cold. They store well in an airtight tin.

To serve, fill with a scoop of ice-cream, decorate with fruits in season and sprinkle a suitable liqueur over the top.

BAKED PASTRY CASES

Recipes in this book and elsewhere which call for baked pastry cases give sizes of tins which correspond to shortcrust pastry made with the following amounts of flour and other ingredients in proportion:

15 cm/6 inch ring: 125 g/4 oz flour
18 cm/7 inch ring: 155 g/5 oz flour
20 cm/8 inch ring: 185 g/6 oz flour
22 cm/9 inch ring: 220 g/7 oz flour
25 cm/10 inch ring: 250 g/8 oz flour

Note: for covered pies, add 50 per cent or more pastry; and use two-thirds for the base and one third for the top.

To line a flan-tin or ring – It is important that the pastry is never stretched or it will shrink during cooking. Lift the rolled pastry using the rolling-pin and cover the ring like a blanket. Using a small piece of dough, gently push the pastry into the shape of the tin, easing and not stretching while keeping an even thickness. With the rolling-pin, roll across the top of the tin to remove the excess pastry.

To bake blind – Pastry cases must often be pre-baked without a filling, so that they are dry and crisp. Prick the pastry in the tin with a fork, then cover with greaseproof paper, easing it into the shape of the tin. Cover the base with a layer of baking beans, any uncooked beans or dry pasta kept specifically for the purpose. Bake for the time stated, generally 15 minutes, until almost cooked. Remove the beans and paper and return to the oven for a further 5 minutes to dry and complete the cooking. Where the case is of pâté sucrée, which is more delicate than other pastries, line with tissue paper and take care not to over-bake. Crumpled foil may be used instead of paper and beans, but care should be taken not to damage the pastry when putting it into the unbaked case.

FRUIT PIES

Fruit pies may have a layer of pastry top and bottom and be baked in a shallow pie-plate or deeper pie-dish. Or you could make a fruitier pie which has only the top crust of pastry.

Plate Pie You will need 350 g/12 oz prepared fruit and 500 g/1 lb Shortcrust Pastry (see page 129). Use a generous half of the pastry to line the pie-plate, then arrange the fruit on top and sprinkle with sugar to taste. Brush the rim of the pastry with water. Roll out the remaining pastry large enough to cover the pie comfortably. Cover the pie, trim and seal the edges securely. Make a small slit in the top to allow the steam to escape, glaze with milk or a little beaten egg and bake at 220°C/425°F/Gas Mark 7 for 15 minutes. Reduce the heat to 180°C/350°F/Gas Mark 4 and cook for a further 25-30 minutes. Serve warm or cold, lightly dredged with caster sugar.

Deep Dish Pie Prepare in the same way as Plate Pie but allow 1-1.5 kg/2-3 lb of prepared fruit and use two thirds of the pastry to line the dish. If necessary add a funnel to prevent the pastry lid from sinking.

Top Crust Pie Use a traditional 1 litre/2 pint pie-dish or casserole with a lip. Arrange 750 g /1½ lb prepared fruit in the dish and sprinkle with sugar to taste. Gently push a pie funnel into the centre of the dish. Roll out 250 g/½ lb pastry large enough to cover the pie comfortably and from the trimmings cut a strip 1 cm/½ inch wide to go around the rim of the dish. Dampen the pastry rim with water and carefully cover the dish with the pastry. Crimp the edges firmly with your thumb and forefinger, or use the prongs of a fork. Make a small slit over the funnel and brush the pastry with milk or egg glaze. Bake at 220°C/425°F/Gas Mark 7 for 10 minutes, then reduce the heat to 180°C/350°F/Gas Mark 4 and bake for a further 30 minutes. Serve warm or cold, lightly dusted with icing sugar.

Double Crust Pastry Pie For a 20 cm/8 inch or 22 cm/9 inch pie, you will need pastry made with 250 g/8 oz flour. Use one half to line the dish and the other, rolled slightly less thinly, for the top. Crimp the edges together or roll flat and press with the prongs of a fork to seal.

GLYNN'S TIP

After baking pastry blind to compensate for the addition of a moist filling, it is common practice to rub the warm pastry with butter to make a seal. I find an egg white works better. While the pastry is still hot, whisk an egg white lightly and paint it on the pastry. Let it rest a few minutes to soak in a little, then put it into the cooling oven to set completely. It doesn't hurt to make two layers.

CHOUX PASTRY

If you've never made pastry before, you may be surprised to find choux pastry coming first, but there's a reason for this — it's the simplest pastry of all to make. The television cook Michael Smith taught me the main secret of choux pastry — it is what you *don't* serve that makes it memorable! There is inevitably some uncooked pastry in the middle of each pastry shape, and you must remove this.

Makes 18 large or 36 small buns

140 g/5 oz strong flour
pinch of salt
300 ml/½ pint boiling water
125 g/4 oz butter
4 eggs, lightly beaten

Sift the flour with the salt on to a sheet of greaseproof paper or into a bowl. Measure the boiling water into a small saucepan and add the butter cut into pieces. Once the butter has melted, increase the heat and bring rapidly to the boil. Take the pan off the heat and shoot the flour into the pan all at once. Stir with a wooden spoon until blended, then return the pan to a low heat and continue to stir until the mixture comes away from the sides of the pan. Stop immediately this happens, take the pan off the heat and allow it to cool a little.

Gradually start to beat the eggs into the mixture, using an electric hand-mixer or a large wooden spoon. Add only a little at a time, making sure that the mixture is smooth after each addition. Depending on the ingredients (especially the size of the eggs), you may not need to incorporate all of the beaten egg. Stop when the mixture looks like very thick batter; if it is too thin it will be difficult to shape.

Wet the baking-trays (the steam water produces in the oven helps the pastry to rise). Pipe or spoon the mixture on to the baking-trays in the required shape (see Options) and bake at 200°C/400°F/Gas Mark 6 until well risen, crisp and brown. Don't open the oven for the first 10 minutes; even small choux buns take 15 to 25 minutes to cook.

Choux pastry always looks cooked before it is thoroughly dried out, so for crisp results make small slits in the sides of the pastry which allow

GLYNN'S TIP

Pamela Harlech taught me that the more eggs choux pastry contains, the softer the pastry will be. If you want your choux pastry to be crisp, cut down the number of eggs to three or even to two if they are large.

GLYNN'S TIP

When filling choux buns and eclairs, don't cut them in half horizontally, but at an angle from the top to the opposite side of the bottom; this leaves them looking more generous when filled and also helps a decoration (half a cherry or piece of strawberry, for instance) to stick into the cream and stay there more securely and attractively.

the steam to escape, then return to a cool (150°C/300°F/Gas Mark 2) oven for an extra 10-15 minutes. Large buns and rings will always have some pastry which has not cooked; this should be spooned out.

Options

Sweet Choux Pastry – Dissolve 30 g/1 oz sugar in the water with the butter.
Spiced and Savoury Choux Pastry – Sprinkle in a little flavouring with the flour — roasted cumin seeds, crushed roasted black peppercorns, coarsely ground green peppercorns, chopped nuts, crushed garlic, very finely chopped onion. (Finely ground spices aren't as exciting as the explosion of flavour that a little piece of a whole spice will create.)
Profiteroles – Pipe small mounds of choux pastry on to a wetted baking-tray (or use a teaspoon) and bake until golden and dried out. Fill with whipped cream flavoured with vanilla and icing sugar, or rose water and icing sugar, rum or liqueur. Whipped cream with an equal quantity of chestnut purée, enhanced with black rum, is a superb combination. For weddings or at Christmas I usually finish each chestnut-cream profiterole with a whole or half black cherry which has languished as long as possible in black rum.
Eclairs – Using a 2 cm/¾ inch plain nozzle, pipe 10 cm/4 inch lengths of choux pastry on to a baking-tray and bake until golden brown. Sweet eclairs are usually filled with whipped cream, as above, then decorated with chocolate or coffee icing. Delicious savoury eclairs can be filled with a mixture of cream cheese or curd cheese beaten with the same amount of strained Greek yoghurt and flavoured with herbs, or with chopped seafood, ham, or cheese.
Savoury eclairs should be glazed with beaten egg yolk before baking, then very lightly dusted with paprika before serving.
Filled with a creamy sauce flavoured with cumin and including lots of crisp, steamed vegetables, large eclairs can be served as a first course or a lunch-time main course. But remember never to fill choux buns too far in

advance or they will lose their crispness.
Gougère – Stir into the savoury choux paste, Gruyère or another hard cheese, cut into small cubes. Form the mixture into a large ring, or pile around the edge of a shallow, ovenproof dish. Bake until well browned (which will take about 30 minutes). Pile a mixture of cooked chicken, fish or meat coated in a well-flavoured sauce into the centre and return to the oven for a further 10 to 15 minutes. Serve hot.
Croquembouche – Cream-filled profiteroles, are piled into a magnificent tower and adorned with spun sugar (fine threads of caramel).

STRUDEL PASTRY

Leaves of strudel dough can be bought ready-made in delicatessens and well-stocked supermarkets, but if you plan to make a really large party-sized pie, here is an opportunity to have fun and make your own. I can recommend it as a wonderfully satisfying and rewarding way of passing a wet afternoon alone, or better still, with someone to help with the exciting bits!

Makes 250 g/8 oz pastry

250 g/8 oz strong white flour
½ tsp salt
1 egg
1 tbls oil
4 tbls water

Sift the flour with the salt on to a board, or into a large bowl. Make a well in the centre and pour in the egg and the oil. Slowly draw in the flour, gradually adding the water and kneading until you have a soft dough. Continue kneading until the surface is covered with tiny blisters; this will take some time (and elbow-grease) but must be done. Cover with a damp cloth and let it recover for an hour — do the same yourself!

Clear a table top and cover it with a clean cloth or sheet. Dust liberally with flour then place the pastry in the centre. Start rolling and when it is about 6 mm/¼ inch thick, abandon the rolling pin and start stretching the pastry with your hands. You'll find your own best way of doing this but, basically, it works better if one hand is under the pastry and one on top. If you are on your own, you'll need to weight down one end of the pastry, otherwise you'll simply be pulling it across the table! If you have assistance, you can get the process well under way by standing together, with fists held slightly apart as if holding a skein of wool, the pastry draped over the top. Now start stretching by extending your arm, at the same time moving away from each other. When the pastry seems about to break out into holes put it on the table and continue stretching, bit by bit, working round the table and easing out the thick bits. The border is prone to develop holes, but these generally disappear when you roll or fold the pastry.

When you're sure that it won't stretch any more (you should be able to read a newspaper through it, although I don't recommend that you try) trim off the thick edge pieces and make a reasonably even shape – a rectangle or oval is best.

If you want to rest or admire it, paint the whole thing with melted butter then cover it with a damp cloth. Otherwise, go ahead and spread the filling over the dough. Make sure that you leave a good border on each side (for folding in) and leave between 25 and 30 per cent of the pastry at either end free from filling so that you will have enough to wrap round, giving the strudel a good shape as well as the added attraction of several layers of crispness. Now roll or fold the cloth back underneath itself, until the roll of cloth is level with the unfilled edge of the strudel. Tuck a baking sheet under this folded edge securely, then to the opposite side of the table and turn in the edge of the strudel by hand to make one roll right along the length. Fold in the sides. Complete the rolling by tipping up the cloth; continue until the strudel finally rolls on to the baking sheet. If your helper is still around, it would be useful to have an extra pair of hands to help you steady the baking sheet.

SUET PASTRY

This is the only pastry where self-raising flour is always used, for a raising agent is needed to give a light texture. Suet pastry is very quick and easy to make but, like scone, it must be handled as little as possible to give a soft dough. This type of pastry is best used for steamed or boiled dishes as it can be rather hard when baked.

Makes 500 g/1 lb pastry

250 g/8 oz self-raising flour
salt
125 g/4 oz beef or vegetarian suet, shredded
150 ml/¼ pint water

Sift the flour with a generous pinch of salt into a bowl and stir in the suet. Use a knife to form a dough while steadily pouring in the cold water. Knead until smooth, taking care not to over-handle. Roll out a suet crust slightly thicker than for other types of pastry (about 6 mm/ ¼ inch).

Options
Although it is a contradiction, butter can be used in place of suet.

For a lighter texture, use 60 g/2 oz fresh white breadcrumbs to replace the same amount of flour.

Add 2 teaspoons finely grated lemon or orange rind to the flour for a sweet pudding, or 1 teaspoon dried herbs for a savoury dish.

ROUGH PUFF PASTRY

If you are looking for value-for-effort, this is the pastry for you (and for me). It is easier to make than conventional puff pastry and few people will be able to tell the difference between rough puff and puff pastry once they are cooked. It looks and tastes professional, requires very little effort and virtually no skill. It is also particularly easy to flavour (see Tip on page 134).

Makes 500 g/1 lb pastry

250 g/8 oz strong plain flour
salt
185 g/6 oz butter, or half butter and half lard or shortening
150 ml/¼ pint water, with a generous squeeze of lemon juice

Sift the flour into a bowl with a pinch of salt and add the fat, cut into small, cherry-sized pieces. Stir well, make a well in the centre and pour in the water and lemon juice. Mix, first with a knife, then with one hand until it forms a ball, but do not knead. Turn on to a floured board and pat into a rectangle; if it looks impossibly messy, is sticky and has lumps of butter sticking through, you have done it right!

Roll out with short, sharp strokes (see Flaky Pastry, page 134), so that it is three times as long as it is wide (about 39 cm × 13 cm/15 in × 5 in). Fold the bottom third up, then the top third down over it, keeping the edges neatly on top of each other. Turn the pastry round so that it resembles a book, with the folded edge on your left. Let it rest for a few minutes and then gently use the rolling-pin to seal both ends and the side seam, thus trapping the air. If you don't do this, you will be wasting at least half of your effort. Still using the short, sharp strokes, roll and fold and rest twice more. By this time it will begin to be recognisable as pastry. Be generous with dredged flour on top and bottom but brush off the excess before folding and be pernickity about resting and sealing the folds each time. Cover the pastry and chill for 10-15 minutes.

Starting with the folded edge on your left again, roll and fold as before. If pieces of fat are still showing through, don't worry, simply dredge with more flour. Fold, roll and turn at least once more. Now wrap and chill for at least 30 minutes before rolling out and using.

Rough puff pastry should be baked in a very hot oven (220°C/425°F/Gas Mark 7) and may be glazed with beaten egg or painted.

PUFF PASTRY

The technique used depends on having the butter and the dough-base at the same texture and temperature; the butter is then continuously rolled out in a sheet between the layers of dough.

Makes 500 g/1 lb pastry

250 g/8 oz strong plain flour
salt
250 g/8 oz butter
150 ml/¼ pint water with a generous squeeze of lemon juice
beaten egg for glazing

Sift the flour into a bowl with a pinch of salt and rub in 30 g/1 oz of the butter to resemble breadcrumbs. Stir in enough water and lemon juice to make a soft, but not sticky, dough and knead until slightly elastic.

Flatten the remaining butter into a rectangle about 2 cm/¾ inch thick. Roll out the dough into a square about 1 cm/½ inch thick and put the slab of butter in the centre. Mark roughly where the butter lies, then remove it. Roll the pastry outside the marked oblong, so that it makes four flaps, each about 6 mm/¼ inch thick. Replace the butter in the centre and fold the flaps over, envelope-style, to cover it completely. Press gently with a rolling-pin, then carefully roll into an even rectangle. Fold the bottom third up, then the top third down over the top and seal the edges gently with the rolling-pin. Wrap and chill the pastry for about 30 minutes. Re-roll and fold and seal the pastry five more times, allowing it to relax for 20-30 minutes after each sequence.

Puff pastry should always be glazed with beaten egg before baking. Take care when brushing not to allow the glaze to drip down the sides, as this will prevent the pastry from rising evenly. Bake in a hot oven, 220°C/425°F/ Gas Mark 7.

FLAKY PASTRY

Flaky pastry is marginally easier to make than real puff pastry, but it does not rise quite so much.

Makes 500 g/1 lb pastry

185 g/6 oz butter
250 g/8 oz plain flour
salt
about 8 tbls water and a generous squeeze of
lemon juice
beaten egg for glazing

Divide the butter into four portions and use one portion to rub into the flour sifted with a pinch of salt. Mix with the water and lemon juice to give a soft but not sticky dough. Knead lightly until it is smooth and slightly elastic. Roll out on a lightly floured board to a neat rectangle three times as long as it is wide.

Using a knife, put flakes of the second portion of butter across the pastry extending two-thirds of the way down from the top. Fold up the bottom (unbuttered) third, keeping the edges neatly together, then fold the top portion over that and seal the edges gently using the rolling-pin. Cover with plastic wrap and chill for 15-20 minutes.

Repeat this rolling, buttering and folding sequence twice more, wrapping and chilling between each one. The pastry will be easier to handle if allowed to chill for at least 30 minutes before use. Flaky pastry should be baked at 200°C/400°F/Gas Mark 6, and is usually glazed with beaten egg, or egg yolk mixed with water, to give a shiny finish.

RE-FLAVOURING READY-MADE PUFF PASTRY

Frozen puff pastry is useful to have in the freezer and, if flavoured, can be as delicious as the finest home-made variety. It is rarely made with more than a small proportion of butter and simply by adding a little more you can give it a home-made or professional flavour that is all too rare and thus always excites comment and appreciation.

For each 250 g/8 oz of chilled (or thawed) pastry you need 60 g/2 oz butter (unsalted Normandy butter is measurably better both in performance and flavour). Try to prise the slab of pastry gently apart along its previous folds; but if this is difficult, roll it out to an even rectangle, about 6 mm/¼ inch thick.

Using half the butter, dot slivers across the pastry from the top, extending two-thirds of the way down (similar to the way in which flaky pastry is made). Fold up the bottom (unbuttered) portion, then fold the top section over the top, keeping the edges even. Seal gently, using the rolling-pin, then turn the pastry so that the fold is on your left, like a book. Roll out again to a rectangle, and repeat the buttering and folding. Wrap and chill the pastry for at least 30 minutes before rolling out and using.

PAINTING PASTRY

Armed with a brush and food colouring, it is possible to re-create the great painted and gilded pies of the past. Provided none of your guests has an allergic reaction to food colouring, use ordinary food colourings available from every supermarket.

The best effects are obtained by the simplest designs; a lattice of bright green on an apple pie, red dots on a pie for a young patient with measles or chicken-pox, a name on a birthday pudding; or place names on individual *mille feuilles* for grown-up diners. The possibilities are endless. (I once made pies for a wedding breakfast which were each painted with an original abstract by a famous French artist and taken hot to the table before being served.

Sensational!) You can also colour pastry decorations, making a rose rose-coloured and its leaves green, for instance.

Painting puff pastries works best but short-crust can also be used. Here is what you do.
● Brush all excess flour from the finished uncooked pie.
● If you must, trace a pattern on to the pastry with the tip of a knife.
● Dip a small watercolour brush into undiluted food colouring, drain well and paint, being careful not to have excess colour on the brush or it will run all over the smooth surface. If you need to join colours, the first will have to be dry before you butt up the second or they will blend.
● Once the pattern is finished, let it dry thoroughly. Then bake the pastry in the usual way.
● If the pastry is going to cook quickly, paint the dried pattern with an egg beaten with a little salt before baking; if it is a pie that will cook for over 30 minutes, apply the egg wash halfway through or it will brown so much that the painting will be hidden.

VOL-au-VENTS and BOUCHEES

Whether you choose vol-au-vents as large as your oven can cope with, or *bouchées* small enough to pop into your mouth in one bite, these puff pastries make really useful standbys. They are easy and quick to make if you have a stock of frozen puff pastry in your freezer.

For a large vol-au-vent, roll the pastry 2.5 cm/1 inch thick, cut into a neat shape and place on a wet baking-sheet. Using a sharp-pointed knife, mark on the pastry a corresponding shape which leaves a margin of about 2.5 cm/1 inch all round. Cut through the pastry to about half its depth, so that this portion may be used as the lid. Glaze with beaten egg, taking care not to let the glaze dribble down the sides of the pastry which will prevent it from rising evenly. Bake at 220°C/425°F/Gas Mark 7 for about 35 minutes, until golden brown. Carefully remove the lid and scoop out any uncooked pastry. Return the base to the oven for a further 5-10 minutes to dry out fully.

Smaller sizes of vol-au-vent should be cut from pastry rolled correspondingly thinner: for 10 cm/4 inch cases the pastry should be 2 cm/¾ inch thick and for 2.5 cm/1 inch cases the pastry should be about 1 cm/½ inch thick. Plain pastry cutters can be used to mark the lids, but take care not to cut further than halfway through the pastry. Glaze and bake as for the large version; they will take from 10-25 minutes, depending on size. Fill with any of the sweet or savoury fillings suggested for *Mille Feuille* (see page 135).

CREAM and SAVOURY HORNS

If you don't already have some, it's worth treating yourself to a set of metal horn-tins, so that you can make the favourite tea-time cream horns and experiment with savoury versions for buffet parties and picnics or as hot or cold starters.

Puff or flaky pastry made with 125 g/4 oz flour will make 8 horns. Roll thinly and cut into strips about 5 cm/2 inches wide and brush with beaten egg, or egg white. Starting at the bottom, with the glazed side outwards, wrap the strip around the lightly greased tins, so that you have a slight overlap each time. Glaze again and bake at 220°C/425°F/Gas Mark 7 for 10-12 minutes. Cool for a few minutes, then ease the tins away from the horns and cool them on a wire rack.

For sweet versions, put a teaspoon of jam, jelly or lemon curd in the tip of the horn and fill with whipped cream. Savoury cold horns can have a teaspoon of lumpfish roe or finely chopped smoked salmon placed in the tip, then be filled with a mixture of cream or curd cheese beaten with an equal quantity of strained yoghurt. Try fillings of a light fish mousse, or soft cheese with masses of fresh chopped herbs beaten into it. For warm starters, the horns can be filled with any well-flavoured sauce containing cooked meat, fish, eggs or vegetables.

THE MILLE FEUILLE

Sandwiches of puff pastry are one of the most effective and quick ways of making a first course or a pudding into something special. As with choux pastry, you must always leave time to excavate the soft, uncooked leaves of pastry before serving.

Roll out the pastry; it should not be more than 6 mm/bare ¼ inch thick.

Generally I cut it into oblongs of pastry for individual servings, about 10 × 5 cm/ 4 × 2 inch. With a sharp-pointed knife, knock back the edges from bottom to top, and mark a pattern into the top, crisscross, wavy or just diagonal lines. Paint with colours and/or a little egg beaten with salt. If it is to be served with a seafood sauce, I always mix saffron powder with an egg yolk and salt.

Place the shapes on to slightly wet trays and bake at 220°C/425°F/Gas Mark 7 until well risen and golden brown. Reduce the heat to dry through, then to be sure, cut each in half, pull out any uncooked pastry and return for the final crisping. These can be served hot or cold but I think they always taste better if at least a little warm.

To serve, sandwich two pastry rectangles together with any savoury filling that you would put into a vol-au-vent. I usually arrange something green (blanched spinach, lettuce etc.) on top of the bottom layer of pastry to stop the sauce softening the pastry too quickly. Here are some ideas to prompt your imagination.

SAVOURY FILLINGS

● Any cooked seafood tossed lightly in butter — even better with a leek cream sauce.
● Poached salmon or quickly cooked thin veal escalopes with a Hollandaise sauce, perhaps flavoured with dill or mint.
● Sautéed leeks or spinach mixed with Ricotta cheese and nutmeg, or perhaps with a cheese sauce.
● Quickly poached monkfish slices on a bed of raw sorrel.
● Dried mushrooms reconstituted in cream, or fresh mushrooms cooked in cream — either is good with snails added. Or simply cook a variety of mushrooms, in a little butter, finish with a dash of Madeira, Cognac or dry vermouth and mix in masses of chopped parsley.
● Beautifully cut vegetables or tiny florets of broccoli and cauliflower in a light sauce — tomato, cumin, cheese or perhaps a *beurre blanc* (see page 14).

SWEET FILLINGS

These will look prettier if served on or alongside a pool of sauce. Only rarely should the sauce be poured over the pastry because it will soften the pastry. If you are using phyllo pastry, moisten only with melted unsalted butter.
● Vanilla-poached pear slices or baked fanned pears with a little honey. Served with thin cream custard, or with melted chocolate.
● Sliced mangoes tossed in lime juice and served with a raspberry *coulis* on the plate.
● Sliced kiwifruit folded into whipped cream or plain yoghurt with chopped pistachio nuts. Grate a little orange or lime zest over the plate.
● Whipped cream or thick yoghurt mixed with lemon or orange curd and sliced strawberries or raspberries.
● Apple purée warmed with a little cinnamon and Cognac and a few fresh blackberries.
● Large chunks of rhubarb stewed gently in its own juice, served with a little orange-flavoured custard on the plate.
● Any fruit fool or Dusky Virgin with a Kick (see page 143).
● Chunks or slices of fresh peach or nectarine in whipped cream with passionfruit pulp.
● Really ripe banana slices tossed in whipped cream with a little passionfruit pulp.
● Whole or sliced strawberries mixed with a little yoghurt or whipped cream and served with a sauce of puréed dried apricots flavoured with orange-flower water.

COLD PUDDINGS

Jewelled jellies and crisp fresh fruit, trembling custards and luscious mousses – or a Dusky Virgin with a Kick in the Bottom. Cold puddings befriend busy cooks and jaded palates alike.

The entertainer's best friends are puddings that can be made in advance of the meal and served cold to balance a hot main course. The simplest are based on the fabulous array of home-grown and imported fruits now found – with a sharp knife and a spray of citrus juice or some suitable alcohol, it's done. A bit more trouble gives you mousses and ice creams, pies to serve chilled with cream or fresh fruit sauces. There's even a pâté of fresh pineapple and chocolate for slicing which should be sufficient for two dinner parties or a whole weekend of family or friends.

FRUIT

Until recently, completing a meal with fresh fruit was considered permissible at lunch but thought to be an easy way out at dinner time. This is no longer true, for two reasons. First, fresh fruit perfectly complements today's style of lighter and more elegant eating, and secondly, the extraordinary range of foreign fruit available throughout the year means that eating fruit can be as memorable and exciting as a dessert that took all day to make. Mangoes and papayas, fresh pineapple, kiwifruit, sharonfruit and persimmons, passionfruit, guava, even the good old banana and orange, can all take pride of place on the dessert plate. Below are some of my suggestions for combining fruits or dressing them up.

Bananas Like most fruits, bananas love orange juice. For quick family puddings, slice ripe bananas and squeeze on fresh orange juice. That's all you need to do. Top with strained Greek yoghurt or whipped cream – unwhipped cream is likely to curdle. For a more exotic touch, replace some or all of the orange juice with passionfruit pulp: but make sure the bananas really *are* ripe.

Dates I often serve chilled fresh dates instead of a sorbet as part of a large meal, on Christmas Day for instance. Peel and stone the dates, then sprinkle very lightly with demerara sugar and a light coating of vodka or white rum, perhaps with orange juice too.

Kiwifruit I prefer kiwifruit when they are still slightly firm and thus retain some acidity; when fully ripe they become sweet but blander in flavour. Basically, you can cut kiwifruit in half and scoop out the flesh as though the fruit was an egg, but that is not very elegant for a dinner party. I prefer to peel and slice them downwards into segments rather than boring slices. They may then be arranged in star patterns on flat plates and dribbled with lime juice, Pernod or *ouzo*. They taste even better if arranged on a puddle of puréed dried apricots, raspberries, blackberries (wonderful with a touch of apricot brandy), prunes or lemony/orangey stewed apples.

Mangoes These need very little attention. Slice off the 'cheeks' by standing the mango on end and cutting down either side of the large, flat stone. Use a sharp-pointed knife to cut a criss-cross pattern through the flesh almost to the skin and then gently turn the mango inside out. A little squeeze of orange juice, lime juice, or a spoonful of an orange-flavoured liqueur is all you need to add – but the adventurous might like to crush some high-quality coffee-beans and sprinkle those on the mango for a contrast of texture. Raspberry and white rum purée, or fresh passionfruit and Cointreau are equally notable with mangoes. For special occasions, place cubes of ripe mango in the bottom of champagne flutes, flavour with a few drops of Cointreau, chill and then top up with champagne. Also see the recipe for Planters Punch Syllabub, page 142.

Oranges Choose seedless navel oranges. Peel and remove the pith completely and slice very thinly. Arrange the slices on a platter or individual plates and sprinkle first with orange-flower water and then with fresh, ground cinnamon.

Fresh strawberries added make a lovely combination, or strew on some lightly toasted flaked almonds. See also Caramel Oranges (page 139).

Papaya (paw-paw) Cut them in half and scoop out the pips which look like caviare. Lime juice or orange juice is a vital accompaniment.

Peaches Few tastes are as delicious as fresh peaches, and they are even better with orange juice or an orange liqueur. Anything with an almond flavour goes well – for instance, crumble on those delicious biscuits from Italy, Amaretto di Saronno. Peaches and raspberries make magic – the famed Peach Melba is vanilla ice cream with peach and a raspberry purée. But the best by far is Peaches in Champagne. It really *is* best with champagne, but you can use sparkling wine – *not* a Muscatel or Spumante. One bottle is enough for six to eight servings and, provided peaches are in season and cheap, it's not really the extravagance it first seems. The delights of first spearing segments of champagne-flavoured peach and then of sipping peach-flavoured champagne are unforgettable.

Allow one large peach per person, more if they are smaller. Wash and dry them, but do not peel. Cut into neat segments (vertical slices), prick them all over with a fork and place in the bottom of tall champagne or wine glasses (not 'saucers'). Sprinkle a very little sugar, or a drop of brandy, or some orange-flavoured liqueur on top (all of these are optional). Just cover the peaches with champagne and leave in the refrigerator for an hour or so while you are enjoying the other courses. Put the glasses on to individual plates, each with a fork, top up with more champagne, serve and enjoy, first toying with the peaches and then sipping the champagne.

Pineapple Cut into slices and dribbled with gin makes a magical combination, or serve it with orange juice and muscovado sugar, or with fresh lime juice and dark rum. Mint goes nicely with pineapple; simply add mint leaves crushed in sugar or a little Crème de Menthe.

Raspberries One of the most elegant of fruits. It is very important not to wash these (unless actually encrusted with filth), for the delicate skin easily punctures and the water dissolves away the juices and flavour. They are perfectly wondrous with a squeeze of orange juice. Instead of cream, I like to serve them with very cold dollops of Petit Suisse, the slightly sharp French cream cheese. These berries also have an astonishing affinity with chocolate and rose water; perhaps serve raspberries with a wedge of really good chocolate cake, or in a pool of thin, cold cream perfumed with rose water and sprinkled with a couple of fresh rose petals.

Strawberries Wonderful, but so frequently abused, being served wet or damp, over-sweetened or drowned in an unsuitable alcohol. If you *must* wash strawberries, this should be done before the green calyx is removed, otherwise you rinse away the sugar content. Wash them very quickly, under running water, and dry them even more quickly.

The only wet strawberries permissible are those marinated in a little alcohol or fruit juice (orange being by far the best). Only use enough to moisten them and don't let them sit in the juice for more than 10 minutes. With the addition of a little sugar, you will create a light syrup. A few drops of orange-flower water, either by itself or in combination with orange juice, is excellent. Red wine is a favourite French way with strawberries, but don't drown them and don't leave them in the wine for hours or the skins will start to dissolve and begin to mush. I would add a little sugar and grate in some orange rind, too.

At party time, make strawberries important by serving prepared whole fruit with a series of bowls containing dips or flavourings. It can make long, lazy lunches or dinners stretch endlessly and deliciously. I serve bowls of the following:

Fresh orange juice of course, but flavour a second bowl with a little pure almond essence.

A choice of sugars – vanilla sugar, rose geranium sugar, mint sugar, rose-petal sugar, cinnamon sugar, black or green peppercorn sugar, elder-flower sugar; all are made by leaving the flavouring ingredients – vanilla beans, rose geranium or fresh mint leaves, elderflowers – in sealed jars of sugar, or by mixing sugar with freshly ground spices.

Whipped and unwhipped cream (unpasteurized yellow Jersey cream is by far the best), both plain and flavoured with orange-flower water, rose water, vanilla and almond. Cream for strawberries may also be flavoured with suitable liqueurs, spirits or wines, or with puréed fruit syrups. I also like to use the haunting flavour of vodka to make a Romanoff dip.

Yoghurt – select thick, strained, plain yoghurt or a mixture of yoghurt and cream as in Dusky Virgins (page 143). Flavour as for cream.

Freshly ground black or green peppercorns give an unusual bite.

Raspberry coulis, a mixture of puréed raspberry and rose water; raspberry and orange juice is equally good.

A choice of liqueurs – Chartreuse, Kirsch, any orange liqueurs, Drambuie, Tia Maria, Crème de Cacao – in fact, virtually all of them. Whatever else you serve, include white or green Crème de Menthe.

Pure fruit syrups are available in all supermarkets. As well as raspberry, strawberry and mint, you might choose blackcurrant, pineapple or mandarin.

Grated dark chocolate or *melted chocolate* makes a wonderful dip.

If organising a series of dips seems too much trouble, stand the whole strawberries in a pool of cream or raspberry purée. You can paint patterns on the raspberry purée or *coulis* with a few drops of cream.

BAKED CUSTARD

A light baked custard, served with fresh fruit or fruit poached in juice, or simply on its own, is one of the nicest hot or, rather, warm puddings I know. Custards may also be served cold, but they should be taken from the refrigerator half an hour beforehand, as over-chilling spoils their delicate flavour. The creamier the milk, the better the custard; you can use half single cream and half milk if you are feeling extravagant.

Serves four

450ml/3/4 pint milk
60 g/2 oz sugar
3 whole eggs
1 egg yolk
1/2 tsp vanilla essence
grated nutmeg (optional)

Heat the milk with the sugar, stirring occasionally, until bubbles appear around the edge. Meanwhile, lightly whisk the eggs and yolk with the vanilla in a large bowl. Gradually pour the scalded milk and sugar over the eggs, stirring with a wooden spoon. This is an important step which 'tempers' the eggs and helps to prevent any misbehaviour by them later. Don't whisk the mixture at this stage, or you will create bubbles which will spoil the custard.

Strain the mixture into a lightly greased ovenproof dish and stand this in a roasting-tin half full of hot water. Sprinkle with nutmeg if used. Bake at 160°C/325°F/Gas Mark 3 for about 40 minutes. Test by inserting a knife-blade into the centre of the custard – it will come out clean when the pudding is baked. The custard should have a definite skin on top, but still wobble.

Options

Orange Custard Add the finely grated rind of an orange with 1 teaspoon of orange-flower water to the custard mixture.

Caramel Custard or **Crème Caramel** Heat 125 g/4 oz granulated sugar with 2 tablespoons of water or fruit juice to make the caramel. When it has turned a rich amber, pour it quickly into an ovenproof dish and, holding the dish with oven gloves, swirl it to coat the sides. Make the custard with just one tablespoon of sugar and strain it on to the caramel.

Coffee Custard Add 2 tablespoons of instant coffee and 2 tablespoons of coffee essence to the milk; decrease the sugar to 30 g/1 oz and omit the vanilla essence.

BAKED APRICOT CREAMS

My first version of this recipe used dark rum, which combines wonderfully with dried apricots and vanilla, but the dish is equally seductive made with Amaretto di Saronno and with the vanilla replaced by almond essence.

Serves six to eight

250 g/8 oz Armadine (apricot sheet) or dried apricots
300 ml/1/2 pint dry white wine
150 ml/1/4 pint double cream
2 tbls dark rum or Amaretto di Saronno
1/2 tsp vanilla or almond essence
3 large eggs, beaten
whipped cream to decorate

Tear the Armadine into small pieces and put in a small pan with the wine. Heat gently, stirring continuously, until you have a fairly smooth purée – purée in a blender or food processor if necessary. Spoon it into a measuring jug; you should have 300 ml/1/2 pint of purée. If there is too little, add more white wine; if there is more, don't worry.

Tip the purée into a bowl and stir in the cream, the rum or Amaretto and the essence. Add the eggs and beat well. Divide the mixture between six or eight ramekin dishes and put them into a roasting-tin. Pour boiling water into the tin so that it comes halfway up the sides of the dishes. Cover the whole tin with foil and cook at 160°C/325°F/Gas Mark 3 for 20 minutes. The Creams should be just set and barely risen. Chill thoroughly.

To serve: top with a little whipped cream flavoured with rum, Amaretto, vanilla or almond essence, or orange-flower water. It's good to serve crisp biscuits or shortbread fingers with these creams.

FRUIT SALADS

These can be dreadful – soggy, oversweet and overburdened with something cheap and boring, usually apples or slices of blackening bananas. There's no excuse; fruit salads can be sensational, even with only a couple of ingredients – indeed, some of the best do have as few as that. It's considered old-fashioned to make fruit salads in sugar syrup, for this rather negates the dietary appeal of fresh fruit, most of which are relatively low in calories. Instead of syrup, make fruit salads in orange juice with a touch of lemon juice – much tastier and healthier. Melon and banana should be added at the last moment, for both tend to overpower other flavours and banana may also turn black.

To make fruit salads look important, even if you are using ordinary fruit, you can do one of two things. Instead of jumbling everything together, you should layer them attractively in a glass bowl. Or, taking a tip from top restaurants, arrange the sliced and cubed fruits prettily on a fairly large flat plate. This is especially effective if done on a fruit purée – raspberry or mango are the most popular but my favourite is dried apricots cooked in white wine, orange juice or plain water and then puréed until smooth.

The most interesting fruit salads are those made with restraint, using just fruits of the same colour or just two of contrasting colour and texture. Here are some combinations that I have enjoyed:

Peaches and blackberries

Peaches and redcurrants

Kiwifruit segments, melon balls and seedless white grapes

Slices of crisp sharonfruit and ripe pear

Strawberries and raspberries – in fact, any mixture of soft, red summer fruits, the more the merrier.

Mango and papaya

Melon and raspberries

Melon and wild strawberries, especially with a sprinkle of white port.

Apple, pear and poached quince

Pear and raspberries

Pear and mango with lime juice

Strawberries and passionfruit pulp

Cherries and sliced oranges

Cherries and pears

GLYNN'S TIP

For special presentation, hide the Chilled Dried Fruit Salad beneath a thick layer of whipped cream, or whipped cream folded into plain yoghurt and sprinkled with nutmeg or cinnamon and chopped almonds and pistachios.

TROPICAL FRUIT SALAD

This is the ultimate in fruit salads as long as you stick to the tropics and do not allow apples and pears, or peaches and plums to find their way into the bowl. Adjust the proportions according to what is in season: if fresh mango or papaya is unavailable, try using the canned varieties; some of them are excellent, especially mangoes of the Alphonse type, usually from India. But don't use any substitutes for fresh passionfruit pulp; there is none which I know of worth your time or money. Passionfruit is actually the secret of any decent fruit salad and the pulp and seeds of one fruit makes a remarkable difference to a large salad.

Serves six

1 pineapple
1 papaya
1 mango
the pulp from 4-6 passionfruit
sugar to taste
Crème de Menthe, white or black rum, gin or a coconut liqueur

Wash the pineapple. Remove the skin and core, and put both in a pan; cover with water and simmer for 20 minutes. Strain and cool the liquid. Cube the pineapple flesh, papaya and mango, mix together and stir in the passionfruit pulp.

Sweeten the liquid from the pineapple skin with a little sugar and add alcohol, or not, according to preference. Pour the liquid over the fruit. Serve lightly chilled. Sliced *ripe* bananas may be added just before serving.

CHILLED DRIED FRUIT SALAD

From the Middle East here's another idea that works just as well from a refrigerator as from a Sultan's palace kitchen. Instead of boiling dried fruits to plump them up, they are left to swell in a flavoured liquid. As they swell, they exchange flavours and their individual sugars blend to make something voluptuous. Although I like to use mixed dried fruits, available ready-packed in most supermarkets, you could use apricots or prunes alone, or make a series of bowls of individual flavours so that you and your guests can mix and match. Serve them as cold as you can.

Serves six

375 g/12 oz whole or halved dried fruits (pears, prunes, apricots, peaches, apples)
600 ml/1 pint fruit juice (orange, apple or pineapple)
a few drops almond essence
2 tsps orange-flower water
chopped almonds or pistachio nuts (optional)

GLYNN'S TIP

If you want to eat the Chilled Dried Fruit Salad in less than 48 hours, heat the fruit juice until very hot, without boiling, before pouring it over the fruit.

Arrange the fruit in a flat, shallow dish and cover with the fruit juice. Add a few drops of almond essence and the orange-flower water. Cover and leave in the refrigerator for at least 48 hours, turning from time to time. The fruit should absorb most of the juice, but if it seems as though this isn't happening, your refrigerator is too cold; take the dish out and leave it somewhere a little warmer. When it is time to serve the fruit, adjust the flavour with more almond essence or orange-flower water.

Serve it alone or with an elegant, buttery biscuit; shortbread would do. *Photograph, p. 114.*

FLOWER WATERS

Readers may be surprised to find that many of these puddings, especially those based on fruit, are flavoured with orange juice, orange-flower water or with rose water. Used properly, each of these acts in the same way as salt with savoury food, enhancing and blending disparate flavours into something new.

The use of orange juice is a modern idea, whereas orange-flower water and rose water are ancient ingredients which should never have been allowed to disappear from the Western kitchen. Brought to Europe from the Holy Land by the Crusaders, they remained top favourites as flavourings until about the time that the gargantuan meals enjoyed by the Edwardians became unfashionable. They are distillations of flowers and both are cheap and long-lasting.

Rose water is wonderful in anything creamy and has a special affinity with raspberries, chocolate, peaches and lychees. It makes a haunting difference to the cream fillings for profiteroles or meringues, to pouring cream for soft red fruit and to baked milk puddings.

Orange-flower water makes buttery and almond-tasting things taste heavenly, especially shortbreads, cakes and the pastry for Christmas mince pies. It is also fabulous on most fruits, particularly strawberries, fresh dates, oranges and all dried fruit.

Once you are familiar with the two flower waters, start mixing them together; this is generally the way they are used in the Middle East where they are still as common as salt and pepper are in the West. There are some very high quality versions about, and some of the national supermarket chains now stock them.

Cheap but good flower waters are usually stocked by Greek, Cypriot or Turkish shops and most of the stores run by Indians and Pakistanis will at least have superior rose water. So will chemists but you must ensure that it is triple-distilled or it will not be strong enough; also, make sure that it is suitable for culinary use.

CARAMEL ORANGES

A personal favourite, which, if you take care to serve attractively, trimming the oranges neatly, is a real treat.

Serves six

500 g/1 lb white sugar
150 ml/¼ pint water
300 ml/½ pint concentrated orange juice or undiluted orange squash
Cognac to taste
6 medium-large seedless navel oranges

Mix the sugar and water in a heavy-based saucepan and heat with care until it turns a rich, golden brown. Remove from the heat and pour in the concentrated orange juice or squash, keeping your face and hands well out of the way. Return the pan to the heat and let it sizzle gently, then simmer for 5 minutes, ensuring that all the caramel has dissolved. Let the syrup cool completely and then add Cognac – you may need up to 150 ml/¼ pint.

Peel the oranges with a long, sharp knife, removing every piece of white pith. Reserve some peel for decoration (see Tip). Put the oranges whole into the syrup and leave in a cool place for at least 6 hours, or in a refrigerator for 12 hours, turning from time to time. As the juice of the oranges mixes with the syrup it will thin a little and change flavour deliciously.

By the time you wish to serve the oranges, the outsides will have darkened considerably. Slice each orange thinly to reveal the contrast of colour and arrange on flat plates. Spoon on some of the sauce and top with your orange-peel matchsticks. Serve with a first-rate ice cream or with a lemon sorbet.

GLYNN'S TIP

It is worth the trouble to make an orange rind garnish for the Caramel Oranges. Slice the pith from the inside of some strips of rind, then cut the rind into thin matchsticks. Plunge into boiling water for a couple of minutes and then spoon directly into very cold water to set the colour.

Options

For more lavish occasions, try using a sharpish orange spirit instead of Cognac – Triple Sec would be good. Or drip some Framboise, raspberry *eau-de-vie*, on to the sliced oranges.

RHUBARB and CINNAMON JELLY

Real fruit jelly is wonderful, and bears very little resemblance to that made from commercial tablets or powders. This one looks good made in a decorative mould, or in individual glass dishes, so that the light can shine through and highlight its glorious colour.

Serves four to six

1.25 kg/2½ lb trimmed rhubarb
250 g/8 oz sugar
1 tsp ground cinnamon
2 tsps grated orange rind
scant 300 ml/½ pint white wine or water
gelatine (see method)
cream to serve

Put the rhubarb into a saucepan with the sugar, cinnamon, orange rind and wine or water and simmer over a low heat until softened. Purée in a blender or food processor, then sieve. Take 1 × 11 g/½ oz gelatine for each 600 ml/1 pint of purée and melt over very low heat or stand the bowl in a pan of simmering water until the liquid is clear and the gelatine dissolved. Whisk it into the rhubarb. Pour into a wetted mould or glass dishes and chill well.

Serve decorated with softly whipped double cream, or with single cream, perhaps flavoured with dark rum. *Photograph, p. 42.*

PAVLOVA

When I was a boy in New Zealand the only times I ever heard ballet mentioned was by people of my parents' generation who had seen Anna Pavlova on tour there; they had gone to see her not as fans of the ballet, but because she was legendary. The Australasians were so enthralled with her that a new pudding was created in her honour (which probably means an old one was renamed).

Serves four to six

4 large egg whites
250 g/8 oz caster sugar
1 tsp vanilla essence
1 tsp malt vinegar

Make sure the egg whites are at room temperature before putting them into a clean, dry bowl. Whisk them, adding the sugar gradually as you go, until the mixture is very thick and glossy and stands in peaks. Beat in the vanilla and vinegar.

Spoon the mixture on to a greased and wetted baking-sheet, or line the sheet with non-stick baking paper. Alternatively, you can line a pie dish (about 20 cm/8 inches diameter) with lightly greased foil and pile the meringue into that.

Bake at 110°C/225°F/Gas Mark ¼ for one hour, then turn off the heat and leave the Pavlova inside the oven until cold. If you prefer your Pavlova to be slightly golden, turn the temperature up a little higher. Turn out, remove the paper and invert so that the crisp crust is on top. If it is on a baking-sheet simply loosen and slide it on to a serving dish. Top with unsweetened whipped cream, plus strawberries, kiwifruit, or passionfruit pulp, about an hour before serving so that the top layer of meringue is dissolved by the cream – you should not be able to tell where the cream stops and the meringue starts.

Options

Praline Pavlova Make praline with 125 g/4 oz each of white sugar and hazelnuts or almonds (see p. 141). Make a Pavlova as above, whip 300 ml/½ pint double cream and add plenty of praline to give a good flavour. Decorate with sliced kiwifruit and extra praline.

Hazelnut Pavlova Use 125 g/4 oz finely crushed hazelnuts and stir into the glossy meringue with the vanilla and vinegar. Top the baked Pavlova with whipped cream and decorate with chopped roasted hazelnuts and fresh raspberries.

Cherry and Chestnut Pavlova Flavour the Pavlova with cherry essence or leave it plain. Top the baked Pavlova with a mixture of whipped cream and vanilla-flavoured chestnut purée, plus black cherries which have been soaked in black rum.

Strawberry and Orange Flavour the Pavlova with grated orange rind or orange-flower water and use a little of either for the cream. Cover the cream with sliced strawberries.

FOOD FACT

Many food writers seem to think that Pavlova is simply a round of meringue on to which you throw cream and fruit. Not so; a Pavlova is a very special type of meringue, which is crisp and fragile on the outside but has a soft marshmallow centre. If it does not have that soft centre, it is not a Pavlova.

MACAROON BASE for FRESH FRUITS

A really special way to serve attractively sliced fruit at the table is on this simple base of coconut macaroon. One large macaroon enables you to arrange a variety of fruits or a single favourite fruit decoratively, or you can make individual bases and serve each person with their own arrangements, perhaps accompanied by a fruit purée on the plate. It makes an ideal change from pastry and is much faster to make.

Serves six

2 egg whites
125 g/4 oz caster sugar
125 g/4 oz desiccated coconut

Whisk the egg whites, then beat in half the sugar until the meringue is glossy and the sugar has dissolved. Fold in the remaining sugar and the coconut. Form into a 20 cm/8 inch circle on non-stick paper or on a non-stick baking-sheet and bake at 150°C/300°F/Gas Mark 2 for 20-25 minutes, by which time the macaroon should be nicely golden and smell of toasted coconut; let it cool before serving.

Flavoured cream may be spread on the cooled base as an anchor if the fruit is wet or very soft. Tropical fruits, bathed in a little lime or orange juice, marry best with the coconut flavour, otherwise raspberries look and taste wonderful, but they do need the accompaniment of cream. *Photograph, p. 113.*

SORBETS

Sorbets have become very popular over the last decade, and are often fallen upon with cries of relief by those professing to be on a diet who don't realise, however, that a serving of sorbet probably contains more sugar than the slice of cake they so self-righteously refused!

Sorbets are relatively easy to make at home but as there are so many excellent ones on the market I'll give you just a couple of ideas that are infallible, and incredibly simple to make. The inclusion of whipped egg white lightens the sorbet's texture, makes it less sweet and, most important, stops it melting too quickly when served.

Canned fruit sorbets The texture and sweetness of canned fruits are perfect for making quick sorbets. Drain the fruit, purée it in a blender or food processor and strain. Meanwhile, reduce the syrup from the can by half its volume over heat but do not let it caramelize. Mix together the syrup and the purée, chill, then freeze, stirring from time to time. When the mixture is mushy in the middle but frozen around the edges, beat it quickly into an even texture and fold in the beaten whites of one or two eggs and return to the freezer until firm.

The best version by far is made with a can of lychees, which really give a marvellous flavour and pale pink colour. Canned mangoes, plums and pears are equally good. Maraschino is an excellent addition to a pear sorbet. Many of the mixtures will benefit enormously from the addition of lemon, lime or orange juice.

Syrup sorbets As the sorbet is essentially a frozen sugar syrup, the pure fruit syrups on the market can be used to make an excellent, quick sorbet. Generally I use 4-6 tablespoons of undiluted syrup to approx 350 ml/12 fl oz of unsweetened fruit purée. A higher proportion of syrup than that makes the sorbet too sweet and you run the risk of the high sugar content preventing it from freezing. One of the most unusual combinations which I have made is rhubarb and strawberry; this is an extraordinarily good old country favourite. It needs 750 g/ 1½ lb of rhubarb cooked with just a splash of water or fruit juice to make the required amount of purée. When cool, flavour with strawberry syrup. Freeze and incorporate whisked egg white as for the tea sorbet (see below).

TEA SORBET

Wonderfully refreshing, tea sorbets can be made with dozens of different flavours, although they'll all be the same colour. Rose Pouchong, Earl Grey and Jasmine tea make the most elegant versions; you can also experiment with a mixture of half tea and half fruit juice – Ceylon tea and pineapple juice, for instance. Choose a quality tea with large leaves if you make it without extra flavouring; if you add fruit juice, a lesser quality tea with smaller leaves can be used.

Serves four to six

60 g/2 oz tea leaves or tea bags, dry weight
600 ml/1 pint boiling water or fruit juice
150 g/5 oz white sugar (optional)
lemon juice (optional)
1 or 2 egg whites

Pour the boiling water on to the tea leaves and brew, 7 minutes for large, whole leaves, 5 minutes for medium leaves. Quality tea bags are suitable and need only brew for a few minutes. Do not over-brew or too much tannin will be released.

Strain the tea through a coffee filter paper if using leaves and make the liquid up to the original 600 ml/1 pint with more water or juice. Add most of the sugar but finish sweetening when the liquid is cool (it will taste less sweet when it is cold and much less sweet when frozen). Only add the lemon juice if the tea you are using is an ordinary blend; it is sinful to put lemon into perfumed teas such as Earl Grey, Rose or Jasmine.

Freeze in a covered container until mushy, beat back to a consistent texture quickly and fold in 1-2 beaten egg whites. Return to the tray and freeze without further interference. Tea sorbets seem especially suited for serving with tropical fruits.

BASIC ICE-CREAM

Basic ice-cream, lightly flavoured with vanilla, is a good standby for the freezer, ready to be flavoured according to the fruits in season and whatever suits your budget and menu. This version cheats a little by including flour, which avoids the horror of a curdled egg custard base.

Makes 600 ml/1 pint

300 ml/½ pint milk
125 g/4 oz caster sugar
1 tbls flour or cornflour
2 egg yolks
pinch of salt
300 ml/½ pint double cream
½ tsp vanilla essence

Scald the milk in a medium saucepan; while it is gently heating, mix together the sugar, flour, egg yolks and salt in a large bowl, and beat these until creamy. Pour the hot milk over the mixture and blend thoroughly, return to the pan and, over a low heat, bring gently to the boil, stirring continuously. Once it boils, and has thickened, let it simmer for 3-4 minutes to remove any floury taste, then strain into a bowl and let it cool. Put a piece of plastic film on the surface of the custard to prevent a skin forming. When it is quite cool, whip the cream until it holds its shape but is not stiff, and fold it in with the vanilla. Pour the mixture into an ice-cream tray or suitable freezer container, cover and freeze for 2-3 hours, until it has begun to solidify around the edges. Turn the ice-cream out into a bowl and beat vigorously until it is creamy, then return to the container and continue to freeze.

Options

Chocolate Use only 150 ml/¼ pint of milk, and add 125 g/4 oz dark chocolate melted in 8 tablespoons water and 2 tablespoons coffee essence.

Tea This is my favourite. Infuse 30 g/1 oz tea leaves or tea bags in 300 ml/½ pint boiling milk according to the packet's instructions (from 2-7 minutes). The best flavours are Rose Pouchong, Lapsang Souchong, Jasmine, Earl Grey, or Green Gunpowder. Be sure to squeeze the leaves to extract all the flavour, and to make up the infusion to the original volume. You might need to add a little extra sugar. *Photograph, p. 149.*

CHILD'S PLAY ICE-CREAM

This is one of the best ice-cream recipes ever! It's economical, and not only is it literally child's play to make, it is extremely popular with all the children I know – and most adults too.

Makes 600 ml/1 pint

200 g/7 oz can sweetened condensed milk
150 ml/¼ pint double cream
2 tbls lemon or lime juice

Refrigerate the condensed milk and the cream overnight to ensure that they are both as cold as possible. Turn the condensed milk into a chilled bowl and whisk it with the lemon or lime juice until very light and frothy. Add the cream and continue beating until the mixture is the consistency of whipped cream. Fold in your fruit flavouring. Pour into an ice-cream tray or plastic container, cover and freeze until solid.

Options

To this basic mixture you can add up to 300 ml/½ pint of an unsweetened fruit purée and other flavourings.

Banana Mash 2 ripe bananas and stir them in with a generous flavouring of vanilla essence. This is also good with some coarsely crushed praline (see page 139) mixed into the ice-cream when it is half frozen; if you do it earlier, the praline will soften and dissolve.

Victoria Plum Add a large can (566 g/20 oz) of plums, drained and sieved, with a teaspoon of ground ginger instead of vanilla essence.

Rhubarb and Cinnamon Use 300 ml/½ pint rhubarb purée with 1 teaspoon ground cinnamon and omit the lemon juice.

Coffee Strudel Use 300 ml/½ pint apple purée, with 1 teaspoon ground cinnamon, 1½ tablespoons of coffee essence and 2 tablespoons of raisins; omit the lemon juice. The raisins can be soaked first in rum or brandy.

REFLAVOURING ICE-CREAM

Home-made or commercial ice-cream can be reflavoured very simply. Let the ice-cream sit in the refrigerator until soft, and chill your chosen flavourings. Quickly mix both together and refreeze. Because commercial ice-cream has a great deal of air beaten into it, you run the risk of reducing its volume if you mess about with it too much, so, rather than attempting to mix the flavouring in evenly, be content with a swirled effect.

Raspberries and Strawberries These should be lightly crushed and flavoured with a little sugar and orange juice, a liqueur, rose water or orange-flower water. Raspberries should really be strained.

Apple This can either be stewed or a pie-filling; add extra spices, brown sugar and mixed peel to make Apple Strudel Ice-Cream.

Gooseberries, Red and Blackcurrants Berry fruits should be poached lightly first.

Liqueurs Swirl in 4 tablespoons of a liqueur such as Crème de Menthe, perhaps also with a touch of food colouring; 2 tablespoons of frozen orange concentrate with the same amount of an orange-flavoured liqueur.

Eggnog Beat 3 egg yolks with 6 tablespoons of rum, brandy or bourbon and swirl it in.

Christmas cake Soak a good slice of rich Christmas cake in sweet sherry, orange juice, rum or Cognac; sprinkle with nutmeg and cinnamon, then lightly crush and stir into good vanilla ice-cream. This is very good in chocolate or coffee ice-cream, too.

Nut-Toasty Any chopped, toasted nuts are excellent in ice-cream, as are crushed peppermint sticks, sticks of rock or chopped up pieces of chocolate. All of these are good in chocolate, coffee or orange ice-cream. The nuts and chocolate are super in strawberry ice-cream.

Cornflake Coating cornflakes in a mixture of brown sugar and melted butter gives them a caramel covering; cool, and crumble them into vanilla, chocolate or fruit-flavoured ice-cream. They stay crisp when you refreeze because of the sugar. Kids love it.

GLYNN'S TIP

Instead of putting the reflavoured ice-cream back into the refrigerator, pile it immediately on to a sponge base, macaroon base, or into a gingernut or digestive biscuit flan base and serve at once as Ice-Cream Pie. You could, of course, freeze the entire concoction for a later occasion. Ice-Cream Pies are even better if you have layered fruit on the base.

FROZEN PRALINE SOUFFLE

This dish isn't as tricky as it first looks and can be prepared well in advance for an impressive dinner-party finale.

Serves six to eight

8 boudoir biscuits
4 tbls Kirsch
8 tbls caster sugar
2 tbls water
4 egg yolks
300 ml/½ pint double cream
6 egg whites
ice cubes (see method)
2 tbls Praline Paste (see below)

Attach a foil collar to a 1.2 litre/2 pint soufflé dish, or to 8 ramekin dishes, by folding a length of foil in half, sticking it to the outside of the dish using a little butter, then tying securely with string.

Cut the biscuits into small pieces and sprinkle the Kirsch over to moisten them. Dissolve 4 tablespoons of sugar in the water in a small pan, then boil the syrup until it reaches the soft ball stage (116°C/240°F using a sugar thermometer). While this is cooking, put the egg yolks into a large bowl and beat until frothy. Pour the syrup over, from a height, in a steady stream, beating all the time. You really need an electric beater to do this successfully, or have someone pouring while you whisk like mad. Avoid letting the syrup drip on to the beaters, or it will solidify and not mix with the yolks. Keep beating until you have a thick, mousse-like mixture and it is quite cold.

Whip the cream until thick, but not stiff. Whisk the egg whites until stiff, then whisk in the remaining caster sugar, a little at a time, until you have a glossy meringue.

Half fill a large bowl with ice cubes and add a little cold water. Stand the bowl containing the mousse mixture inside this, resting on the ice, then stir the Praline Paste into the cool mousse and blend well. Fold a third of the meringue into this mixture, followed by a third of the cream. Repeat until all the ingredients are blended, taking care not to overmix. Gently stir in the soaked biscuits. Transfer to the prepared dish or ramekins and freeze for at least 2 hours.

PRALINE PASTE

125 g/4 oz almonds
125 g/4 oz hazelnuts
250 g/8 oz sugar
8 tbls water
1 tbl oil

Lightly oil a large sheet of foil, or a marble or formica surface. Roast the nuts at 200°C/400°F/ Gas Mark 6 for 5-10 minutes until they are golden and shiny. Put the sugar and water in a small saucepan and dissolve over a medium heat, shaking once or twice. Boil the sugar, without stirring, until it turns to an amber caramel, then remove from the heat and stir in the nuts. Spread the mixture over the oiled surface. When quite cold, break into pieces, then put into a blender or food processor and blend or process to a paste. Do this in short bursts, which is both more effective and less wearing on the machine. I make some of the mixture quite fine for sprinkling and some more coarse for putting into ice-cream and icings. Use just almonds or hazelnuts if you like.

SIMPLE CHOCOLATE MOUSSE

One of the simplest of all desserts to make, this remains one of the most popular cold puddings. If you plan to serve it alone, do so after a light meal or it will not be appreciated and enjoyed, and serve only small quantities. Better still, serve the mousse in individual ramekins with a little fresh fruit in the base (raspberries are a particularly good choice).

Makes six small ramekins; eight with a fruit base

90 g/3 oz unsalted butter
155 g/5 oz plain, dark chocolate
3 eggs, separated
1 tsp vanilla essence
150 ml/¼ pint double cream for decoration (optional)

Break the butter and chocolate into a bowl and stand this over a pan of very hot water but turn off the heat. Stir from time to time until the chocolate and butter are well blended. Remove from the heat and beat in the egg yolks, one at a time; the mixture will then thicken slightly. Stir in the vanilla or other flavourings (see Options below).

Allow the mixture to cool slightly; meanwhile, whisk the egg whites until they are stiff, but not dry. Stir a couple of tablespoons of the egg white into the chocolate mixture, then fold in the remainder, using a spatula or large metal spoon, working with a figure-of-eight movement and taking care not to overmix. Spoon the mixture into individual dishes; work as speedily as possible, for the less you handle the mousse, the lighter it will be. Chill for at least 4 hours, overnight if possible, to mature.

Options

Mocha Mousse Dissolve 1 tablespoon instant coffee powder in 1 tablespoon very hot water and add to the chocolate mixture with ½ teaspoon vanilla essence.

Grand Marnier Mousse Add the finely grated rind of 1 orange, with 1½ tablespoons Grand Marnier, to the chocolate mixture. Omit the vanilla essence.

GLYNN'S TIP

Take care when melting chocolate; if it becomes too hot it will thicken and be useless. Never let it come into contact with steam or the same thing will happen. Always turn off the heat once you have placed the bowl containing the chocolate over the pan of simmering water.

GLYNN'S TIP

It is possible to make a chocolate mousse without butter; the result is lighter and wetter and very suitable for small servings (as in the French petits pots au chocolat) but large mousses need the body that the butter gives.

My Favourite Mousses The flavours I like best are the unsweetened *eaux-de-vie*, especially the raspberry flavoured Framboise. Put some raspberries in the individual dishes and sprinkle with a touch of Framboise. The next best flavouring is Poire William, and, as pears and raspberries have an affinity, you may consider serving a pear and chocolate mousse over raspberries, a chocolate mousse over pears flavoured with Framboise, or a chocolate and pear mousse over pears flavoured with Poire William! Two teaspoons of rose water replace the vanilla wonderfully.

LEMON MOUSSE

Once you have mastered the technique of making a good lemon mousse, you can adapt the recipe to use other citrus fruits.

Serves six to eight

grated rind and juice of 2 lemons
11 g/½ oz gelatine
4 large eggs, separated
125 g/4 oz caster sugar
300 ml/½ pint double cream
chopped roasted hazelnuts to decorate

Tie a band of non-stick baking parchment or lightly oiled greaseproof paper round the outside of a 1 litre/2 pint soufflé dish, so that it stands about 7.5 cm/3 inches above the rim. Use string or an elastic band to hold the paper securely in place.

Put 4 tablespoons of the lemon juice into a small bowl and sprinkle in the gelatine. Allow it to form a sponge until all the liquid has been absorbed. Melt over very low heat or stand the bowl in a pan of very hot, but *not* boiling water until it dissolves. Remove the bowl and cool.

Beat the egg yolks with the sugar until they are very pale and thick, then gradually beat in the lemon juice. Stir in the rind followed by the cool gelatine. Leave the mixture until it is just beginning to set. You are aiming for the same texture as whipped cream, so keep checking and don't let the mixture get too stiff or the mousse will be lumpy.

Whip the cream until thick, but not stiff. Whisk the egg whites until stiff, but not dry.

Using a large metal spoon, or a spatula, fold the cream and whites into the lemon mixture, alternately, taking care not to over-mix or you will lose all the air that has been beaten in. Spoon the mixture into the prepared soufflé dish, and refrigerate until set. Gently pull away the paper collar and press finely chopped roasted hazelnuts into the exposed mousse.

Options

Use any other citrus fruits – pink grapefruit is delicious; a mixture of orange and lemon; or fresh lime.

Fruit Mousses Instead of citrus juice and rind, use 150 ml/¼ pint of fruit purée. Soft summer fruits, such as raspberries, strawberries, or blackcurrants, are best, and only the blackcurrants need to be slightly cooked. The purée should be fairly sharp, or the finished mousse will be bland, so add just enough lemon juice to give 'bite' without overpowering the fruit; and incorporate an *eau-de-vie* of suitable flavour.

PLANTER'S PUNCH SYLLABUB

Rum Punch is one of the few flavours as sensuous as a fresh mango, and thus marries perfectly with it.

Serves four

2-3 generous tbls dark rum
2 tsps caster sugar (or to taste)
1-2 tbls fresh lime, lemon or orange juice
1 tsp freshly grated lime, lemon or orange rind
2 ripe mangoes (or any other tropical fruits)
150 ml/¼ pint chilled double cream
freshly grated nutmeg

Mix together 2 tablespoons rum, the sugar, 1 tablespoon citrus juice and grated rind and leave in a cool place (but not a refrigerator) overnight. An hour or so before the meal, slice the mangoes and place in the bottom of attractive glasses. Sprinkle them with the extra rum and juice.

Pour the cream into the rum mixture and whip until it holds its shape but is still rather soft and floppy. Ensure that you scrape back any pieces of the rind which may be clinging to the whisk or beaters.

Spoon the syllabub over the fruit and put the glasses to chill until needed. Just before serving, grate on some nutmeg. I sometimes serve these with unfilled ginger crisps (see page 166).

CREME BRULEE

Whatever the season or occasion, this is a party dessert which will always be received enthusiastically. If you like the idea but would prefer something less rich, try the Dusky Virgins version below.

Serves six

4 egg yolks
2 tbls caster sugar
450 ml/3/4 pint double cream
1 tsp vanilla essence
3-4 tbls brown sugar

Beat the egg yolks with the caster sugar until creamy. Heat the cream in a double boiler to scalding point, then gradually pour it over the egg yolks, stirring all the time. Return the mixture to the pan and heat gently, stirring constantly, until the mixture thickens and coats the back of a spoon. Take care not to let the mixture get too hot; if it boils the mixture will curdle. Add the vanilla essence and then strain the custard into a large ovenproof dish, or into six individual ramekins. Cool thoroughly in the refrigerator, preferably overnight.

Preheat the grill. Spoon the brown sugar evenly over the cold creams and stand them under the hot grill until the sugar melts and forms a crust. Chill thoroughly before serving.

Options
You may use a combination of egg yolks and whole eggs but both the texture and the flavour will be a little coarser.
Crème Brûlée with Fruit In a sensible effort to serve lighter sweets, many restaurants are put-ting fruit at the bottom of their ramekins.
Crème Caramel This mainstay of the catering profession on either side of the Channel could be described as burnt cream turned upside down, a layer of caramel topped with a baked custard. Use the same custard mixture as above and put as much or as little caramel as you like in the bottom of the small ramekins. (Use one large dish, if you prefer.) Let the caramel set, pour on the ready-thickened custard — or bake them. This pudding is better if left for a day to ensure that the caramel at the bottom has dissolved. The caramel is specially good if the sugar is first melted with orange juice and you might also grate some orange rind into the custard. Truly yummy!

DUSKY VIRGINS

I don't know the origins of this name, but the simplicity with which the dish is made and its intriguing flavour more than compensate for any confusion. You can adjust the proportions of the two main ingredients according to your budget or store cupboard, but with these quantities you will enjoy a pudding that is better for you than it looks, and few people will recognise the flavour of cream and yoghurt combined.

At its simplest, the mixture is covered with muscovado sugar or fruit (see Options). If you swirl a purée of fruit through the mixture, you have a modern version of the creamy fool. Flavoured with a sweet wine or sherry and some grated lemon and orange rind, the mixture becomes a latter-day (and more sensible) version of a syllabub.

Serves four to six

300 ml/1/2 pint unsweetened plain yoghurt
150 ml/1/4 pint double cream
muscovado sugar for topping

Tip the yoghurt into a small sieve and leave for at least 20 minutes to drain away excess liquid. Turn the yoghurt gently from time to time but not too much or it will thin. Transfer the yoghurt to a bowl. Lightly whip the cream and fold it into the yoghurt; the acid content of the yoghurt will immediately make it stiffen.

Spoon the mixture into individual ramekins and sprinkle with muscovado sugar, which gives the pudding a rum-like flavour. Leave it to chill thoroughly, by which time the sugar will have started to melt here and there.

Options
If you're really health conscious, and would rather not eat sugar, chopped fresh fruit or a fruit purée is just as good a topping. My favourite is fresh passionfruit pulp. Alternative-ly, put fruit in the base of the dishes and flavour with juice or a liqueur — the dish then becomes a Dusky Virgin with a Kick in the Bottom.

THE GREAT BRITISH TRIFLE

Where have all the good trifles gone? A trifle used to be described as any pudding based on layers of cake and topped with cream or a syllabub-type concoction. There was only one important criterion — it should be impossible to slice a trifle. The flavours, textures and colours should blend deliciously and it should be fairly soft without being pappy. So, if you like the cake at the bottom set with jelly, use more liquid than usual in the jelly so it does not become too solid. Don't over-thicken the cus-tard and don't overbeat the cream.

Should we be eating trifle at all in these health conscious days? Of course we should, using rather more fruit than we might have done once, using fruit juice instead of wine to soak the cake, and reducing the amount of custard and cream on top. If you don't want to make any of these changes, then simply plan to serve a trifle after a light meal or salad instead of after a roast beef blow-out. You'll actually enjoy it more that way.

Without doubt, sherry trifle is today's most popular trifle.
The base Use large cubes of sponge-cake that are split and spread generously with raspberry jam, or you could slice up a jam roll or two. Arrange the sponge in a serving bowl and soak more than generously with either a cream or sweet sherry (or you could try using port). You must use enough to seduce the cake into passive repose; a sprinkle and a promise of better things to come is no use to anyone.
The middle Use a mixture of fruit. This is one place where canned fruit, especially canned fruit salad, seems to work better than fresh; partially drain the fruit but do not leave it parched. Of course, if you have your own home preserved fruit, so much the better.
The custard A true egg custard or *crème Anglaise* never tastes quite right on a trifle — far too posh. Ordinary custard made with commer-cial powder is best; make it a little less thick than you might usually do. For a richer flavour, you can either whisk a couple of egg yolks into the finished custard or boil some double cream until reduced by at least half and stir that in.
The topping Cream whipped lightly with a little vanilla and sugar. Do not whip it until really stiff. The rich totally cover the trifle; the sensible dot the cream about or make a ring around the edge. Toasted whole or flaked almonds add the final touch. Chill thoroughly, but take it out of the refrigerator 30 minutes before serving so that it is not too cold to enjoy. If you can cut it into even slices that stay together, you have failed to make a great trifle.

GLYNN'S TIP

If you find it difficult to make an egg custard without curdling it (something I understand only too well!), try the following method for making the Crème Brûlée. Mix all the ingredients together except for the brown sugar and strain into the ramekins. Place them in a roasting-tin and half fill it with boiling water. Bake the creams gently at 150°C/ 300°F/Gas Mark 2 for about an hour or until a knife blade inserted in the centre of one of them comes out clean. Allow them to chill before sprinkling with the brown sugar and grilling. Don't try to make Crème Brûlée with Fruit by this method; they usually curdle and become unsightly.

A PERSONAL SUMMER PUDDING

This recipe is one of the finest tributes to fresh fruit from the garden; every time I make it, I change the ingredients and proportions according to what is in season. If the fruit is very ripe, you will not need to heat it until the juice runs, something I prefer not to do anyway. I put in white currants if I can find them. Make your Summer Pudding a day in advance, use the very best ingredients, and the result will be a pudding which cannot be bettered.

Serves six

half a large loaf of white bread (two days old)
juice of 1 lemon
60 g/2 oz caster sugar (optional)
500 g/1 lb raspberries
250 g/8 oz redcurrants, with stalks removed
250 g/8 oz strawberries, halved

Lightly butter a 1.2 litre/2 pint pudding-bowl. Take the crusts off the bread and slice thinly. Line the bowl with the slices, reserving a few for the lid. Try to make the lining as even as possible; dab the bread with a little butter if it won't stay in position. Squeeze the lemon juice over the fruit and mix together with the sugar, if you are using it. Fill the bread shell with the fruit and top with a bread lid.

Compress the pudding by resting a saucer on the lid and weighting it with about 500 g/1 lb weight consisting of some suitable cans or kitchen weights. Refrigerate for at least 8 hours, preferably overnight. Remove the weight and saucer, then invert a serving plate on top and turn over gently to unmould.

Serve on pools of chilled single cream (yes, it is better if flavoured with orange-flower water or rose water) and decorate with something summery – a few mint leaves, rose petals, or some borage flowers.

Options

Having advised you to make an all-red Summer Pudding, it is only fair to say that an all-black one is equally effective, and perhaps more surprising. In this case, it is best to cook the fruit very gently for about 5 minutes, to promote extra juice. Mix the fruit with the sugar, if you are using it, let it stand for a while, then simmer with no extra liquid. Take care with the lemon juice – with differing types and ripeness of fruits, the amount needed will vary each time.

I find that the flavour of blackcurrants is too intrusive, swamping the sweetness of the raspberries and strawberries. If you want to use blackcurrants, do so with caution and remember that they need to be cooked slightly. Blackberries are better to use if you just want some darkness of colour.

PINEAPPLE TRUFFLE LOAF

A slicing dessert that may be presented as simply or as dramatically as you choose. You could use canned pineapple but would then miss the enticing contrast of sharp and sweet.

Serves twelve or more

375 g/12 oz fresh pineapple, trimmed
4 tbls dark rum
1 tsp vanilla essence
220 g/7 oz Bournville chocolate
185 g/6 oz cream of coconut (solid)
125 g/4 oz unsalted butter
220 g/7 oz packet gingernut biscuits

Chop the pineapple into small chunks and marinate it in the rum and vanilla for 2 hours. Melt together the chocolate, cream of coconut and butter over gentle heat. Crush the gingernut biscuits finely and stir evenly into the hot mixture. Stir in the pineapple marinade and then the flesh.

Lightly oil a 500 g/1 lb loaf tin then line the base with greaseproof or waxed paper. Pile in the mixture and press down lightly to ensure it is even. Cover and chill overnight. Unmould and slice thinly. *Photograph, p. 80.*

ICED CHRISTMAS PUDDING

My iced Christmas pudding can be made by anybody with a refrigerator or chilly window ledge. Make the pudding a few days in advance so that the flavours blend well, and serve it very cold with just a lapping of cream – oh, well, with lots of whipped cream, if you really must! I made this as a really big pudding so that it looks the same size as a decent-sized steamed pudding; you could make a smaller one by halving the ingredients.

Serves at least eight, probably twelve

625 g/1¼ lb soft, 'no need to soak' dried stone fruits (apricots, prunes, figs or dates)
125 g/4 oz large, seedless raisins
30 g/1 oz currants
30 g/1 oz chopped mixed peel, or chopped glacé cherries
1 medium lemon
1 cinnamon stick
70 cl bottle rich ruby wine or port
up to 150 ml/¼ pint dark rum or orange liqueur
2 × 11 g/½ oz sachets gelatine powder

First assemble the dried fruits in a bowl, letting the apricots dominate – I use 250 g/8 oz apricots (halved) and 125 g/4 oz of each of the other fruits. Put the raisins, currants and peel or cherries into a small saucepan with the thinly-pared rind of the lemon and the cinnamon stick. Add 300 ml/½ pint of the wine, bring *very* slowly to the boil, simmer for 5 minutes, then remove from the heat.

Squeeze the juice from the lemon and make the amount up to 150 ml/¼ pint with the rum or orange liqueur. Pour this over the fruit. Remove the lemon peel from the raisin mixture and stir that into the fruit as well.

Add a further 300 ml/½ pint of your ruby wine, cover and leave overnight in a warm, but not hot, place. In the morning, drain the liquid off and remove the cinnamon stick. Measure the liquid and make it up to 450 ml/¾ pint with ruby wine. If there is a little left over, use it for the next step.

Take a few spoonfuls of ruby wine or the liquid from the soaked fruit and put it into a small saucepan. Sprinkle the gelatine on top and allow it to become sponge-like until all the liquid has disappeared. Heat very gently until the liquid is clear. Remove from the heat and add to the soaking mixture.

Arrange the prepared fruit in a 1.5 or 1.75 litre/2½ or 3 pint pudding-basin, perhaps making a pattern on the base with some of the apricots. Pour in the liquid, cover, and leave to set and chill for several days.

To serve, plunge the bowl up to the rim in hot water for a few seconds, cover with a serving plate, then quickly invert and turn out the pudding. To cut this you need a very sharp or serrated knife. First cut the pudding in half, then into neat segments. *Photograph, p. 51.*

CONTINENTAL FRUIT PIE

It took me a long time to find a recipe for the sort of pie you find in Europe, with thick, crisp pastry that lasts well without going soft, and which is perfect for picnics and parties where it can be eaten in the fingers. The technique of pre-baking the base is the secret.

Serves eight to ten

PASTRY
315 g/10 oz self-raising flour
105 g/3½ oz caster sugar
few drops vanilla essence
½ egg yolk
1 egg white
1 tsp milk
155 g/5 oz butter
FILLING
1.5 kg/3 lb peeled trimmed fruit, flavoured with sugar and spice to your taste

Sieve half the flour on to a clean, cool surface and make a well in the centre. Mix together the sugar, vanilla, the half yolk, white and milk and mix evenly with the flour. Rub the butter into the remainder of the flour, then knead the two mixtures into a consistent dough. If it is a little sticky, let it rest in the refrigerator.

Use half the dough to line the base only of a 23 cm/9 inch springform baking tin, prick all over and bake at 180°C/350°F/Gas Mark 4 for

15-20 minutes. Roll out the remaining dough and cut a circle the same size as the springform tin. Reshape and roll out the trimmings to make an inside rim for the springform at least 2.5 cm/1 inch high. Damp this and seal it well on to the cooled base. Spoon in your filling, pop on the pie top, seal it and brush with milk. Bake at 180°C/350°F/Gas Mark 4 for 20-30 minutes and let the pie cool in the tin before removing. *Photograph, p. 79.*

RASPBERRY BLACK BOTTOM PIE

Black Bottom Pies are an American speciality, a layer of rich chocolate custard topped with a light rum-flavoured chiffon. Here the chocolate layer is given freshness and fascination by being combined with puréed fresh raspberries, and the top is flavoured with another great friend to both chocolate and raspberries – rose water. Make this your own recipe by using a variation on the raspberry-flavoured *eau-de-vie* I suggest, or by using none at all.

Serves eight to twelve

large brioche or boudoir biscuits
1 capful framboise or Cognac
60 g/2 oz Bournville chocolate, melted
570 ml/1 pint milk
20 g/³/4 oz cornflour
3 eggs, separated
2 × 11 g/¹/2 oz sachets gelatine powder
185 g/6 oz Bournville chocolate
90 g/3 oz unsalted butter
290 ml/¹/2 pint fresh raspberry purée
60-90 g/2-3 oz sugar (optional)
rose water, framboise or Cognac to taste

Lightly oil a 25 cm/10 inch springform pan. If you have a large brioche loaf, slice it thinly and lay it evenly over the base, standing slices around the pan to make a brioche crust. If you are using sponge fingers, ensure the sugared side faces outwards. Sprinkle the base layer with alcohol then paint with the melted chocolate.

Heat the milk to simmering point, meanwhile mixing together the cornflour, gelatine and egg yolks. Pour on the hot milk, whisking continuously, then return the mixture to the pan and cook over gentle heat until it has thickened. Leave on the heat to cook for at least 5 minutes, stirring continually. Remove from the heat. While still hot, divide into two even portions. Press cling film on to the surface of one portion and leave to cool to room temperature. Cut up the chocolate and the butter and stir into the other portion. Let them melt into the custard, stirring regularly. Once cool, but before setting, stir in the raspberry purée, taste for sweetness and add sugar if you like, then ladle carefully on to the prepared base. Arrange

any leftover brioche or sponge fingers on top, sprinkle with a little more alcohol, then leave to set in the refrigerator.

Once it has set, flavour the remaining custard with rose water or with more alcohol and sweeten slightly if you must. Then whisk the egg whites and fold them into the mixture. Ladle evenly over the chocolate and raspberry layer. Chill for at least 4 hours; overnight is better. Serve in wedges with a little un-sweetened whipped cream or decorate with more raspberries and curls of chocolate.

Note You will need about 500 g/1 lb of fresh raspberries, forced through a sieve, to give you the required amount of purée; do not cook it or put it into a hot mixture or you will lose its fresh taste. *Photograph, p. 44.*

Option
You can also make this with a purée of fresh pears, flavoured with either framboise or Poire William, the pear-flavoured *eau-de-vie*.

A MERINGUE MAKER'S PRIMER

Meringue for topping pies should be very glossy and smooth. Follow the basic rules for making meringue and you should have no problems:
● Use a clean, grease-free bowl and clean beaters.
● Make sure there are no traces of yolk with the whites.
● Add 1 teaspoon white wine vinegar and a pinch of salt for every 3 egg whites, to give a mallow-like texture to the meringue, to break down the whites and speed up whisking.
● Whisk the whites until soft peaks have formed; only then add the sugar (60 g/2 oz per medium-sized egg white), a tablespoon at a time, whisking well between each addition.
● Use the meringue as soon as it is made or it will separate.
● To prevent the meringue 'weeping' after it is cooked, you must always seal it well to the pastry by first making a rim of meringue round the edge touching the pastry, pile the remainder

in the middle, with extra height in the centre.
● Bake meringue-topped pies at 180°C/350°F/Gas Mark 4 for 12-15 minutes. Cool thoroughly before serving but do not refrigerate.

MERINGUES

These meringues have a marshmallowly texture in the centre, a sign they are home-made.

Makes 12-14

4 egg whites
pinch of salt
¹/2 tsp cream of tartar
250 g/8 oz caster sugar

Line two baking-sheets with non-stick silicone paper, or with lightly oiled greasproof paper.

Put the egg whites with the salt and cream of tartar into a large, clean, dry bowl and whisk until soft peaks form. Gradually add the sugar, a tablespoon at a time, and keep whisking until the mixture forms very stiff peaks. Using two dessertspoons, form the meringue into egg-shapes on the sheet. You can pipe them if you like but I always suspect these of having been bought. Heat the oven to 150°C/300°F/Gas Mark 2, put in the sheets, then immediately turn the oven down to 140°C/275°F/Gas Mark 1 and bake for 1 hour. If possible, leave the meringues in the cooling oven to dry out completely. If it isn't possible to leave them there undisturbed, put them in an airing-cupboard or warm place for an hour or so. When quite cold, remove from the baking-sheets and store in an airtight tin.

To make meringues special: sandwich them together with unsweetened cream and orange-flower water. *Photograph, p. 152.*

Options
Raspberry Meringues Stir into the meringue mixture 2 tablespoons of best-quality raspberry jam and a few drops of red food colouring.
Coffee Nut Meringues Stir 2 teaspoons of instant coffee powder into the caster sugar. Fold 90 g/3 oz finely chopped roasted hazelnuts into the meringue mixture.
Fig and Walnut Meringues Fold 125 g/4 oz chopped dried figs and 60 g/2 oz finely chopped walnuts into the meringue mixture.
Chocolate-dipped Meringues Break 90 g/3 oz plain chocolate into a small bowl, add 15 g/¹/2 oz white cooking fat and melt gently over a pan of barely simmering water. Remove the bowl from the heat, dip cooked and cooled meringues quickly into the chocolate and dry on a rack. Chocolate-dipped nut meringues are very good.
Nutty Meringues Fold 185 g/6 oz finely crushed nut brittle into the meringue mixture.
Chocolate Nut Meringues Fold 90 g/3 oz grated chocolate and 60 g/2 oz chopped, toasted hazelnuts into the meringue mixture.

GLYNN'S TIP

Quantities of meringue required for pies:

For a 20 cm/8 inch pie use 2 egg whites and 4 rounded tablespoons of sugar.

For a 22-23 cm/9 inch pie use 3 egg whites and 6 rounded tablespoons of sugar.

For a 25 cm/10 inch pie use 4 egg whites and 8 rounded tablespoons of sugar.

GLYNN'S TIP

For parties or festive occasions, don't hesitate to make rainbow-coloured meringues. Add a few drops of food colouring or give them mystery with a few drops of flavouring; I like to use a cherry essence and fill the meringues with a mixture of chestnut purée and whipped cream.

PLUM PIE with CINNAMON MERINGUE

Serves six

PIE
250 g/8 oz puff or shortcrust pastry (see page 129)
6 tbls fresh white breadcrumbs
3-4 tbls butter
3 egg yolks, beaten
2 tbls muscovado sugar
750 g/1½ lb plums, greengages, or damsons, halved and stoned
1 tbls lemon juice
ground allspice
MERINGUE
4 egg whites
1 tsp ground cinnamon
90 g/3 oz caster sugar
pinch of salt

Preheat the oven to 220°C/425°F/Gas Mark 7. Line a 23 or 25 cm/9 or 10 inch pie-dish with pastry, making a double layer round the edge and crimping decoratively.

Fry the breadcrumbs in 2 tablespoons of butter until crisp and golden brown. Mix with the beaten egg yolks and spread this mixture over the base of the pastry case. Sprinkle half the sugar on top.

Arrange the plum halves, cut-side down, on the pastry, cutting some into slivers to fill the gaps. Sprinkle the rest of the sugar and the lemon juice over, dot with the remaining butter and dust with allspice.

Bake at 220°C/425°F/Gas Mark 7 for 10 minutes, then reduce the heat to 180°C/350°F/Gas Mark 4 and continue cooking for another 20 minutes. Remove the pie and allow it to cool.

While the pie is cooling, whisk the egg whites until stiff. Stir the cinnamon into the caster sugar and add the egg whites a tablespoon at a time, whisking until you have a glossy meringue. Spread the mixture around the edge of the pie, making sure that there are no gaps, then pile the remainder in the middle and swirl to make peaks. Return to the oven for about 5 minutes, until the meringue is just beginning

to brown. Leave for at least 2 hours before serving cold. *Photograph, p. 41.*

Option
Before covering the pie with meringue, warm 250 g/8 oz strained apricot jam and spread this over the plums.

BUTTERSCOTCH MERINGUE PIE

This is as ubiquitous in America as lemon meringue pie in Britain.

Serves eight to ten

3 large egg yolks
250 g/8 oz light muscovado sugar
2 generous tbls cornflour
¼ tsp salt
600 ml/1 pint milk
60 g/2 oz butter
1 tsp vanilla essence
one baked 23 cm/9 inch shortcrust pastry case (see page 129)
MERINGUE
3 large egg whites
185 g/6 oz caster sugar

In a large bowl combine the yolks, brown sugar, cornflour and salt and mix to a paste with a little of the milk. Pour the remaining milk into a saucepan, heat to scalding point, then pour over the egg mixture, stirring all the time. Return all the mixture to the pan and cook over a low heat, stirring continuously, until it thickens well. Remove from the heat and stir in the butter and vanilla. Pour the filling into the pastry case and allow it to cool so that a skin forms on top.

Make a meringue by whisking the egg whites until stiff, then gradually whisking in the caster sugar a tablespoon at a time until you have a glossy, stiff mixture. Spread this over the cooled butterscotch filling, taking it right to the edges, then swirl it into peaks. Bake at 220°C/425°F/Gas Mark 7 for 15 minutes, or until the meringue is lightly browned. Serve cold, but if you chill it for too long it will collapse.

RHUBARB MERINGUE PIE

Serves four to six

750 g/1½ lb rhubarb
280 g/9 oz caster sugar
3 eggs, separated
60 g/2 oz ground almonds (or very finely crushed gingernuts)
one 18 or 20 cm/7 or 8 inch flan dish lined with shortcrust pastry (see page 129)
60 g/2 oz dried fruit, chopped (apricots are by far the best)

Cut the rhubarb into even lengths of no more than 2.5 cm/1 inch, then cut any thick stalks lengthwise so that all the pieces are approximately the same size. Put the rhubarb into a bowl with 90 g/3 oz caster sugar and leave for 1 hour or so to allow the juices to run. Turn the fruit from time to time, then drain it in a colander standing over a bowl, reserving the juice.

Mix the egg yolks with the almonds or crushed gingernuts and add enough of the rhubarb juices to make a paste. Spread this over the bottom of the pastry case and sprinkle with the chopped dried fruit. Arrange the drained rhubarb on top and bake at 190°C/375°F/Gas Mark 5 for about 35 minutes; the rhubarb should then be tender and the pastry will be golden. Remove the pie from the oven and turn the heat down to 150°C/300°F/Gas Mark 2.

Make a meringue by whisking the egg whites until stiff, then gradually whisking in the remaining caster sugar a tablespoon at a time until you have a stiff, glossy mixture. Spread the meringue over the pie, taking it right up to the edge, then pile the remainder in the middle, swirling it around to make attractive peaks. Return the pie to the oven for a further 10-15 minutes or until the meringue is crisp on the outside and golden brown. Serve cold.

If you have plenty of leftover rhubarb juice, you could heat it to serve as a sauce with the pie; also, a little added to whipped cream makes an accompaniment to plain stewed fruit.

Option
Gooseberry Meringue Pie Use gooseberries, halved, with a little chopped stem ginger to replace the dried fruit.

SWEET TREATS

It makes a dinner seem extra special if the guests are offered home-made chocolate sweetmeats with the coffee; it shows so much more care, and style, than handing round mints in paper cases. So, if you have the time, try preparing one of the following specialities.

GLORIOUS TRUFFLES

This recipe uses butter to enrich and soften the chocolate and has always been a hit when I've included it in a demonstration or broadcast. Once you are committed to eating a hunk of chocolate and butter I reckon you may as well go all the way and add cream or liqueur.

Makes about 12 truffles

5 tbls double cream
185 g/6 oz dark, bitter chocolate
4 tbls unsalted butter
2 tbls liqueur, spirit or fruit syrup (optional)
Cocoa powder to finish

Reduce the cream over gentle heat until it is half its original quantity. Remove from the heat and stir in the chocolate and butter, which should both have been broken up into small pieces. If the mixture does not emulsify satisfactorily, stand it over hot, but not boiling, water until it behaves as you wish. It may be left plain or you can flavour it with liqueurs, fruit syrup (which are sweet, remember), Cognac or another spirit. All of them will make the final truffle a little bit softer.

Let the mixture set for about 40 minutes in the refrigerator then shape roughly and roll in cocoa powder. Keep refrigerated until 10-15 minutes before serving.

Options

If you have any preserved summer fruits in vodka or Cognac, you could wrap truffle mixture around these. Equally good are some exotic dried fruits again used as a centre or chopped into the truffle mixture — a really sharp dried apricot is fabulous, but it is even better if it has been reconstituted in a little Cognac first. My absolute favourite flavourings may be guessed — rose water, orange-flower water, Framboise *eau-de-vie*, Calvados and black rum.

NUT TRUFFLES

In this American recipe hazelnuts are specified though any nut may be used; all should be lightly toasted first, however, to give both flavour and resistance to softening. The exceptions are pistachios.

Makes about 36

185 g/6 oz toasted hazelnuts (or your favourite alternative)
185 g/6 oz dark chocolate
155 g/5 oz icing sugar
1 egg white
1 tbls orange liqueur or rum
ground hazelnuts or cocoa powder, to finish

Grind the hazelnuts finely. Chop the chocolate into a small bowl; heat gently over a pan of simmering water until it melts. Mix the ground nuts, icing sugar, egg white, liqueur or rum in a bowl then add the chocolate mixture. Stir to blend thoroughly and chill for at least an hour. Shape into small balls and roll in ground hazelnuts or cocoa powder. Store in the refrigerator, covered.

Option

Almond Truffles Use ground almonds and Amaretto or an orange liqueur with ¼ teaspoon of almond essence. Roll the truffles in finely chopped toasted almond flakes.

WHITE TRUFFLES

Although white chocolate isn't chocolate at all but cocoa butter which has been played about with, it is simpler to call it white chocolate for then everyone knows what you mean. It isn't very easy to find in Britain, so when you go to Paris or anywhere else in France, keep a look out for it and bring some home.

Makes about 20 truffles

125 g/4 oz slivered almonds
155 g/5 oz white chocolate
60 g/2 oz unsalted butter
1-2 tbls fruit liqueur or spirit
icing sugar, to finish

Chop the almonds roughly. Put the chocolate into a small bowl and stand it in a pan of hot water until it melts. Stir in the butter and nuts then pour in the liqueur or spirit and blend thoroughly. Chill until firm, then form into small balls and roll in icing sugar. Store in the refrigerator, covered.

CHOCOLATE-COATED FRUIT and NUTS

Chocolate Liqueur Dates for 250-375 g/8-12 oz fresh dates, stoned, make a filling by mixing 1 tablespoon of ground almonds with 1 tablespoon of finely-grated orange rind, 90 g/3 oz dark chocolate melted with 45 g/1½ oz unsalted butter and 2 teaspoons Grand Marnier or other liqueur. Chill the mixture, then use to fill the date cavities.

Melt 90 g/3 oz dark chocolate with 15 g/½ oz white vegetable fat and pour into a deep glass or mug. Skewer the dates then dip into the liquid chocolate and leave to dry on a foil-lined tray.

Chocolate-coated Almonds Roast 60 g/2 oz whole blanched almonds in a moderate oven (180°C/350°F/Gas Mark 4) until light brown, then cool. Wrap each nut in almond paste (you'll need about 125 g/4 oz) and allow them to dry out on a wire rack. Melt 125 g/4 oz dark chocolate and use for dipping the almonds, leaving them to dry on a foil-lined tray at room temperature.

Chocolate Strawberries Melt 125 g/4 oz dark chocolate with 15 g/½ oz white vegetable fat in a bowl over simmering water. Using fingers or tongs to hold the strawberries (wiped but not hulled), dip them to coat the bottom half of the fruit. Drain off excess chocolate then put on a foil-lined tray to set at room temperature.

Chocolate Orange Sticks Peel 2 large, thick-skinned oranges, taking off the skin with the pith intact. Cut into even strips about 1 cm/½ inch thick. Drop the orange strips into a pan of boiling water, return to the boil then drain. Repeat this twice more. Put 250 g/8 oz sugar in a pan with 300 ml/½ pint water and stir over a low heat until the sugar dissolves. Add the orange strips, bring to the boil then simmer, uncovered, for 5-10 minutes, stirring from time to time, until the peel becomes translucent. Using two forks, arrange the orange strips on a wire rack to dry overnight. Melt 125 g/4 oz dark chocolate and dip the orange strips to cover. Put on a foil-covered tray to dry at room temperature.

HOT PUDDINGS

A rapid increase in sales of home freezers and the introduction of a vast range of instant puddings seemed to forecast the demise of the hot pudding. Restaurants adopted the 'sweet trolley', thus popularizing the mousses and cakes which soon became 'gâteaux'. But the British weren't prepared to let some of their favourite dishes disappear so easily. And quite right too!

Winter Sunday lunches are simply not the same without a hot pudding and lighter meals in other seasons often need something warm to avoid a sense of anti-climax. Many of the newer styles of hot puddings, like *gratins* of summer fruit, are quick and simple to prepare. It's the traditional ones which take more time, another reason why some of them have disappeared.

What about all the considered advice of those who tell us to eat less fat, more fibre and less sugar? Don't let these prophets of gloom deter you from enjoying steamed puddings with custard *and* jam. But, as you are tying down the cloth over the pudding-basin, it is worth reflecting that it might be more sensible if you served it after a light main course rather than a fat-saturated roast. And instead of the usual custard and sauces which accompany puddings, you might instead serve a hot, unsweetened fruit purée, grilled fruit, or fruit poached in apple or orange juice rather than in sugar syrup.

The simplicity of baked fruit should never be overlooked, no matter how formal or smart the occasion. It is an important sign of the times that simple food perfectly cooked is more appreciated than complicated desserts which muddle myriad flavours in search of something new.

These are, perhaps, the most important style of hot pudding for modern tastes, for they generally favour a much higher proportion of fruit to sugar than any other type – indeed, some need none at all. But from time to time you will need a sharp knife to help with the presentation.

There's no need to feel guilt-ridden about serving hot fruit pies and crumbles either – increase the proportion of fruit to pastry or topping, and incorporate some wholemeal flour into the recipe; use fresh rather than canned or preserved fruits and consciously add less sugar. Do all this and serve old-fashioned puddings after more contemporary, lighter courses and you've nothing to worry about!

HOT SUMMER FRUIT GRATINS

Fruit gratins are a modern classic, mainly because they offer the busy cook an elegant way to ring the changes with fresh fruits without drowning them in cream or cooking out their essential sweetness. They are the summer equivalent of a fruit crumble. But this is also an exceptionally good way to serve the sort of fruits you would put under a crumble topping, such as apples, gooseberries and plums.

Serves four to six, according to ramekin size

500 g/1 lb mixed summer fruits (raspberries, strawberries, redcurrants, and blackberries)
light rum for flavouring
60 g/2 oz ground almonds
1 egg, separated
4 tbls double cream
30 g/1 oz caster sugar
1 tsp orange-flower water

Divide the fruit between 4-6 ramekin dishes and pour 2 teaspoons rum into each. Blend the almonds, egg yolk, cream, sugar and orange-

flower water to a thick paste. Whisk the egg white until stiff and gently fold it into the mixture. Spoon the mixture over the fruit in the ramekins and stand them on a baking-sheet. Bake at 230°C/450°F/Gas Mark 8 for 10 minutes. Serve immediately. I try to make an extra one (unnoticed!), for I find these delicious when cold. ⓠ *Photograph, p. 77.*

HONEYED-ALMOND *and* CARDAMOM STUFFED APPLES *with* APRICOT COULIS

A simple old fashioned recipe bearing the treasured flavours of the Old World – almonds, honey, cardamom and orange-flower water. Preparation can be done in advance and the apples cooked in the oven at the same time as your main dish – ideal for Sunday lunch.

Serves six

6 small apples, preferably Golden Delicious or Cox's Orange Pippin
90 g/3 oz ground almonds
1 tsp honey
30 g/1 oz butter, softened
crushed seeds from 3 cardamom pods
SAUCE
125 g/4 oz dried apricots (ideally not the soft ready to eat type for they are generally too sweet)
2 tsps honey
300 ml/½ pint fruity white wine
300 ml/½ pint water
1 tbls orange-flower water

AUTUMN ELEGANCE
From top, clockwise: Tea Ice-Cream with Pistachio Nuts and Dates, p. 140; Smoked Salmon Shells on
Watercress Sauce, p. 32; Duck Breasts with Fresh Pear and Cumin, p. 91.

NEW GAME RULES
From top, clockwise: Casseroled Pheasant with Cranberry Sauerkraut, p.94; Warm Salad of
Saddle of Venison, p.107; Mallard with Turnips and Kumquats, p.93.

CHRISTMAS ALTERNATIVES
From top, clockwise: Baby Turkey Breasts in a Cranberry and Pecan Overcoat, p.98;
Iced Christmas Pudding, p.144; Potted Prawns, p.71.

HOME BAKING for TEA

From top, clockwise: Pierrot Cake, p.171; on plate with Old World Chocolate Cake, p.171, Fruit Loaf, p.168, and
Cardamom Loaf, p.169; Assorted Meringues, p.145; Down-Under Lemon Cake, p.170, with Coconut Macaroons, p.165; Orange Scones, p.164;
Chocolate Praline Cake with Raspberry Purée, p.171; Apricot Bran Loaf, p.169, and Date Loaf, p.169.

Prepare the sauce well in advance so it can chill well. Rinse the apricots then put into a saucepan with the honey, wine and water. Bring to the boil. Reduce to a simmer, cover and cook until really tender, up to 40 minutes depending on type and size. Pass through a sieve to make a really fine purée. Flavour with the orange-flower water and chill, covered. Before serving, check that the texture is supple enough – it should flow like thick double cream. If it doesn't, thin with more wine, water, or, if you are being naughty, some single or double cream.

To prepare the apples, core neatly and score the skin through to the flesh evenly about one-third of the way down. Mix together the stuffing ingredients and divide evenly between the apples. Stand them in a baking dish or enamelled dish and add 150 ml/¼ pint water and 1 teaspoon of honey. Bake for 40-45 minutes at 180°C/350°F/Gas Mark 4.

To serve, gently peel away the top skin to reveal the snowy white cooked apple. Stand the hot apples on a generous puddle of the chilled apricot coulis and just before serving dribble some of the honeyed cooking water over the white part of each apple. *Photograph, p. 116.*

Option
You could also bake quinces this way.

BAKED QUINCES

If you can buy fresh quinces, or know someone who has a tree, this is probably one of the oldest treats there is, still enjoyed enormously throughout the Middle East where quinces remain much more popular than here. But their varieties vary in flavour and aroma far more than apples, from the heady perfume of pineapple and mango to a rather woody blandness. Generally, the better they smell the better they'll bake.

Serves four

4 small or 2 large quinces
lemon juice
125 g/4 oz butter
3 tbls cream
155 g/5 oz icing sugar

Peel the quinces neatly then cut off the tops so that they are the same height.

Remove the core from the top, using a sharp knife and taking care not to pierce the bottom of the fruit. Brush with lemon juice, inside and out, then arrange in a shallow, buttered oven-proof dish. Mix together the butter, cream and icing sugar and when well blended pour into the quinces and sprinkle the tops with extra icing sugar. Bake at 180°C/350°F/Gas Mark 4 for about 35 minutes. Serve hot.

Options
Large quinces are better cut in half as for pears

and baked with a lump of sweetened butter on them and an occasional basting with fruit juice or wine.

A sprinkling of currants, almonds or pine kernels and a spoonful or two of rose and orange-flower water would give an Eastern flavour, and help to cut down on the sugar worked into the butter.

PEARS à la MINUTE

Choose ripe, unblemished pears, allowing one per person. Peel the fruit, cut them in half lengthways, and remove the core neatly. Rub all over with a little lemon juice, place cut side down and slice finely almost to the necks; push down lightly and the pears will fan out. Brush with a tiny amount of melted butter and grill until the outsides are just brown and the pears are heated through.

The appearance can be enhanced by a light sprinkling of sugar (vanilla sugar ideally), which you allow to caramelize under the grill. You may also pour on just a touch of Cognac or Poire William. ⓠ

Options
For a richer version, pour some cream into the dish when the pears are half cooked.

Peaches or nectarines may be treated in just the same way, with or without the cream.

FRUIT on TOAST

I am particularly pleased with this recipe, which I perfected from an idea found in an old cookbook many years ago. It's a simple way to make a little fruit into something special. It is important to use good bread; milk bread or Vienna loaf are both fine, but sliced brioche is best of all. You can use wholemeal bread if it has a firm, heavy texture but don't bother with pappy, sliced white 'bread' or light, supermarket wholemeal.

The fruits I find most successful are plums and greengages, but apricots, peaches and nectarines are also good. Generously butter one slice of bread per person and sprinkle with demerara sugar. Dust with ground cinnamon, then remove the crusts.

Halve and stone the fruit, then arrange, cut-side down, on the bread. Make deep cuts in the fruit and into these insert slivers of butter. Sprinkle with more sugar and cinnamon. Lay the slices in a baking-tin or an ovenproof dish and bake at 180°C/350°F/Gas Mark 4 for about 15-20 minutes, until the fruit has softened and glazed with syrup and the bread is crisp and brown around the edges. Serve the slices warm, with cream. If you want the dish to be really special, spoon a suitable liqueur over the fruit before serving. *Photograph, p. 43.*

REAL APPLE STRUDEL

More and more supermarkets are stocking frozen strudel pastry, which works well and can be used if you haven't time to enjoy the fun of making your own.

Serves eight to twelve

250 g/8 oz strudel pastry (see page 132)
125 g/4 oz butter, melted
FILLING
60 g/2 oz butter
90 g/3 oz fresh breadcrumbs
125 g/4 oz sugar
3 tsps mixed spice
1 small orange
750 g/1½ lb cooking apples

Roll out the pastry to a rectangle about 45 × 60 cm/18 × 24 inches. Trim the edges and lay it out on a lightly floured cloth or sheet; paint the pastry liberally with some of the melted butter.

For the filling, melt the butter in a pan and fry the breadcrumbs until golden brown. Add the sugar, spice and the grated rind of the orange, stir, then take off the heat. Squeeze the juice from the orange into a bowl. Peel, core and thickly slice the apples and toss them in the orange juice.

Sprinkle the spiced breadcrumbs over the pastry, leaving a good border down the short sides and stopping two-thirds of the way down the pastry overall. This is to leave a good wrap-around for the finished strudel. Spread the apple over the crumbs, taking care to leave the borders free and making a good solid line on the closest (crumbed) side which will give a sub-stantial middle to the strudel. Dribble the remaining melted butter over.

Fold in the short sides, then tip the floured cloth and roll up the strudel evenly, flopping it on to a baking-tray. Turn in the ends neatly. Bake at 180°C/350°F/Gas Mark 4 for 50 minutes. Check from time to time and spoon the buttery syrup over the strudel; this will caramelize and make an attractive decoration.

Serve warm, or cold, with cream. You can, if you like, dredge a little icing sugar over the top, but try not to hide the caramel cascades. Ⓔ

Options
Cherry Strudel Use fresh or drained canned cherries instead of apples, with 2 teaspoons of cinnamon to replace the mixed spice.
Pineapple Strudel Mix 750 g/1½ lb curd or cream cheese with 3 eggs, sugar to taste and vanilla essence, then stir in 375 g/12 oz of drained chopped pineapple (*not* crushed pineapple) and a handful of raisins. Sprinkle with 30 g/1 oz of butter-fried breadcrumbs flavoured generously with ground cinnamon, and proceed as above. When baked, sprinkle with a mixture of cinnamon and caster sugar.

DEEP-DISH FRUIT PIES

These are the modern versions of fruit pie, incorporating lots of fruit, minimum added sugar and pastry topping. Use a traditional deep pie dish, with a lip, or any suitable casserole dish of about 1 litre/2 pint capacity. If the dish doesn't have a lip, take care to attach a dampened strip of pastry around the rim before putting on the pastry lid, so that it can be securely sealed. Replacing the water with fruit juice will reduce the amount of sugar required and it is better to underestimate the quantity and have a dredger on the table for people to help themselves, if they have a sweet tooth.

DOUBLE-CRUST FRUIT PIES

These can be made in pie plates which are shallow and hold only a small amount of fruit (approximately 375 g/12 oz) or in a deeper pie dish which will accommodate two or three times the quantity but with a similar amount of pastry, making it a healthier proposition.

BASIC FRUIT PIE

500 g/1 lb shortcrust pastry (see page 129)
375 g-1 kg/12 oz-2 lb fruit, peeled, cored and sliced
as necessary
sugar to taste
milk or beaten egg to glaze
a little caster sugar for dusting

Depending on the dish chosen, use up two-thirds of the pastry to line it. If it is shallow, use only a generous half and have the topping thicker, otherwise the pastry base will not cook through. Arrange the prepared fruit on the pastry and sprinkle with sugar mixed with spices if used. A deep pie can have a funnel in the middle to prevent the pastry lid from sinking. Roll out the remaining pastry large enough to cover the pie comfortably; lay over the fruit, seal the edges securely and make a small slit in the top. Glaze the pastry with milk or beaten egg and bake at 220°C/425°F/Gas Mark 7 for 15 minutes, then lower the heat to 180°C/350°F/Gas Mark 4 and cook for a further 25-30 minutes. Serve warm or cold, lightly dredged with caster sugar.

BASIC APPLE PIE

750 g/1½ lb apples, peeled, cored and thickly sliced
125 g/4 oz sugar, or to taste
2 cloves, optional
5 tbls water or fruit juice
250 g/8 oz shortcrust pastry (see page 129)
milk or beaten egg to glaze
a little caster sugar for dusting

Lightly butter a pie dish or casserole of at least 1.2 litre/2 pint capacity and in it arrange the fruit, sugar, and cloves if you like. Pour over the water or fruit juice. Gently push a pie funnel into the centre of the dish. Roll out the pastry large enough to cover the pie comfortably and from the trimmings cut a strip 1 cm/½ inch wide to go around the rim of the dish. Dampen the pastry rim and carefully cover the dish with the pastry. Crimp the edges firmly with thumb and forefinger, or use the prongs of a fork. Make a small slit over the funnel and brush the pastry with milk or egg glaze.

Bake at 220°C/425°F/Gas Mark 7 for 10 minutes, then reduce the heat to 180°C/350°F/Gas Mark 4 and continue cooking for 30 minutes. Serve warm or cold, lightly dusted with caster sugar.

Options

Add the finely grated rind of an orange and its juice, or include chopped orange peel or chopped crystallized ginger.

Add sultanas or raisins to the fruit and use a tablespoon of golden syrup to replace the sugar.

Include 2 or 3 tablespoons of chopped toasted hazelnuts, and the same amount of cream sherry if you have any, to replace some of the liquid.

Spiced apple pie can include ginger, cinnamon, nutmeg, ground cloves or mixed spice, and is nicest made with brown sugar.

APPLE PIE with SPICED BEER

If you like apple pie, you'll love this recipe. It takes a little longer to make, but the result is well worth the trouble.

Serves six

500 g/1 lb short or rough puff pastry (see pages 129 and 133)
750-1 kg/1½-2 lb Bramley apples, peeled
150 ml/¼ pint good beer
food colouring
1 small egg, beaten
up to 1 tsp spices of your choice
1½ tbls butter
sugar to taste

Line a 23 cm/9 inch pie dish with about two-thirds of the pastry. Core and slice the apples, dip each piece into the beer and arrange in the lined dish. Put a pie funnel in the centre, then cover with the remaining pastry. Paint the pie with food colouring to give it additional colour then glaze lightly when dry with beaten egg.

Bake at 220°C/425°F/Gas Mark 7 for 20 minutes, then reduce the heat to 180°C/350°F/Gas Mark 4 and continue cooking for another 15-20 minutes, or until the pastry is cooked through.

Meanwhile, put the beer, spices and butter into a saucepan and boil to reduce by half. Sweeten to taste. Once the pie is baked, either strain out the spices from the liquid (you will probably have to use muslin if the spices were ground) or leave them in. Pour the liquid into the pie through the pie funnel swirling the dish around to ensure that it is well distributed. Serve warm with cream.

WET BOTTOM SHOO-FLY PIE

There are many styles of shoo-fly pie, supposedly made by Pennsylvanian Dutch settlers to attract the summer flies, thus shoo-ing them away from other foods. This is my favourite version because of the silly but accurate name, and the combination of textures and flavours. It is very sweet and rich. Although designed for six, this pie will serve up to twelve. It also lasts very well so I have known it serve just two people – over 3 days.

Serves six

1 quantity shortcrust pastry (see page 129)
FILLING
1 egg yolk
300 ml/½ pint mixed molasses and boiling water (see below)
1 tsp baking soda
185 g/6 oz plain flour
½ tsp ground cinnamon
⅛ tsp each of ground nutmeg, ginger and cloves
125 g/4 oz demerara or muscovado sugar
2 tbls butter

Line a pie-dish (at least 4 cm/1½ inches deep and 23 cm/9 inches diameter) with shortcrust pastry.

Beat the egg yolk. Pour boiling water on to enough molasses to make up a quantity of the flavour you prefer – I like to use slightly less than half molasses, that is, under 150 ml/¼ pint. Blend the liquid into the egg yolk; stir in the soda and leave to cool. Combine all the dry ingredients, then work in the butter to make crumbs. Pour the liquid directly on to the unbaked pastry base and sprinkle the crumbs over evenly. Bake at 200°C/400°F/Gas Mark 6 for 10 minutes and then reduce to 180°C/350°F/Gas Mark 4 for a further 35 minutes. Let the pie cool a little before serving. Serve with unsweetened cream.

FOUR FRUIT PIE

The delicious combination of the tartness of fresh cranberries with the rich fruitiness of naturally sweet dried apricots, prunes and raisins in the filling of this pie means that it is packed with goodness. If you make the pastry case with half wholemeal flour, you'll have a wonderful whole-food pudding.

375 g/12 oz shortcrust pastry (see page 129)
FILLING
125 g/4 oz granulated sugar
2 tbls flour
150 ml/¼ pint water
300 ml/½ pint orange juice
125 g/4 oz dried apricot halves
250 g/8 oz fresh or frozen cranberries
125 g/4 oz raisins
125 g/4 oz ready-to-eat prunes
1 tsp vanilla essence

Mix the sugar and flour in a large saucepan and gradually blend in the water and orange juice. Bring to the boil and cook over a moderate heat, stirring constantly, until thickened. Add the apricots, snipped in half, cover and simmer for 10 minutes, stirring from time to time. Remove from the heat and stir in the cranberries, raisins, roughly chopped prunes and vanilla essence and cool.

Roll out the pastry and line a 23 cm/9 inch pie plate. Pile the mixture into the pie shell and roll out the pastry trimmings to make 1 cm/½ inch wide strips. Twist these and arrange, lattice fashion, over the pie. Bake at 220°C/425°F/Gas Mark 7 for 30 minutes, or until the pie crust is golden. Cool on a rack. Serve with a mixture of softly-whipped cream and strained yoghurt.

APPLE and MARMALADE TART

Here is a very new recipe, based on a prize-winning idea from a Nottinghamshire teenager, Andrew Foss. The marmalade suggested by Andrew was grapefruit, but you can use any thick-cut marmalade, as long as it is sharp-tasting rather than sweet.

Serves six

315 g/10 oz wholemeal or shortcrust pastry (see page 129)
1 egg, separated
375 g/12 oz peeled, cored and thickly sliced Bramley apples
2 generous tbls marmalade
300 ml/½ pint plain yoghurt, drained
30 g/1 oz walnut pieces

Roll out the pastry to line an 18 cm/7 inch flan dish and bake blind at 200°C/400°F/Gas Mark 6 for 10-12 minutes. Brush the bottom of the flan with the egg white and return to the oven for 3-4 minutes to make sure that it is set. Reduce the oven heat to 180°C/350°F/Gas Mark 4.

Mix the apples with the marmalade and the egg yolk and pile into the baked case. Return to the oven and cook for 30 minutes. While the tart is cooking, strain the yoghurt through a fine sieve or a sieve with muslin inside.

Let the tart cool for 10-15 minutes, then spread the yoghurt on top and sprinkle with the walnuts. Serve at once.

Options

The apples make a delicious syrup as they cook, and a little of this should be put on each plate as the tart is served. If you prefer, you can top the tart with whipped cream or soured cream, but the tart should be only *just* warm.

UPSIDE DOWN TART

The ribaldry associated with the name of this dessert is part of the fun and must be borne with fortitude. The combination of caramel, butter and apple is hard to beat, unless you make it with caramel, butter and pears. My Upside Down Caramel-Orange Tart is even more spectacular – but first the real thing.

Serves four to six

125 g/4 oz white sugar
120 ml/4 fl oz water
1 kg/2 lb Golden Delicious apples
60-125 g/2-4 oz butter
250 g/8 oz shortcrust pastry (see page 129)

Lightly butter an ovenproof dish about 20 cm/8 inches in diameter which has straight sides at least 6 cm/2½ inches deep.

Mix the sugar and water and cook over a low heat until a rich golden caramel has formed. Pour this immediately into the bottom of the dish, where it will set quite firmly.

Peel and core the apples, cut them in half and then into thickish but even slices. Arrange a layer of apples on the caramel, remembering that the bottom will be the top when it is turned out – so make it as attractive as you can. Fill the dish with the remaining apples, keeping the edges neat and the filling as even as possible. Dot with as much butter as you like. With Golden Delicious, which is the best apple to use, or with Cox's Orange Pippins, you will not need extra sugar.

Roll out the pastry and let it rest a minute, then lay it over the apples. If you have chosen a shallow, wide dish, you might have to use more pastry than suggested so that it cooks to a thick, firm base; a thin layer is useless.

Cook for 20 minutes at 180°C/350°F/Gas Mark 4 or until you are sure that the pastry is cooked through. Turn down the heat to 90°C/175°F/Gas Mark 2 and cook for another 10 minutes to crisp up the pastry without burning. Cool for at least 20 minutes so that it is warm rather than hot. Put a large plate over the dish and quickly invert it. Cut the tart at the table so that everyone can see how clever you have been.

Options

Upside Down Caramel-Orange Tart Make the caramel with orange juice rather than water, and incorporate a few tablespoons of butter too.

Use puff pastry and give it a few extra turns (see page 133), adding freshly grated orange rind and a little butter each time. When you cover the fruit, turn the pastry up around the edges or make a rim so that when it is turned over it will sit high above the plate.

Bake for 30 minutes at 200°C/400°F/Gas Mark 6, or until you are sure that the pastry is cooked through. This calls for even more cream.

Although pears are the only alternatives usually seen, any of the fruits used for a sponge upside down cake, that will form a firm pattern when cooked, could be used. Quinces are the next obvious fruit, followed by peaches, nectarines, plums, greengages – or a mixture – or dried fruits plumped up with fruit juice and perhaps some rose or orange-flower water.

FRUIT CRUMBLES

Here is the basic recipe for a traditional crumble, which, when properly made, is delicious cold and excellent as a party dish.

Serves four to six

90 g/3 oz butter
185 g/6 oz plain flour
185 g/6 oz white sugar
500-750 g/1-1½ lb prepared fresh fruit (apples, rhubarb, gooseberries, blackcurrants, plums, blackberries)

Rub the butter into the flour until it is half done, then add the sugar and keep rubbing in until you have a loose crumbly mixture. Place the uncooked fruit into an ovenproof dish and sprinkle most of the crumble over the top. Press down a little, then loosely scatter the remainder on top so that it will crisp more easily. Bake for 40 minutes at 190°C/375°F/Gas Mark 5.

Options

Substitute wholewheat flour for up to half the white flour and use demerara sugar in place of the white sugar. Add ground cinnamon, or ground mace, to the crumble mixture.

Flapjack Topping For a 18 cm/7 inch dish, melt 60 g/2 oz butter with a tablespoon each of demerara sugar and golden syrup, then stir in 125 g/4 oz rolled oats and a teaspoon of mixed spice. Use and bake as for the crumble topping.

FRUIT BATTER PUDDING

Clafoutis, France's batter pudding of black cherries from the Limousin, has lasted longer and more famously than its British counterpart. The closest pudding to *Clafoutis* was probably that baked in Kent, where cherry trees flourish, but almost any fruit can be baked in what is essentially a pancake batter.

Serves four to six

60 g/2 oz plain flour
salt
60 g/2 oz caster sugar
2 eggs, beaten
300 ml/½ pint single cream or creamy milk
30 g/1 oz butter, melted
500 g/1 lb ripe black cherries
icing sugar

Sieve the flour with a pinch of salt into a large bowl and stir in the caster sugar. Gradually add the eggs and blend thoroughly. Warm the cream or milk and pour it slowly on to the mixture, beating all the time to give a smooth, light batter. Sift in the melted butter. Cover and allow to stand for 20-30 minutes if you can.

Stone the cherries and place them in the bottom of a well-buttered 600 ml/1 pint baking dish. Carefully pour the batter over and bake at 200°C/400°F/Gas Mark 6 for 20 minutes; turn the oven down to 180°C/350°F/Gas Mark 4 and continue to cook for a further 20 minutes, until well-risen and golden. The pudding should have a soft, creamy texture in the middle. Serve warm.

Options

Add a few tablespoons of black rum or cherry brandy either to the batter or the cherries.

Use 500 g/1 lb peeled and sliced pears, with 60 g/2 oz blackcurrants instead of the cherries and replace the cherry brandy with Crème de Cassis, or Poire William.

Use sliced fresh peaches or drained peaches which have been canned in fruit juice or their own juice; perhaps flavour with apricot brandy or, more unusually, with Marsala. If you have time, marinate the fruit in the wine with four or five cloves for an hour or so, but remove the cloves when you make the pudding.

GLYNN'S TIP

What is the difference between pancakes and crêpes? The words are used indiscriminately but, generally, pancakes are thicker and larger in diameter and sometimes are served with a savoury filling; crêpes are very thin, sometimes rather small and always sweet.

TRADITIONAL PANCAKES

Pancakes shouldn't be confined to Shrove Tuesday; they are a good base for all kinds of sweet fillings and sauces, whether you cook them in a pan and toss them, or bake them in the oven. I don't think that you can fry pancakes in anything other than butter; most margarines are unsuitable for frying and most oils don't have a good flavour. Remember that it's butter for batter, even if you do use a non-stick pan.

Makes about eight to ten

125 g/4 oz plain flour
salt
1 egg
300 ml/½ pint milk
grated rind of ½ lemon
1 tbls melted butter
butter or lard for frying
lemon juice and caster sugar to serve

Sieve the flour with a pinch of salt into a bowl. Make a well in the centre and break in the egg. Gradually stir in the milk, adding half the liquid a little at a time until you have a smooth batter. Add the remaining liquid and the lemon rind and beat well. Leave the batter to stand for 30 minutes. Just before cooking, stir the melted butter into the batter.

Heat a very little butter in a crêpe, omelette or small frying-pan until it is very hot. Pour in some batter and tilt the pan so that it covers the bottom. If you've added too much, tip it out before it has time to set.

Cook until the top of the pancake turns from creamy white and wet to yellowish and dry and a few holes start to appear. Turn over or toss and cook the other side. If you think it is too thick, thin the batter with a little extra milk. Stack on a warm plate, covered, until all the batter is cooked. The most usual way to serve pancakes is sprinkled with sugar and lemon juice and rolled.

Options

Add finely grated orange rind to the batter and serve with orange juice. Try spreading the pancakes thinly with lemon curd and roll up.

Jungle Gin Drain the juice from a 425 g/15 oz can of crushed pineapple. Make 6 large pancakes and spoon the drained fruit into one corner of each. Fold in half, then into half again, making a fan shape. In a frying-pan melt 125 g/4 oz butter and stir in 60 g/2 oz sugar; let it caramelize to a rich brown, then stir in the juice from the pineapple and simmer for a few minutes. Add 3-4 tablespoons of gin. Gently place the folded pancakes in the syrup and heat through quickly. Serve with whipped cream.

Crêpes Suzette Make 2-3 very small, thin crêpes per person. Put a teaspoon of butter sweetened with sugar and flavoured with grated orange rind on to each and fold in half and half again. Make a syrup of sugar and orange juice in a small frying-pan and sharpen it slightly with lemon juice. Flavour it further with Cognac and orange liqueur if you have some. Carefully put the stuffed pancakes into the hot sauce and, when heated through, flame with additional Cognac or serve as they are. This is not the classic recipe, but the flavour is very similar.

OVEN PANCAKE

This is a dramatic pudding to bring to the table and can be different every time you make it.

Serves four to six

90 g/3 oz plain flour
pinch of salt
2 eggs
scant 150 ml/¼ pint milk

Make up the batter following the instructions above. While it is standing, heat the oven to its maximum temperature. Put 4 tablespoons of butter in a large ovenproof dish (at least 25 cm/ 10 inch diameter). At this stage you can also add fresh or drained canned fruits (black cherries, chopped pineapple or mandarin oranges) together with 2 tablespoons of a brandy, liqueur or spirit and 2 tablespoons of demerara sugar. Put the dish into the oven until the butter and other ingredients are sizzling, then quickly pour the batter over and return to the oven *immediately* to bake for 15 minutes. If you have done everything right it will puff up like a monstrous Yorkshire pudding; if you have not it will still be good.

Meanwhile, if you are using canned fruit, heat the syrup to reduce by half. Serve the wedges of pancake with this sauce poured over and cream.

If the pancake has been baked with no fruit, top with fresh fruit and cream, or serve with hot lemon juice, orange juice or maple syrup.

BREAD and BUTTER PUDDING

Anton Mosimann, super-chef at London's Dorchester Hotel, baked this pudding on television, making this simple way to use left-over bread into an overnight star. I don't suppose it is necessary to tell you that the bread used must be of the very highest quality, and is better for being a day or two old.

Serves six

6 slices of white bread, without crusts
60 g/2 oz butter
60 g/2 oz sultanas or raisins
1 tbls chopped peel (optional)
3 tbls sugar
2 large eggs
600 ml/1 pint milk
grated nutmeg

Spread the bread thickly with the butter and cut each slice into four fingers, squares or triangles. Lightly butter a 1.2 litre/2 pint baking-dish and put half the bread pieces in the bottom, butter-side down. Sprinkle the fruit over, with half the sugar. Arrange the remaining bread on top, butter-side up, and sprinkle with the rest of the sugar. Beat the eggs into the milk with a fork and strain over the pudding. Top with nutmeg, freshly ground if possible, then leave the pudding to stand for at least half an hour before baking, giving it the odd prod to ensure that the milk is well absorbed. Stand on a folded sheet of newspaper in a roasting-tin and pour in boiling water to come half way up the container. Bake at 180°C/350°F/Gas Mark 4 for about 45-50 minutes, until the top is golden and crisp. Serve warm.

Options

Use lightly toasted bread and try substituting single or double cream for some of the milk.

Flavour the milk with spirit or liqueur, with vanilla or another favourite essence. You could use wholewheat bread, in which case a good demerara sugar, the darker muscovado sugar, or honey, and some cinnamon or nutmeg would be appreciated.

Banana Bread and Butter Pudding Slice a large, ripe banana and arrange over the first layer of bread with the dried fruit. Omit the nutmeg and instead use two or 2-3 teaspoons of ground cinnamon, sprinkling it over the buttered bread.

QUEEN of PUDDINGS

Provided you use enough lemon to give a sharp but not overpowering flavour, and a really good quality jam, this thoroughly deserves its name.

Serves four to six

125 g/4 oz cake or breadcrumbs
1 tbls sugar
600 ml/1 pint milk
grated rind of 1 lemon
3 eggs, separated
generous quantity raspberry jam
3 tbls caster sugar

Put the crumbs with the sugar into a large bowl. Bring the milk to the boil and pour it over the crumbs, then stir in the lemon rind and the egg yolks. Pour the mixture into a buttered piedish and stand this in a roasting tin half full of hot water. Bake at 180°C/350°F/Gas Mark 4 for about 30 minutes, or until the centre is quite firm.

Take the pudding out of the oven, reducing the heat to 150°C/300°F/Gas Mark 2, and spread an even layer of jam over the top. Whisk the egg whites until stiff and fold in the caster sugar. Spread over the pudding and sprinkle

with a little extra caster sugar. Return to the oven and bake until the top is crisp and a pale gold colour. Serve warm.

Options

Flavour the base with orange rather than lemon. Use lemon or orange curd, marmalade or apricot jam instead of raspberry jam.

Prince of Puddings Melt 125 g/4 oz dark chocolate with 30 g/1 oz butter and spread this over an orange-flavoured base. Use cubed, rather than crumbled bread. The combination of orange with the chocolate sauce makes a flavour called jaffa – a Prince among Puddings.

Rather than slow baking, cook the base at 180°C/350°F/Gas Mark 4 for 20 minutes, then the meringued pudding for a further 10 minutes at the same temperature. This is a useful point to bear in mind if your oven happens to be at a higher temperature for cooking something else.

MUD WIZARDRY

From looking an absolute mess when they go into the oven, these puddings turn themselves inside out to please you – the horrid mixture on top becomes a rich sauce upon which a delightful sponge pudding floats.

Serves one to six depending on the greed factor!

SPONGE BASE
125 g/4 oz self-raising flour
125 g/4 oz sugar
1/2 tsp baking-powder
1/2 tsp salt
1 tbls cocoa powder
2 tbls butter
150 ml/1/4 pint milk
1 tsp vanilla essence
FUDGE MUD SAUCE
250 g/8 oz demerara sugar
5 tbls cocoa powder
450 ml/3/4 pint milk

Sift together the dry ingredients for the base. Melt the butter in a mixture of the milk and vanilla essence and beat into the dry ingredients. Turn into a deep ovenproof dish or heatproof pudding-bowl. Mix together the sugar and cocoa powder for the sauce and sprinkle over the base. Then pour on the milk – but don't do a thing to make it look attractive. Simply bake it at 180°C/350°F/Gas Mark 4 for 60 minutes, by which time a wonderful sponge will have emerged through that primeval-looking mud mixture you put on top.

Option

Mocha Mud Wizardry Make the base the same way, but substitute 1 tablespoon of instant coffee powder for 1 tablespoon of cocoa in the topping and use all white or half white and half brown sugar.

EVE'S PUDDING

This pudding of apple baked with sponge on top is a perennial favourite. If you use a sweet apple such as Cox's Orange Pippin, you can probably leave the sugar out of the filling. My recipe is the accepted balance of sponge and fruit but do add more fruit if you like. Whatever you do, don't cook the apples beforehand.

Serves four to six

125 g/4 oz butter
250 g/8 oz caster sugar
grated rind and juice of 1 lemon
2 eggs, beaten
125 g/4 oz self-raising flour
salt
500 g/1 lb apples, peeled, cored and thinly sliced
1/4 tsp ground cloves

Cream the butter with half the sugar until light and fluffy, then add the lemon rind and the eggs and beat well. Fold in the flour, sifted with a pinch of salt. Grease a 1.2 litre/2 pint ovenproof dish and lay half the sliced apples in the bottom. Stir the ground cloves into the remaining sugar and sprinkle this over the apples, with the lemon juice. Cover with the remaining slices of apple and spoon the sponge mixture over the top. Bake at 180°C/350°F/Gas Mark 4 for about 40-45 minutes, when the top should be golden and firm and the apples soft.

Options

Substitute grated nutmeg, mace, cinnamon or a good mixed spice in place of the cloves. I've used a mixture of ginger and orange peel with great success. Other fruits can be used, although then it is not strictly Eve's pudding but Your Fruit Sponge. Rhubarb is particularly good, with 1/2 teaspoon ground ginger stirred into the sugar instead of the cloves. Stoned plums are also successful, with ground cinnamon. You may prefer to replace the lemon juice with water when using slightly more tart fruits; try using the rind and juice of an orange instead, which is my favourite, especially with rhubarb, apples, pears, or fresh pineapple, which is marvellous. Adding spice to the sponge topping as well as putting it on to the fruit is a tasty alternative.

Orange or Lemon Sponge Add the grated rind of an orange or a lemon to the sponge mixture. Use 155 g/5 oz flour, and enough orange or lemon juice to give a dropping consistency. Serve with orange or lemon sauce, unsweetened apple sauce, fresh raspberry, strawberry or blackberry purée, or a chocolate sauce.

Chocolate Sponge Sift 3 level tablespoons of cocoa powder with the flour and add a little milk to give a dropping consistency.

Fig Sponge Sift 1/2 teaspoon of mixed spice with the flour. Chop 125 g/4 oz dried figs and stir them into the mixture.

FRUIT UPSIDE DOWN PUDDING

This recipe (often called an Upside Down Cake, although served as a pudding) is made usually with sliced pineapple but is just as successful with any canned or fresh fruit that has an affinity with brown sugar.

Serves four to six

FRUIT TOPPING
2 tbls butter
4 tbls dark soft brown sugar
425 g/15 oz can pineapple rings or other fruit
1 tbls chopped nuts (optional)
1 tbls glacé cherries (optional)
SPONGE BASE
125 g/4 oz softened butter
60 g/2 oz caster sugar
2 eggs
½ tsp vanilla essence
185 g/6 oz self-raising flour
2-3 tbls fruit juice

Lightly grease an 18 cm/7 inch cake-tin or straight-sided ovenproof dish and melt 2 tablespoons of butter in the bottom. Sprinkle over the sugar and arrange slices of drained pineapple, or other fruit, on top. You can be artistic and include nuts and glacé cherries to make a pattern if you like, or simply pack in the fruit, which will taste just as good.

To make the sponge, cream the butter and sugar, then beat in the eggs with the vanilla. Stir in the flour with the juice and spoon the mixture on top of the fruit. Bake at 180°C/350°F/Gas Mark 4 for about 45 minutes, or until the sponge is golden and firm to touch. Allow it to stand in the tin for 3-4 minutes before turning out on to a warmed serving dish. Serve warm with cream.

Options
Use pears in place of pineapple and replace 30 g/1 oz of the flour with cocoa powder. Try using stoned cherries with or without a slurp of black rum. For a special treat, stuff peach or apricot halves with macaroons, crushed and moistened with a little wine, sweet vermouth or fruit juice, and omit the brown sugar; some strips of angelica for decoration make this dish look particularly pretty.

With fresh sliced peaches, an orange-flavoured sponge would be nicer. Dried fruit, say apricots or a mixture of apricots and prunes, makes a delicious and unexpected change. Reconstitute the fruit in cider, red or white wine, apple or some other fruit juice; the fruit will be sweet enough and colourful enough not to need the brown sugar on the base, but the butter is always good; perhaps flavour the sponge with cinnamon for this version.

A STEAMED PUDDING PRIMER

Suet – that is, beef fat – is the traditional fat for steamed puddings but butter gives both a better flavour and a lighter texture and will be preferable to modern palates.

Serves four to six

125 g/4 oz butter or shredded beef suet
125 g/4 oz caster sugar
2 eggs, beaten
125 g/4 oz self-raising flour
salt
1-2 tbls milk or water
butter for greasing the basin

Generously butter a 1 litre/1¾ pint pudding-basin, and add to the basin whatever you have chosen to flavour your pudding (see Options). Cream the butter (or stir the suet) with the sugar and beat in the eggs little by little. Sieve the flour with a pinch of salt, fold it into the mixture and then stir in milk or water to achieve a soft dropping consistency. You can also flavour the sponge mixture itself (see below). Spoon the mixture into the bowl and cover with buttered foil folded into a pleat in the middle to allow for expansion during cooking. Tie string securely round the rim of the bowl.

Stand the pudding on a trivet in a large saucepan and pour in boiling water up to the bottom of the rim of the basin. A butter pudding should steam for 1½ hours; a pudding made with suet will need up to 30 minutes longer. Leave it in the basin to shrink and cool slightly before running a knife around the inside of the bowl.

You can serve the pudding directly from the bowl, but it is more attractive turned out on to a warmed plate – run a knife around the inside of the bowl first.

Options
For a lighter texture, try using fresh breadcrumbs. Either replace all of the flour with 185 g/6 oz fresh white breadcrumbs or use a mixture of 60 g/2 oz flour and 90 g/3 oz breadcrumbs.

Golden Syrup Pudding This is perhaps the most popular steamed pudding. Put at least 3 tablespoons of golden syrup into the basin. I put a few knobs of butter in too. Some people add a little ginger to the mixture or to the golden syrup. The fudgy flavour of maple syrup makes a change, if you can afford it.

Jam Pudding Add 3-4 tablespoons of a favourite jam or marmalade to the basin before adding the mixture. It's simple but good!

Raisin Pudding Stir some seedless raisins into the sponge or put a layer of them in the bottom of the basin, sprinkle with a little brown sugar and cinnamon, and add some knobs of butter.

It's especially delicious if the sponge is flavoured with orange or lemon rind.

Sugar and Spice Pudding Instead of mixing the pudding with milk or water, use warmed treacle or golden syrup and stir in rather a lot of ground ginger, nutmeg or mixed spice; you may need a generous tablespoon or more because the long cooking time will lessen its flavour.

RUM *and* TOFFEE PEAR PUDDING

This one will make you feel really wicked!

Serves six

FRUIT BASE
90 g/3 oz butter
2 tbls dark rum
185 g/6 oz muscovado sugar
500 g/1 lb firm pears, peeled, cored and sliced
SPONGE
125 g/4 oz butter
125 g/4 oz caster sugar
2 eggs, beaten
1 tbls lemon juice
1 tbls grated lemon rind
125 g/4 oz self-raising flour

In a small pan, gently heat the butter, rum and sugar together until melted and stir to blend. Put one third of this mixture in the bottom of a well-buttered 1.5 litre/2½ pint pudding-basin. Put the sliced pears into a bowl and pour the remaining syrup over them, stirring very gently to coat them without breaking up the slices.

Make a sponge mixture by creaming the butter and sugar, beating in the eggs, lemon juice and rind, then folding in the flour. Mix the sponge into the pears, without fussing too much – the unevenness of colour and flavour is part of this pudding's appeal. Ladle the mixture into the basin, cover and tie. Stand the basin in a large pan on a trivet and pour in boiling water up to the basin rim. Steam for at least 1½ hours.

Run a knife around the inside of the basin, turn out on to a warmed dish and serve. A little cream flavoured with rum makes the perfect accompaniment.

HOLY LAND PUDDING

Although this pudding needs to cook for at least four hours, it is made much more quickly than the usual Christmas pudding. The pudding has a crisp suet crust surrounding plump, moist fruits from the eastern Mediterranean which, in turn, cradle a whole orange. The orange will cook so thoroughly that you can eat the peel – as with the lemon of the traditional Sussex Pond pudding. If you cannot find a thin-skinned navel orange, seedless mandarins will do, but the effect won't be quite so succulent.
The dried fruits should include at least 250 g/ 8 oz apricots, plus dates, figs and prunes. All must be soft and 'ready-soaked'; if you cannot buy these, soak the drier ones in fruit juice just long enough to soften.
This recipe is for a very large pudding because the cold leftovers are equally sensational. For a smaller size (1.75 litre/3 pint basin), reduce everything by one-third but keep the cooking time the same, or the orange won't be soft.

Serves twelve

SUET CRUST
375 g/12 oz self-raising flour
185 g/6 oz shredded beef suet
185 g/6 oz caster sugar
3-4 tsps grated lemon rind
milk and water to mix
FILLING
1 kg/2 lb mixed dried fruits (see above)
1 navel orange or 2-3 seedless mandarins
3 tsps ground cinnamon
185 g/6 oz demerara sugar
3 tsps orange-flower water
3 tsps rose water
60 g/2 oz butter

To make the crust, mix together the dry ingredients in a large bowl and stir in enough milk and water to make a soft dough. Roll out on to a lightly floured surface and use two-thirds of it to line a 2.5 litre/4½ pint pudding-basin which has been lightly buttered. Reserve the remaining dough for the lid.
Mix the dried fruits and put a good layer at the bottom of the lined basin. Prick the orange or mandarin skin all over and place in the centre. Mix the remaining fruit with the cinnamon, sugar and flower water and pack loosely around the whole fruit. Cut the butter into small pieces and arrange on top of the fruit. Brush the edges of the pastry with water. Roll out the remaining pastry to make a lid and cover, sealing firmly with finger and thumb. Cover with a double layer of pleated foil (butter the underside) and tie securely to the top of the basin with string.
Steam for at least 4 hours, preferably 5-6, to ensure that the orange is well cooked. Use a really large pan of boiling water, covered, to make sure that no steam escapes. Check during cooking and top up with water as necessary.
When you are ready to serve, run a knife around the inside of the bowl and turn out the pudding on to a warmed plate; accompany with a little thin cream or custard. You don't have to wait for Christmas to enjoy this! ⓣ

CHRISTMAS PUDDING

It's a brave man who declares that he has solved the problems of making a Christmas pudding which will please everyone! This is a recipe which blends and marries together the best ideas from a number of old family favourites.
The pudding is not especially dark in colour, but the high proportion of citrus flavourings and spice gives it a clean, honey-like taste that does not clog the palate.
I find that 1 kg/2 lb is about right for serving six people but with this recipe you can make a bigger pudding or a number of small ones; few things are more appreciated than a pudding as a very special homemade gift. They are best made several months before Christmas and kept in a cool place, but extra-long cooking will make a younger pudding taste almost as good as a mature one.

Makes 3 kg/6 lb cooked pudding mixture

250 g/8 oz self-raising flour
185 g/6 oz coarse, homemade breadcrumbs
440 g/14 oz dark demerara sugar
15 g/½ oz mixed spice
scant 8 g/¼ oz ground nutmeg
2-3 pinches ground cloves
315 g/10 oz shredded beef suet
125 g/4 oz butter
1 orange, unpeeled, roughly chopped
1 lemon, unpeeled, roughly chopped
150 ml/¼ pint Guinness
6 tbls port or brandy
4 eggs, beaten
185 g/6 oz mixed glacé citrus peel
375 g/12 oz sultanas or seedless Californian raisins
250 g/8 oz currants
185 g/6 oz grated apple
250 g/8 oz treacle
caramel or flavourless browning for colouring
4-5 tbls Cognac or dark rum to serve

Mix together thoroughly the flour, bread-crumbs, sugar, spices and suet. Rub the butter in evenly.
Remove the pips from the orange and lemon. Put both fruits into a blender or food processor and work until they are puréed but with still some texture left in the peel. Stir into the mixture with the Guinness, port and brandy and eggs, adding a little extra liquid if using metric measurements. Add the peel, dried fruits, grated apple and treacle. Stir in a little caramel to darken, if you like.
Leave the mixture overnight in a cool place so that the moisture begins to plump out the dried fruits and the flavours begin to blend. Fill a suitable basin about three-quarters full, cover, then tie and place on a trivet in a large saucepan. Add hot water and cook for 2 hours per 500 g/1 lb weight of pudding. There is a school of thought which recommends that the cloth or foil should be changed if you are going to keep the pudding for a while. If you wish to do this, you must let the pudding cool completely and then chill it, for the moment you take off the covering you exchange sterile air for dirty air, and if moisture or condensation is trapped, the pudding will certainly develop mould. Generally, it is best to leave it alone and, if appearances matter, tie a clean piece of cloth or foil over the original cover.
To serve, boil the pudding for at least 30 minutes per 500 g/1 lb or longer. Remove the covering and run a knife around the inside edge of the basin and turn out the pudding on to a plate or platter that has a rim (which is important). Heat some Cognac or dark rum in a small saucepan and, when you can smell the fumes strongly, touch a flame to the fumes at the top of the saucepan; *do not* plunge your hand into the pan or you will burn it as the flames explode. Gently pour the flaming spirit on to the pudding little by little, tipping the plate to ensure that it continues to flow and flame. Carry the platter into the room (wearing oven gloves) and keep tilting it slightly to ensure a continuation of the show. To extinguish the flames, blow gently; a bigger blow will almost certainly result in a conflagration of the table, its contents and your guests! Cut the pudding in half and then into wedges.
Serve Christmas Pudding with a thin, Rich Custard Sauce (see page 19) rather than with brandy or rum butter which properly belong to mince pies.

GLYNN'S TIP

If you wish to revive the habit of placing a coin in the pudding, which symbolizes prosperity for the person lucky enough to find it, first sit the coin in household bleach for a few minutes to sterilize it, rinse it well, then wrap it securely in a small piece of greaseproof paper. Stir it into the mixture just before spooning into the bowls.

HOME BAKING

Don't let the campaigners for healthy eating put you off baking. Apart from the delicious smells wafting throughout the house, home-baked cakes, biscuits and bread are a touchstone of hospitality and welcome in a world where it is all too easy to buy shop-baked goodies. Here are just a few of my special favourites . . .

Not long ago a book such as this would have had long separate chapters on bread and yeast cookery, on biscuits and small cakes and on large cakes – and quite right, too. Almost the only way to get decent bread was to bake it yourself, and where did you buy croissants or brioche? Today, bakers are much more aware of the importance of wholegrain breads and, as well as offering a stunning variety of breads, even supermarkets now supply croissants and brioches. Nonetheless, it is immensely satisfying to bake yeast-raised goodies from time to time – pizza is probably the simplest – even if only for the gorgeous smell that permeates the house.

Home-makers and entertainers used to bake cakes and biscuits for more than the welcoming aroma. Sugar for 'energy' was how mums explained tins full of biscuits for the kids, and cakes were an accepted badge of a home cook's ability. Now we know that a diet with plenty of fresh fruit and vegetables gives children and adults all the sugar they need, and they will give them extra when needed, too. So, cakes and biscuits belong firmly in the realm of treats and long may they reign as such, for no family gathering or special tea, no picnic or party is complete without them. And when stretched budgets make gift-giving a problem, a batch of lovingly baked biscuits or a perfectly risen cake is much more appreciated than anything you can buy from a shop, edible or not.

I love cakes and biscuits of all kinds and no-one will ever convince me to stop eating them. As part of a varied diet they add excitement, offering rewards both to baker and eater, and what else makes a house smell quite so deliciously welcoming and comfortable?

A BREAD-MAKER'S PRIMER

Bread baking is not important to master because it's increasingly easy to buy good breads. Even so, there is a special earthy pleasure in knowing that you could, if you wished, produce perfect breads and fill the house with delicious baking smells.

Basic bread needs wheat flour, water, yeast and a little salt. The wheat must be of the type known as 'hard', which has a high protein or gluten content. When wet, gluten becomes very elastic, and as the yeast feeds on the starch of the flour, converting it into sugar and carbon dioxide, the gas stretches the gluten, causing the dough to rise. Salt helps prevent souring and improves flavour but is not essential. While these processes are under way, usually referred to as proving the yeast, other complex enzymic actions work on the dough and develop subtle changes of flavour. The longer and slower the process and the less yeast used to achieve it, the better the eventual flavour and texture of the dough.

Other liquids, such as milk or beer, can be used instead of the water, and butter, oil, eggs, flavourings or other grains can be added to alter the appearance and flavour of the bread, but the process remains that of simple, natural interactions.

Bread-making is spread over a number of hours, the more the better generally, but the time it expects your presence is negligible and bread-making can be fitted around any routine. Unlike cake mixtures or soufflés, a yeast dough can be speeded up, slowed down or postponed according to what you are doing. Kneading is the part of the yeast cookery that most worries the inexperienced; but it shouldn't. It requires balance and rhythm rather than strength. Anyway, there are some yeasted wholemeal and chemically raised breads which require no kneading.

Types of Flour
Wholemeal and wholewheat flours are made from 100 per cent of the wheat grain. Once you could have been certain that nothing had been added, but now they may contain improvers, so look at the label carefully before you buy.

Extraction flours Sometimes sold as **farmhouse** flour, these have had a proportion of the wheat fibre removed to make a lighter-looking and lighter-baking flour. The usual percentage removed is either 19 or 15 per cent, which give an 81 or 85 per cent flour respectively. These flours used to be called wheatmeal, but this is no longer a legal term.

White flours White flour, which is simply wholemeal flour with all the bran and fibre sieved away, is creamy yellow when freshly milled but gradually whitens if stored for some months. Manufacturers can't afford this prolonged storage and therefore bleach flour so that they can sell it more quickly. As part of the movement back to a more natural way of eating, unbleached white flour is now generally available; I think that the creamier colour of the bread it makes is reassuring. Any apparent difference in flavour between breads made with bleached and unbleached flours will be caused by the baking technique rather than the flours themselves. As long as you use strong white flour, you will get good results. A proportion of wholemeal flour adds nuttiness and texture to a white loaf. I often knead white dough with wholemeal flour and sprinkle the inside of the baking-tins with a little more.

Yeasts

There are three types of yeast available – fresh, dried and easy-mix. The first two must be mixed with a warm liquid to prove that they are active before being incorporated into a dough. Add a pinch of sugar when activating dried yeast but sugar inhibits the action of fresh yeast. Easy-mix yeast is a new product that is mixed directly into the dough.

For normal bread doughs, 15 g/½ oz of fresh yeast will leaven up to 1 kg/2 lb of flour but the larger the quantity of flour, the longer the yeast will take to enable the dough to rise. Add 7 g/ ¼ oz or equivalent of fresh yeast for every extra 500 g/1 lb of flour.

Weight for weight, dried yeast is twice as powerful as fresh yeast, so you use half as much. It has a reputation for making a drier loaf, which keeps less well than one made with fresh yeast, but this is because it is easy to use too much. If in doubt, always use less rather than more yeast.

Materials for Bread-Making

Barley Once used on its own for bread-making, barley contains little gluten so makes a very heavy loaf. Barley flour or pre-soaked grains added to a white or wholemeal dough give a deliciously sweet and nutty flavour.

Buckwheat This is actually the seeds of a grass and is better known for its use in the pancakes of Brittany or the United States. However, buckwheat flour adds a warm, homely flavour to dough that is very welcome with winter's hearty dishes. It contains no gluten of its own, so add no more than 20 per cent of the overall weight of the flour used.

Corn In Britain this used to be a generic word for all grains, including wheat, but it is now mainly used for maize. It contains no gluten and, therefore, will not make yeasted doughs on its own but adds a sweet flavour and a cake-like texture. Corn-meal breads and sticks are always leavened with chemicals.

Millet Sweet and bland, millet meal (which you can make in a blender or food processor) is an interesting addition to wholemeal and to white bread dough. As millet is a staple of northern China, such breads are good with the spicy Chinese dishes of this region.

Oats This gives crunch and flavour if used as a topping for bread or as a lining for bread-tins.

Potato The addition of thoroughly dried potato purée makes marvellous bread that keeps for ages. The simplest way to benefit from the effects of potato is to use the water in which you have cooked potatoes for making the dough. Alternatively, you can use up to equal quantities of flour and potato. You can use any leftover cooked potatoes but the best results require more attention to preparation. Boil potatoes in their skins until really soft, chop and place them over a very low heat to steam dry. Sieve out the skins and any lumps, and weigh. Use 125 g/4 oz potato prepared in this way to 500 g/1 lb of white flour; make the dough with milk rather than water and use the normal amount of yeast.

Rice Cooked rice, particularly if it has been allowed to sour, is a popular addition to 'healthy' breads, but rice flour gives a dry texture to dough and is not recommended.

Rye It is impossible to make bread with rye

flour alone but replacing up to 20 per cent of your normal flour with rye flour makes a delicious loaf with excellent keeping qualities.

Soya Flour made from the soya bean is an important way to enrich bread and its oil extends considerably the life of bread. Soy and soya flours add different flavours, for the latter is made from beans which have been toasted. Too much full-fat soya flour will make bread cake-like, so the maximum proportion I recommend is 60 g/2 oz to 500 g/1 lb.

Whole grains Malted grains are the simplest and most popular types. These have been soaked to start germination (which makes them naturally sweeter), then toasted. But you can do the same with whole wheat, cracked wheat, barley and other grains. Soak them overnight before adding to your dough.

Eggs Eggs enrich breads but they make the dough heavier. In my opinion, no more than 2 eggs per basic bread mixture should be added, unless you are making brioche.

Fats Any fat added to dough will make a loaf more cake-like but it will increase the lasting quality of the bread. Just a little makes a big difference, so to 1.5 kg/3 lb of flour add no more than 60 g/2 oz of butter or lard or 4 or 5 tablespoons of oil. Alternatively, up to a maximum of 20 per cent of the liquid required for most breads can be full-cream milk.

Fruit and Nuts Bread dough does not need to be sweet to have fruit and nuts added to it – far from it. Walnuts are the best addition to a mixed-flour dough and are often also accompanied by some raisins; the resulting bread is very good served with cheese.

Liquids Beer, orange juice, wine, cider and vinegar all turn up in bread recipes, so feel free to experiment.

WHOLEMEAL and OAT SODA BREAD

This recipe was sent to me from Dun Laighaire, County Dublin; it was the first one I had seen which used rolled oats in a soda-raised bread, and it's delicious.

750 g/1½ lb wholemeal stone-ground flour
250 g/8 oz plain white flour
185 g/6 oz rolled oats
4 tsps salt
4 tsps sugar
4 tsps baking-powder
600 ml/1 pint warmed milk
300 ml/½ pint water

Mix the dry ingredients in a large bowl. Add the milk and water to make a dough which will hold its shape for a few minutes before starting to spread. Working quickly, form the dough into a round shape, cut a cross over the top, then put it on to a floured baking-tray. Bake at 220°C/425°F/Gas Mark 7 for 35-40 minutes, and turn on to a wire rack to cool.

THE YEASTED WHITE LOAF

Makes one large or two small loaves

1 kg/2 lb strong white flour
2 tsps fine sea salt
15 g/½ oz fresh yeast or 7 g/¼ oz dried yeast with a pinch of sugar
450-600 ml/¾-1 pint warm water

Sift the flour and 1 teaspoon of salt together and warm it in the oven while you activate the yeast. Dissolve the yeast in a little of the warm water and stand in a warm place until it is frothing. Make a well in the warmed flour and strain the yeast mixture into it. Using your hands, slowly start to work in the rest of the warmed liquid with the remaining salt dissolved in it. Once the dough is starting to cling together and come away from the sides of the bowl it is time to start kneading. Use either a large, wide bowl or a warm work-surface. (Marble is the most unsuitable surface; wood is good provided that it is clean, dry and un-tainted.)

Rhythm is the secret of good kneading. This is how I do it, but you must find the order and method that suits you best. Start by picking up the far edge of the dough with both hands and folding it back towards you. When the dough is folded in half, push it forwards with the heels of both hands. As you pull at the far end again, turn the dough through a quarter or half turn (it can be clockwise or anti-clockwise) and then repeat the action.

That's all there is to it; once you get started, it is soothing and not hard work at all. Keep going until the outside of the dough is silky smooth (this should take about 10 minutes). If in doubt, continue for a little longer.

Place the dough in a lightly oiled bowl, turning it to oil it all over, then cover most of its top surface lightly with plastic wrap to prevent a crust from forming. Cover the bowl with a damp cloth and then wrap in a thick one and leave it in a warm place for about an hour, or 2-3 hours at room temperature. The dough should double in size. Do not leave it in a hot place, for this encourages the dough to rise too fast and gives a tough, dry bread.

Once the dough has risen, knead for a few minutes more to knock it back, or expel any air.

You now need to let the bread dough rise once more. The longer and slower the proving, the better the flavour and texture of the baked loaf. Knock back again, shape the dough and stand on a baking-sheet, or put it into lightly oiled and floured loaf-tins. Cover with a damp cloth and leave to rise until doubled in bulk once more. Bake at 230°C/450°F/Gas Mark 8 for 45-50 minutes for a single loaf and about 30-40 minutes for two small loaves. Reduce the heat a few degrees (to about 200°C/400°F/Gas Mark 6) after 15 minutes. Turn the loaves out of their tins and place directly on the oven shelf for the last 10 minutes to crisp. A cooked loaf will sound hollow when tapped with the knuckles.

Options

The mixture makes a good base in which to incorporate other flours; or you may mix in a little butter or lard (about 15-20 g/½-¾ oz), or use 1-2 tablespoons of milk to replace some of the water.

Ascorbic acid strengthens gluten, so if you add a little you can virtually omit the proving process. Crumble a 25 mg tablet of ascorbic acid (vitamin C) into the yeast liquid. Once the bread has been well kneaded, let it recover under a damp cloth for 10 minutes, then knead for further 5 minutes. Shape, leave it to double in bulk, then bake at the same temperature.

THE NO-KNEAD WHOLEMEAL LOAF

Also known as the Grant Loaf after the lady who popularized the recipe earlier this century, this is the recipe to start with if you are nervous about bread-making. The dough is marginally softer and wetter than you might expect, so do not be alarmed. For the lightest results, make three small loaves rather than one large one.

1.5 kg/3 lb wholemeal flour
30 g/1 oz fresh yeast or 15 g/½ oz dried yeast with a pinch of sugar
1.2 litres/2 pints lukewarm water
2-3 tsps muscovado sugar
4 tsps fine sea salt

Place the flour in a large bowl and put to warm in the oven while activating the yeast. Stir the yeast into about 150 ml/¼ pint of the water, cover, and leave in a warm place until frothing well. Dissolve the sugar and salt in the rest of the water.

Lightly oil or butter 3 × 1 litre/2 pint loaf-tins. When the yeast is frothy (about 15-20 minutes), sift the flour into a large mixing-bowl, make a well in the centre and pour in the two liquids. Mix well with a wooden spoon or by hand to obtain a pliable dough which leaves the sides of the bowl. Add a little extra water or flour if you think it necessary. Divide the dough between the tins, cover with a damp cloth and place in a warm place to rise – it should double in size, and, if you have used the recommended tin size, it will be above the top of the tin. (Unlike white bread, wholemeal bread does not rise much more in the oven.) Bake the loaves at 200°C/400°F/Gas Mark 6 for about 40 minutes. For a crisper crust, take the loaf out of the tin some 10 minutes before the end of the baking time and finish the baking directly on the oven shelf. A firm rap with the knuckles on the base of the loaf will sound hollow when the bread is cooked.

Options

A single loaf Use 500 g/1 lb of flour with up to 450 ml/¾ pint of warm water, 15 g/½ oz of fresh yeast, 1 teaspoon of sugar and 1 heaped teaspoon of salt.

Vitamin C Bread A 25 mg ascorbic acid or vitamin C tablet dissolved in the warm water with the yeast will strengthen the protein and give a better-than-average rise. Accordingly, you might also add up to 30 g/1 oz of butter, lard or margarine, which would make the loaf too heavy if a normal dough mixture is used.

Kibbled Wheat Bread To a 1.5 kg/3 lb mixture, add 2 cups of kibbled wheat which has been covered with 600 ml/1 pint of boiling water and left to get barely lukewarm. Dissolve 30 g/1 oz yeast in another 300 ml/½ pint of lukewarm water and, once the yeast is working, stir in 2 tablespoons of honey. This will make 2×20 cm/8 inch loaves.

Wheat 'n' White Bread The most popular mixed-flour bread is made from half wholemeal flour and half white flour. Such loaves can stand the addition of butter or the replacement of some 10-20 per cent of the water with milk.

Bran Bread Add 45 g/1½ oz of bran for every 500 g/1 lb of wholemeal flour and 1 scant teaspoon of molasses, honey or brown sugar to the mixing liquid. A vitamin C tablet would probably help to give a lighter loaf (see above).

Oatmeal Bread For every 500 g/1 lb of wholemeal flour, add about 125 g/4 oz of medium or coarse oatmeal and also, if you like, about 60 g/2 oz of toasted wheatgerm. The chewy sweetness of oatmeal bread is even better if you use a proportion of milk in the mixing liquid, or stir in a few tablespoons of skimmed-milk powder.

THE PIZZA

Pizza means pie in Italian but we generally think of it as squares or circles of bread dough covered with tomatoes and other goodies. At least, it should be dough, but it is as likely to be thin and crisp or a sort of scone mixture. Make this deep-dish real pizza for supper, or for a late-night filler for parties, and you'll never bother with other versions again.

Makes six to eight large pieces in a roasting-tin measuring about 30 × 23 cm/12 × 9 inches

500 g/1 lb strong white flour
30 g/1 oz fresh yeast or 15 g/½ oz dried yeast, with a pinch of sugar
300 ml/½ pint warm milk
good olive oil
TOPPING
397 g/14 oz can plum tomatoes
125 g/4 oz sliced Mozzarella cheese
16 small stoned black olives
salt and pepper
dried oregano to taste
good olive oil
8 anchovy fillets (optional)

Sift the flour and warm it in the oven while activating the yeast in a little of the warm milk. Make a dough and knead it well as for Yeasted White Loaf (see page 162). Smear a little olive oil all over, place it in a bowl covered with a damp cloth, and leave to prove in a warm place until the dough has doubled in size.

Lavishly bathe the inside of the roasting tin with olive oil (this is the most important part of pizza making and baking). Knock back the dough and use your knuckles to squash the dough evenly into the tray. It is an advantage if the olive oil gets worked into the dough and covers the top surface as you do so. Do not make the edges thicker than the centre – if anything, do the reverse.

To make the topping, take each of the whole tomatoes from the can and, after squashing them gently in your palm, arrange them evenly over the dough. Then pour on all the juice from the can. The Mozzarella slices must then be distributed over the dough but pushed under the tomatoes so that they are covered, or they will shrivel away during baking, wasting your money. Scatter on the olives, salt and pepper and oregano, then more olive oil. Arrange the anchovy fillets (if you are using them) evenly.

If your kitchen is warmish, the dough will already be starting to rise again, and if the edges are starting to swell, you can bake at once. If not, leave the prepared pizza just long enough for this to happen, then bake at 220°C/425°F/Gas Mark 7 for 20-30 minutes.

Options

Cheddar cheese has no real place on pizza – but if you do use it, slice rather than grate it and put it under the tomato as for the Mozzarella above; it will bubble through in places and brown. For more 'bite', scatter Parmesan on to the pizza half way through baking.

Onion lovers could cook two or more large chopped onions in olive oil until really soft and use that as a base for the tomatoes. If you want to use fresh tomatoes, peel and slice and add them to the cooked onions and heat through until they start to soften.

MONKEY BREAD

I'm puzzled over the derivation of the name of this bread recipe, which consists of lumps of dough separated by butter or other fat and baked together. The marvel is that you do not need to slice it because the pieces separate easily after baking. It is perfect for parties.

500 g/1 lb strong white or 85 per cent extraction flour
150 ml/¼ pint soured cream
150 ml/¼ pint warm water
15 g/½ oz fresh yeast or 2 tsps dried yeast with ½ tsp sugar
1 tsp salt
2 tsps sugar
90-125 g/3-4 oz butter, melted

Sift the flour into a large bowl and put this into the oven to warm while activating the yeast. Mix the soured cream and warm water, pour about a quarter of it into a small warm bowl and crumble the fresh yeast on top, or add the dried yeast and ½ teaspoon of sugar if using. Stir the salt and the 2 teaspoons of sugar into the rest of the diluted soured cream and keep warm. When the yeast is working and frothy, add it to the remaining liquid and stir into the warmed flour. Using your hands, mix to a dough which comes cleanly away from the bowl, adding extra flour or water as necessary. Knead thoroughly (see page 162) for about 8-10 minutes, until the texture becomes smooth and elastic, then return it to the bowl, cover with a damp cloth and let it rise in a warm, but not hot, place. Once the dough has doubled in bulk, turn it on to a lightly floured board and knock it back to its original size by kneading. Pat or roll it to about 1-2 cm/½-1 inch thick and cut it into shapes; squares, circles, triangles, about 5 cm/2 inches long. Generously grease a large ring-mould, or deep *gugelhopf* mould, with some of the melted butter; use more of the butter to brush the tops of the dough. Make a ring of the pieces of dough in the mould, building up layers and buttering each one generously. If you have any butter left, pour it over the top. Cover with a damp cloth and let the dough prove in a warm place for 15-20 minutes until risen, then bake at 200°C/400°F/Gas Mark 6 for about 30 minutes. Take care when turning the bread out of the tin, or you'll find yourself with lots of small pieces! Put a plate over the mould, hold tight, invert, then remove the tin gently. Ⓔ *Photographs, p. 78-9.*

Options

Use butter flavoured with lots of crushed garlic, with Italian seasoning (especially good served with Ratatouille), with cumin and coriander to accompany Indian dishes, with dill to serve with fish, with saffron to give a wonderful colour and extravagant touch to anything, or almost any other herb or spice alone or in a combination. Add grated strong cheese to the layers for an extra-savoury 'bite'.

Sprinkle the layers with lots of brown sugar mixed with cinnamon and chopped nuts for an excellent sweet version.

GLYNN'S TIP

Whatever flavour Monkey Bread you make, be sure to butter each layer generously or the pieces will stick together. You may think that it is swimming in fat when it goes into the oven, but all the butter will be absorbed while baking.

A CAKE-MAKER'S PRIMER

As long as a few basic rules are observed, anyone can make cakes successfully. The recipes which follow include the most popular styles of home-baked cakes and some special ones which I have discovered or created over the years.

Always preheat the oven and follow instructions carefully, but not rigidly. Ingredients, equipment and conditions vary and it is important to use common sense in judging the consistencies of mixtures and cooking times, adjusting them where necessary.

Always sift flour. Even so-called super-sifted flour needs sifting. The point is not to remove lumps, which are rarely found these days, but to aerate the mixture to give a lighter result. Sifting other dry ingredients with the flour helps to distribute them evenly throughout the cake.

Prepare the cake-tin correctly. Sponges require oiled and floured tins, and tins used for heavier mixtures should be lined. Cakes are easier to remove from springform or loose-bottomed tins. For cooks who worry about sinking centres in their cakes, ring-tins are the answer, for there are no centres! They also make slicing neater, give an ideal shape for 'drizzle' icing and look attractive when served filled with fresh fruits. If you choose a ring-tin, reduce the cooking time to compensate for the lesser density.

Always test for done-ness. Until you are familiar with a recipe and the length of cooking time needed in your oven, always test a cake to see if it is cooked through. A powerful smell from the oven usually indicates that it is time to test! Sponges will spring back when pressed lightly with a finger and will have shrunk away from the sides of the tin. Fruit cakes can be tested with a skewer, which should come out clean when inserted in the centre of the cake; listen to the cake by putting your ear close to it – if it is 'singing', it needs a little more time.

Allow cakes to rest. Always allow cakes to sit in the tin for a few minutes before turning out on to a wire rack to cool. Don't put cakes in storage tins until they are quite cold. Cakes which require maturing before eating, such as gingerbreads, should be wrapped in greaseproof paper or foil, not in plastic film or plastic bags.

SCONES

The important thing to remember when making scones is to have everything warm; the ingredients, bowl and baking-sheets should all be heated slightly; the oven should be preheated and very hot at 220°C/425°F/Gas Mark 7. Don't follow an exact recipe but cook them as I was taught:

For each large cup of sifted plain flour add 1 teaspoon of baking-powder, a pinch of salt and a little sugar. Warm through and mix quickly to a soft but not sloppy dough with warm milk in a warm bowl. Tip on to a warm surface, pat quickly into a neat shape a few inches thick without pressing the top (which would release the trapped air), cut the dough into squares with an extremely sharp knife.

The use of cutters is silly; it invariably ruins the scones by sealing the edges and preventing them from rising. Avoid handling the cut scones; transfer them to a warmed baking-sheet.

Bake for 15-20 minutes. Cool on a wire rack, covered with a cloth if you like them soft. Scones, like bread and rock cakes, should never be cut but pulled apart when they are cold. *Photograph, p. 152.*

Options
The inclusion of eggs or butter makes a mixture that keeps better but which is much heavier; the only flavouring is a few drops of vanilla essence which adds sweetness without having to use too much sugar.

For a mixture using 2 cups of flour . . .
Coconut Scones Add 6 tablespoons of desiccated coconut and a little extra milk; this is especially good if the coconut is lightly toasted.
Lemon Crisp Scones Mix together 1 teaspoon of lemon juice, 1 teaspoon of lemon rind and 4 tablespoons caster sugar; brush this mixture over the scones before baking.
Orange Raisin Scones Add 1 tablespoon of dried milk powder to the flour, and stir in 90 g/3 oz raisins. Make up the dough using the juice and finely grated rind of one orange, with sufficient milk to give a soft dough, plus 1 teaspoon of vanilla essence.
Fruit & Spice Scones Add finely grated rind from half an orange and half a lemon, ½ teaspoon each ground cinnamon, ground nutmeg and vanilla essence, with 90 g/3 oz chopped dates or dried apricots.
Cheese Scones Omit any sugar and add 90 g/3 oz finely grated strong Cheddar and sprinkle more over the top with a little hot or sweet paprika.

ROCK CAKES

Most of us enjoyed making rock cakes or buns as children, probably more than the unfortunate family and friends who were obliged to eat them, especially when they turned out to be aptly named. In fact, rock cakes are so called because of their rugged shape. They have many interesting variations and, if well made, are a welcome change from scones.

Makes about 18

250 g/8 oz self-raising flour
125 g/4 oz butter, or a mixture of butter and lard
90 g/3 oz caster sugar
90 g/3 oz currants or mixed dried fruit
1 egg, beaten with a pinch of salt
milk to mix

Sift the flour into a large bowl and rub in the fat until it resembles coarse breadcrumbs. Add the sugar and fruit; then stir in the beaten egg and just a little milk in order to give a very stiff dough. Put rocky heaps of the mixture on to a greased baking-sheet and bake at 200°C/400°F/Gas Mark 6 for about 15 minutes.

CUP CAKES

This is the most basic style of small cake but it has numerous variations. Cup cakes can be cooked in lightly greased patty-pan tins, but paper cases keep them more moist.

Makes 18 cakes

125 g/4 oz butter, softened
125 g/4 oz caster sugar
2 eggs
½ tsp vanilla essence
125 g/4 oz self-raising flour
pinch of salt
decoration (see below)

Cream the butter and sugar together until light and fluffy. Beat the eggs and vanilla until frothy, then add to the creamed mixture and beat again until well mixed. Sift the flour and salt and gently fold in, using a metal spoon, taking care not to overmix. Put about 2 teaspoons of the mixture into the paper cases, or greased tins, and bake at 190°C/375°F/Gas Mark 5 for 12-15 minutes.

Cool on a wire rack and decorate when cold; thin vanilla icing sprinkled with 'hundreds and thousands', or thick chocolate icing topped with silver balls are favourites with children of all ages.

Options
Chocolate Cup Cakes Dissolve 3 tablespoons of cocoa powder in 2 tablespoons of very hot water and beat with the eggs and vanilla. Sift 1 teaspoon of baking-powder with the flour. Decorate with melted dark chocolate and top with nuts.
Buckingham Cakes Omit the vanilla. Sift 1 teaspoon of ground ginger with the flour and stir 2 tablespoons of chopped stemmed ginger or ginger marmalade into the mixture at the end.
Golden Betty's Omit the vanilla. Warm 2 tablespoons of golden syrup and beat with the eggs: sift 2 teaspoons of ground ginger with the flour.
Nutty Cakes Stir 125 g/4 oz chopped nuts into the mixture at the end; use toasted hazelnuts, walnuts, pecans or mixed nuts.
Queen Cakes Omit the vanilla. Increase the amount of flour to 185 g/6 oz; beat the juice and finely grated rind of one lemon and 1 tablespoon of brandy with the eggs. Fold in 60 g/2 oz currants at the end.
English Madeleines Bake the mixture in very well greased dariole moulds. When cool, turn

out and coat with warmed, sieved apricot or raspberry jam and roll in desiccated coconut. Decorate with halves of glacé cherries.

Butterfly Cakes Make the basic mixture. When cold, slice off the top of each cake and cut that slice in half. Place a dab of whipped cream, butter cream or glacé icing on the cake and stick the two 'wings' into it at slight angles. The 'wings' can be further decorated with a drizzle of icing or jam, or dusted with sifted icing sugar.

ECCLES CAKES

This is one of my favourite cakes; I find the deep, dark, spicy filling in the buttery pastry case irresistible. If you haven't time to make flaky pastry, frozen puff pastry is almost as good.

Makes about 24

375 g/12 oz made weight puff pastry
FILLING
60 g/2 oz butter
125 g/4 oz soft brown sugar
250 g/8 oz currants
60 g/2 oz candied peel, chopped
1 tsp ground cinnamon
1/2 tsp ground nutmeg
grated rind of 1 orange
TO GLAZE
1 egg white
little caster sugar

Soften the butter, then mix in the rest of the filling ingredients. Roll out the pastry and cut into rounds about 8 cm/3½ inches diameter. Put 1 teaspoon of filling in the centre of each round and brush the edges of the pastry with water. Draw up the pastry to cover the filling and pinch together to seal well. Turn the parcel over and gently form into a neat, round shape. Lightly press with the rolling-pin to flatten, but don't roll too thinly (1 cm/½ inch deep).

Brush the tops with egg white and sprinkle with caster sugar. Transfer the cakes to a greased baking-sheet and bake at 220°C/425°F/ Gas Mark 7 for 10 minutes, then reduce the heat to 190°C/375°F/Gas Mark 5 and bake for a further 10 minutes, until golden brown. ℚ

MACAROONS

Depending on their size, macaroons make a delightful tea-time treat, ideal partners for ice-cream or dainty *petits fours*.

125 g/4 oz ground almonds
185 g/6 oz caster sugar
1 tsp rice flour
2 egg whites
few drops almond essence
split almonds to decorate

Mix together the ground almonds, sugar and rice flour in a bowl, then stir in the unbeaten egg whites and beat until well mixed. Add the almond essence and beat until blended.

Line two baking-sheets with non-stick silicone paper, or rice paper. Pipe or place teaspoons of the mixture on to the paper allowing plenty of room for spreading. Top with a piece of almond and bake at 170°C/325°F/Gas Mark 3 for 20-25 minutes or 10-15 minutes for tiny ones. Cool on a wire rack and store in an airtight container.

COCONUT MACAROONS

You will discover devotees of these cherry-topped pyramids among all age groups.

Makes about 20

3 egg whites
185 g/6 oz caster sugar
30 g/1 oz granulated sugar
250 g/8 oz desiccated coconut
glacé cherries (optional)

Line baking-sheets with non-stick silicone paper or rice paper.

Whisk the egg whites until stiff, then whisk in the caster sugar to make a meringue; gently fold in the granulated sugar and coconut. Spoon about 20 small mounds of the mixture on to the baking-sheets. With wetted fingers, gently draw up the mixture to make pyramid shapes and top each one with a piece of glacé cherry if you wish. Bake at 180°C/350°F/Gas Mark 4 for about 20 minutes. If you are using two baking-sheets, change their positions in the oven halfway through cooking. The macaroons should be slightly golden brown. Cool on a wire rack and store in an airtight tin. *Photograph, p. 152.*

ICED LIQUEUR BROWNIES

Makes nine

90 g/3 oz butter
90 g/3 oz plain chocolate
2 eggs
2 tbls orange liqueur or rum
1/2 tsp vanilla essence
250 g/8 oz granulated sugar
60 g/2 oz plain flour
FROSTING
60 g/2 oz softened butter
155 g/5 oz icing sugar, sifted
2 tbls orange liqueur or rum
GLAZE
30 g/1 oz plain chocolate
small knob of butter

Melt the butter and chocolate in a small pan over a very low heat, stirring until blended and

taking care not to overheat. Cool completely.

Beat the eggs with the liqueur, essence and sugar in a large bowl, using an electric mixer, until very thick and pale. Add the chocolate mixture and blend well. Sift the flour and fold in.

Transfer to a buttered 18 cm/7 inch square tin and spread the top level. Bake at 180°C/350°F/Gas Mark 4 for about 30 minutes, or until a knife inserted in the centre comes out clean and the mixture has shrunk away from the sides of the tin. Cool completely before frosting.

To prepare the frosting: beat the butter until light and fluffy, stir in the icing sugar and liqueur and beat until smooth and creamy. Spread over the cool brownies.

For the glaze: melt the chocolate and butter in a small pan over very low heat, or put in a bowl over a pan of barely simmering water. Drizzle the chocolate over the frosted brownies. Cut into 9 squares.

APRICOT SQUARES

Makes 16 squares

250 g/8 oz dried apricots, chopped
4 tbls lemon juice
155 g/5 oz plain flour
1/2 tsp baking-powder
pinch of salt
125 g/4 oz butter
90 g/3 oz soft brown sugar
125 g/4 oz rolled oats
60 g/2 oz walnuts, chopped
3 tbls honey

Generously grease one 20 cm/8 inch square tin.

Put the apricots and lemon juice with 2 tablespoons water in a small pan, cook gently until soft, then cool. Sift the flour and baking-powder with the salt into a bowl and rub in the butter. Add the sugar, oats and walnuts and mix well. Press half the oat mixture into the bottom of the prepared tin, then cover with the apricots. Warm the honey and pour over. Cover evenly with the remaining oat mixture.

Bake at 180°C/350°F/Gas Mark 4 for about 40 minutes. Allow the cake to get quite cold in the tin before cutting into squares.

Option
Date Squares Use dates intead of apricots, chopped and cooked in 4 tablespoons of orange juice. Omit the honey.

Streusel Fruit Bars

The unexpected flavour of bananas in these bars lifts them up out of the ordinary. Remember to store them in a cool place.

Makes 16-20 bars

185 g/6 oz dried fruits (apricots, peaches, pears or prunes), chopped
150 ml/¼ pint orange juice
1 tsp ground cinnamon
pinch of ground nutmeg
2 tsps ground ginger
2 ripe medium bananas, chopped
250 g/8 oz soft brown sugar
185 g/6 oz butter, softened
185 g/6 oz wholemeal flour
185 g/6 oz quick-cooking rolled oats

Grease a 33 × 23 cm/13 × 9 inch square tin.

In a small saucepan combine the chopped fruits, orange juice, cinnamon, nutmeg and ¼ teaspoon ginger. Simmer for 5 minutes, remove from the heat, stir in the bananas and cool. Beat the sugar and butter until light and fluffy, then stir in the flour, oats and remaining ginger. Reserve a quarter of the oat mixture for the top and press the remainder into the bottom of the prepared tin.

Bake at 200°C/400°F/Gas Mark 6 for 15 minutes. Spread the fruit mixture evenly over the warm base and sprinkle with the reserved oat mixture. Return to the oven and bake for a further 15-20 minutes until the top has browned. Allow the cake to cool in the tin, marking into bars while still warm.

Chocolate Afghans

These crunchy chocolate biscuits topped with chocolate and half a walnut were a firm childhood favourite of mine.

Makes about 24

90 g/3 oz cornflakes
185 g/6 oz butter
60 g/2 oz sugar
90 g/3 oz dark chocolate, melted
185 g/6 oz plain flour
1 tbls cocoa
TOPPING
125 g/4 oz chocolate
knob of butter
walnut halves

Put the cornflakes briefly into a low oven to ensure they are crisp and dry, then crush them fairly finely. Beat the butter and sugar together until light, then beat in the melted chocolate. Sift the flour and cocoa together and stir into the mixture. Finally add the crushed cornflakes.

Put generous teaspoons of the mixture on to greased baking sheets, allowing room for expan-sion and bake in the oven for 15 minutes at 180°C/350°F/Gas Mark 4. Allow the biscuits to cool for 10 minutes before removing them to a rack to cool completely.

To make the topping, melt the chocolate and beat in the butter. Drizzle a little on the top of each biscuit and top with a walnut half.

Ginger Crisps

These thin, crisp biscuits are essentially flat brandy snaps. If brandy snaps are what you want, roll them, while still warm, round the handle of a wooden spoon. They keep well in an airtight tin, but handle with care as they are rather fragile.

Makes 12

60 g/2 oz butter
60 g/2 oz golden syrup
60 g/2 oz soft brown sugar
60 g/2 oz plain flour
1 tsp ground ginger
1 heaped tsp grated lemon rind
1 tsp brandy

Line one Swiss roll tin or 30 cm/12 inch square baking-sheet with non-stick silicone paper.

In a large saucepan, gently melt the butter with the syrup and sugar. Stir in the flour, sifted with the ginger, then add the lemon rind and brandy. Spoon 4 generous teaspoons of the mixture on the prepared baking-tin or sheet, spacing them well apart. Flatten into circles using the back of a spoon. Bake one tin at a time, at 190°C/375°F/Gas Mark 5 for 8-10 minutes, until golden brown and gently bubbling all over. Cool for just 1 minute, then carefully lift off the paper. If you allow the non-stick silicone paper to cool down a little, you can re-use the same lined trays for the rest of the mixture. Cool on a wire rack, flat, or mould as described above.

Glynn's Tip

Warm Ginger Crisps can be moulded round the bottom of an inverted cup or glass to make an edible dish for such puddings as ice-cream or mousses. Also, they can be made large enough to mould around a basin to be filled with scoops of ice-cream or sorbet for a spectacular party dish.

If you have a microwave oven, it is a simple matter to warm cooled Ginger Crisps for 30 seconds and then mould them as you will.

Grantham Gingerbreads

I know of nothing quite like these biscuits, which are like a cross between meringues and gingernuts. The outside is crisp, the inside hollow.

Makes about 36

125 g/4 oz butter, softened
375 g/12 oz caster sugar
1 egg, beaten
280 g/9 oz self-raising flour
1½ tbls ground ginger

Grease several large baking sheets.

Beat the butter until very creamy and grad-ually add the sugar, beating until light. Add the egg and blend well, then sift the flour and ginger into the mixture and stir to form a soft dough.

Make into walnut-sized balls and place them on greased baking sheets, allowing 5-7.5 cm/2-3 inches between them for spreading. Bake at 170°C/325°F/Gas Mark 3 for 35-40 minutes. Cool on a wire rack and store in an airtight tin when quite cold.

Option

Use 220 g/7 oz flour sifted with 60 g/2 oz cocoa and 2 teaspoons cinnamon for a spicy, crunchy, chocolate biscuit.

Kisses

These dainty, melt-in-the-mouth biscuits are popular in Australia and New Zealand. They are ideal for the experimental cook as the options I've given can inspire a huge variety of flavours.

Makes about 12

125 g/4 oz butter, softened
125 g/4 oz caster sugar
2 eggs
125 g/4 oz plain flour
125 g/4 oz cornflour
1 tsp baking-powder
1 tsp vanilla essence

Grease several large baking sheets.

Cream the butter and sugar until light and fluffy, then beat in the eggs one at a time until well blended. Fold in the sifted dry ingredients and vanilla essence and place teaspoons of the mixture on the prepared baking sheets, allowing some room for spreading. Bake at 190°C/375°F/Gas Mark 5 for 10 minutes. Cool on a wire rack and, when cold, sandwich together with rasp-berry jam. Dust with sifted icing sugar before serving.

Options

Replace the vanilla with 2 teaspoons orange-flower water and sandwich the biscuits together with apricot or peach jam.

Add 1 teaspoon finely grated lemon rind to the mixture and sandwich the biscuits together with lemon curd.

Add 1 teaspoon instant coffee powder and 2 teaspoons cocoa powder dissolved in 1 tablespoon boiling water. Sandwich the biscuits together with chocolate icing or butter cream.

Add 60 g/2 oz flaked almonds to the mixture and sandwich the biscuits with apricot jam.

LAMINGTONS

Though little known in Britain, Lamingtons are more Australasian than Foster's lager and rival the Pavlova in popularity. You don't have to bake the sponge base yourself; most people 'Down Under' buy it.

Makes 24

CAKE BASE
*250 g/8 oz sugar
125 g/4 oz butter, softened
1 whole egg
1 egg yolk
1/2 tsp bicarbonate of soda
8 tbls milk
185 g/6 oz plain flour
1 tsp cream of tartar*
CHOCOLATE ICING
*60 g/2 oz butter
60 g/2 oz cocoa powder
6 tbls boiling water
375 g/12 oz icing sugar, sifted
few drops vanilla essence*
TO FINISH
250 g/8 oz desiccated coconut

To make the cake, beat half the sugar with the butter in a large bowl until light. In a separate bowl, beat the remaining sugar with the eggs, add to the butter mixture, and mix until blended. Dissolve the bicarbonate of soda in the milk and fold into the mixture alternately with the flour and cream of tartar sifted together. Transfer the mixture to a 30 × 20 cm/12 × 8 inch tin, greased and with the base lined, and bake at 180°C/350°F/Gas Mark 4 for 25-30 minutes. Allow the cake to get quite cold before cutting into 5 cm/2 inch squares.

To make the icing, warm the butter gently until just melted; dissolve the cocoa powder in the boiling water. Mix the two together in a large bowl then gradually stir in the icing sugar and vanilla essence and beat well.

Dip the squares of cake in the icing, which should be very liquid, and allow it to soak into the cake. Roll in coconut and leave the squares to dry on a wire rack.

Options
Split each square in half and fill with whipped cream. Instead of a chocolate syrup as the base of the icing, try using a fruit syrup – strawberry or raspberry flavour goes particularly well.

CRISP BISCUITS for DRINKS

These elegant biscuits are just right for handing round with drinks of any description when you feel like a change from olives, peanuts and other savoury nibbles. They are truly superb with a glass of champagne! But if your budget will only run to sherry, or a cup of tea, you'll still enjoy them.

Makes about 20

*125 g/4 oz plain flour
90 g/3 oz butter
60 g/2 oz icing sugar
30 g/1 oz ground almonds
1 egg yolk
1 tbls unsweetened spirit (Calvados, Marc, and Pernod work particularly well)*

Lightly grease several large baking-sheets. If you have a food processor, place the flour and butter in the bowl and process until crumbs are formed. Add the sugar and almonds and mix for a few seconds, then add the egg yolk and spirit and process for just long enough to form a dough. Wrap in plastic film and chill for 20 minutes before using.

If you are mixing by hand, rub the butter into the flour, stir in the sugar and almonds, then mix in the yolk and spirit with a fork until you have a soft dough – it will be a little sticky at this stage. Chill for 20 minutes before using.

After chilling, roll out on to a floured board, as thinly as you can without over-flouring and making the dough tough. Cut into fingers, or crescents, or any other shape you fancy. Transfer to the baking-sheets. Bake at 190°C/375°F/Gas Mark 5 for 5 minutes. Take care not to overcook the biscuits, or the flavour will be lost. Check them after 4 minutes; you may need to remove some of the biscuits close to the edges of the sheets which are already tinged with brown and return the rest for the last minute. Cool the biscuits on a wire rack and store them when quite cold in an airtight tin.

Options
Increase the ground almonds to 45 g/1½ oz and replace the spirit with 1½ tablespoons of orange-flower water, or with 1 tablespoon of rose water and ½ teaspoon orange-flower water.

FATLESS SPONGE

The absence of fat in this basic whisked cake means that it will not store well and is best eaten as soon as it is cool. Its slightly dry texture makes it ideal for desserts such as Trifle, when the cake is soaked with fruit juice or alcohol. It is lovely as a dessert filled with slightly softened ice-cream and served with a warm chocolate sauce.

*60 g/2 oz caster sugar
2 eggs
60 g/2 oz self-raising flour
1/4 tsp vanilla essence*

Grease and lightly flour two 15 cm/6 inch sandwich-tins, or one 20 cm/8 inch tin.

For best results, the ingredients should all be at room temperature.

Put the sugar and eggs into a bowl set over a pan of barely simmering water. Whisk the mixture until it is pale, fluffy and a clear trail is left on the surface when the whisk is lifted. Remove the bowl from the pan and continue to whisk until the mixture is cool; this is an important step, for if the flour is added to the warm mixture the result will be heavy.

Sift the flour once, then sift again over the egg mixture. Gently fold in the flour with a metal spoon, using a figure-of-eight movement. Don't overmix, or all the air laboriously beaten into the mixture will be lost. Add the vanilla as you finish folding in the flour. Divide the mixture between the two prepared tins (if used), level off the top and bake both (on the same shelf) at 180°C/350°F/Gas Mark 4. It will need 18-20 minutes if in two tins or 20-25 minutes for the single cake.

Even if you have made a single cake, it should be treated as a sandwich cake and split so that you can fill it with whipped cream, jam or fresh fruits.

Option
Grated orange or lemon rind or a generous tablespoon of cocoa or coffee powder can be added.

GLYNN'S TIP

If you are using a powerful tabletop mixer when making a fatless sponge, there is no need to beat the eggs and sugar over hot water; simply whisk until really thick and fluffy.

POUND CAKE

If well-made, the moist, mellow flavour of a Pound Cake does not need to be fussed about with very much. I think that a flavoured butter icing is better than a water icing, and specially like the contrast of a dark icing, say coffee- or praline-flavoured, with this creamy cake, or an orange, sharp lemon or lime icing, or one made with mashed bananas. With its richness, smooth texture and reliability, this is probably the best of all cake mixtures with which to experiment.

250 g/8 oz butter, softened
250 g/8 oz caster sugar
250 g/8 oz eggs (4 or 5), beaten
250 g/8 oz self-raising flour

Grease and base-line with lightly oiled grease-proof paper one 20 or 23 cm/8 or 9 inch round or springform tin.

Beat the butter in a large bowl, add the sugar and continue beating until light and fluffy — don't be tempted to skimp on this stage, which is important for a good result. Gradually add the eggs, beating until really smooth. If the mixture curdles while the eggs are being added, add a spoonful of flour. Sift the flour over the mixture and, using a metal spoon, fold in gently but thoroughly. The mixture should be a soft dropping consistency, requiring just a light shake to fall from the spoon.

Transfer the mixture to the prepared tin and bake at 160°C/325°F/Gas Mark 3 for 80-90 minutes. When cooked, the cake will spring back when pressed lightly with a finger and should have shrunk away from the sides of the tin; it should not 'sing' if held close to the ear. Cool for a few minutes before turning out on to a rack.

Options
Victoria Sandwich Make half the quantity given above and bake in two 18 cm/7 inch sponge-tins for 25-30 minutes. When quite cold, sandwich together with jam and dust the top with sifted icing sugar.
Madeira Cake Add the grated rind of a lemon to the creamed butter and sugar; put a slice or

two of citron peel on top of the cake before baking.
Seed Cake Add 3 teaspoons of caraway seeds with the flour, with 2 tablespoons of ground almonds. Add enough milk to give a soft dropping consistency.
Almond Cake Add 90 g/3 oz ground almonds with the flour, a ¼ teaspoon of almond essence with the beaten eggs, and enough milk to give a soft dropping consistency (1-2 tablespoons). Sprinkle the top with a few flaked almonds before baking.
Coconut Cake Reduce the amount of flour to 220 g/7 oz, add 90 g/3 oz desiccated coconut and enough milk to give a soft dropping consistency. This cake keeps particularly well.
Hazelnut and Chocolate Chip Cake Add 60 g/2 oz chocolate chips and 60 g/2 oz toasted chopped hazelnuts to the mixture.

FRESH FRUIT POUND CAKE

There are as many possibilities for this recipe as there are fresh fruits available. The most successful tins to use are springforms or rings. They should be well oiled and lightly dusted with flour, then with caster sugar.

250 g/8 oz butter, softened
250 g/8 oz caster sugar
250 g/8 oz eggs (4-5), beaten
125 g/4 oz potato flour
125 g/4 oz self-raising flour
1 tsp orange-flower water
1 tbls orange juice
finely grated rind of 1 orange
500 g/1 lb fresh fruit (see below)

Make the cake as for the basic Pound Cake (given above), sifting the flours together and adding the orange-flower water, juice and rind at the end.

Spoon the mixture into the prepared tin, then arrange fresh fruit on top: slices of apple or pear (not too thin), halved plums or apricots, medium slices of kiwifruit, pineapple slices, etc. Bake for 60-70 minutes, by which time the fruit will have sunk to the bottom of the cake. Allow the cake to cool slightly before turning out on to a rack. The cake is served upside down, fruit-side up, and dusted with sifted icing sugar.

If served warm, these cakes make remarkably good puddings served with a fruit sauce, thin, rich custard or thickly whipped cream.

FARMHOUSE FRUIT CAKE

Made by the simple 'rubbing-in' method, this is generally regarded as a midweek, economy cake. It will keep well for up to 2 weeks in an airtight tin.

125 g/4 oz butter
250 g/8 oz self-raising flour
125 g/4 oz granulated sugar
125 g/4 oz mixed dried fruit
2 eggs
1-2 tbls milk to mix

Grease and line one 15 cm/6 inch square or 750 g/1½ lb loaf-tin.

Cut up the butter and rub it into the flour until it resembles coarse breadcrumbs. Stir in the sugar and the dried fruit. Beat the eggs with 1 tablespoon of the milk and add to the dry ingredients, adding the extra milk, if needed, to give a stiff dropping consistency (that is, mixture which will drop reluctantly from a spoon if shaken). Take care not to overmix or the cake will have a tough crust.

Turn into the prepared tin and bake at 180°C/350°F/Gas Mark 4 for 50-60 minutes or until a skewer inserted in the middle of the cake comes out clean and the cake does not 'sing' if held close to the ear. Cool for a few minutes in the tin before turning out on to a wire rack.

Options
Wholemeal Farmhouse Cake Use half wholemeal and half white flour, with 2-3 tablespoons of milk to mix.
Honey Farmhouse Cake Replace 30 g/1 oz of the sugar with 1 tablespoon of warm honey, mixed with the eggs.
Raisin Farmhouse Cake Use all raisins and add the grated rind of 1 orange and 1 tablespoon of orange juice to replace the milk.

FRUIT LOAVES

These cakes, made by the 'soaking' method, have origins in the Irish bracks and Welsh bara briths, and are often served sliced and buttered. The soaking liquid is usually cold, milkless tea.

To get a good tea flavour you must use tea made with the proportion of 30 g/1 oz of tea to 600 ml/1 pint of water. Milk, strong cold coffee, ginger-ale, cider or beer also give reasonable results but there is nothing wrong with plumping up the fruit in plain water.

500 g/1 lb mixed dried fruit
220 g/7 oz soft brown sugar
300 ml/½ pint cold soaking liquid (see above)
1 egg, beaten
2 tbls chunky orange marmalade
500 g/1 lb self-raising flour
2 tsps ground cinnamon

Soak the fruit and sugar in the chosen liquid for several hours, preferably overnight. Grease and base-line one 1 kg/2 lb loaf-tin. Stir in the beaten egg, the marmalade, then the flour sifted with the cinnamon. Transfer to the prepared tin, level the top and bake at 180°C/350°F/Gas Mark 4 for 90-100 minutes (to test for doneness, see page 164).

Cool for a few minutes in the tin before turning out on to a wire rack. Serve sliced, with butter. *Photograph, p. 152.*

Options
Fruit and Ginger Loaf Soak the fruit in ginger-beer; use all sultanas or raisins and 1 teaspoon of ginger to replace the cinnamon.
Date Loaf Use half wholemeal and half white flour, sifted with 1 teaspoon of baking-powder and 1 teaspoon of cinnamon. Replace the fruit with 250 g/8 oz dates, chopped. Use demerara sugar, saving 2 tablespoons to sprinkle over the cake before baking. *Photograph, p. 152.*

CARDAMOM LOAF with CHOCOLATE and RAISINS

A sensational loaf that will disappear faster than anything else on the table, this recipe is recommended even to amateur bakers.

Makes a 1 kg/2 lb loaf

250 g/8 oz butter
250 g/8 oz golden granulated sugar
4 eggs (size 4)
440 g/14 oz self raising flour
seeds from 10 cardamom pods, crushed and ground
150 ml/¼ pint milk
125 g/4 oz dark chocolate (chopped into fairly large pieces)
90 g/3 oz raisins

Grease and base line a 1 kg/2 lb loaf tin. Cream the butter and sugar until light. Add the eggs one at a time, beating well between each addition. Stir in the flour and cardamom alternately with the milk, mixing well without overbeating. Stir in the chocolate and raisins. (The mixture will be stiff dropping consistency.) Spoon into the prepared tin and bake at 190°C/375°F/Gas Mark 5 for about 1 hour, covering with a sheet of greaseproof paper during the last 10 minutes or so if it looks too brown on top. Allow the loaf to cool in the tin for 10 minutes before turning out onto a wire tray. This cake improves for days and needs no icing. Its elegant, slender lines make it particularly suitable for serving with a fresh raspberry or other fruit sauce, and cream. *Photograph, p. 152.*

APRICOT BRAN LOAF

It is now accepted that a high fibre intake encourages better health, and this fact is reflected by the emergence of a number of cake recipes, which make use of whole ingredients.

185 g/6 oz light soft brown sugar
125 g/4 oz dried apricots, chopped
1 tbls runny honey
125 g/4 oz All-bran breakfast cereal
300 ml/½ pint milk
125 g/4 oz self-raising flour
½ tsp ground cinnamon

Soak the sugar, apricots, honey and breakfast cereal in the milk overnight. Grease and base-line one 500 g/1 lb loaf-tin.

Sift the flour and cinnamon, then stir into the fruit mixture. Transfer to the prepared tin and bake at 180°C/350°F/Gas Mark 4 for 1 hour. Cool for 5 minutes in the tin before turning out on to a wire rack. Serve sliced. *Photograph, p. 152.*

Option
Fig Bran Bread Replace the apricots with chopped dried figs; use only 90 g/3 oz soft brown sugar and 1 tablespoon of golden syrup instead of the honey.

NUT BREADS

The old-fashioned walnut bread is popular again as an accompaniment for cheese, and very good it is too. The oil in the nuts means that nut breads keep for a very long time and can be eaten without butter. The addition of raisins or even of cranberries makes a wonderful bread to serve hot with poultry and light meat dishes.

Makes a 25 cm/10 inch loaf

250 g/8 oz plain flour
4 tsps baking powder
½ tsp salt
1 egg
125 g/4 oz demerara sugar
155-185 g/5-6 oz walnuts, coarsely chopped
250 ml/8 fl oz milk
1½ tbls walnut oil

Butter the loaf tin well. Stir together the dry ingredients. Cream the egg and sugar well then mix in the dry ingredients and the nuts. Gradually add the milk to form a soft batter. Fold in the walnut oil and turn the mixture gently into the prepared loaf tin. Bake in the oven at 170°C/325°F/Gas Mark 3 for at least an hour (it may need up to 15 minutes extra) until a skewer inserted in the centre comes out clean. Turn on to a wire tray after 10 minutes resting and serve cold; it improves enormously if left for a few days.

Options
The flavour is more intense if the nuts you use are slightly toasted before use; this is especially true of pecans, hazelnuts and cashew nuts. In fact any nut can be used, even the simple peanut. Up to half can be replaced with raisins, currants and the like. The use of nut oil helps both flavour and keeping quality. If you have none use melted butter instead. I like a mixture of half white and half wholewheat flour for a change and have also added ground cinnamon – marvellous.

AUSTRALIAN SULTANA CAKE

Sultanas from Turkey, or Smyrna raisins as they were once called, are the sweetest and most syrupy of the dried vine fruits used in baking. Sultanas from other countries taste well and bake beautifully, of course, but try those from Turkey just once to see what I mean. Crushed pineapple is a favourite Australasian way of adding moisture to cakes.

155 g/5 oz butter
250 g/8 oz granulated sugar
500 g/1 lb sultanas
250 g/8 oz drained, canned, crushed pineapple
1 tsp bicarbonate of soda
2 eggs, beaten
280 g/9 oz self-raising flour
1 tsp ground mixed spice
good pinch of salt

Grease and line a 20 cm/8 inch tin. Put the butter, sugar, sultanas and pineapple into a saucepan, bring to the boil and simmer for 15 minutes. Remove from the heat, stir in the bicarbonate of soda (it will froth) and allow the mixture to get quite cold. Stir in the beaten eggs, then the flour sifted with the spice and a good pinch of salt. Transfer to the prepared tin and bake at 170°C/325°F/Gas Mark 3 for about 2 hours, until a skewer inserted in the middle comes out clean and the cake no longer 'sings' when held close to the ear. Cool for several minutes in the tin before turning out on to a wire rack. This cake improves if wrapped and kept airtight for two to three days before cutting.

ALL-IN-ONE CAKES

This one-stage method of making cakes is ideal if you have a mixer – or a strong arm and a wooden spoon! They can be very successful and do save time, but the important point to remember is not to overmix or the result will be tough and leathery. The method works for most creaming-method recipes, but I've found fruit cakes to be most successful. Remember to put the dry ingredients into the bowl first, so they are buried by the rest and do not fly all over the room once the mixing starts. Most recipes suggest using soft margarine, which certainly works, but even better, I think, would be the new spreads of butter blended with oil, which gives the moistness and flavour. But can anything really beat the flavour of butter in cakes?

QUICK FRUIT CAKE

250 g/8 oz self-raising flour
185 g/6 oz soft butter or margarine
185 g/6 oz soft brown sugar
3 eggs
1 tbls treacle or golden syrup
375 g/12 oz mixed dried fruit
60 g/2 oz glacé cherries, chopped
1½ tsps ground mixed spice

Put all the ingredients into a warm mixing bowl (flour first); beat on low speed until combined, then on medium speed for just a few seconds to blend thoroughly but DO NOT OVERMIX.

Transfer to a greased and lined 20 cm/8 inch round cake tin and bake at 170°C/325°F/Gas Mark 3 for 1¼-1½ hours or until a skewer inserted in the middle comes out clean and the cake does not 'sing' if held close to the ear.

DOWN-UNDER LEMON CAKE

This cake is quite expensive to make but it is truly a star of any table.

250 g/8 oz butter, softened
500 g/1 lb caster sugar
3 eggs, beaten
440 g/14 oz self-raising flour, sifted
175 ml/6 fl oz milk
grated rind of 2 lemons
2 tbls lemon juice
ICING
500 g/1 lb icing sugar
125 g/4 oz unsalted butter, softened
grated rind of 3 lemons
6 tbls lemon juice

Well grease one 23 cm/9 inch ring-tin or a 20 cm/8 inch square tin.

Cream the butter and sugar until very light, then beat in the eggs gradually. Gently stir in the sifted flour alternately with the milk, then add the lemon rind and juice. Spoon the mixture into the prepared tin and bake at 180°C/350°F/Gas Mark 4 for 60-70 minutes until golden, springy to touch and slightly shrunken around the edges.

While the cake is cooking, make the icing. Beat together the icing sugar and butter, and stir in the lemon rind and juice. Leave the cake to cool for 10 minutes in the tin, then turn it out on to a rack standing over a plate. Pour the icing over. Ⓢ *Photograph, p. 152.*

Decorate with crystallised violets and fine julienne strips of lemon or orange peel. (These should be blanched in 1 cm/½ inch of boiling water for 5 minutes, then immediately plunged into cold water to set the colour.)

THE BEST ORANGE CAKE

I published this recipe first over ten years ago and it was a great success. It's only drawback is that it must be kept for three days before cutting.

185 g/6 oz butter, softened
185 g/6 oz caster sugar
3 eggs, beaten
185 g/6 oz self-raising flour
1 tsp grated orange rind
2-3 tbls fresh orange juice
ICING
250 g/8 oz icing sugar
150 ml/¼ pint fresh orange juice
1 tbls orange liqueur or brandy (optional)
1 tsp grated orange rind

Grease one 18 cm/7 inch round tin or one 20 cm/8 inch ring-tin.

Cream the butter and sugar until light and fluffy, then gradually add the beaten eggs. Sift the flour over the mixture and fold it in gently. Add the grated orange rind and enough of the juice to give a soft, dropping consistency. Transfer to the prepared tin and bake at 180°C/350°F/Gas Mark 4 for about 1 hour. Cool for 10 minutes in the tin.

While the cake is cooling, prepare the icing. Sift the icing sugar and dissolve it in the orange juice and liqueur (if used); stir in the grated rind.

Turn the cake out on to a wire rack standing over a plate and using a knitting needle or very fine skewer, make holes all over the cake, then spoon on the icing. Retrieve the icing which collects on the plate and keep spooning it over until it has all been absorbed. When quite cold, wrap the cake in foil and keep it for three days in an airtight tin before cutting.

FESTIVE BANANA CAKE

There is no disguising the pungent smell and taste of bananas in this cake. It is a surprise to anyone who knows the more usual Banana Cake, which is rather dark and flecked with black – the result of including baking-soda. This one is pale and unfreckled.

185 g/6 oz butter, softened
280 g/9 oz caster sugar
3 eggs, beaten
3-4 ripe medium-sized bananas
3 tbls milk
1 tsp vanilla essence
375 g/12 oz plain flour
3 tsps baking-powder

Grease and lightly flour a 23-25 cm/9-10 inch round tin. Cream the butter and sugar together until light and fluffy. Gradually add the eggs and beat well. In a separate bowl, mash the bananas until frothy (using only really ripe, mottled-skinned fruit), then stir in the milk and vanilla essence. Sift the flour with the baking-powder and gently fold it alternately with the bananas into the creamed mixture, taking care not to overmix. Transfer the mixture to the prepared tin and bake at 160°C/325°F/Gas Mark 3 for 45-60 minutes depending on the depth of the tin. Cool for 10 minutes in the tin before turning out on to a wire rack.

Eat it just as it is, or emphasise the banana flavour by splitting the cake and filling it with a mixture of banana mashed with a little orange or lemon juice, and some whipped cream.

Option
Chocolate Iced Banana Cake Mash a ripe banana into 500 g/1 lb icing sugar, then gradually add softened butter (about 60 g/2 oz) until you have a spreading consistency. Add about 2 tablespoons cocoa powder to give a good chocolate colour (don't use drinking chocolate). Spread this icing over the top and sides of the cake, using the prongs of a fork.

OATMEAL GINGERBREAD

The oatmeal gives a marvellous texture to this variation on gingerbread from the Isle of Man. This cake improves for weeks.

60 g/2 oz butter
500 g/1 lb plain or wholemeal flour
125 g/4 oz medium oatmeal
60 g/2 oz muscovado or moist dark brown sugar
1 tsp ground ginger
¾ tsp bicarbonate of soda
1 tbls golden syrup
1-2 tbls treacle
1 egg
buttermilk or soured milk to mix

If you have no buttermilk, add a few drops of lemon juice to ordinary milk; or use 1 teaspoon baking-powder and ordinary milk.

To measure syrup and treacle without waste, place the saucepan on the scales, note the weight of the pan and measure the ingredients into it.

Grease a small roasting-tin or a 20 cm/8 inch square tin and line the base. Rub the butter into the flour and stir in the other dry ingredients, including the ginger and bicarbonate of soda. In a small pan, melt the syrup and treacle slightly, then beat the egg into it. Mix with the dry ingredients, adding buttermilk or soured milk to achieve a soft dropping consistency. Turn into the prepared tin and bake at 180°C/350°F/Gas Mark 4. It will take at least an hour and maybe up to 30 minutes longer, depending on your ingredients.

STEM GINGER CAKE

This is rather an up-market cake with a superior taste. It makes an excellent alternative to fruit cake at Christmas, or you might like to try making it in the New Year with any stem ginger left over from the festivities.

2 tbls golden syrup
2 tbls stem ginger syrup
3 eggs, beaten
185 g/6 oz butter, softened
185 g/6 oz caster sugar
250 g/8 oz self-raising flour
2 tsps ground ginger
30 g/1 oz ground almonds
60 g/2 oz stem ginger, chopped

Grease and line one 20 cm/8 inch square tin, or grease generously one 23 cm/9 inch ring-mould.

Warm the syrups slightly, and add to the beaten eggs. Cream the butter and sugar in a large bowl until light and fluffy, then gradually beat in the egg and syrup mixture until well blended. Sift the flour with the ginger and gently fold in, together with the ground almonds. Stir in the chopped ginger, taking care not to overmix. Transfer the mixture to the prepared tin and bake at 180°C/350°F/Gas Mark 4 for 50-60 minutes, or until springy to the touch and slightly shrunk. Allow to cool in the tin for a few minutes before turning out on to a wire rack. When cold, decorate with lemon icing and pieces of stem ginger or crystallized ginger.

CHOCOLATE PRALINE CAKE

This cake is an absolute winner and is better for being made in advance.

125 g/4 oz granulated sugar
125 g/4 oz hazelnuts
125 g/4 oz butter (unsalted)
220 g/7 oz chocolate
4 eggs, separated
2 tbls caster sugar
60 g/2 oz self-raising flour, sifted

Make praline with sugar and hazelnuts: Put nuts and sugar into a heavy bottomed pan and heat very gently *without stirring*, until the sugar melts. Increase the heat and cook until the mixture turns a good, rich brown, tossing the pan occasionally so that the nuts do not stick. Have ready a lightly oiled baking tray (or clean formica top) and tip the caramel nuts onto this in a thin layer. When cold and brittle crush with a rolling pin and either continue rolling until a fine powder or transfer to a food processor.

Melt the butter with the chocolate and beat until very smooth. Whisk the egg yolks with the caster sugar until pale and fluffy. Fold the praline into the chocolate mixture, then gently stir in the egg yolks and sugar, the flour and lastly the stiffly beaten egg whites. Transfer to a lined 25 cm/10 inch springform tin and bake at 180°C/350°F/Gas Mark 4 for about 30 minutes, until the cake has shrunken from the sides of the tin and springs back when pressed lightly with a finger. Cool in the tin for 10 minutes before turning out on to a wire tray to cool.
Photograph, p. 152.

OLD WORLD CHOCOLATE CAKE

175 g/6 oz butter
175 g/6 oz caster sugar
150 g/5 oz Bournville dark chocolate
juice of medium orange
1 tsp grated orange rind
2 tsps orange flower water
1 tsp rose water
5 medium sized eggs
75 g/3 oz ground almonds
50 g/2 oz cornflour
75 g/3 oz self raising flour
1 tsp ground cinnamon
100 g/4 oz ground almonds
100 g/4 oz icing sugar
1 egg yolk
1 tbls orange flower water
1/2-1 tsp ground cinnamon
3-4 tbls apricot jam

Grease and line 20 cm/8 inch square or 23 cm/9 inch round tin.

Cream butter and sugar well. Melt chocolate gently then stir in juice, orange rind, orange flower and rose water. Beat in eggs one at a time. Stir in the chocolate and then blend in the dry ingredients. Spoon into tin and level the surface. Bake at 160°C/325°F/Gas Mark 3 for 60-70 minutes and allow to cool 15 minutes before turning out onto rack.

Knead together marzipan ingredients, ensuring you have enough cinnamon to balance the sweetness. Cut the cold cake in half and brush the cut sides with warmed, sieved apricot jam. Roll out marzipan and cut to shape using the cake tin. Sandwich together. Leave for a day.
Photograph, p. 152.

PIERROT CAKE

WHITE BATTER
5 egg whites
250 g/8 oz caster sugar
125 g/4 oz butter, softened
250 g/8 oz plain flour
2 tsps baking-powder
4 tbls milk
1 tsp vanilla essence
CHOCOLATE BATTER
4 tbls golden syrup
4 tbls milk
60 g/2 oz cooking chocolate, broken
1 tbls coffee essence
1 tsp bicarbonate of soda
125 g/4 oz butter, softened
125 g/4 oz caster sugar
5 egg yolks
250 g/8 oz plain flour
2 tsps baking-powder
2 tbls cocoa powder

Grease and line a 23 cm/9 inch round tin. To make the white batter: make a meringue by whisking the egg whites until stiff and then whisking in half the sugar. In a large bowl, cream the butter with the remaining sugar until light and fluffy. Sift the dry ingredients together and add to the creamed mixture alternately with the milk and vanilla. Lastly, fold in the meringue.

To make the chocolate batter: in a saucepan, gently warm the syrup, milk, broken chocolate and coffee essence until melted and well mixed; stir in the bicarbonate of soda and allow the mixture to cool. Cream the butter with the sugar until light and fluffy, then gradually beat in the egg yolks. Sift the remaining dry ingredients together and add alternately with the cool chocolate batter.

Put alternate spoonfuls of the two mixtures into the prepared tin and very lightly fork together. Bake at 180°C/350°F/Gas Mark 4 for 60-70 minutes. Cool in the tin for 10 minutes before turning the cake out on to a wire rack.
Photograph, p. 152.

CHOCOLATE FUDGE CAKE

To the uninitiated or critical, the centre of this cake may seem uncooked. To others, the inside is like a fudgy-chocolate mousse – the chocoholic's dream! This is especially suitable for serving in wedges on a pool of raspberry purée as a dessert.

185 g/6 oz dark unsweetened chocolate
185 g/6 oz unsalted butter (preferably Normandy)
185 g/6 oz caster sugar
5 large eggs, separated
90 g/3 oz ground almonds or walnuts
60 g/2 oz plain flour
flavourings (see below)

Butter a deep 20 cm/8 inch or 25 cm/10 inch tin or two sandwich-tins of the same diameter and dust with cocoa powder.

Melt the chocolate in a bowl over a pan of hot but not boiling water. Slowly add the butter in small pieces until you have an unctuous combination of the two. (Be careful, as too much heat will over-thicken the mixture and you will have to start again.) Remove the mixing-bowl, stir in the sugar and let the mixture cool to room temperature. Beat in the egg yolks one by one, then the nuts and the flour. If you are happy to have a plain chocolate cake, carry on; otherwise, add a complementary flavouring (see below).

Whisk the egg whites until firm but not dry and fold them into the chocolate mixture. Ladle (*do not pour*) the mixture gently into the prepared tin(s) and bake at 180°C/350°F/Gas Mark 4 until the cake just begins to shrink away from the tin. It will take about 40 minutes in a 20 cm/8 inch single tin, 30-35 minutes in a 25 cm/10 inch tin, or about 25 minutes if you are using two sandwich-tins. Remember that the cake should remain a little moist in the middle and, as it cools and settles, a thicker moister layer will form. Let it rest in the tin for 10 minutes before turning out on to a cooling rack.

Options

Flavour the cake mixture with 1-2 tablespoons of either brandy, Cognac, whisky or black rum. Calvados and Crème de Menthe also work well but a larger quantity may be needed. Lashings of vanilla is delicious, but rose water is the most unusual and successful of all, particularly if the cake is to be served with raspberries.

The sandwiched version of this cake can remain unflavoured if you prefer, for you can flavour the filling or cream instead. Strained apricot jam folded into whipped cream is good, especially with a touch of Cognac, and you can never go wrong with raspberry jam on chocolate cake, preferably the more expensive seedless variety.

GRAND FRUIT CAKE

My Grand Fruit Cake was adapted from a wedding-cake recipe of Francatelli, one of Queen Victoria's famous chefs. It is moist and rather light in colour; the almonds and high fruit content keep it moist for months and the citrus and orange-flower flavours prevent it from being over-sweet and sickly. Use only the best ingredients and, whatever else you change, please don't cut down on the almonds.

This quantity makes about 2.5 kg/5 lb in weight. The quantity may be reduced for a smaller occasion, or increased for larger parties.

375 g/12 oz butter, softened
250 g/8 oz caster sugar
4 eggs, beaten
375 g/12 oz plain flour
½ tsp each of ground nutmeg and cinnamon
¼ tsp ground cloves
finely grated rind of 2 oranges and 1 lemon
500 g/1 lb currants
185 g/6 oz sultanas
185 g/6 oz mixed peel, chopped
125 g/4 oz glacé cherries, chopped
125 g/4 oz ground almonds
2 tbls orange-flower water
8 tbls brandy

Grease and double-line one 25 cm/10 inch tin. Wrap two layers of brown paper around the outside rising well above the cake tin. Tie with string.

Cream the butter and sugar until light and fluffy. Gradually add the beaten eggs, with a tablespoon of the flour if the mixture begins to curdle. Sift the flour with the spices and fold in, then add the fruit rind, the dried fruits, the ground almonds and the orange-flower water and brandy. The mixture should be a stiffish dropping consistency; adjust with extra liquid, if necessary.

Turn into the prepared tin, make a slight depression in the top so that the finished cake has a flat surface, bake at 150°C/300°F/Gas Mark 2 for 1 hour, then turn the oven down to 140°C/275°F/Gas Mark 1 and bake for a further 1½-2 hours. It is done when a skewer inserted in the centre comes out clean and the cake does not 'sing' when held close to the ear. Cool in the tin before turning out.

Once the cake is cool, remove the papers and

> ### GLYNN'S TIP
> *When calculating the size of a rich fruit cake required for special occasions remember that 500 g/1 lb of mixture will serve eight.*

> ### GLYNN'S TIP
> *Rich fruit cakes need a few weeks in which to mature before you ice them. During this time it is a good idea to 'feed' them with extra flavour and moisture, either alcohol or mixtures of fruit juices, alcohols and flower waters.*

skewer it fairly thoroughly from top to bottom. Line the cleaned baking-tin with fresh grease-proof paper and replace the cake. Spoon on the equivalent of 1 tablespoon of soaking liquid per 500 g/1 lb of cake, and use the back of a spoon to encourage the liquid to soak in. I turn the cake over every 4 or 5 days and repeat the operation in reverse. It is amazing how much liquid this cake can take, and this all helps both its keeping qualities and moisture content. My favourite mixture is of Cognac and orange-flower water to enhance what is already there, or half Cognac and half of any orange liqueur; I find the sharp but less commonly found Triple Sec gives the best results.

Home-made marzipan, again flavoured with orange-flower water, should be used to cover the cake and when that is dry use Royal icing to complete it. You can now buy ready-made icing that you roll out and apply, then smooth down with the palms of the hands (slightly damp).

CAKE ICINGS

ROYAL ICING

This durable icing is hard, pipes well and helps to keep the cake and almond paste moist underneath. The amounts needed to give two thin coats of icing are shown below; allow extra for elaborate decoration. It is most important to allow the icing to stand, covered, for a few hours before adding the final amount of icing sugar.

18 cm/7 inch square: 20 cm/8 inch round:
750 g/1½ lb icing sugar
20 cm/8 inch square: 23 cm/9 inch round:
900 g/2 lb icing sugar
23 cm/9 inch square: 25 cm/10 inch round:
1 kg/2¼ lb icing sugar
25 cm/10 inch square: 28 cm/11 inch round:
1.2 kg/2½ lb icing sugar
28 cm/11 inch square: 30 cm/12 inch round:
1.4 kg/3 lb icing sugar

For each 500 g/1 lb icing sugar, stir 2 large egg whites in a bowl to break them up lightly without incorporating air bubbles. Sift the icing sugar twice and fold half of it into the egg whites, stirring until it is well mixed. Cover the bowl with a clean damp teatowel and allow to stand for at least 1 hour so that the air bubbles rise to the surface. Gradually stir in the remaining icing sugar until the desired consistency is achieved. For rough icing it should form stiff peaks, for a flat coating a wooden spoon should stand upright for a few seconds before slowly falling over. If possible, cover and leave the icing for 24 hours before serving.

If the icing has slackened too much while resting, beat in a little extra sugar. If it seems a little stiff, take a spoonful of it and stir in a teaspoon of water then mix with the rest until smooth.

If you prefer a slightly softer icing, add 2 teaspoons of glycerine for every 500 g/1 lb icing sugar.

A simple but attractive effect can be achieved by tinting half the icing pale green, pink or blue, then covering the cake randomly with the white and coloured icings before swirling and peaking using two forks.

GLACE ICING

This quantity is sufficient to cover the top of an 18 cm/7 inch-20 cm/8 inch cake. Use double quantity if you want to ice the sides as well.

185 g/6 oz icing sugar, sifted
3 tbls warm water or syrup made with equal
quantities of golden syrup and water
few drops of food colouring (optional)

Put the icing sugar into a bowl and gradually beat in the warm water or syrup until the icing is smooth and coats the back of the spoon. Spoon over the cake and spread evenly using a palette knife dipped in a jug of hot water. To coat the sides as well, stand the cake on the base of an upturned plate and have the icing soft enough to run down without too much use of the palette knife. Pour about three-quarters of the icing over the cake and use the remainder to fill any gaps.

Warm water makes a quick and easy icing; the addition of golden syrup gives an extra gloss and softer texture.

Options

Chocolate Icing Add 30 g/1 oz melted dark chocolate to the finished icing, *or* dissolve 1 tablespoon of cocoa powder in a little of the hot water or syrup. Glazing the cake with a little apricot jam, sieved and warmed, before icing gives an extra glossiness and improved flavour.
Coffee Icing Add 2 teaspoons coffee essence to the sifted sugar before the water or syrup, *or* dissolve 1 tablespoon of coffee granules in a little of the hot water or syrup.
Mocha icing Melt 20 g/¾ oz dark chocolate with 1 or 2 teaspoons of coffee essence and add to the finished icing, *or* dissolve ½ tablespoon

coffee granules and 1 teaspoon cocoa powder in a little of the hot water or syrup.
Orange or Lemon Icing Warm 1 or 2 tablespoons of orange or lemon juice and add to the sifted icing sugar before the warm water or syrup. A combination of the two juices is good, as is lime juice, and in this case you may like to tint the icing a very pale green.

AMERICAN FROSTING

American frosting which doesn't require a sugar thermometer to make it successfully is usually called 'Seven Minute Frosting' or 'Eight Minute Frosting' depending on the power of the electric or rotary whisk being used. You can probably achieve a good result in 5 or 6 minutes; be sure the peaks are really stiff and the icing is a good spreading consistency.

This quantity is sufficient to fill and frost a
20 cm/8 inch cake

375 g/12 oz caster sugar
2 egg whites
¼ tsp cream of tartar
4-5 tbls cold water
1 tsp vanilla essence

Put the sugar, egg whites, cream of tartar and water into a bowl and set over a pan of simmering water. Beat until stiff peaks form, which will take anything from 4 to 8 minutes. Remove from the heat, add the vanilla and beat until the frosting is a good spreading consistency.

Options

Orange or Lemon Frosting Replace some or all of the water with orange or lemon juice.
Coffee Use half soft brown sugar and half caster sugar and *either* replace 1 tablespoon of the water with coffee essence, *or* dissolve a heaped tablespoon of coffee granules in a little of the water.
Chocolate Make the basic vanilla frosting then stir in 30 g/1 oz melted dark chocolate before using.
Nut Add 2 or 3 tablespoons of finely chopped toasted nuts to the basic frosting.
Rock Candy Frosting Replace the vanilla essence with ½ teaspoon peppermint essence, tint the frosting pale pink and stir in 60-90 g/2-3 oz crushed peppermint rock before using.
Coconut Frosting Tint the basic frosting pale green and stir in 60 g/2 oz lightly toasted desiccated coconut.

BUTTER CREAM

The following amount is sufficient to cover the top and sides of an 18 cm/7 inch cake, or to cover the top and fill. For a 23 cm/9 inch cake, filled and iced all over, double the quantities given.

125 g/4 oz butter, softened
250 g/8 oz icing sugar, sifted
2-3 tbls single cream or milk
1 tsp vanilla essence or other flavouring
salt (optional)

Beat the butter until light, then gradually beat in the icing sugar, adding a little of the cream or milk as you go. Mix in the vanilla or other flavouring and taste; you may like to add a little salt depending on the butter used. The icing should be a good spreading consistency – add a little more cream or milk if it is too stiff.

Options

Chocolate Melt 30 g/1 oz dark chocolate and beat into the butter before adding the sugar, *or* dissolve 1 tablespoon of cocoa powder in a little warm water and substitute for the same amount of cream or milk.
Coffee Beat 1 tablespoon of coffee essence with the butter before adding the sugar, *or* dissolve 1 tablespoon of coffee granules in a little warm water and substitute for the same amount of cream or milk.
Mocha Melt 20 g/¾ oz dark chocolate with 2 teaspoons coffee essence and beat into the butter before adding the sugar, *or* dissolve 1 teaspoon cocoa powder and 2 teaspoons coffee granules in a little warm water and substitute for the same amount of cream or milk.
Nut Beat 2 or 3 tablespoons of finely-chopped toasted nuts into the butter cream before using. Hazelnuts and almonds are both very good, as are pecans or walnuts.
Orange or Lemon Beat 1 or 2 teaspoons of very finely grated rind in with the butter and use half orange or lemon juice to replace the same amount of cream or milk. It is important to beat this butter cream very well or it may curdle.

See also the Banana Chocolate icing used on the Festive Banana Cake on page 170.

JAMS and PRESERVES

Preserving is one aspect of cooking where the rewards come quickly and last long. Little equals the sense of achievement in producing jars of jam, glowing with jewel colours, or bottles of perfect pickles which invite the admiration of guests.

More and more people are experimenting with jam-making, bottling, pickling, even drying and salting, methods which are centuries old and were developed to allow cooks flexibility in using foods both in and out of season.

Much of the credit for this growing interest is due to the proliferation of pick-your-own farms and market-gardens. The great advantage when picking your own is that you can select fruit or vegetables in perfect condition for preserving: that is, undamaged and slightly under-ripe. This is probably the single most important point to bear in mind when choosing produce for preserving, whether from a farm, a super-market or your own garden.

Equipment

A preserving pan (maslin) is not essential, although if you are going to make a lot of jams and pickles it is well worth investing in one. Any large, heavy-based pan will do – the only proviso is that it should have a large surface area to enable unwanted water to steam off rapidly.

Unless you have a very steady pouring arm, you will find that a funnel is useful and the least wasteful way to fill jars. For bottling, proper Kilner or Continental preserving jars are essential; they should be clean, undamaged and have new seals. Jams can be stored in any glass jar, with waxed discs and paper seals. However, modern houses usually don't have cold pantries or larders, and if the jam is going to be stored in a warm place it is safer to use screw-top jars. Wash and keep all the empty jars you buy; you'll soon build up enough for your needs. Take a tip from gift shops and cut out circles of gingham or pretty floral cloth to cover the jars; they make perfect presents – if you can bear to part with them.

LEMON CURD

Curds are made from eggs and butter and are not intended to keep for longer than a week or two in the refrigerator. For this reason, the amount made at one time shouldn't fill more than a couple of jars. The texture should be like velvety honey. If you are not expert at judging egg-thickened goodies, it is better to undercook than overcook, otherwise curd becomes curdle! The following recipe is the best known of all.

Makes about 750 g/1½ lb

3 lemons
185 g/6 oz unsalted butter
375 g/12 oz sugar
3 large eggs, well beaten

Finely grate the lemon rind directly into the top of a double saucepan (or a basin that will fit into a saucepan), then squeeze out all the juice, strain and add with the butter and sugar. Set over simmering water. Cook gently, stirring, until the sugar dissolves. Remove from the heat and strain in the beaten eggs. Return to a low heat and stir continuously until the mixture thickens. You may strain out the peel. Pour into warmed jars, cover and label. Store in the refrigerator.

Options

Lime, orange and grapefruit all make admirable curds, but there are some mixtures which are less well known but even better, especially the first:
Blackberry Curd Cook, purée and sieve 500 g/1 lb of blackberries and cook and purée 125 g/4 oz of sharp, peeled and cored apples. Mix together the purées with the sugar and then proceed as above. You can also include the juice and rind of a lemon or orange for flavour.
Lime Curd You'll need the grated rind and juice of 250 g/8 oz of fresh green limes, 185 g/6 oz of sugar, 60 g/2 oz of butter and 2 eggs or 4 egg yolks.
Apple and Lemon Curd Simmer 500 g/1 lb peeled and cored cooking apples with the grated rind of 2 lemons and 4 tablespoons of water until reduced to a pulp, then sieve or purée in a blender. Add the juice of the 2 lemons, 500 g/1 lb of sugar and heat very gently, stirring, until the sugar has dissolved, then remove from the heat. Beat 4 eggs and strain them into the mixture, then add 155 g/5 oz of unsalted butter. Cook over very low heat, stirring, until the mixture is thick and creamy. Pour into warmed jars, cover and label.
Orange and Lemon Curd Use 1 lemon, 1 orange, 155 g/5 oz of unsalted butter and 2 eggs. Follow the basic recipe.

FRUIT BUTTERS and CHEESES

These are soft, often spicy, spreads which are made from fruit pulp. Butters are usually spread on cake-like breads or scones; cheeses are harder and can be cut into wedges to be served with biscuits, scones or slices of cake. They are the perfect solution to using up a glut of fruit in the autumn. Both butters and cheeses rely on a certain amount of caramelizing of the sugar which darkens the colour.
Fruit Butters Cook such fruit as apples, pears or plums in just enough water to cover until softened, and strain to make a purée. Measure the volume of the purée. To each 500 g/1 lb of fruit pulp add 375 g/12 oz sugar. Cook gently, stirring regularly, until the mixture looks like a custard or thick cream. Pour into warmed jars and seal with metal lids. Once opened, keep in the refrigerator.

Fruit Cheeses To each 500 g/1 lb of fruit pulp (blackberries, plums and quinces are good) add 375 g/12 oz of sugar and heat gently to dissolve. Continue to cook, stirring occasionally, over a low heat until the mixture is so thick that the wooden spoon drawn through the mixture will leave a clear channel. You must be extremely careful when cooking this, for it is so concentrated that it burns very easily. Pour the mixture into very lightly greased moulds, such as ramekins, and unmould the cheese to serve.

JAM PREPARATION PRIMER

The most important, and potentially the most difficult, aspect of successful jam-making is achieving a good set. This depends upon the amount of sugar added plus the pectin and acid content of the fruit. Jam sugars are available which have added citric acid and apple pectin, in a formula which the makers recommend for use in low-pectin fruits such as strawberries, blackberries and cherries. Used with unsweetened fruit juice, it makes fruit jelly after just one minute's boiling.

Helpful though this will be, it is not necessary to pay almost double the price for this special sugar, provided you follow the rules given below, adding lemon juice or commercial pectin (or both) where necessary. Granulated or preserving sugar can be used for jam making. Caster sugar and, to a lesser extent, ordinary granulated sugar are both slightly more tricky than large crystals of preserving sugar, tending to form a heavy, sand-like mass at the bottom of the pan, which is more difficult to dissolve.

FRUIT FOR JAM-MAKING: GUIDE TO PROPORTIONS AND TIMING

NAME	AMOUNT	WATER	SUGAR	SIMMERING	BOILING	YIELD	EXTRAS
Apple and Ginger	1.5 kg/3 lb	600 ml/1 pint	1.5 kg/3 lb	30 mins	20 mins	2.5 kg/5 lb	1½ level tsps ground ginger; grated rind and juice of 2 lemons
Apple and Pineapple	1.5 kg/3 lb (apples)		1.5 kg/3 lb	30 mins	20 mins	2.75 kg/5½ lb	600 ml/1 pint pineapple juice (unsweetened); grated rind and juice of 1 lemon; 250 g/8 oz crushed pineapple
Apricot (fresh)	1.5 kg/3 lb	600 ml/1 pint	1.5 kg/3 lb	20 mins	20 mins	2.5 kg/5 lb	blanched kernels from stones (optional)
Apricot (dried)	500 g/1 lb	1.75 litres/3 pints	1.5 kg/3 lb	30 mins	20 mins	2.5 kg/5 lb	90 g/3 oz blanched almonds; juice of 1 lemon
Blackberry	1.5 kg/3 lb	5 tbls	1.5 kg/3 lb	10 mins	15 mins	2.5 kg/5 lb	juice of 2 lemons or 150 ml/¼ pint liquid pectin
Blackberry and Apple	500 g/1 lb (blackberries) 1 kg/2 lb (apples)	600 ml/1 pint	1.5 kg/3 lb	20 mins	20 mins	2.5 kg/5 lb	juice of 1 lemon
Blackcurrant	1 kg/2 lb	900 ml/1½ pints	1.5 kg/3 lb	30 mins	10 mins	2.5 kg/5 lb	
Damson	1 kg/2 lb	450 ml/¾ pint	1.25 kg/2½ lb	20 mins	10 mins	2 kg/4 lb	
Gooseberry	1.25 kg/2½ lb	450 ml/¾ pint	1.5 kg/3 lb	30 mins	10 mins	2.5 kg/5 lb	
Gooseberry and Orange	1.5 kg/3 lb	300 ml/½ pint	1.5 kg/3 lb	30 mins	10-15 mins	2.5 kg/5 lb	grated rind and juice of 2 oranges
Plum	1.5 kg/3 lb	300 ml/½ pint	1.5 kg/3 lb	15 mins	15 mins	2.5 kg/5 lb	
Raspberry	1.5 kg/3 lb		1.5 kg/3 lb	15 mins	5 mins	2.5 kg/5 lb	
Rhubarb and Orange	1 kg/2 lb		1 kg/2 lb	10 mins	5 mins	2 kg/4 lb	rind and juice of 3 oranges and ½ lemon
Strawberry	1.75 kg/3½ lb		1.5 kg/3 lb	15 mins	10-15 mins	2.5 kg/5 lb	juice of 1 lemon
Strawberry and Gooseberry	1.5 kg/3 lb (strawberries) 250 g/8 oz (gooseberries)	300 ml/½ pint	1.5 kg/3 lb	15 mins	10 mins	2.5 kg/5 lb	

Acidity Lemon juice should be added to such fruits as strawberries or pears which are naturally low in acidity. As well as helping the jam to set, by releasing the pectin present in the fruit, it will help prevent crystallization and will also give the jam a good colour. As a general rule, allow the juice of one lemon for every 2 kg/4 lb of fruit; for low pectin soft fruits use the juice of 1 lemon to 500 g/1 lb.

Pectin test If the pectin level of the fruit is high enough, adjusted either with commercial liquid pectin or by adding high-pectin fruit such as cooking apples or gooseberries, there should be no difficulty in achieving a good set.

Take 1 teaspoon of the juice from the softened fruit before the sugar is added. Put it in a clean, clear glass and add 1 tablespoon of methylated spirits. Shake gently, and if there is very little clotting, the pectin level is low; if there are medium-sized clots, it is medium; if one large clot forms, the pectin level is high. Add either pectin or lemon juice and test again.

Preparing the jam Choose fruit which is just ripe or slightly under-ripe, never bruised or over-ripe. Weigh the fruit and calculate the amount of sugar required (see individual recipes). Don't try to make too much jam at once; as a rule, 1.5 kg/3 lb of fruit is a manageable amount, anything over 3 kg/6 lb should be split into batches.

Warm the sugar in a low oven – this helps it to dissolve more quickly. It's a good idea to wash the jam-jars and dry them in the oven at the same time.

Put the fruit with the lemon juice and water, if needed, into the pan and simmer, covered, until soft.

Remove the stones from plums, damsons, greengages etc. which will have floated to the surface with a slotted spoon. Check the pectin level of the fruit. If commercial pectin is needed, it should be added at this stage.

With the pan over a low heat, add the sugar and keep stirring until the sugar has completely dissolved. This is important, as any undissolved sugar will cause crystallization in the jam. Stir in a knob of butter; this makes the jam clear and bright and also helps prevent scum from forming.

When you are sure that all the sugar has dissolved, increase the heat and bring the jam to a rapid, rolling boil. Boil, uncovered, until the setting-point is reached. The chart and individual recipes give an indication of how long this will take, although the size of the pan and amount of jam being made will cause some variations.

To test for a set Put a saucer into the refrigerator. When you think that the jam is ready, put 1 teaspoon of it on to the saucer. (While you wait for it to cool, take the pan off the heat or you may over-boil the jam.) When cool, push the surface of the jam in the saucer with a finger; it should crinkle, and a channel made across the bottom of the saucer should remain visible, with the sides staying apart.

If the jam has not reached setting-point, continue to boil it for a few more minutes. Give it an occasional stir with a wooden spoon to prevent it from sticking on the bottom, but don't overdo it or you will delay the setting-point being reached.

When the setting-point is reached, remove any scum with a slotted spoon, then allow the jam to cool for 10-15 minutes. This is especially important with whole fruit jam, as it helps to prevent the fruit from rising in the jar and also ensures a more even distribution of fruit.

Ladle, or pour, the jam into the warmed jars, filling them to within 3 mm/⅛ inch of the rim. It is important to minimize the air between the top of the jam and the lid, in order to prevent a mould from forming. If you are using paper covers, put a wax disc on top of the jam immediately. These discs prevent mould from forming. If you are using metal lids, cut circles of greaseproof paper and put these on top of the hot jam. For each jar, dampen a cellophane cover on one side and stretch it over the rim, then secure with a rubber band. If using jars with metal lids, screw these on when the jam is cold. Clean the jars, label and store.

GLYNN'S TIP

Conserve is the name given to a soft, syrupy jam which is produced mainly from low-pectin fruits, such as cherries, pears and strawberries. Often the fruit is allowed to marinate overnight with the sugar. It is easy to make because you do not need to worry about setting.

JELLY PREPARATION PRIMER

The principles of jelly-making are broadly the same as for jam, but the rules are different and important to follow if you want a clear, sparkling and flavoursome jelly. Jellies made from wild fruits are my particular favourites to make and to give as gifts. They are always sharper in flavour than the commercial jellies, and are wonderful served with game, poultry or cold meats. They can also play an important part in finishing and balancing gravies and sauces too.

Fruits rich in pectin make the best jellies, particularly those with a distinctive flavour such as redcurrants, quinces and crab-apples; old favourites are hard to beat. Hedgerow fruits are also good for jelly-making; rowan-berries, mulberries, medlars, hips and haws are all suitable.

Use slightly under-ripe fruit for jelly-making. If windfalls, or slightly damaged fruit, are used, cut off the bruised parts. There is no need to remove the stalks from the berries, but large fruit should be cut up.

Place the washed fruit into a pan and add the water. Allow 150 ml/¼ pint water per 500 g/ 1 lb of soft fruit, 450 ml/¾ pint water for hard fruits. Simmer until it is very soft; tough-skinned fruits can take about 1 hour. Turn the softened fruit into a jelly-bag and allow the juice to drip into a bowl. *Do not* force the juice through or squeeze the bag as this will make the jelly cloudy. Measure the strained juice into a large pan and calculate the required amount of sugar. Test also for pectin level.

As a general rule, add 500 g/1 lb of sugar for each 600 ml/1 pint of juice. High-pectin fruits will need slightly more sugar per 600 ml/1 pint of juice (around 625 g/1¼ lb).

Bring the juice to the boil, remove from the heat, add the sugar and stir until it has dissolved. Return to the heat, bring to the boil and boil rapidly until the setting-point is reached (see above).

During the boiling stage it is important *not* to stir the mixture as this can cause bubbles which will spoil the appearance of the jelly. It shouldn't be necessary to boil for more than 10 minutes in order to reach the setting-point. The saucer method is not as accurate for testing the set in jellies; if possible, use a jam thermometer and stop boiling when it reaches 105°C/220°F.

When the setting-point is reached, carefully remove any scum and pour very gently into small, clean, warm jars. Avoid air bubbles forming while pouring by tilting the jar, resting the lip of the pan on its rim. Cover the jars immediately as for jam. Leave the jelly to get cold and set before moving the jars. Clean, label and store them.

Here are some successful mixtures for jellies:

Gooseberry and Elderflower Add 12 elderflower heads to every 1.5 kg/3 lb of fruit. Check each flower head, avoiding any with an unpleasant smell. Never gather them close to a busy road.

Hips and Haws Use equal quantities of each, with the juice of 1 lemon for each 500 g/1 lb of fruit.

Apple and Herb Add a handful of fresh mint leaves and the juice of 2 lemons to each 1.5 kg/ 3 lb of fruit. Rosemary, thyme, lavender (honestly!), lemon balm, sage or tarragon are also delicious flavourings for savoury jellies.

GLYNN'S TIP

Don't leave the fruit dripping for too long, or the quality of the juice will suffer. Aim to have the jelly made within 24 hours from start to finish.

Crab-apple and Sage Add 12 stems of fresh sage to each 1 kg/2 lb of crab-apples.

Rowan and Crab-apple Use equal quantities of both fruits. You can also use cooking-apples with rowan-berries. Of course, either rowan-berries or crab-apples are marvellous as jellies by themselves.

Elderberry and Apple Use equal quantities of elderberries and apples plus pieces of cinnamon stick, a little lemon rind and a few cloves. Don't be tempted to make elderberry jelly by itself – it is boring.

MARMALADE

The origins and development of marmalade are difficult to chronicle accurately, although it is agreed that this preserve was first made using quinces. In Britain it is made only from the pulp and skin of oranges or other citrus fruits. In Europe almost everything is called 'marmalade'.

The classic fruit for marmalade-making is the Seville orange, a thick-skinned, acidic fruit which is bursting with pips that are, in turn, bursting with extra pectin. But the Seville orange, which still comes almost exclusively from Spain, has only a short season of a few weeks in February. However, it is possible to make very successful marmalades using most citrus fruits, alone or combined, and you could also try orange with carrots.

The principles and rules are as for jam-making. The main difference lies in the preparation and cooking of the fruit. Many recipes recommend mincing the orange skins. Whether you do this in a hand-mincer or a food processor, there is no denying that it is time-saving when compared with shredding or slicing by hand, but the result looks awful. If you *are* going to make marmalade, buy a sharp knife and set aside the time to slice the peel by hand. Slightly chunky strips of peel are more suitable for the robust flavour of a Seville orange marmalade; leave fine peel for the lighter-flavoured versions.

The cardinal rule for marmalade is to be absolutely certain that the peel is cooked – so soft, in fact, that you can crush it against the roof of your mouth with your tongue; once you add the sugar the peel tends to get harder, if anything. Be prepared for the rind to take an hour or more to become soft, unless you have a pressure-cooker, which is the only modern assistance I recommend for marmalade-making.

There is a great deal of pectin in the pith and pips of citrus fruit, so cook them with the fruit. Make a bag of muslin, old (clean) net curtain, or new kitchen cloth, secure the pith and pips inside and hang it over the side of the pan, tied to the handle so that you can remove it easily. Give it a good squeeze to extract all the juices before discarding. Lemon juice should always be added to help extract the pectin; allow 2 lemons for each 1.5 kg/3 lb of prepared fruit.

GLYNN'S TIP

A number of techniques may be used for preparing the fruit for marmalade. Some recipes suggest cooking the fruit whole, but I have found the best results and greatest satisfaction (which is not unimportant) from following 'the tradi-tional way', where a lot of the pith is included in the finished marmalade. It gives more body to the jelly and reveals more of the citrus flavouring. My method is to quarter the fruit, extracting the pips over a bowl which also collects the juice. Then I cut the rind and flesh across, as finely or thickly as it pleases me on the day, so that some of the rind is rather short and some, from the middle, rather long. If it were all the same size, no one would think it was homemade! Add the juice to the peel, flesh and water and tie the pips in muslin.

SEVILLE ORANGE MARMALADE

Makes 4.5 kg/10 lb

1.5 kg/3 lb Seville oranges
3.5 litres/6 pints water
juice of 2 lemons
3 kg/6 lb sugar, warmed

Prepare the fruit (see page 176). Tie the pips in a bag, dangle it in the pan and secure the string to the handle. Add all the juice which has been expressed and the water and lemon juice. Bring to the boil and then reduce to a gentle simmer until the peel is soft and the pan contents have reduced by half. This process may take as long as 2 hours.

Remove the pan from the heat, squeeze the bag of pips and discard. Add the sugar and stir until completely dissolved. Return to the heat, bring to a rolling boil and continue to boil rapidly until setting-point is reached (see page 176). Remove any scum, then cool for 10 minutes before pouring or ladling into clean, warm jars. Cover and label (see page 174).

Options

Grapefruit Marmalade Use 1.5 kg/3 lb of grapefruit, juice of 2 lemons, sugar and water as above. Because the pith is a little tougher than that of the orange, you should remove most of it from the skin before cutting the rind into

---

shreds, and add it to the bag of pips.

Dark Chunky Marmalade Use 1.25 kg/2½ lb Seville oranges, with the rind and juice of 2 lemons. Cut all the rind into thick chunks. Proceed as above but stir in 1 heaped tablespoon of black treacle with the sugar.

Three Fruit Marmalade This is a particularly useful recipe when Seville oranges are not available. Use 2 grapefruit, 4 lemons, 2 large, sweet oranges with the water and sugar. Include the shredded rind of all the fruit and proceed as above.

Carrot Marmalade Carrots help the fruit to go further and give a wonderful colour to the marmalade. Use 500 g/1 lb each of peeled carrots, sweet oranges and lemons. Grate the carrots finely and slice the fruit peel. Simmer in 3.5 litres/6 pints of water until soft. Discard the pips, and stir in 2 teaspoons of ground cinna-mon with the 3 kg/6 lb of sugar.

PRESSURE-COOKER MARMALADE

You can cook any of your favourite recipes in a pressure-cooker but you must reduce the water by half to allow for the shorter cooking time. If your recipe calls for 3.5 litres/6 pints of water, you should only use 1.75 litres/3 pints. Cook the peel and the bag of pips in the pressure-cooker with only 600 ml/1 pint of the measured amount of water. Thickly cut peel will take 10-12 minutes on high pressure, thin strips will take about 8 minutes. Test to ensure that the skin is really soft before adding the sugar. When the peel is soft, discard the bag, add the other 1.2 litres/2 pints, bring to the boil and stir in the warmed sugar and boil, uncovered, until setting-point is reached.

PINK GRAPEFRUIT MARMALADE

This marmalade is particularly successful if cooked in a pressure-cooker. For a total weight of 625 g/1¼ lb of pink grapefruit, you'll need the juice of 1 lemon. Cook the prepared grapefruit rind and flesh, together with the bag of pips, in 600 ml/1 pint of water in the pressure-cooker as given above. Warm 1 kg/2 lb of preserving sugar, stir it into the peel and boil rapidly until setting-point is reached. Let it rest for at least 10 minutes, stirring just once before bottling in warm jars. This will give a yield of about 1.5 kg/3 lb.

MINCEMEAT

Concern over cholesterol levels has led to a new wave of mincemeat recipes, where the amount of suet is greatly reduced, or even omitted altogether. Vegetable suets are a compromise, if you like the texture but would prefer to cut down on animal fats.

Makes about 750 g/1½ lb

125 g/4 oz raisins
125 g/4 oz currants
125 g/4 oz grated apple
125 g/4 oz brown sugar
125 g/4 oz sultanas
grated rind and juice of 1 lemon and 1 orange
60 g/2 oz suet (optional)
60 g/2 oz chopped mixed peel
30 g/1 oz blanched almonds, chopped
1 tsp mixed spice
2-3 tbls rum or brandy

Mince all the fruits together with the nuts, then stir in the remaining ingredients. Leave covered in a cool place for several days, turning from time to time. Pack into clean jars and cover with waxed discs or circles of greaseproof paper. Store in a cool place if you include the suet; without suet it is best kept in the refrigerator.

Option
Omit the raisins or sultanas and add 60 g/2 oz dried apricots, soaked overnight in orange juice, then chopped finely.

'BREAKFAST TIME' MINCEMEAT

For my first Christmas on *Breakfast Time* I spent a lot of time researching old mincemeat recipes and discovered that many of them included a purée of cooked lemon peel. I added my favourite ingredient, oranges, and called the result St Clement Dane's Mincemeat, of course. It was a smash hit in mince pies up and down the country, particularly because the cleaner citrus flavour made them more suitable for accompanying wine and less cloying and heavy at the end of a meal or with coffee. These quantities will make enough mincemeat for several batches of pies and some to give away as well.

Makes about 3.5 kg/7 lb

BASE MIXTURE
2 sweet navel oranges
2 lemons (thin skinned if possible)
1 kg/2 lb Bramley cooking apples
500 g/1 lb dark Barbados or muscovado sugar
500 g/1 lb stoned raisins
500 g/1 lb currants
500 g/1 lb shredded beef suet
125 g/4 oz glacé citrus peel, chopped

GLYNN'S TIP

Too much mincemeat? Use it in fruit pies. Layered over the pastry and with sliced fruit on the top, it makes a quick pudding to be served hot or cold. If you have used none in the mincemeat, add a little orange-flower water to the pastry, and so discover a terrific way to give individuality to Christmas mince pies.

My favourite combination with mincemeat in a pie is thin slices of fresh pineapple.

Squeeze the juice from the oranges and lemons, strain and reserve in a bowl. Put the skins and pulp into a saucepan, cover with water and cook gently until soft enough to purée in a blender; don't drown them with water or you will lose too much of the flavour. Meanwhile, peel and core the apples, chop finely and add to the citrus juice. Add the sugar, raisins, currants, suet and chopped peel plus the cooled purée. Mix well, cover and leave for several days, stirring occasionally, and then put into jars and keep for at least another 2 weeks.

Option
This is very good as it is but the addition of 150 ml/¼ pint of dark rum, brandy or an orange liqueur and 2 teaspoons each of ground mace, cloves and allspice makes it both better tasting and longer lasting.

CANDIED CITRUS PEEL

Once you have taken the time to make your own candied peel, you'll never again want to buy the commercial kind. It also makes a wonderful present.

Peel oranges, grapefruit or lemons, leaving the inner pith intact, and cut the peel into even-sized pieces, strips or larger chunks. Put it into a pan, cover with cold water and bring to the boil. Drain, and repeat five times. After the sixth boiling, cover again and boil until the peel is tender. Discard the liquid.

Weigh the peel and put it into a pan with an equal weight of sugar. Add just a little water and bring to the boil, stirring to dissolve the sugar. Simmer until you have a thick syrup, which may take 2-3 hours. Drain and cool the peel. Sprinkle caster sugar on greaseproof paper and roll the peel in it until it is well coated. Let it stand overnight to dry out before putting it into an airtight container.

FLAVOURED VINEGARS

An increasing variety of speciality vinegars is now available commercially, but it is great fun, and much cheaper, to make your own.
Herb Vinegars Half fill a screw-top, wide-necked jar with clean, freshly gathered herbs, roughly torn if the leaves are large. Fill the jar to the top with white vinegar and steep for at least 14 days. Strain into a clean bottle, with a choice fresh sprig of the chosen herb, which should be picked just before the plant starts flowering. Tarragon, thyme, basil, mint and rosemary are all excellent.
Fruit Vinegars Choose soft fruits such as blackberries, raspberries or cherries, and for each 500 g/1 lb pour over 600 ml/1 pint of white wine or cider vinegar. Cover and steep for 5-7 days, stirring occasionally. You can leave the fruit in for as long as you like, or strain it off; if you have a lot of fruit, add more to concentrate the flavour. Use as you would any other vinegar.

Raspberry and rose-petal vinegar (use fragrant petals from which you trim the bitter white base) may also be sweetened with sugar over heat and used as a cordial, diluted with water or soda water, for a refreshing summer drink.
Spiced Vinegars To each 600 ml/1 pint malt or wine vinegar add 15 g/½ oz mixed whole spices (pickling spice), with 6 peppercorns and 2 chillies if you want a hotter flavour. Allow it to steep for 1-2 months before using, shaking from time to time. Use straight from the bottle, strained. By heating the ingredients gently for 5 minutes, you can speed up the process – it will be ready in a few weeks. Don't make such vinegars for everyday use, for really hot condiments disguise rather than enhance food. A clove or two of garlic or sliced onion can be included in this vinegar.

BLACKBERRY or ELDERBERRY KETCHUP

Put the fruit in a pan with water to come halfway up. Simmer until soft, then push through a fine sieve and measure the pulp. To each 600 ml/1 pint, add 125 g/4 oz white or brown sugar, ¼ teaspoon dry mustard, 1 teaspoon ground ginger, pinch of ground cloves and 300 ml/½ pint vinegar. Simmer gently, stirring to dissolve the sugar, for about 30 minutes, until a good thick, pouring consistency. Transfer to clean, warm bottles and cover securely.

The elderberries may just be seeped in the vinegar overnight, standing in a warm place such as an airing cupboard, and not cooked. In this case, simply strain off the liquid (do not squash the berries) and boil this for 10 minutes with the spices and half the sugar. Let it cool, then taste and add more sugar if you like. Bottle without straining.

SPICED PLUM or PLUM and TOMATO SAUCE

This is one of the old fashioned store-cupboard sauces which all households once made and makes a marvellous change from tomato ketchup on the table, especially with the cold meats of summer. Made only with red-fleshed plums, it was my maternal grandmother's speciality and variations are enormously popular throughout Australasia. This version combines plums with tomatoes, but you can make it just with plums or just with tomatoes. It improves in the bottle for many months.

Makes about 1.5-2 kg (3-4 lb)

750 g/1½ lb ripe red plums
750 g/1½ lb ripe red tomatoes (or use all plums or vary the proportions of the two)
500 g/1 lb white or brown sugar
2-3 garlic cloves, chopped
125 g/4 oz onion, chopped
185 g/6 oz Bramley apple, cored and chopped
1 heaped tsp mixed spice or allspice
15 g/½ oz black peppercorns
½ tsp ground cloves
6-12 dried chillis
3-4 fresh or 2 dried bay leaves
600 ml/1 pint red wine vinegar

Put all the ingredients into a large pan and bring slowly to the boil. Simmer gently for up to 2 hours, until the mixture is a sloppy pulp.

Cool a little then strain through a colander to remove the stones and skins. You can then sieve the purée if you prefer a really smooth sauce. If the sauce is too runny, reduce over a gentle heat to the desired consistency.

CRANBERRY SAUCE

The secret in making this simple sauce is to add the sugar *after* the cranberries have cooked; otherwise the skins will be tough.

500 g/1 lb fresh or defrosted cranberries
150 ml/¼ pint red or white wine, port or orange juice
1 cinnamon stick
185-250 g/6-8 oz white sugar

Put the cranberries into a saucepan with the wine, port or fruit juice and the cinnamon stick. Bring slowly to the boil and simmer gently until the skins begin to pop. Remove from the heat and stir in the sugar to taste. For a smooth sauce, cook until the fruit is soft, then strain.

Options

Stir in blanched matchsticks of orange rind. Even better, toast some pecans or walnuts, chop them coarsely and mix into the cold sauce.

CRANBERRY ORANGE RELISH

The warm pink colour and rich but sharp flavour of this American condiment for cold meats is a welcome change at the Christmas table; but as cranberries are available from freezers all year round, it can also make an appearance at summer spreads too. This relish requires no cooking and can be prepared in minutes if you have a blender or food processor. Excellent with hot or cold turkey or pork and open to a great number of variations; in fact these measurements are arbitrary and may be adapted according to what you have or prefer.

Makes about 375 g/12 oz

1 large orange
1 large sharp apple
250 g/8 oz raw cranberries, fresh or frozen
sugar to taste

Wash the orange, quarter and remove the pips, but do not peel. Put the orange into a blender or food processor and blend until roughly chopped; work in two batches if necessary. Core but do not peel the apple and add to the orange followed by the cranberries. Continue to blend until finely chopped.

Turn into a bowl and add sugar to taste, but with discretion at this stage. Cover and store in a cool place for 24 hours, then taste again. The relish will have softened in texture and sweetened in flavour. If it is too sweet for you, add a little lemon juice.

Options

A sprinkle of ground cinnamon is liked by some people. Other additions which are good include a half lemon, peel included, some chopped celery or toasted nuts. A generous slurp of vodka, Cognac or port is very good for special occasions.

APPLE CHUTNEY

Chutneys are wonderful standbys for the larder. They add interest and flavour to the plainest of meals; fresh bread, good cheese and a home-made chutney is a lunch fit for a lord, not just a ploughman!

Makes about 3.5 kg/7 lb

1.5 kg/3 lb sour apples
1 kg/2 lb onions
500 g/1 lb large raisins or sultanas
750 g/1½ lb soft brown sugar
grated rind and juice of 2 lemons
2 tsps ground ginger
2 tsps mustard seed
½ tsp cayenne pepper
1 tsp salt
1.25 litres/2 pints white vinegar

Peel, core and finely chop the apples. Peel and finely chop the onions. Put the apples and onions into a large saucepan or preserving-pan with the raisins, sugar, lemon rind and juice, spices, salt and vinegar. Bring to the boil and simmer gently, stirring from time to time, until the mixture is thick and a wooden spoon drawn across the bottom of the pan leaves a distinct channel for a few seconds. Pour into warm, clean jars, cover securely and label.

Options

The apples and onions may be minced or grated.

GREEN TOMATO CHUTNEY

Makes about 4 kg/8 lb

2 kg/4 lb green tomatoes
500 g/1 lb cooking apples
500 g/1 lb shallots or onions
15 g/½ oz dried root ginger, bruised
8-10 chillies
250 g/8 oz large raisins
500 g/1 lb soft brown sugar
600 ml/1 pint vinegar
2 tsps salt

Peel and chop the tomatoes, apples and shallots finely, or mince. Tie the bruised ginger and chillies in muslin. Put all ingredients into a large saucepan or preserving-pan and heat gently, stirring, until the sugar has dissolved. Continue to simmer, until the mixture is thick and a wooden spoon drawn across the bottom of the pan leaves a channel visible for a few seconds. Remove the bag of spices. Transfer to clean, warm jars, cover securely and label.

BANANA CHUTNEY

This makes a pleasant change from mango chutney as an accompaniment for curries.

Makes about 1 kg/2 lb

500 g/1 lb onions
250 g/8 oz dates
125 g/4 oz crystallized ginger
8 ripe bananas, mashed
2 tsps salt
300 ml/½ pint vinegar
250 g/8 oz black treacle
1 tbls pickling spice

Mince the onions with the dates and ginger. Put these ingredients into a preserving-pan with the bananas, salt, vinegar, black treacle and pickling spice (tied in a muslin bag). Stir, while heating gently, until the sugar dissolves, then simmer until the mixture is thick enough. Remove the spice-bag and transfer the chutney to clean, warm jars. Cover securely and label.

CONFITURE D'OIGNONS

Savoury *confitures* are very popular as a garnish throughout France and this one comes from Provence. It is especially good served, hot or cold, with pâtés and terrines.

1 kg/2 lb onions
7 tbls peanut oil
2 tsps salt
6 peppercorns
2 whole cloves
250 g/8 oz caster sugar
150 ml/1/4 pint raspberry vinegar
200 ml/1/3 pint fragrant red wine (ideally from Provence)

Peel and slice the onions finely; cook covered, with the oil, salt, peppercorns and cloves. After 15 minutes' gentle cooking, stir well, then continue cooking for a further 15 minutes. Add the sugar, vinegar and wine and cook uncovered for a further 45 minutes. Adjust the sweetness by adding more raspberry vinegar if needed, cooking further to ensure that the flavour has been fully absorbed.

PICKLES

There are two basic forms of pickle, either cold or sweet. The two methods used are cold pickling, for fresh young vegetables, or small fresh herrings, and hot pickling for sweet pickles.

Pickled Red Cabbage Choose small, brightly coloured, fresh cabbages; remove the cores and slice finely. Arrange in a bowl with plenty of salt between each layer, cover and steep for 24 hours. Drain thoroughly under cold running water and rinse very well. Drain again, removing all surplus water (a salad drier is useful for this), then pack loosely into clean jars. Cover with cold, spiced vinegar, cover and label. This is ready to eat after 7 days and best eaten within 3 months.

Mixed Pickle Use a selection of small onions, cauliflower florets, chunks of cucumber and marrow, and proceed as for Pickled Red Cabbage.

Pickled Onions The onions should be small and even-sized. Peel them, then steep for 24 hours in brine made with 250 g/8 oz salt to 2.25 litres/4 pints of water, weighted down with a plate to keep them under the water. Drain, pack into clean jars and cover with cold, spiced vinegar. Leave for 2 weeks before eating.

Pickled Mushrooms Choose small button mushrooms and wipe carefully. Put into a saucepan with 1 teaspoon of salt, cover with water and bring to the boil, drain and dry on kitchen paper. Prepare vinegar as for Pickled Damsons (see below). Pack the dried mushrooms into clean jars and pour the hot vinegar over. Cover securely.

MARINATED AUBERGINES

These are especially good with cold fish.

Makes 1 kg/2 lb

1 kg/2 lb aubergines
salt
300 ml/1/2 pint white wine vinegar
4-6 garlic cloves, crushed
1 tbls dried oregano
olive, or other oil, to cover

Peel and slice the aubergines and arrange in a colander, sprinkling each layer with salt. Set aside for 2-3 hours so that the bitter juices drain away. Place the aubergines in a pan and add the vinegar to cover the slices; poach for 5 minutes, then drain well. Arrange the slices in a large glass jar, sprinkling the crushed garlic and oregano between the layers. Fill the jar with oil and cover securely with a lid. The pickle can be eaten after a week, but it keeps indefinitely.

PICKLED DAMSONS

Pickled fruit is excellent with picnic food of all kinds, especially pies and cold meats.

Makes about 3 kg/6 lb

2 kg/4 lb damsons
1 kg/2 lb sugar
1 cinnamon stick
3 whole cloves
2 tsps whole allspice
piece of fresh ginger
600 ml/1 pint white vinegar

Wash the damsons, prick all over with a needle and place in a non-metallic bowl. Heat the sugar and spices with the vinegar until the sugar dissolves, then pour over the damsons. Cover, and leave to stand for 2-3 days. Strain off the vinegar into a pan, bring to the boil, then pour back over the damsons. Leave for another 2-3 days. Repeat this process once more. Strain off the vinegar into a pan and simmer until it has reduced to a thick syrup. Pack the drained fruit into jars, pour the hot syrup over and cover. These are best stored for 3-4 weeks before use.

SPICY PICKLED PEACHES

Makes about 750 g/1 1/2 lb

500 g/1 lb peaches, ripe but firm
300 ml/1/2 pint cider, or other white, vinegar
6 tbls white sugar
4 tsps pickling spice
1 cinnamon stick

Cut the peaches in half and remove the stones, but do not peel. Cut each half into three or four

segments and prick all over with a skewer or fork. Heat the vinegar with the sugar, pickling spice and cinnamon. Simmer together for 10 minutes, then add the sliced peaches. Continue simmering, allowing 2-3 minutes if you intend to keep the pickle for a few weeks, 7-8 minutes if you want to eat it immediately. Transfer to clean, warm jars and cover securely. Once opened, the jar should be kept in a refrigerator. If you prefer, you can remove the spices from the vinegar before adding the peaches.

SWEET-SPICED PRUNES

An accompaniment to make for a special occasion. Store in the refrigerator and serve hot or cold with game, roasts or cold meats.

12 large prunes
250 ml/8 fl oz red wine
250 ml/8 fl oz port wine or cream sherry
2 dry or 3 fresh bay leaves
1 cinnamon stick
6 juniper berries
large strip lemon rind
1 tbls muscovado sugar

Place all the ingredients in a saucepan and simmer gently until the prunes are plump and the syrup is reduced until almost none remains.

SPICED PICKLED ORANGES

Makes about 2 kg/4 lb

6 large oranges
500 g/1 lb white sugar
450 ml/3/4 pint white vinegar
5 whole cloves
cinnamon stick
blade of mace
pared rind of 1 lemon

Wash the oranges and cut into fairly thick slices, discarding the ends. Put into a saucepan and cover with water. Simmer gently until the fruit is tender (about 2 hours), then drain. Warm the sugar in the vinegar in the pan, stirring until it dissolves, then add the spices and the lemon rind, all tied in a muslin bag. Simmer for 10 minutes, then add the oranges and continue to simmer for a further 60-70 minutes. Strain off the vinegar into a clean saucepan, discarding the bag of spices, and boil rapidly. Pack the drained orange slices into clean jars and add the vinegar when it is syrupy. Cover tightly. These make a perfect accompaniment to cold ham and game.

ENTERTAINING FOOD

Ideas for creating individual styles and moods with food – whether
in the kitchen through choice of ingredients or at the table, where the
ambience should fit the fare and compliment your guests.

THE CONTEMPORARY STORECUPBOARD

In the so-called good old days anyone with the space had a storecupboard, without which they could not get by. It was stocked with dried herbs and preserves, potted meats, summer fruits in syrup, and, once the idea had been brought back from India, chutneys and piquant sauces. Some people preserved beans in salt and pickled meat in brine and kept them beside the great sacks of wheat or dried peas that kept them going during the winter. Others stored less robust items such as homemade rose-petal honey, elderflower wine or wild berry jellies. Nowadays we have shops to provide much of this for us. But nonetheless there is something comforting in knowing you have a store of goodies to fall back on, particularly if some of them are homemade.

These days it is more useful to base such a store on flavourings and condiments and treats rather than on basics; to create, in fact, a personal palette with which you can transform simple foods into something original and appetizing in minutes, often by using an ingredient that may be expensive to buy but is used in only small amounts. Equally, you need only change the flavour or appearance of something inexpensive to make a mark. Take black peppercorns: if you roast them until they 'pop' and are smelling like spicy coffee grounds, you can completely change the flavour of a dish and double your repertoire; use them in or on anything, from simple salads to jacket potatoes with soured cream, on poached fish or in stews. Make them every couple of weeks and store them in an airtight jar. Alternatively, exchange the peppercorns for coriander seeds in your peppermill and every one of your favourite recipes will taste brand new. With very little thought and a few minutes' work from time to time you will gradually build up a terrific range of individual flavours and flavourings, many of which simply aren't available in shops. There's an extra advantage, too: you always have really personal gifts to give.

I've always found spices more useful than herbs for flavouring; they store better and are more capable of being surprising. You might try stocking some green peppercorns in brine, but be aware that, once opened, they tend to turn black. Rinse them of brine and put them into vodka and store the container in the refrigerator. The pepper-flavoured vodka can be used separately to point sauces or simply to dribble onto plainly cooked food or into sauces – even over scrambled eggs.

The whole spices in your cupboard should include nutmeg, for grating fresh over anything including cheese, sweet or savoury, for roasted pork, or for green vegetables. The same goes for allspice, which is better to buy whole and to grind as you need it; use it whenever you would traditionally use cinnamon, and enjoy a little more bite and flavour. Cumin seeds are really fabulous when roasted and scattered on things – on a grilled fan of pear to accompany poultry, in a salad, on soured cream for a baked potato. Cardamom gives a truly wonderful flavour crushed into coffee or used in syrups for fruit salad, and can impart mysterious fragrance to any mixture of spice, whether used in Christmas cake, curries or dips for hard-boiled eggs.

Ground cumin and ground coriander are vital. They form the basis of all the cuisines of North Africa and everywhere east of Suez until you get past India. Flavour-wise, think of cumin as peppery and lemon-like, coriander as orange-like. The beauty of them is that they may be used in any proportion one to the other, and by subtle adjustments of balance give you thousands of flavour possibilities. Add some ground cinnamon and/or sweet paprika to a dish and you can go anywhere. Add also saffron, which you should never be without, and you have as many possibilities of voluptuous fragrance as you will ever need. Saffron magically transforms rice for anything, butter for fish or vegetables, and combines with tomato to make amazingly colourful dishes and satisfying flavours; Poussins with Tomato, Saffron and Coriander is an excellent example (see page 94). Marvellous in mayonnaise for potatoes, for fish or for vegetables, too; and it is always better with garlic.

A festoon of garlic bought in summer is a must and so is a good few inches of fresh ginger root, which keeps forever in the bottom of the refrigerator. Grated or finely chopped with garlic it makes an archetypal oriental flavour for the base of anything cooked in a wok, or sprinkled into or onto steamed or baked fish or poultry.

Another instant oriental trick is to paint cooked poultry or fish with a touch of sesame oil. I also dribble a little onto strips of turkey or chicken breast before microwaving them for a few minutes, and then sprinkle on soya and toasted sesame seeds. The seeds are indispensable and perfectly finish both savoury or sweet dishes. If you see them, always buy moon-pale pine nuts, which are far more exotic to strew than flaked almonds; but lightly toast or roast them first. American pecan nuts – which are always better for being lightly toasted before use – can top cakes, add crunch to stuffings, bulk out sauces and be chopped for scattering onto rice dishes, especially if wild rice is included.

As well as sesame oil you'll need a decent olive oil, of course, and walnut or hazelnut oil, to use solo or in combination with cheaper, blander edible oils. Individualists should make their own oils. Pop three or four high-class bags of mixed herbs (the ones that look like tea bags) into 600 ml/1 pint of oil, perhaps adding some lightly crushed garlic, strips of lemon and a couple of chilli peppers. Keep the oil in a warm place for a few weeks until it tastes the way you like it, then remove the flavourings. If you have the time and the choice, use fresh herbs and make yourself a series of different-flavoured oils.

A good vinegar is another indispensable item. Rich, rounded Balsamic vinegar from Italy or Sherry vinegar from Spain give fabulous lifts to salads and can be used to enliven pan sauces (reduced cooking liquid), which you then thicken by whisking in butter off the heat. Raspberry and black cherry are equally useful on salads and in hot sauces, but I use them on fresh fruit for first courses; dripping raspberry vinegar onto peach slices with parma ham for instance. To make your own, put about 500 g/1 lb of fruit into 600 ml/1 pint of white or cider vinegar for a few weeks, test and replace the fruit with more, if you like. Victorians used to sweeten raspberry vinegar and use it as the base of a summer drink with sparkling water. Remember never to boil your vinegar to dissolve the sugar or you get jam rather than a fresh flavour.

Fruit, herbs and spices also flavour alcohols, used mainly for very special aperitif drinking, for mixing with champagne or flavouring sauces, or finishing simple puddings, fruit or cake. Virtually any fruit can be put into vodka or brandy. I recommend any sort of plum, including damsons and sloes, for gin. For Christmas, stuff some chilli peppers, garlic, lemon, allspice and bay into a bottle of vodka and greet guests with a strained, well-chilled snort on arrival; this is also marvellous for cooking.

I like to have rose water and orange-flower water in bottles, too. Rose water has amazing affinities with cream, with chocolate and with raspberries. Drip some into a raspberry coulis or flavour icing for a chocolate cake; use it in cream for meringues, for baked apples, pears and quinces. Orange-flower water particularly likes anything to do with butter or almonds and most fruits, too. Simply sprinkle it on sliced chilled oranges, and serve with a touch of cinnamon. Rub it lightly over your hands before kneading shortbread or patting out scones. Put it into any cream for any dessert with fruit.

On a more mundane level I like a choice of rices, long-grain Basmatti for fragrance and for pilaffs, short-grain Italian Arborio for real, runny risottos, some wild rice for adding to either, using in stuffings, or simply to sprinkle (it's very expensive) over vegetables or into salads. I keep a range of pasta shapes and types and a few things with which to make sauces. Plum tomatoes in their own juice in several sizes are a must, and some of the exorbitantly priced but fashionable sun-dried tomatoes from Tuscany; just a teaspoonful adds wonderful figgy flavour to sauces. Other 'musts' include dried ceps or porcini mushrooms from France or Italy; whole fruits in their own juices or in syrup – pineapples, peaches, mandarines and the like – and some packets of hummous mixture. Add olive oil to the hummous, sprinkle with cumin, coriander, saffron and paprika from the cupboard and you have one of the best first courses in the world.

In the deepfreeze I like to have several packets of frozen raspberries, mainly for making hot or cold sauces, and some blackcurrants for making quick stews. I cook them with a splash of white wine and vanilla essence, which gives the effect of sweetness, and add sugar only if they are particularly sharp. As they are cooling I stir in some toasted walnuts or pecans and serve them with clotted cream, which I also keep in the deepfreeze. It's always a sensation.

In addition to clotted cream I like to have some really good French unsalted butter, in case I want to bake a cake or produce really special vegetables and sauces. There's phyllo pastry always, for squares of that painted with olive oil for savoury or butter for sweet, cook in minutes and look so wonderful as they float on the plate, filled with whatever you have to hand. Finally, I always have in stock a couple of special jams, plus a herbed-apple jelly or two to serve with meat instead of redcurrant jelly – but homemade rowanberry jelly is always so much better.

Once you start to store your cupboard with such goodies, you'll be amazed at how simple it is to compose new dishes.

SERVING and PRESENTATION

The appearance of food is certainly important, but it should never be allowed to become the star of an occasion. If it does, it may be at the expense of good hospitality, or you may have forgotten that the *taste* of food is more important than its presentation, the designer kitchen where it was prepared, etiquette or surroundings. Too many cooks these days are cooking for the plate rather than the palate, a plastic image rather than for the joy of entertaining their friends by cooking interesting food – hence the current avalanche of boring restaurant fare and uninspired home cooking.

First the table. Even a few wild flowers unfussily arranged in a water glass look nice, but if you don't like them or are allergic, put any interesting object that you like on to the table. But keep it simple – over-decorated tables, particularly those with 'themes', belong to magazines and people who need to impress. For more formal occasions always ensure that any large flower arrangements won't hide guests from one another; you can quickly check this beforehand by sitting in all the chairs yourself. Similar care should be taken with candles, which should either be very high or very low so they won't dazzle people. If you aren't certain of the effect they will create, it would be better to have some other form of low-key lighting somewhere else in the room – I often move a standard lamp into a corner.

When the size of the table makes it impossible to have both flowers and candles, combine them. I stand candles in small bowls, securing them by melting their bottoms, fill the bowls with water and then tuck flowers or leaves with very short stems around the candle to hide the water and the bowl; use violets to surround a pink candle, roses around white ones, and so on. Soup bowls are useful containers for this. At Easter I fill the bowls with small easter eggs, and at Christmas with tree decorations. I have had enormous success at both very casual and very formal meals simply by strewing flowers directly onto the table or the cloth. The most spectacular, I recall, was at a grand country house in the Borders, where two round tables for 12 in the dining room were almost groaning with silver, crystal and linen. The candleholders were so spectacular they brooked no competition, so I sent two guests outside each with instructions to pick only white or purple crocuses. I sprinkled the flowers generously in a circle around the candelabra and no-one talked of anything else, which was a pity because the food was pretty good that night and deserved a mention at least.

When it comes to utensils the rules are simple, start with those for the first course on the outside and work in. Although it is becoming a more acceptable practice, it is better not to arrange the spoon and fork for pudding across the top of the setting. If there is not enough space on the table to put them either side of the table mat, leave them off altogether. When it is time for pudding, clear the table of everything but the decorations, take off all the used glasses, set new glasses if needed, set the spoon and fork, then serve.

Even if you have staff, so-called silver service (when someone serves you with everything separately) has little place in the private home for there is rarely enough space for them to work in and by the time everyone is served the food is cold or spoiled. Far better to adopt modern serving practice and put everything on the plates in the kitchen (remember when this method was called 'dog's dinner'?) or on the sideboard if you have the space. Otherwise, the host or hostess should serve the main part of the meal – meat, poultry, etc – and let guests help themselves to vegetables by passing around dishes at the table.

Whatever you do don't fall for the fifties pretension of thinking you must never abandon your guests for the kitchen. By not doing so you will have to serve food which has been kept warm and thus has lost its texture and goodness. It is a compliment to your guests that you think enough of them to want to cook vegetables at the last minute; if you don't, serve salads instead but dispense with the hostess trolley for heaven's sake.

If you have produced something which looks spectacular, make sure your guests see it before it is cut up. You are not showing off, but allowing them to share the excitement and making all your effort worthwhile – a little touch of stardom for the cook is vital. I usually try to serve pudding at the table, for conversation should be buzzing by then and why should the cook miss out?

The French custom of serving cheese before the pudding is more sensible than the British will allow, and enables diners to finish their main course wine, which is very important if it is a red one. An excellent way to avoid the hassle of plates with biscuits and cheese and the like is to follow the rather good American habit of serving cheese with salad, and eating them with a knife and fork. Whatever the cheese it *must* be wrapped tightly until just before being served to keep the air from it, but be allowed to return to room temperature or just below if it is midsummer or if the central heating is at full blast.

The rules about wine are essentially simple – drink what you prefer and what you like. The accepted norms of red with red meat and white with white meat or fish are based on centuries of experience, but are by no means written in stone. There are many strongly flavoured white burgundies, or white wines from hot countries, which stand up perfectly well to light red meats such as lamb or the small, sweeter game birds. Fruity Beaujolais and light Bordeaux wines (the true *clairettes*) are fabulous with fattier fish (like salmon) or with rich fish dishes, especially if lightly chilled. In summer and in hot winter dining rooms, red wines are probably better for being chilled lightly before being served. It is better for them to be like this and to flower in the glass than to be too warm and flabby.

With more people caring about their health these days, provision should always be made for water glasses on the table. If people have had to drive to you, consider not serving spirits at all but offering good white wine or champagne as an aperitif. This is an especially good way to simplify entertaining, for the aperitif wine can continue in the same glasses at the table for the first course, or you can choose to serve the first course in the sitting room, with guests helping themselves. Incidentally, if you are serving good wine, *never* serve raw onion or chives in the meal. You might also like to consider contemporary restaurant practice of leaving the vinaigrette off the salad, and using a very good oil and a scatter of freshly grated lemon zest instead.

In the end, though, you must entertain in the way that suits you and your guests best. Make your guests the stars rather than the food and they'll feel both welcome and happy to repay the compliment.

INDEX